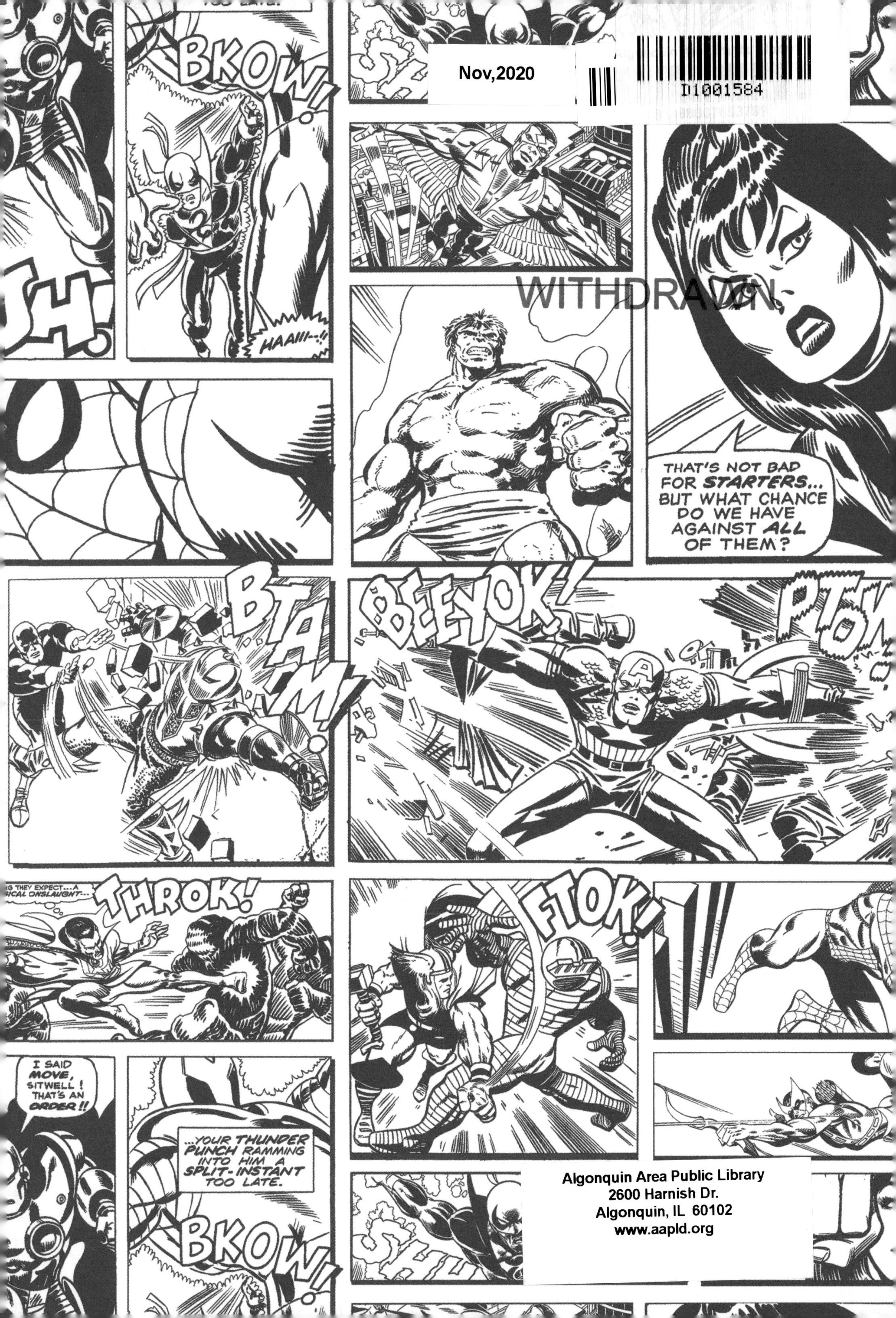
BKOW!
HAAIII--!!
THAT'S NOT BAD FOR STARTERS... BUT WHAT CHANCE DO WE HAVE AGAINST ALL OF THEM?
BTAM!
BEEYOK!
THROK!
FTOK!
I SAID MOVE, SITWELL! THAT'S AN ORDER!!
...YOUR THUNDER PUNCH RAMMING INTO HIM A SPLIT-INSTANT TOO LATE.
BKOW!

INTRODUCTION

The power of Marvel lies in the human qualities displayed by its legion of comic book characters... in the spirit of the stories that they star in... in the realism that they inhabit. Millions of readers around the world have found themselves part of a virtual community, enchanted by amazing adventures within a universe populated with extraordinary characters that are as realistic and credible as they are super-powerful. Marvel is a modern-day mythology, a parallel dimension that is as close to everyday life as possible; a powerful combination of art, literature, and legend. Perhaps in the future, Marvel lore will share the same appeal for scholars as the ancient Greek gods and heroes have for today's great minds. But for now, take a journey back in time to explore the first 80 years of Marvel. And here's to 80 more!!

THE OFFICIAL MARVEL STUDIOS MOVIE SPECIALS

Thor: Ragnarok
Black Panther: The Official Movie Special
Black Panther: The Official Movie Companion
Ant-Man and The Wasp
Marvel Studios: The First 10 Years
Avengers: Infinity War
Captain Marvel
Avengers: Endgame
Spider-Man: Far From Hone
Avengers: An Insider's Guide to the Avengers Films
Black Widow: The Official Movie Special

DISNEY PUBLISHING WORLDWIDE
Text Fabio Licari, Marco Rizzo
Additional Text & Editing Steve Behling
Design and Editing Ellisse s.a.s. di Sergio Abate & C. Valentina Bonura (Designer) Tiziana Quirico (Editor)
Translation John Rugman
Thanks to Guy Cunningham, Joseph Hochstein, Mark Long, Caitlin O'Connell, Brian Overton, Jeff Youngquist.

Originally created by Disney Publishing Worldwide

TITAN EDITORIAL
Editor Jonathan Wilkins
Managing Editor Martin Eden
Art Director Oz Browne
Assistant Editor Phoebe Hedges
Senior Production Controller Jackie Flook
Production Controller Caterina Falqui
Sales and Circulation Manager Steve Tothill
Press and Publicity Assistant George Wickenden
Marketing Manager Ricky Claydon

Publicist Imogen Harris
Editorial Director Duncan Baizley
Operations Director Leigh Baulch
Executive Director Vivian Cheung
Publisher Nick Landau

DISTRIBUTION
U.S. Newsstand: Total Publisher Services, Inc.

John Dziewiatkowski, 630-851-7683

U.S. Newsstand Distribution: Curtis Circulation Company

PRINTED IN THE U.S.
U.S. Bookstore Distribution: The News Group

U.S. Direct Sales: Diamond Comic Distributors
For more info on advertising contact adinfo@titanemail.com

Marvel: The First 80 Years published November 2020 by Titan Magazines, a division of Titan Publishing Group Limited, 144 Southwark Street, London SE1 0UP.

For sale in the U.S. and Canada.

ISBN: 9781787734487

Thank you to Christopher Troise, and Eugene Paraszczuk at Disney, plus Guido Frazzini. Titan Authorized User. No part of this publication may be reproduced, stored in a retrival system, or transmitted, in any form or by any means, without the prior written permission of the publisher. A CIP catalogue record for this title is available from the British Library.
10 9 8 7 6 5 4 3 2 1

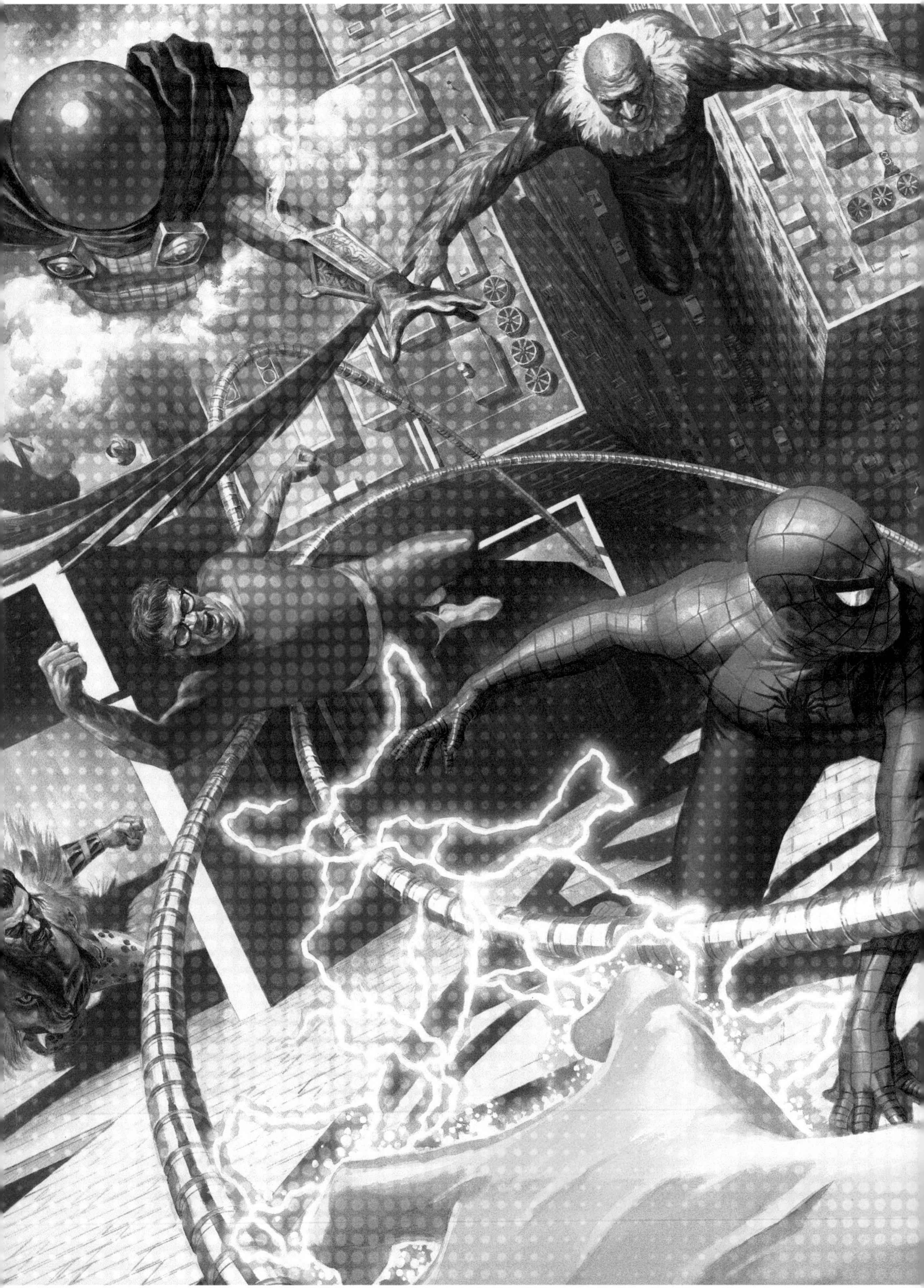

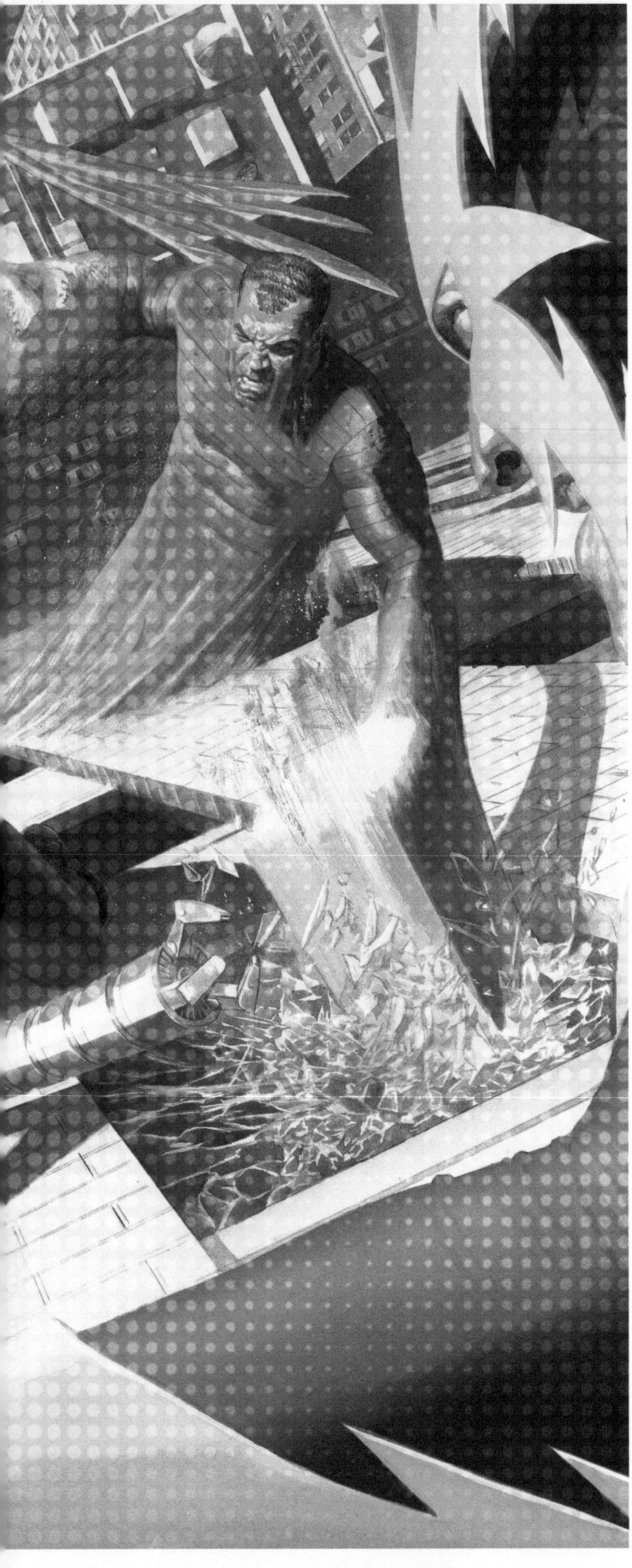

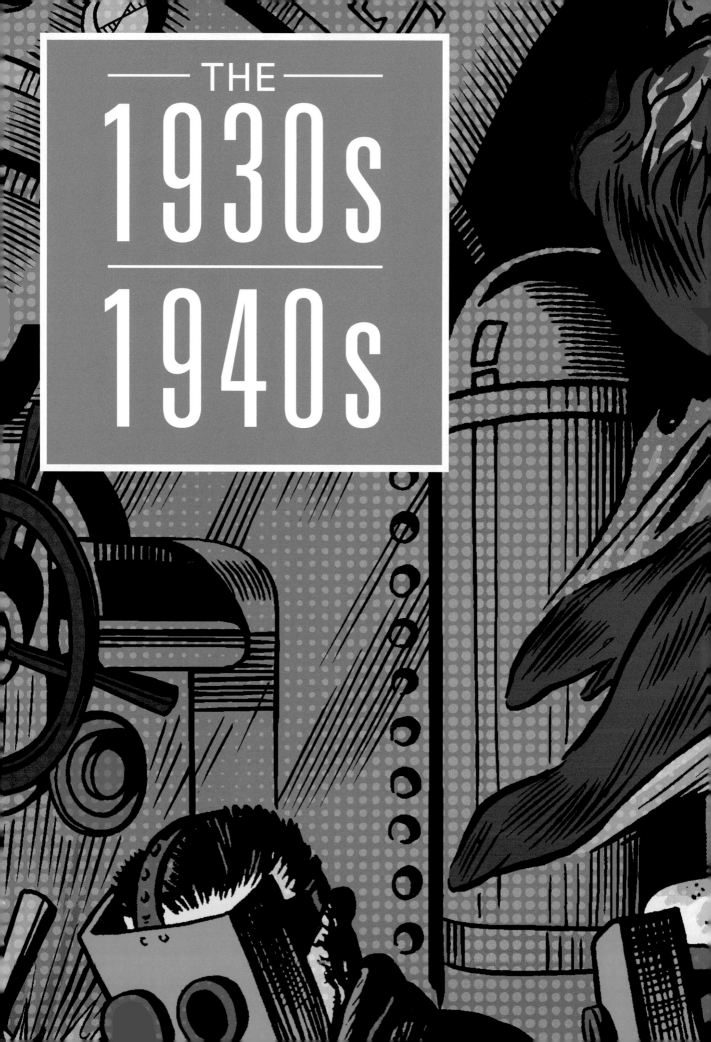

THE
1930s
1940s

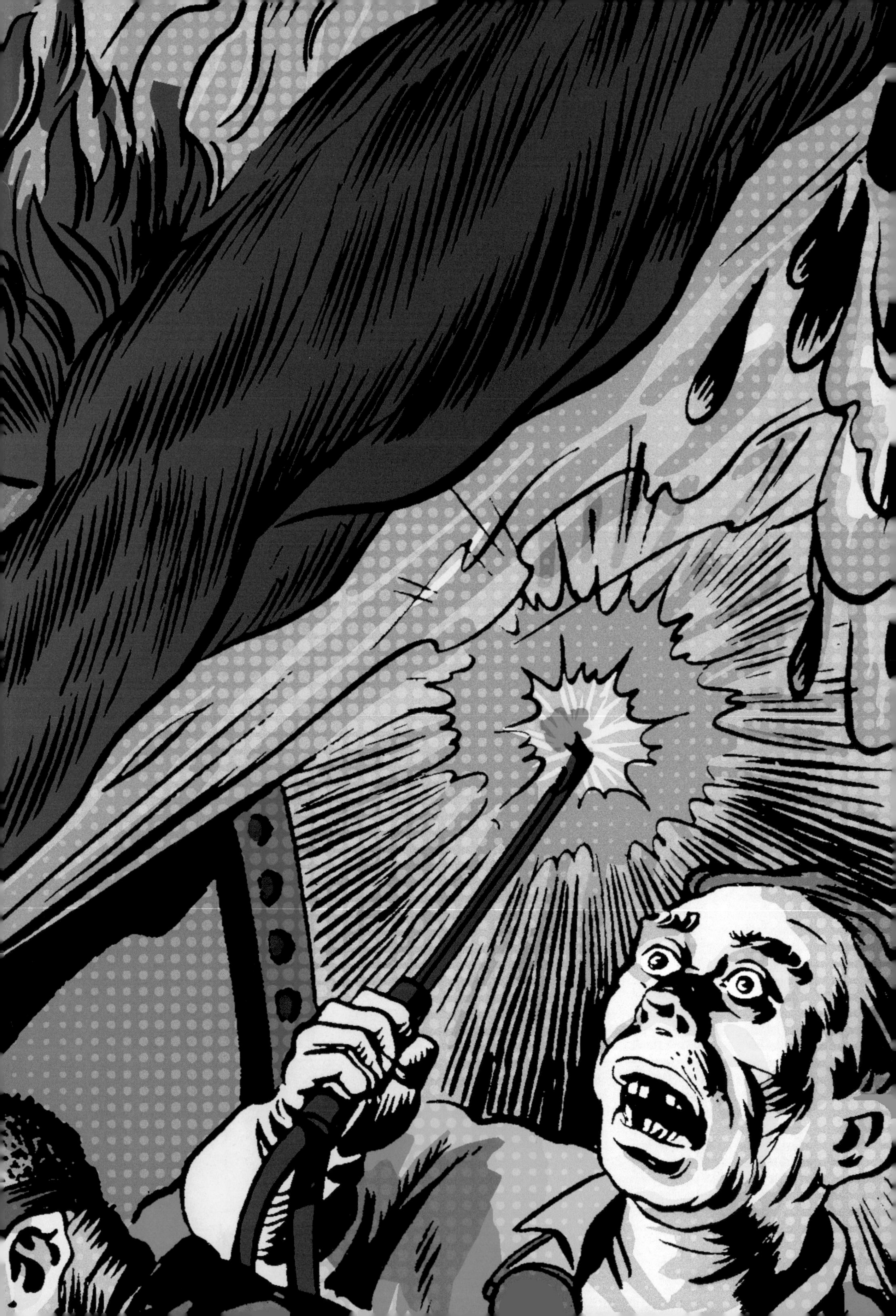

WHEN IT ALL BEGAN

A man, draped in the patriotic colors of the United States of America, delivering a crushing right to the jaw of the fascist dictator Adolf Hitler. The image was indelible, instantly unforgettable.

Nestled in that punishing blow dealt to Hitler was a dream: a free world where America would send the latest Super Villain packing for good, a Doctor Doom (another nasty chap in dictator mode and the Fantastic Four's most dreaded enemy) who unfortunately was no pen-and-ink creation, but an unparalleled enemy in the flesh. *Der Führer* would be made sport of, yes, to the applause of some readers, while others were moved to tears. The slipstream effect of that blow, the movement, even the "sound" that resonated made it so palpable that it transcended what was simply the cover of a comic book, *Captain America Comics #1.* But what a cover it was!

The year was 1940, and Captain America, the new red-white-and-blue Super Hero, burst onto the scene, waylaying the world's archenemy. But such bravado alone wouldn't have been enough to win the hearts of a million readers without the eerily compelling stories that revealed the talents of a pair of iconic artists like Joe Simon and Jack Kirby, who in the process made comic book history. It was a combination of emotion, emphasis, action, and narrative flair that encapsulated what was to come, in the form of Marvel Comics, then known as Timely Comics.

Captain America Comics #1, however, was not Timely's first comic book. It all started with *Marvel Comics #1,* which debuted on August 31, 1939.

America had just shrugged off the Great Depression, which first reared its ugly head in 1929 and left millions of people grappling with poverty. The attack on Pearl Harbor in 1941 propelled America into World War II.

THIS PAGE: Bucky (left) and Captain America, from the splash page to *Captain America Comics #1* (March 1941). Art by Jack Kirby and Joe Simon,

OPPOSITE PAGE: *Captain America Comics #1* (March 1941). Cover by Jack Kirby and Joe Simon.

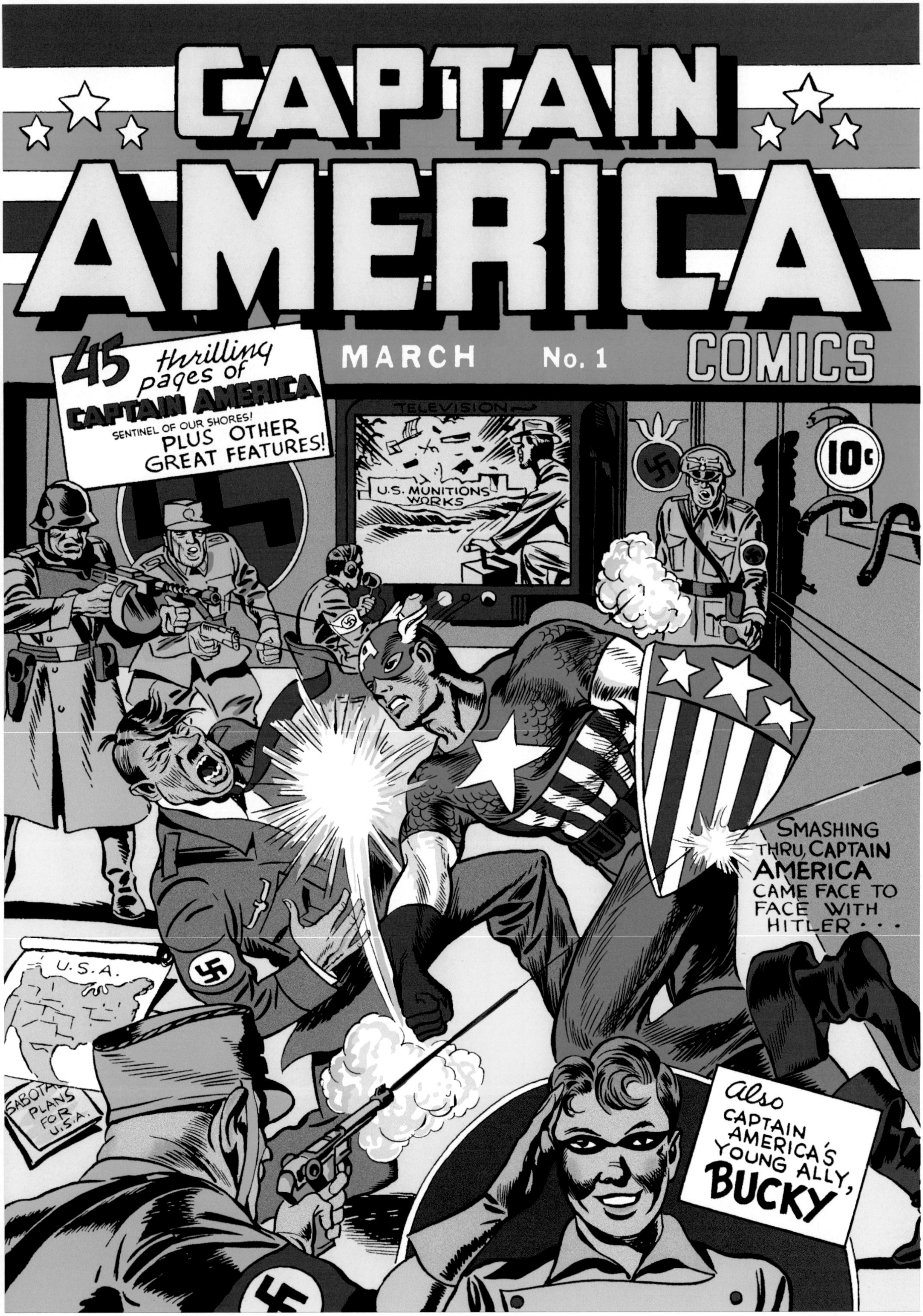
CAPTAIN AMERICA
COMICS
MARCH
No. 1
45 thrilling pages of
CAPTAIN AMERICA
SENTINEL OF OUR SHORES!
PLUS OTHER GREAT FEATURES!
10¢
TELEVISION
U.S. MUNITIONS WORKS
SMASHING THRU, CAPTAIN AMERICA CAME FACE TO FACE WITH HITLER . . .
U.S.A.
SABOTAGE PLANS FOR U.S.A.
Also CAPTAIN AMERICA'S YOUNG ALLY, BUCKY

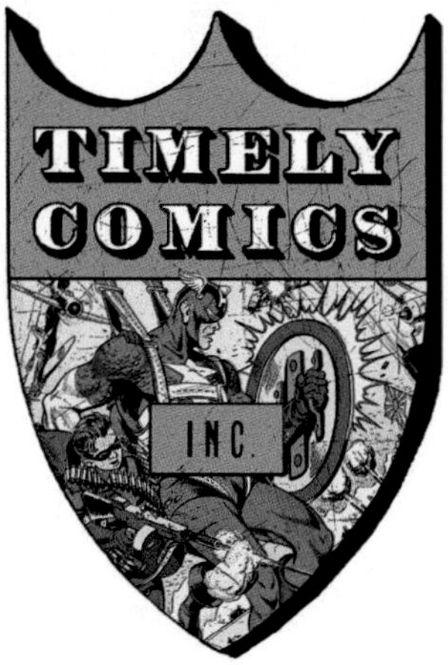
TIMELY
COMICS
INC.

Goodman could sense what markets were longing for...

But even at the time, a 10-cent comic book was accessible to nearly everyone: kids and their families with little money to be spared on "extravagances" like movies, soldiers heading off to this or that front. And comic books were something new. Until then, there were only the syndicated comic strips that appeared in newspapers by renowned artists like Alex Raymond and Hal Foster, who indeed considered their work an artform.

But in 1934 Max "Charlie" Gaines came up with the brilliant idea of publishing those strips in a new format, the size of a newspaper folded twice over—and thus the birth of comic book that we know and love to this day, give or take a few millimeters. Reprinted comic strips would soon give way to all-new original stories and characters.

One of the most active publishers at that time was Martin Goodman, a tireless workhorse in his own right with a masterful editorial instinct. Goodman could sense what markets were longing for, and doggedly sought to hone in on the latest trends. His endeavors were not limited to comics—Timely Publications, the publishing house he launched in 1939, was also involved in pulp fiction that featured westerns, sci-fi, horror, mysteries, romance, and detective and adventure stories.

Sales boomed. But it would have been hard for him to imagine that one day Timely would spawn what turned out to be the world's premier publisher of comic books, Marvel Comics. So that's how it all started, in those wonder-filled years that would come to be known as the Golden Age of Comic Books.

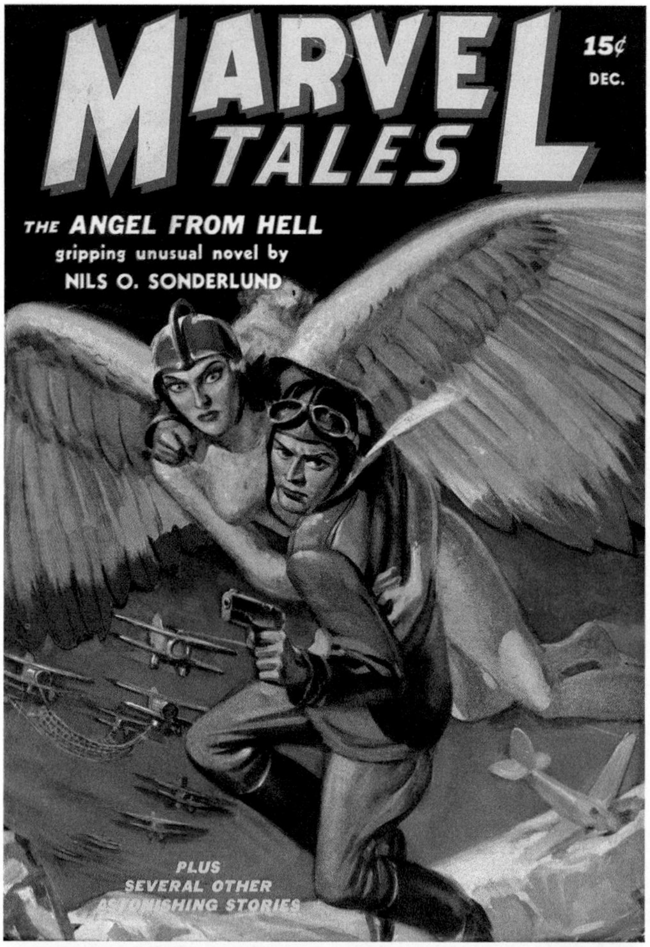
MARVEL TALES
15¢
DEC.
THE ANGEL FROM HELL
gripping unusual novel by
NILS O. SONDERLUND
PLUS
SEVERAL OTHER

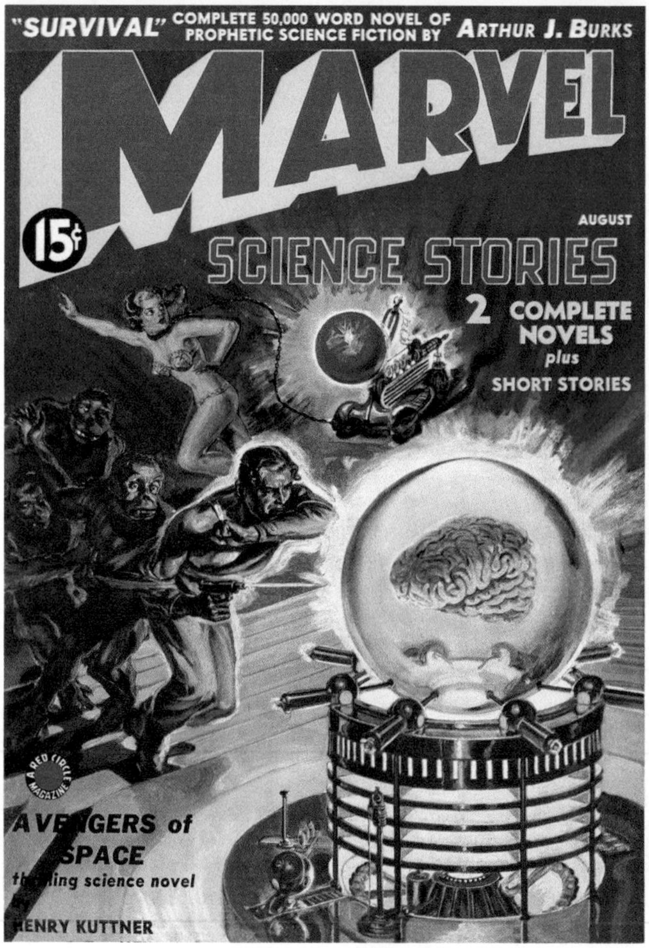
"SURVIVAL" COMPLETE 50,000 WORD NOVEL OF PROPHETIC SCIENCE FICTION BY ARTHUR J. BURKS
MARVEL
15¢
AUGUST
SCIENCE STORIES
2 COMPLETE NOVELS plus SHORT STORIES
A RED CIRCLE MAGAZINE
ENRY KUTTNER

ABOVE:
A shield emblem bearing the Timely Comics logo, early 1940s.

ABOVE RIGHT:
Marvel Tales vol. 1 no. 6 (December 1939).

RIGHT:
Marvel Science Stories vol. 1 no. 1 (August 1938), the first Timely publication to bear the name "Marvel".

OPPOSITE PAGE:
Marvel Comics #1 (October 1939). Art by Frank Paul.

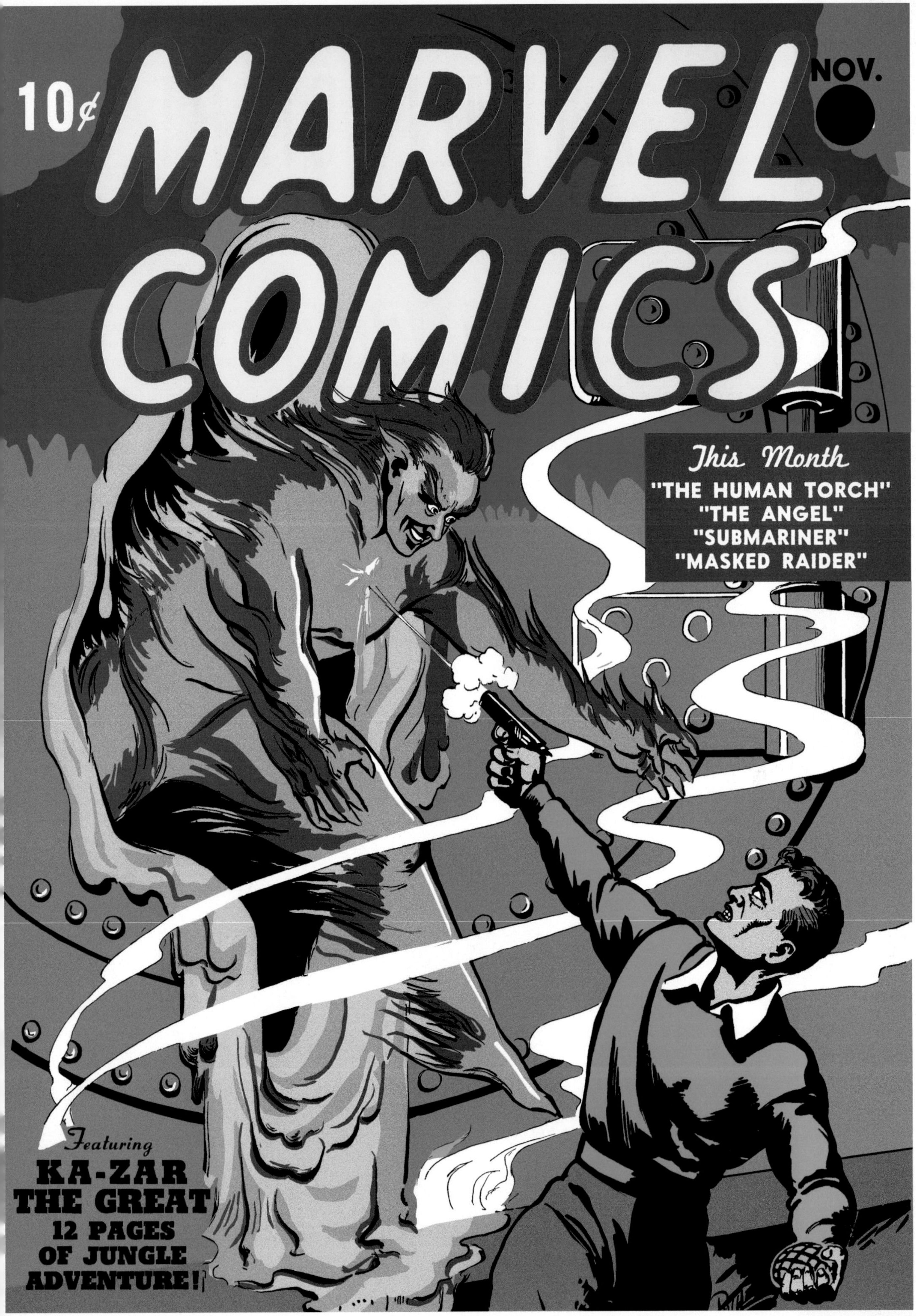
10¢
MARVEL COMICS
NOV.
This Month
"THE HUMAN TORCH"
"THE ANGEL"
"SUBMARINER"
"MASKED RAIDER"
Featuring
KA-ZAR
THE GREAT
12 PAGES
OF JUNGLE
ADVENTURE!

A TIMELY START

Before the world could marvel at Marvel, they would be in awe of the Super Heroes from Timely.

Timely's first comic book release featuring Super Heroes was *Marvel Comics #1*. In the upper right corner of the cover—sporting extraordinarily powerful artwork by Frank R. Paul—there appeared the month of publication, "Oct."

However, historians consider the official publication date to be August 31, 1939, inasmuch as comic book publication dates were always (and still are) postdated, for reasons linked to distribution.

By postdating their releases, comic books had a longer shelf life at newsstands. As for the artwork, the scenic impact is riveting. It shows a flaming android bursting through a steel wall and attacking a man who in vain fires a pistol at his assailant. The red banner at the bottom promises "Action Mystery Adventure." The top screamer shows the names of the issue's protagonists in quotes: The Human Torch, The Angel, Sub-Mariner and Masked Raider; the screamer in the lower left corner presents Ka-Zar The Great in bold.

DARING
10 MYSTERY COMICS
JANUARY
THE FIERY MASK

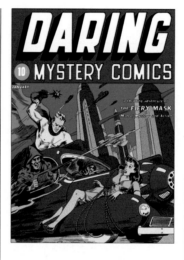

The issue was reprinted the following month and sold some 900,000 copies all told. A huge hit. Timely Publications, with offices at 330 West 42nd Street in Manhattan, had opened its doors in 1933 with the release of the pulp collection *Complete Western Book Magazine. Marvel Comics #1* was Goodman's very first comic book release. Beginning with issue #2, which hit newsstands two months later, *Marvel Comics* became *Marvel Mystery Comics*, which continued until 1949, amassing a total of 92 issues before morphing into *Marvel Tales*, which kept up the pace throughout most of the 1950s.

It was clear to Goodman that comic books were potentially big business, and he wasted no time in setting up his own staff of writers and illustrators, headed by Joe Simon and Jack Kirby, two emerging artists who worked in tandem. Simon became Timely's Editor in Chief, and together with Kirby created the Captain America character for the imprint that bore his name, *Captain America Comics*. The first issue, dated March 1941, hit newsstands on December 20, 1940, and sold for 10 cents. It sold a million copies, Goodman's biggest seller to date. Legend has it that the publisher quaked at the thought of Hitler's untimely death as the issue went into print. "What if *Der Führer* is killed in the meantime?" he reportedly wondered.

THIS PAGE: *Daring Mystery Comics #1* (January 1940). Art by Alex Schomburg.

MIDDLE: *Red Raven Comics #1* (August 1940). Art by Jack Kirby and Joe Simon.

FAR RIGHT: *Young Allies Comics #1* (Summer 1941). Art by Jack Kirby.

1930

A NEW COMPLETE 2ND NOVEL—15¢
WESTERN
15¢ SUPERNOVEL Magazine
MAY
JESS ROUNDTREE, TEXAS RANGER
STEVE PAYNE
CLEE WOODS

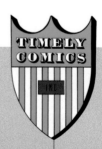

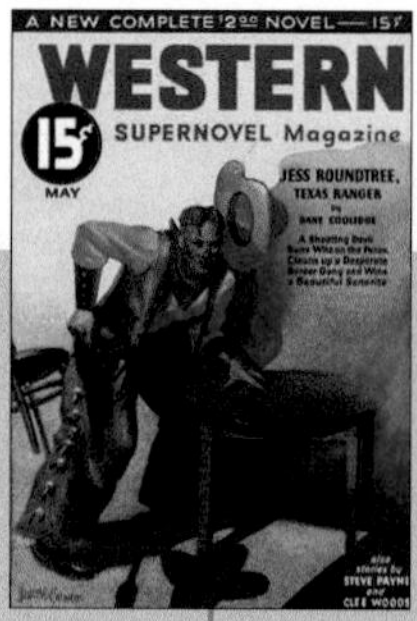

MAY 1933

It all begins with *Western Supernovel Magazine*, the first pulp magazine published by Martin Goodman, future head of Timely Comics, which would go on to become Marvel Comics.

JANUARY 1939

Timely Comics is officially founded on January 12, 1939. Its logo: a blue-and-white shield. Offices were initially located in Manhattan's McGraw-Hill Building.

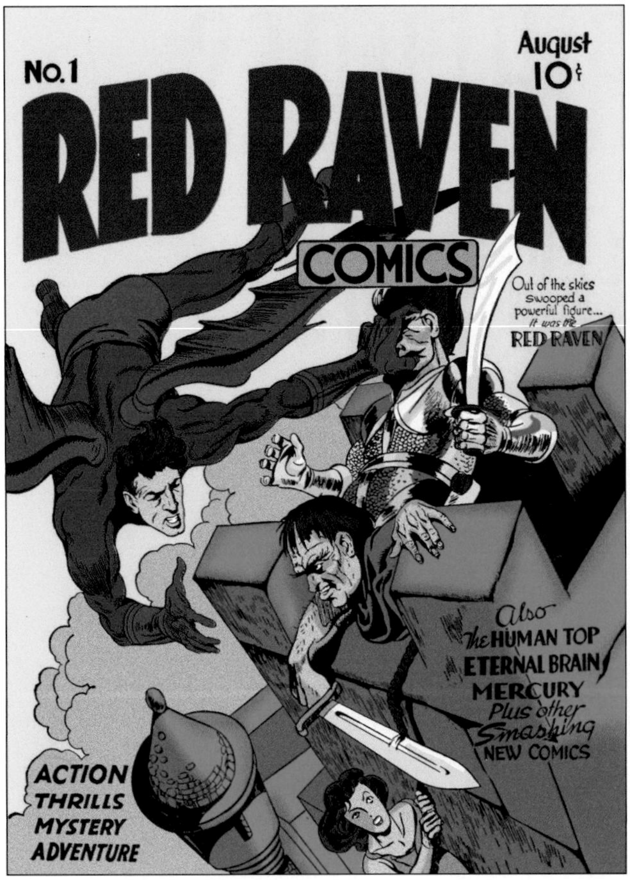
No.1
August
10¢
RED RAVEN
COMICS
Out of the skies swooped a powerful figure... It was the RED RAVEN
Also
The HUMAN TOP
ETERNAL BRAIN
MERCURY
Plus other Smashing NEW COMICS
ACTION
THRILLS
MYSTERY
ADVENTURE

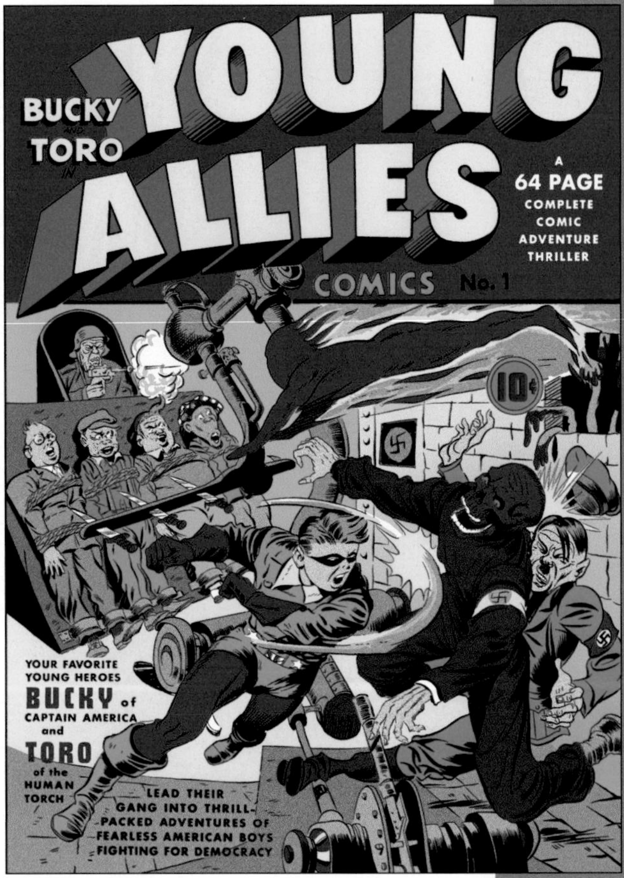
BUCKY AND TORO IN
YOUNG ALLIES
COMICS No. 1
A 64 PAGE COMPLETE COMIC ADVENTURE THRILLER
10¢
YOUR FAVORITE YOUNG HEROES
BUCKY of CAPTAIN AMERICA
and
TORO of the HUMAN TORCH
LEAD THEIR GANG INTO THRILL-PACKED ADVENTURES OF FEARLESS AMERICAN BOYS FIGHTING FOR DEMOCRACY

His fear was that the artwork for the cover might be obsolete before readers could get their hands on it. That first issue contained half a dozen stories: four starring Captain America, one featuring Hurricane, and the last turning the spotlight on Tuk the Caveboy.

Meanwhile, by 1940 The Human Torch had gotten his own comic book, dubbed *Human Torch Comics*, which began with issue #2, since it followed in the wake of the short-lived *Red Raven Comics*, yet another Timely publication. In the years 1940-42, Goodman's young publishing house had flooded the market with a host of new titles, including *All Select Comics, Daring Mystery Comics, Mystic Comics, Submariner Comics, Young Allies Comics,* and *All Winners Comics.*

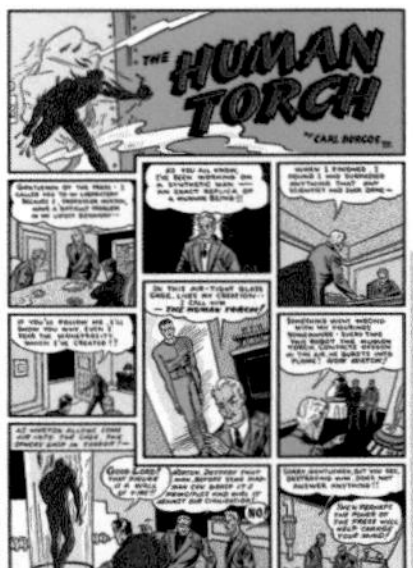
THE HUMAN TORCH

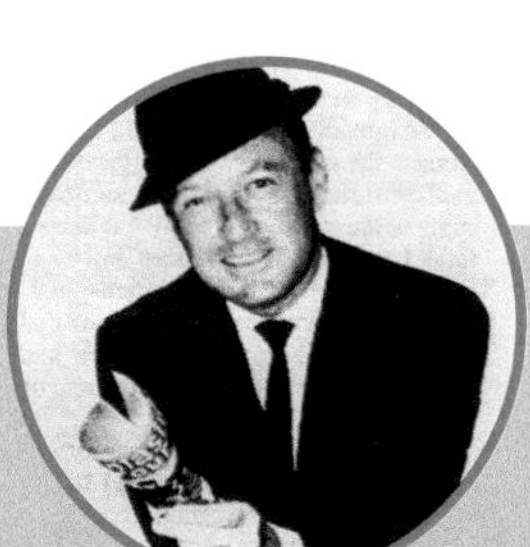

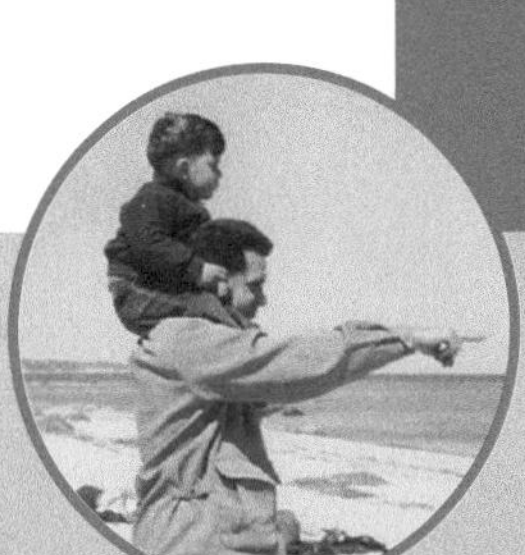

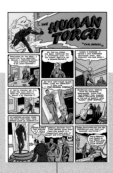

AUGUST 1939

Timely's first comic book featuring Super Heroes, *Marvel Comics* #1, hits the newsstands. It stars Carl Burgos's Human Torch, Bill Everett's Sub-Mariner, and Ka-Zar.

1939

17-year-old Stanley Lieber, better known as Stan Lee, is hired by Goodman as an assistant to Simon and Kirby. His first published story appeared in *Captain America Comics* #3 in 1941.

1940

Jack Kirby joins the staff of Timely Comics invited by Joe Simon, previously hired by Goodman. The team of Simon and Kirby became legendary in the annals of comic book storytelling.

SUPER HEROES AMONG US

They were dark, desperate times, and the call for heroes had never been stronger. Timely was ready to answer that call.

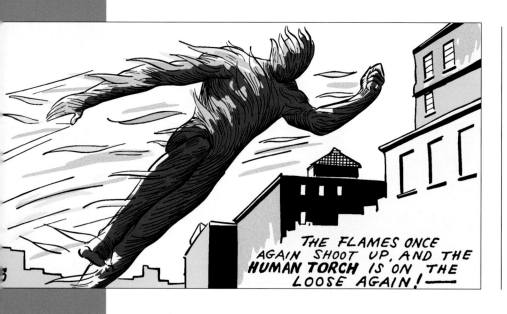

THE FLAMES ONCE AGAIN SHOOT UP, AND THE HUMAN TORCH IS ON THE LOOSE AGAIN!—

The key to Marvel's greatness has always been the humanity of its protagonists. There are no invincible, perfect, immaculate heroes among its ranks. Instead, they tend to be human beings much like us, possessed of commonplace weaknesses and fragility. They reveal contradiction after contradiction, focusing on characters who may lose even when they win, and often wind up being defeated by life. From the very beginning the seeds of restlessness, incompatibility with the world, diversity and solitude had already been sown, especially when it came to the three big names from Timely's Golden Age: Captain America, the Sub-Mariner, and the Human Torch.

AS THE TORCH LANDS ON THE BRIDGE, SUB-MARINER PICKS UP A STEEL GIRDER—
AND HURLS IT AT HIM.
HOW'S THIS, SUB-MARINER?

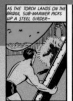

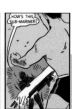

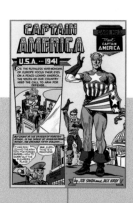

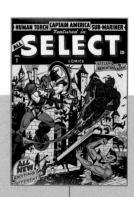

JUNE 1940

Timely's first crossover appears in *Marvel Mystery Comics* #8 featuring a clash between the Sub-Mariner and the Human Torch. The battle rages on in #9 and #10.

CAPTAIN AMERICA
CASE No. 1
Meet CAPTAIN AMERICA
U.S.A. ... 1941
by JOE SIMON and JACK KIRBY

DECEMBER 1940

Captain America, created by Simon and Kirby, makes his debut in *Captain America Comics* #1. The Super-Soldier sends Hitler reeling and declares war against the Nazis.

HUMAN TORCH CAPTAIN AMERICA SUB-MARINER
Featured in
ALL SELECT
No. 1
10¢
COMICS
HITLER'S BERCHTESGADEN
ALL NEW EXCITING DIFFERENT

FALL 1943

The release of *All-Select Comics*, a comic book featuring the adventures of Timely's top three Super Heroes: Captain America, the Human Torch and the Sub-Mariner.

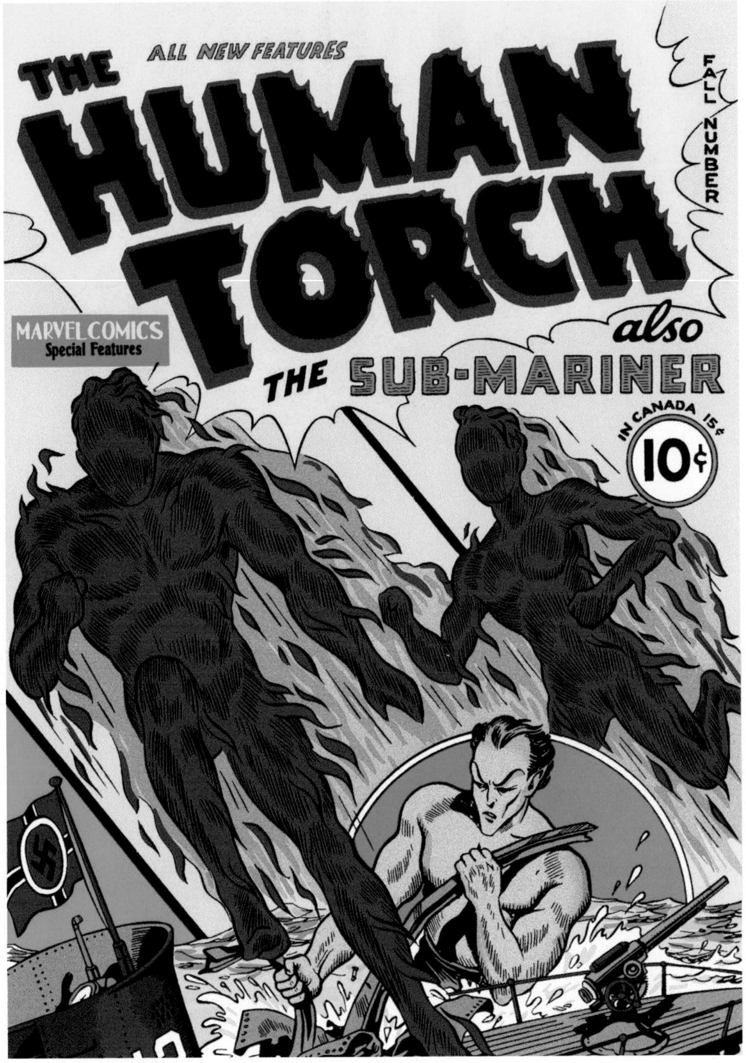
ALL NEW FEATURES
THE HUMAN TORCH
FALL NUMBER
MARVEL COMICS
Special Features
also
THE SUB-MARINER
IN CANADA 15¢
10¢

Indeed, they have remained household names even today. Captain America is a living legend straight out of World War II, who after a period of hibernation, sprung back into action in the 21st century. Namor the Sub-Mariner, a deep-sea prodigy, tends to be scornful and resentful in his dealings with humans; his hybrid nature allows him to age at a snail's pace. Lee and Kirby revamped him in stories that date to the 1960s. In the 1940s the Human Torch was depicted as a heroic android (i.e., an automaton with human features) created in a laboratory. In the 1960s, a hero with the same name joined the Fantastic Four, while the original would later be reworked.

The original Human Torch, created by Carl Burgos, was a creature born in scientist Phineas Horton's laboratory. Misunderstood, he inevitably terrorized the denizens of New York, where he had been created, because he was not yet able to control his fiery flare-ups. But soon he would convince people he was on their side in the fight against evil. He enrolled in the police academy and was often helped by his sidekick, Toro.

Namor the Sub-Mariner, a character conceived by artist Bill Everett, was half human with Atlantean blood coursing through his veins. His mother, Princess Fen, daughter of the Emperor of Atlantis, fell in love with Leonard McKenzie, a surface dweller. Theirs was a strained romance which came to an end with Fen's forced return to Atlantis, along with her son, Namor. As Prince of Atlantis, Namor would

OPOSITE PAGE: *The Human Torch* (October 1939). Script, pencils, and inks by Carl Burgos.

RIGHT: *The Human Torch Comics* #2 (October 1940). Art by Alex Schomburg.

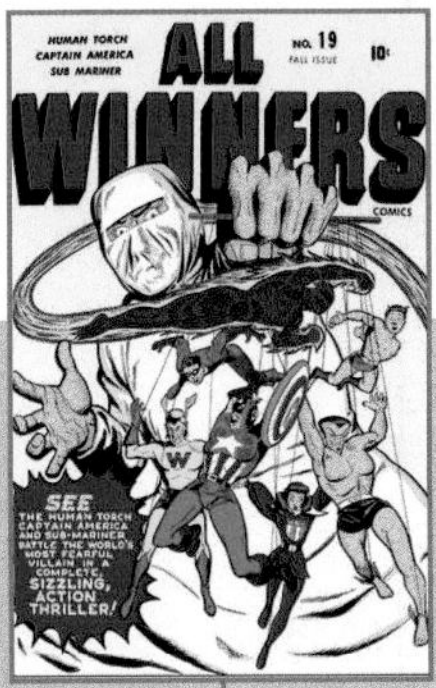
HUMAN TORCH
CAPTAIN AMERICA
SUB MARINER
ALL WINNERS
NO. 19
10¢
COMICS
SEE
THE HUMAN TORCH CAPTAIN AMERICA AND SUB-MARINER BATTLE THE WORLD'S MOST FEARFUL VILLAIN IN A COMPLETE SIZZLING, ACTION THRILLER!

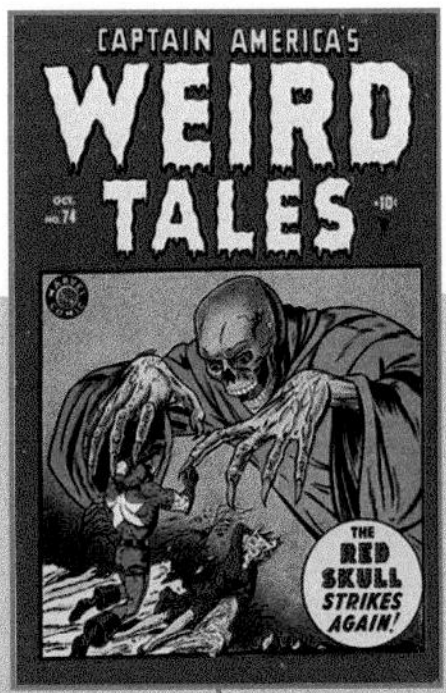
CAPTAIN AMERICA'S
WEIRD TALES
10¢
THE RED SKULL STRIKES AGAIN!

1950

FALL 1946

All-Winners Comics #19 contains the first story featuring the All-Winners Squad, a team with Captain America, Bucky, the Human Torch, Toro, the Sub-Mariner, Whizzer, and Miss America.

OCTOBER 1949

For Timely, the end of the Golden Age of Comic Books is generally thought to coincide with the release of *Captain America* #74. After, the comic had been retitled *Captain America's Weird Tales*.

have many an occasion to unleash his ire against the surface dwellers. He came off as haughty and presumptuous but, like the Human Torch and Toro, joined the fight against the Nazi war machine, together with Captain America and his sidekick, Bucky. Later on, Namor would often find himself straddling that thin, barely perceptible line that separates the good guys from the villains.

Then there's Captain America—the young and unassuming Steve Rogers, an illustrator deemed physically unfit to serve in the army. His dogged spirit and sense of patriotism were unmatched. Steve signed on to take part in an experiment whose outcome had the potential to turn the tide of the war. It involved receiving massive doses of the Super-Soldier Serum that had been perfected by Dr. Erskine (called Dr. Reinstein in the early stories). The experiment was a success—Steve was transformed into a superhuman, although shortly thereafter Erskine was murdered by a Nazi spy and took his secret formula with him to the grave. Captain America was born and, with his young sidekick Bucky, took on the Axis powers in Simon and Kirby's never-ending saga.

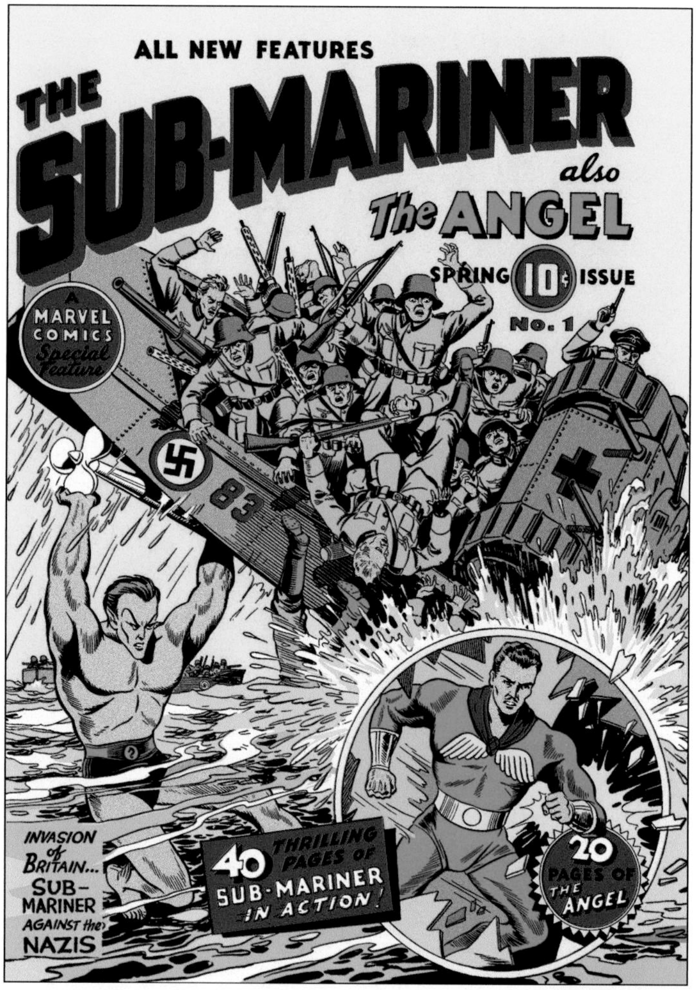
ALL NEW FEATURES
THE SUB-MARINER
also
The ANGEL
SPRING 10¢ ISSUE
No. 1
A MARVEL COMICS Special Feature
INVASION of BRITAIN... SUB-MARINER AGAINST the NAZIS
40 THRILLING PAGES OF SUB-MARINER IN ACTION!
20 PAGES OF THE ANGEL

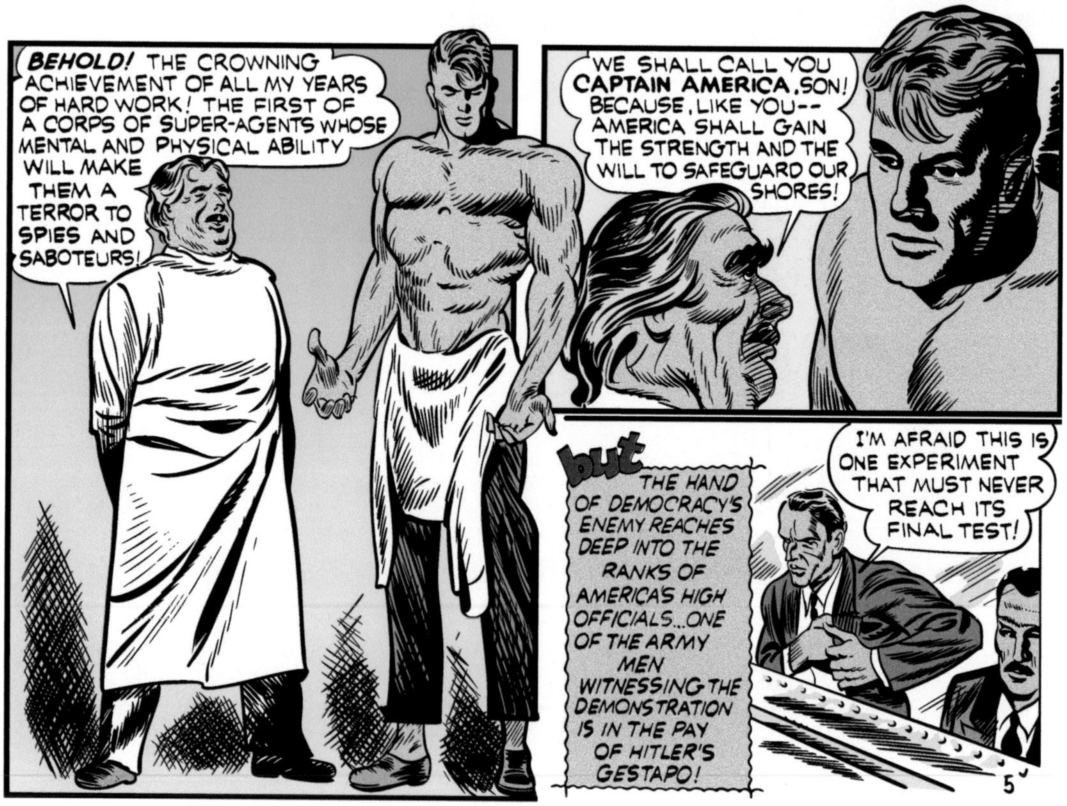
BEHOLD! THE CROWNING ACHIEVEMENT OF ALL MY YEARS OF HARD WORK! THE FIRST OF A CORPS OF SUPER-AGENTS WHOSE MENTAL AND PHYSICAL ABILITY WILL MAKE THEM A TERROR TO SPIES AND SABOTEURS!
WE SHALL CALL YOU CAPTAIN AMERICA, SON! BECAUSE, LIKE YOU-- AMERICA SHALL GAIN THE STRENGTH AND THE WILL TO SAFEGUARD OUR SHORES!
but... THE HAND OF DEMOCRACY'S ENEMY REACHES DEEP INTO THE RANKS OF AMERICA'S HIGH OFFICIALS...ONE OF THE ARMY MEN WITNESSING THE DEMONSTRATION IS IN THE PAY OF HITLER'S GESTAPO!
I'M AFRAID THIS IS ONE EXPERIMENT THAT MUST NEVER REACH ITS FINAL TEST!
5

ABOVE: *The Sub-Mariner Comics* #1 (April 1941). Art by Alex Schomburg.

RIGHT: The results of the Super-Soldier Serum are revealed. Captain *America Comics #1* (dated March 1941, released December 20, 1940). Script by Joe Simon and Jack Kirby. Art by Joe Simon and Jack Kirby (pencils), and Al Liederman (inks).

THE MEN BEHIND THE MAGIC

It took a team of brazen young men with brash ideas and bold pencils to bring the new Timely Super Heroes to life.

The history of a publishing house and its characters is inevitably the history of the creative minds behind the scenes, especially in an age when being a comic book artist was neither a stepping stone toward social and cultural respectability, nor a way to get rich. But now that they were stars in the world of comic books, Joe Simon and Jack Kirby weren't doing so bad for themselves. Simon was born in 1913 in Rochester, New York. His passion for drawing was matched by a keen sense of business acumen. He went to work straight out of high school, and was eventually recommended to Lloyd Jacquet, head of Funnies, Inc., which Timely Publications had commissioned to create another flaming Super Hero along the lines of the Human Torch.

Soon Simon would meet up with another young comic art prodigy, Jack Kirby (born Jacob Kurtzberg, 1917–1994), who, like Simon, was the son of an immigrant tailor. Kirby grew up on Manhattan's Lower East Side, the same working-class neighborhood where Steve Rogers (A.K.A. Captain America) was from. What a coincidence! Simon took an immediate liking to Kirby— who in all likelihood had grown up in circumstances even more humble than his own—and his artistry. Looking at them, this dynamic duo made an odd match: Joe was a tall, handsome young man with a certain *savoir faire* about him, while Jack was a scrappy little fellow who took no lip from anyone.

Many years later, people still remembered the day when Kirby literally kicked a messenger from the mob out of the publisher's offices when the punk showed up to "ask" whether Goodman and company might be interested in using suppliers affiliated with the underworld. Almost as if Kirby

LEFT:
Jack Kirby unleashes his imagination, circa 1949/early 1950.

"I was eleven when the first issue was published. My friends in Brooklyn, all comics traders, were unaware that it was not the usual Super Hero book. My own reactions foreshadowed my future in comics. I showed them how different it was from all the others they had seen, and noticed the figures leaping out of the panels making every page so exciting. It was clear to me that this 'Simon and Kirby' were not doing the ordinary comics we'd known."

—John Romita, Sr., artist

ABOVE:
Illustration featuring Jack Kirby (left) and Joe Simon at work in the 1940s, from Marvel's in-house fan magazine *FOOM #8* (1973). *FOOM* stood for Friends of Ol' Marvel.

OPPOSITE PAGE:
Interior page from Marvel *Mystery Comics #8* (June 1940). Script by Bill Everett, art by Bill Everett and Carl Burgos.

had been one of the Super Heroes that he himself had created. Captain America was their biggest hit at Timely, where Simon had become editor in chief (the very first at Goodman's storied publishing house) and Kirby worked as art director. Before moving on, the two had been responsible for Captain America's first 10 issues, and continued working together for a decade and a half. It was hard to tell where one's work finished and the other's began. Kirby would later return to the Marvel Comics fold for a stint in the 1960s and again in the 1970s.

It so happened that in those days another young hopeful began working for Timely, a distant relative of Goodman's by the name of Stanley Martin Lieber (1922– 2019). He too

was the son of European immigrants, and dreamed of becoming an acclaimed novelist. He worked under the pen name of Stan Lee, figuring he'd save his real name for the novel that, alas, never got written (though at the time he hardly realized that the Marvel odyssey itself would become a great American novel). Once Simon and Kirby set out on their own, Goodman made Lieber hwis editor in chief, even though he was only 19 years old. A move Goodman would never regret.

In those days, more great talent had come to the fore. Besides Simon and Kirby, A-list comic book artists included the likes of Carl Burgos and Bill Everett. Both worked for Funnies, Inc. Burgos (whose real name was Max Finkelstein) had created the first

Marvel Super Hero ever to appear on a comic book cover, the Human Torch, which of course had been a tremendous success right off the bat. Burgos got his start at what had been dubbed Harry "A" Chesler's studio, where he specialized in drawing backgrounds and inking, but soon evolved into an artist with his own very distinct personality. Everett's art was even more celebrated.

A virtuoso illustrator, Everett also had an eye for humor (among his many collaborations, he worked for *Cracked* magazine), although he would go down in history as one of the greatest Silver Age comic book artists. In 1964, he co-created Daredevil with Stan Lee. Unfortunately, Everett met an untimely end in 1973.

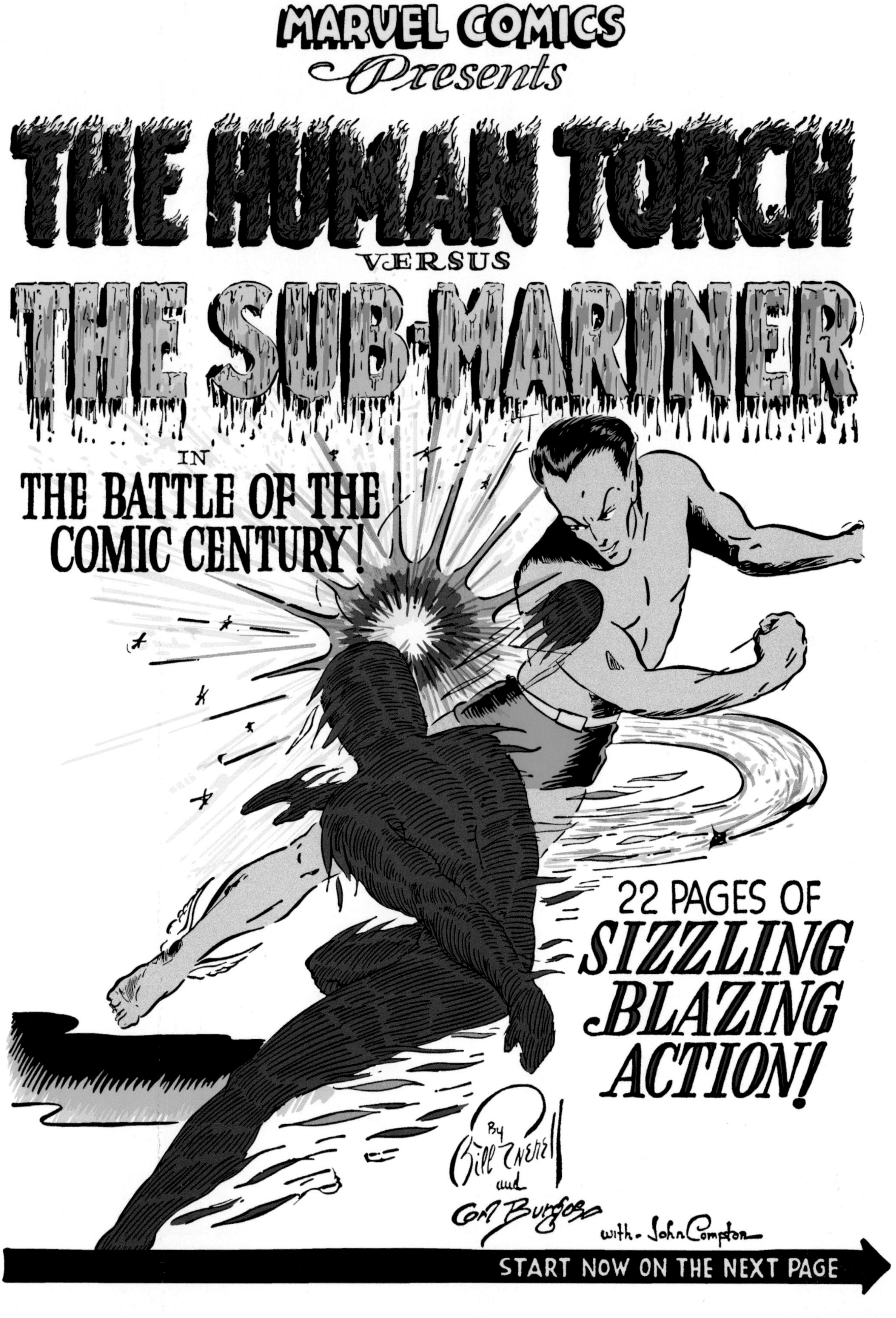
MARVEL COMICS
Presents
THE HUMAN TORCH
VERSUS
THE SUB-MARINER
IN
THE BATTLE OF THE COMIC CENTURY!
22 PAGES OF
SIZZLING BLAZING ACTION!
START NOW ON THE NEXT PAGE

OUTSIDE INFLUENCES

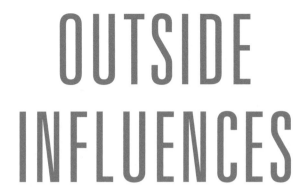

The characters and stories of Timely Comics were swayed by the sentiments of the era—and almost immediately, they affected the world of popular culture. The image was indelible, instantly unforgettable.

THIS PAGE: Readers who joined Captain America's Sentinels of Liberty club in 1941 could receive this badge, along with a membership card.

BELOW: *All Winners Comics #1* (dated June 1941, released July 10, 1941). Cover by Alex Schomburg.

OPPOSITE PAGE: The Human Torch, Captain America, and Sub-Mariner get ready to take on the Axis Powers in a house ad for *All-Winners Comics #5* (featured in *Marvel Mystery Comics #34*, August 1942).

Martin Goodman's comic books spoke his readers' language, providing precious minutes of escape from the harshness that plagued their existences and a promise of deliverance. On an emotional level, this was something readers could identify with. That's why the first issue of *Captain America Comics* sold a million copies, and the year before Marvel Comics #1 had hit the 900,000 mark. In 1941, 30 U.S. publishers cranked out 150 comic books, with some 15 million copies sold to 50–60 million loyal readers—an immense market, the likes of which had never been dreamed of in the burgeoning comic book sector.

CAPTAIN
AMERICA
A
SENTINELS OF LIBERTY

ALL
WINNERS
COMICS
10¢
No. 1
5 NEW FAMOUS
ACTION
FEATURES
CAPTAIN AMERICA and BUCKY
HUMAN TORCH and TORO
SUB-MARINER
THE ANGEL · BLACK MARVEL
SUMMER ISSUE

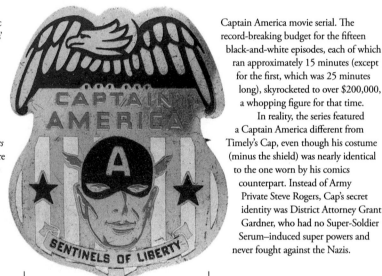

Targeting younger readers, comic books were the heirs of pulp literature—pop culture stories and novels usually on the lower end of the quality spectrum, whose authors were paid by the word, which often attained best-seller status. The "pulp" moniker took its cue from the cheap paper used to print them, which was made from low-grade pulpwood. The soon-to-yellow pages featured the debuts of characters like the Shadow and Doc Savage, who would go on to become comic book staples, even if pulp fiction content was more adult-oriented.

By the 1940s radio and film adaptations had made their way onto the scene, which meant that once again Timely's Super Heroes played their part in pioneering the latest developments in mass entertainment. In 1944, with the defeat of the Axis powers on the horizon, Republic Pictures created the Captain America movie serial. The record-breaking budget for the fifteen black-and-white episodes, each of which ran approximately 15 minutes (except for the first, which was 25 minutes long), skyrocketed to over $200,000, a whopping figure for that time.

In reality, the series featured a Captain America different from Timely's Cap, even though his costume (minus the shield) was nearly identical to the one worn by his comics counterpart. Instead of Army Private Steve Rogers, Cap's secret identity was District Attorney Grant Gardner, who had no Super-Soldier Serum–induced super powers and never fought against the Nazis.

Timely's Super Heroes played their part in pioneering the latest developments in mass entertainment.

By the second half of the 1940s, America was on the eve of its post-war economic boom. The days of Super Heroes bashing enemies like Adolf Hitler had come to an end. Comic book print runs began to shrink, forcing Timely to come up with new formulas for success. Dangers of a different kind lurked just around the corner, and the comic book industry was already gearing up to meet the challenges of the next decade. ■

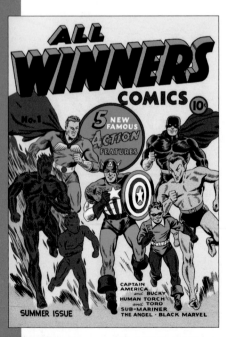

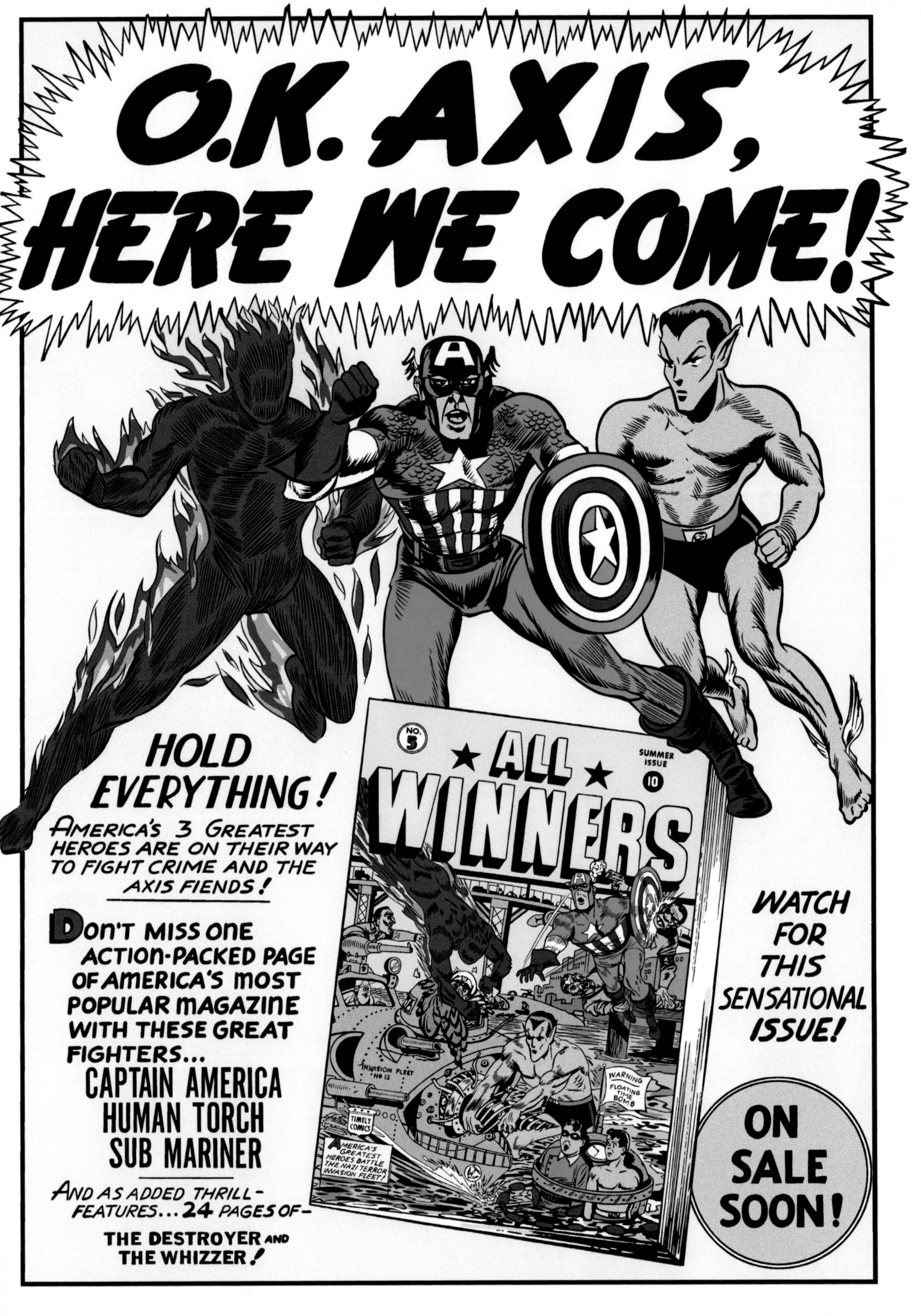
O.K. AXIS, HERE WE COME!
HOLD EVERYTHING!
AMERICA'S 3 GREATEST HEROES ARE ON THEIR WAY TO FIGHT CRIME AND THE AXIS FIENDS!
DON'T MISS ONE ACTION-PACKED PAGE OF AMERICA'S MOST POPULAR MAGAZINE WITH THESE GREAT FIGHTERS...
CAPTAIN AMERICA
HUMAN TORCH
SUB MARINER
AND AS ADDED THRILL-FEATURES... 24 PAGES OF-
THE DESTROYER AND THE WHIZZER!
NO. 5
ALL WINNERS
SUMMER ISSUE
10
INVASION FLEET NO 12
WARNING FLOATING TIME BOMB
TIMELY COMICS
AMERICA'S GREATEST HEROES BATTLE THE NAZI TERROR INVASION FLEET!
WATCH FOR THIS SENSATIONAL ISSUE!
ON SALE SOON!

THE 1950s

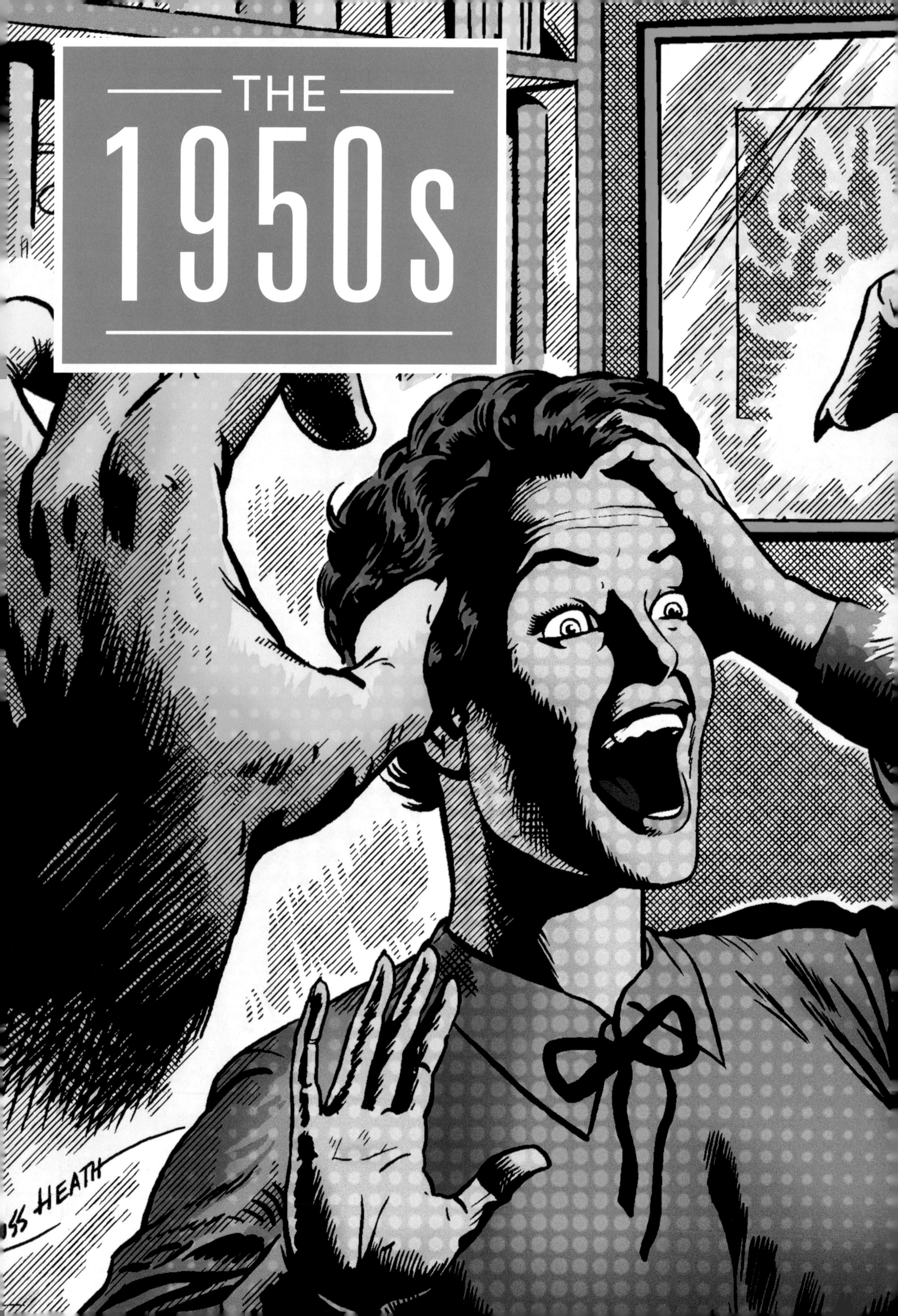

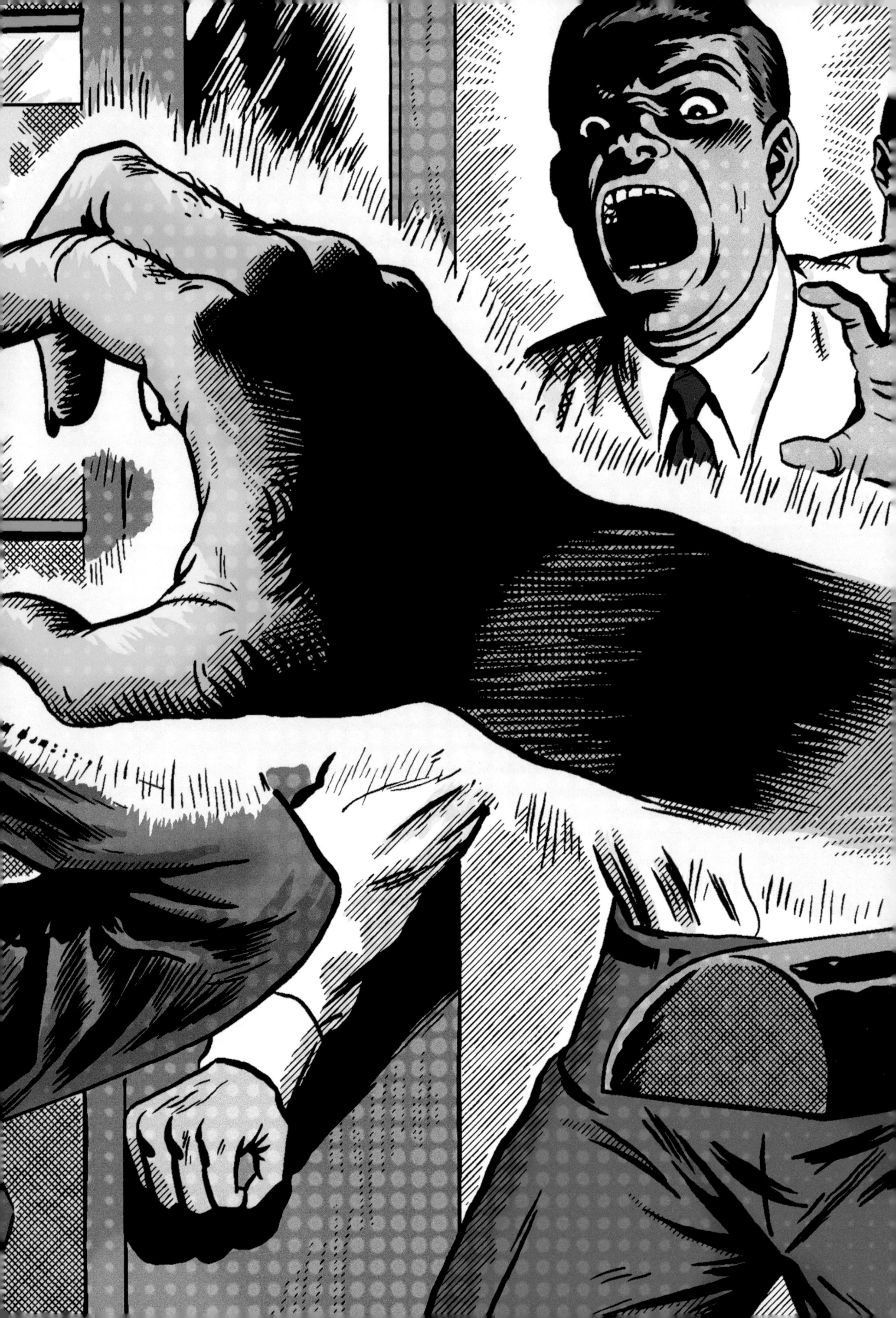

NEW THREATS

By the dawn of the 1950s, new and complex scenarios were coming into play that would be of concern not only to nations, but to the publishers of comic books as well. Among them, Martin Goodman's Timely Publications.

Mankind was gripped by fears that unbridled progress in atomic energy would go unchecked, with potentially disastrous consequences, while tensions were escalating between the United States and the Soviet Union (already engaged in the Cold War). It was hardly a time when people could rest easy. But as the events unfolded, they provided new angles for the creators of comic book stories.

Other factors threatened the very existence of comic books, even if they were by no means on a par with the arms race. Enter: Dr. Fredric Wertham, a child psychiatrist and author of a 1954 study on comic books and their presumed negative influence on young readers.

In America, his *Seduction of the Innocent* sparked an ethical and moral crusade that, as we shall see, pretty much held the entire industry hostage, forcing publishers to adopt a code of self-regulation to keep from going under.

Not even Goodman and company could eschew this sudden and violent about-face. Meanwhile, beginning with comic books cover-dated November 1951, the old Timely shield was replaced with a new logo, Atlas. The logo—a white globe crisscrossed by black lines indicating longitude and latitude—belonged to Martin Goodman's own distribution company. The logo appeared on most of the company's comic books during this time, and it came to be known as the Atlas era.

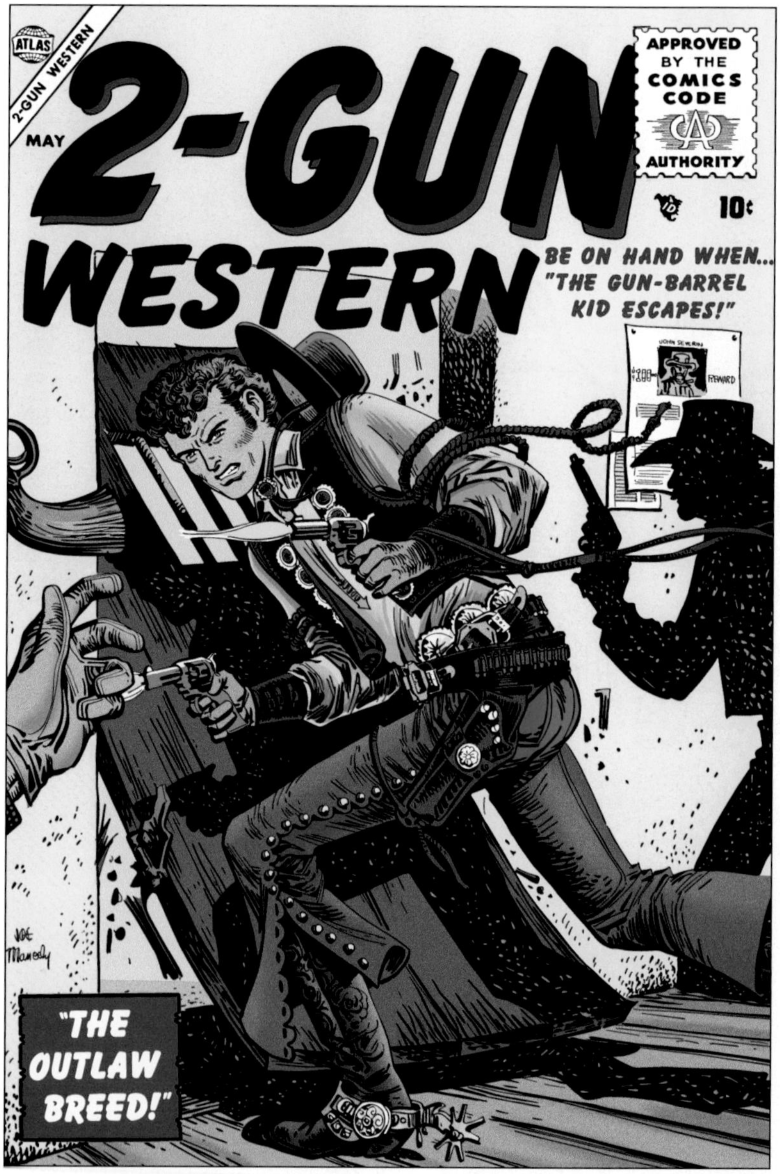
ATLAS
2-GUN WESTERN
MAY
2-GUN WESTERN
APPROVED BY THE COMICS CODE AUTHORITY
10¢
BE ON HAND WHEN... "THE GUN-BARREL KID ESCAPES!"
"THE OUTLAW BREED!"

THIS PAGE: *2-Gun Western* #4 (May 1956). Art by Joe Maneely (pencils, inks).

OPPOSITE PAGE: *Astonishing #30* (Feb. 1954). Art by Joe Maneely and Stan Goldberg.

What's more, by this time Super Heroes were on their way out. Readers were now more interested in romance, westerns, horror, war, crime, and humor. Soon they'd also be turning their attention to adventures featuring aliens and monsters, as an all-new genre was about to embark upon its own Golden Age: Science Fiction.

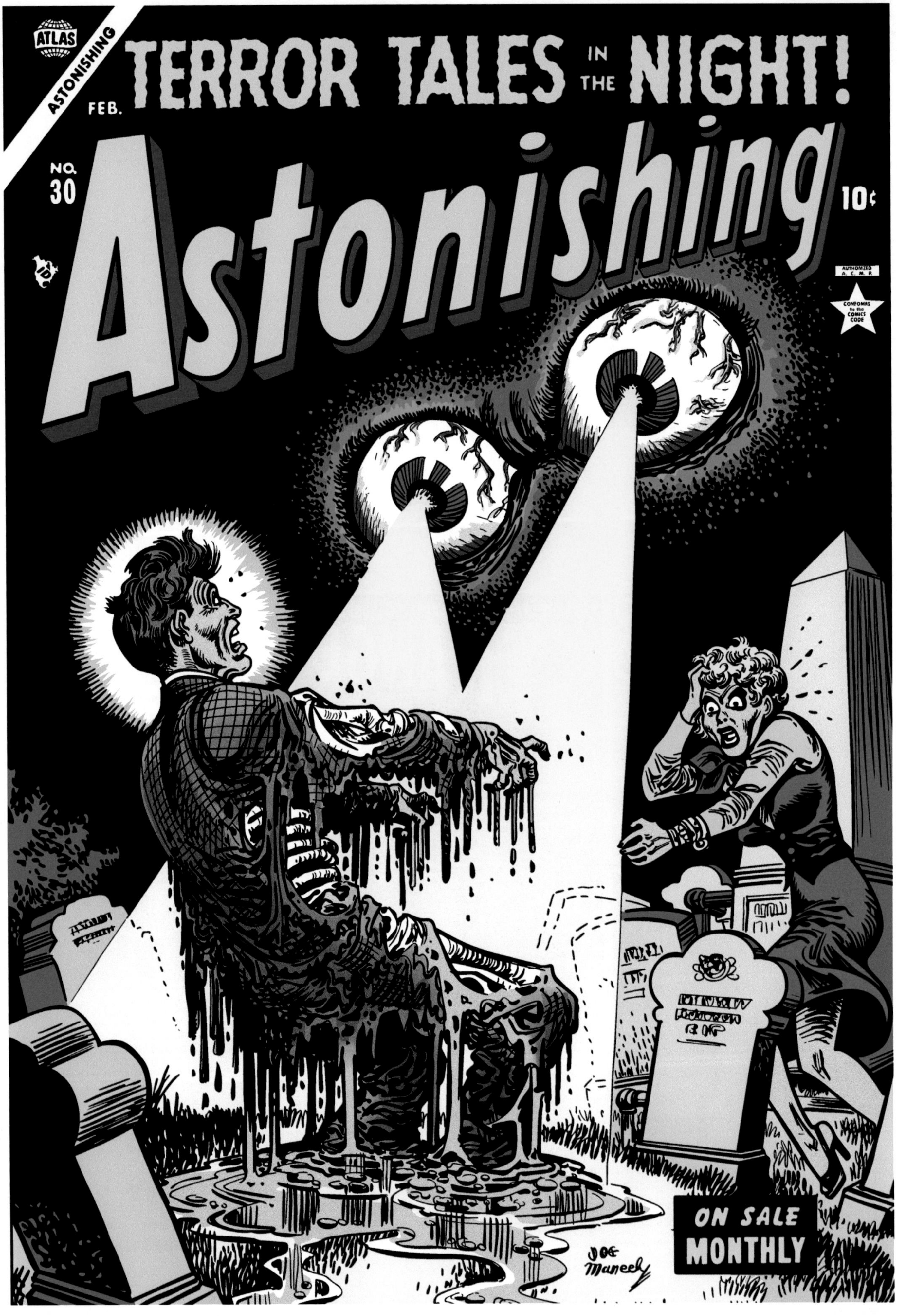

ATLAS
ASTONISHING
TERROR TALES IN THE NIGHT!
FEB.
NO. 30
Astonishing
10¢
AUTHORIZED A. C. M. P.
CONFORMS to the COMICS CODE
ON SALE MONTHLY
JOE Maneely

MODELS, MONSTERS, AND BLACK KNIGHTS

As the popularity of Super Heroes waned in the 1950s, other genres came to the forefront—with a vengeance.

MILLIE
NO. 1 the MODEL 10¢
COMICS
WATCH ME THROW A PERFECT STRIKE!

STRANGE TALES OF STARTLING SUSPENSE!
STRANGE TALES
10¢
JUNE
NO LIVING CREATURE KNEW THE TERRIFYING SECRET OF "THE ROOM!"
ALSO IN THIS ISSUE
"THE STRANGE MEN!"
"A CALL IN THE NIGHT!"
"THE BEAST!"
KEEP WALKING, RESTON! THAT'S IT... JUST A LITTLE FURTHER! ONE MORE STEP AND ALL YOUR WORRIES WILL BE OVER!
NO...NO! YOU CAN'T MAKE ME GO IN THERE!

THE GREATEST KNIGHT OF THEM ALL!
APPROVED BY THE COMICS CODE AUTHORITY
APR. NO. 5
BLACK KNIGHT
10¢
THRILLS FROM KING ARTHUR AND HIS KNIGHTS OF THE ROUND TABLE!
ALL NEW STORIES
CAN THE MIGHTY BLACK KNIGHT DEFEAT "THE INVINCIBLE TARTAR!"

BELOW LEFT: *Millie the Model #1* (December 1945). Written by Stan Lee, art and cover by Stan Goldberg,

MIDDLE: *Strange Tales #1* (June 1951). Art by Carl Burgos (pencils).

ABOVE RIGHT: *Black Knight #5* (April 1956). Art by Joe Maneely (pencils)

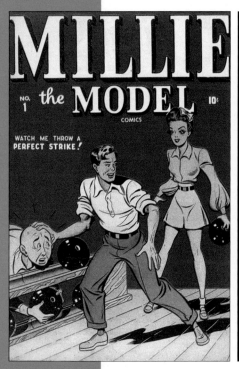

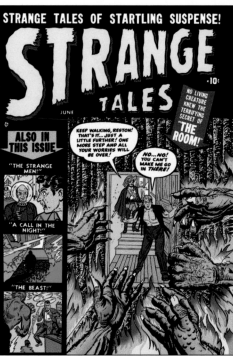

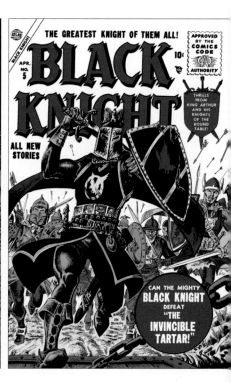

The last of Timely's Super Hero titles, *Captain America Comics*, came to an end with issue #75, cover-dated February 1950. An entire fictional universe had disappeared, although characters with super-powers, dressed in tight suits, would be making a comeback soon enough.

Atlas began releasing a diversified array of comic book genres in an attempt to win over new audiences. They targeted girls with *Millie the Model*, a series that reached its height in popularity during the 1950s (though it had been created in the 1940s).

Among the hundreds of titles churned out at this time, four played a crucial role in expanding Goodman's empire, and continued until the 1960s, when they helped to launch a handful of Lee, Kirby, and Ditko's Super Heroes with super problems. The first of these was *Strange Tales* (#1 cover-dated June 1951), a monthly horror show featuring creepy monsters with outrageous names like Fin Fang Foom

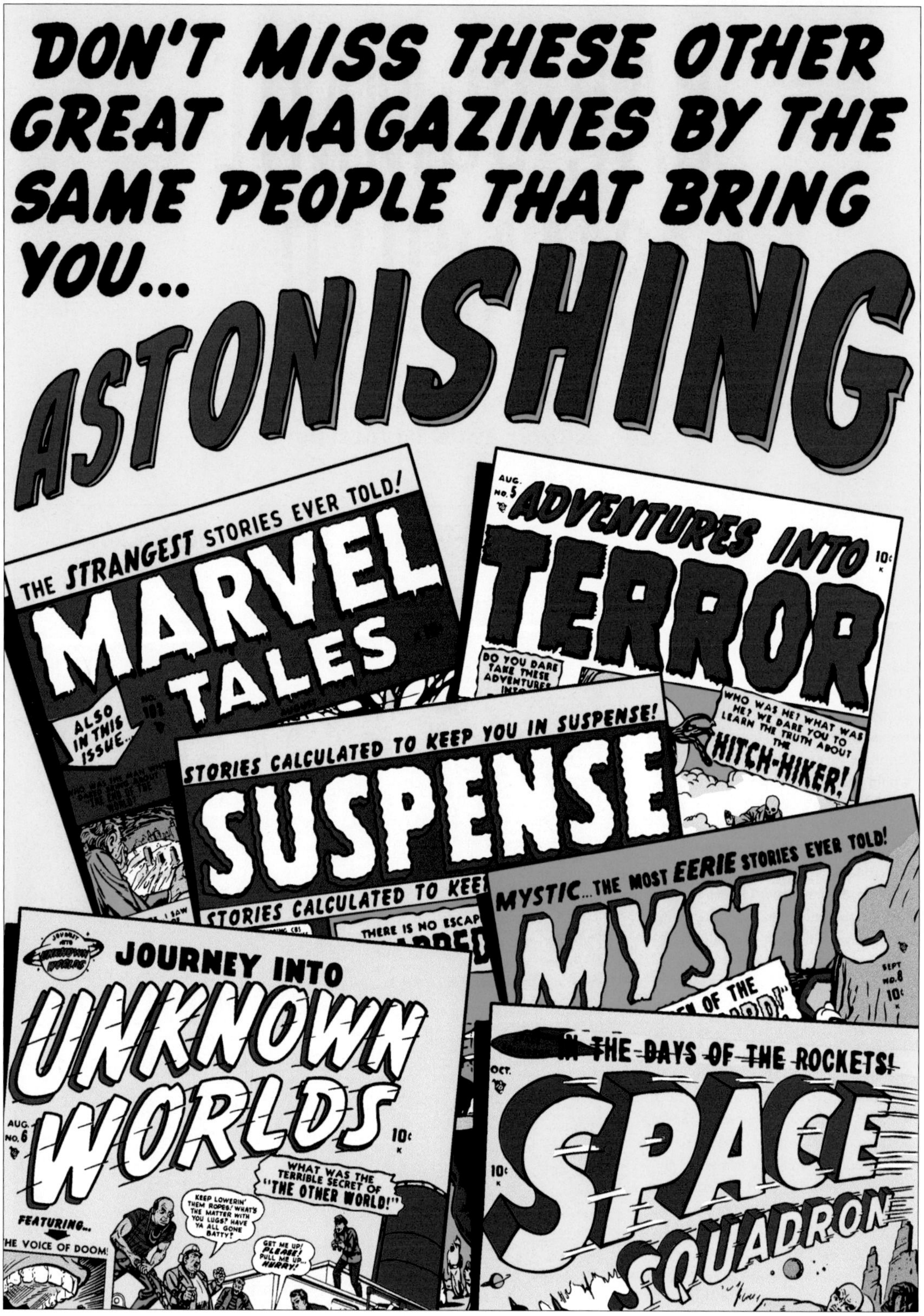
DON'T MISS THESE OTHER GREAT MAGAZINES BY THE SAME PEOPLE THAT BRING YOU...
ASTONISHING
THE STRANGEST STORIES EVER TOLD!
MARVEL TALES
ALSO IN THIS ISSUE...
AUG. NO. 5
ADVENTURES INTO TERROR
10¢
DO YOU DARE TAKE THESE ADVENTURES
WHO WAS HE? WHAT WAS HE? WE DARE YOU TO LEARN THE TRUTH ABOUT THE HITCH-HIKER!
STORIES CALCULATED TO KEEP YOU IN SUSPENSE!
SUSPENSE
STORIES CALCULATED TO KEE
THERE IS NO ESCAP
MYSTIC... THE MOST EERIE STORIES EVER TOLD!
MYSTIC
SEPT NO. 8
10¢
JOURNEY INTO UNKNOWN WORLDS
AUG. NO. 6
10¢
WHAT WAS THE TERRIBLE SECRET OF "THE OTHER WORLD!"
KEEP LOWERIN' THEM ROPES! WHAT'S THE MATTER WITH YOU LUGS? HAVE YA ALL GONE BATTY?
GET ME UP! PLEASE! PULL ME UP... HURRY!
FEATURING...
THE VOICE OF DOOM!
IN THE DAYS OF THE ROCKETS!
OCT.
10¢
SPACE SQUADRON

THIS PAGE: An assortment of Atlas comic book offerings from 1951..

and Orrgo. *Journey Into Mystery* was next. It debuted in June 1952 and featured more monsters and scary stories.

Then came the sci-fi titles *Tales of Suspense* and *Tales to Astonish*, both of which hit newsstands in June 1959. The wild names and the imaginative cover art sparked audiences' curiosity. Other titles from that time, including *Jungle Action*, *Black Knight*, *Love Romances*, *War Comics*, *Kid Colt*, and *Rawhide Kid*, reveal the depth of genres then available.

But that didn't mean it was all over for the Super Heroes. In 1954, Goodman opted for a relaunch. He put Stan Lee in charge of writing and editing new stories. Short runs featured old favorites like the Human Torch (three issues), Captain America (three issues), and the Sub-Mariner (ten issues). But readers weren't hooked the way they had been in the 1930s and '40s, and it looked like this chapter in comic book history had come to an end for the moment.

CAP, COMMIE SMASHER

The Super Heroes reappear mid-decade, but they aren't exactly the same as their 1940s counterparts.

The return of Captain America excited readers who still remembered his feats of World War II heroism. But times had changed. The new Cap, in stories written by Stan Lee and illustrated by the young artist John Romita, Sr.—whom we'll be hearing a lot more about—was a man of the 1950s, fighting the Red Menace instead of the Nazis. He had become a "commie smasher" in stories that Marvel would later decide to attribute to another character entirely. At any rate, the Cold War Captain America came to symbolize an age whose concerns proved long lasting. Even in the stories starring the new Super Heroes of the 1960s, especially those revolving around the Avengers and Iron Man, the Red Menace still loomed large.

Meanwhile, the character from this "Super Hero revival" that seemed to have the most going for it was none other than the Sub-Mariner. After the first film appearance by Captain America in the 1940s, it was very nearly the Sub-Mariner's turn to make the leap to the screen. But not the big screen—in this case, certain producers figured the Prince of Atlantis would be perfect for a new TV series. They had even chosen actor Richard Egan (of *Love Me Tender* fame), for the part. But for reasons lost to time, the project never got off the ground (not even a pilot was made).

Millie the Model, however, remained a hit. One reason behind her continued success was cartoonist Dan DeCarlo. Besides Millie, another female star had joined the ranks—the pretty young redhead Patsy Walker, who, like Millie, often found herself involved in love stories with comic overtones. In the decades that followed, Marvel would revamp Patsy and transform her in ways that 1950s Patsy could only imagine.

ATLAS
SUB-MARINER
SUB-MARINER...SCOURGE OF THE SEA!
AUG.
NO. 35
SUB-MARINER

THIS PAGE: *Sub-Mariner Comics* #35 (August 1954). Art by Russ Heath.

OPPOSITE PAGE: *Captain America* #78 (September 1954). Art by John Romita, Sr. (pencils).

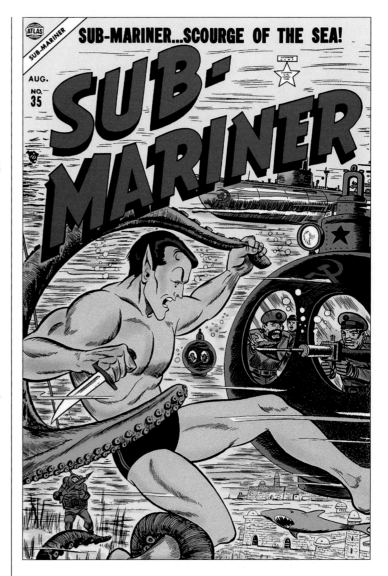

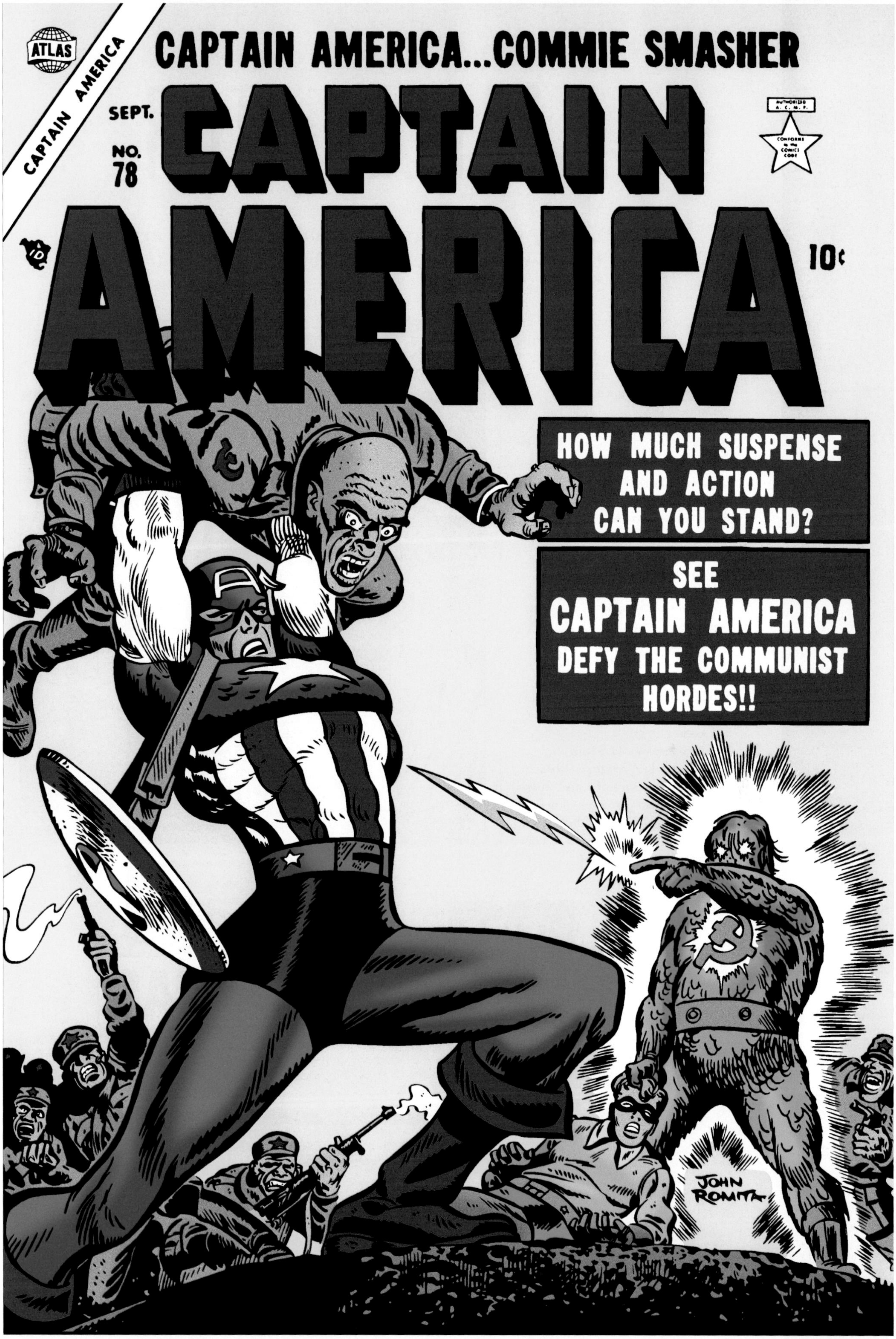
ATLAS
CAPTAIN AMERICA
CAPTAIN AMERICA...COMMIE SMASHER
SEPT.
NO. 78
CAPTAIN AMERICA
10¢
HOW MUCH SUSPENSE AND ACTION CAN YOU STAND?
SEE CAPTAIN AMERICA DEFY THE COMMUNIST HORDES!!
JOHN ROMITA

A FALLEN STAR

Joe Maneely was among Atlas' stable of amazing artists in the 1950s—but his career would be cut short by tragedy.

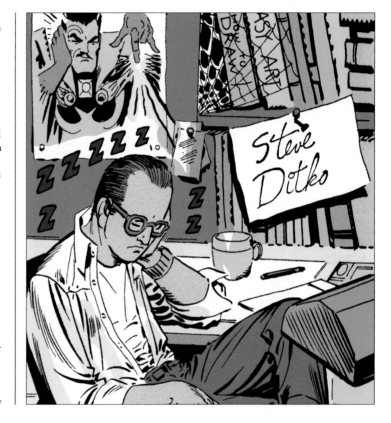

Stan Lee remained as editor in chief at Atlas Comics, Martin Goodman's small but feisty Manhattan-based publishing outfit, where he scripted most of the stories. As a writer, Lee had an uncanny knack for changing gears, and could move from Super Heroes to westerns and beyond with ease. He had an inborn talent for dialogue, and brilliantly molded his characters' often slangy speech patterns.

Lee worked alongside three artists who themselves epitomized comic book creativity. One was Jack Kirby, who in the late 1950s returned to Atlas after setting out on his own a few years prior. Next was Steve Ditko, an amazing visual storyteller with just the right touch of weirdness for the times. Together, Kirby and Ditko illustrated hundreds of stories for Atlas Comics in genres that included horror, adventure, and sci-fi.

Then there was Joe Maneely, arguably Stan Lee's favorite collaborator of the era. An extremely talented artist, Maneely was known to work without pencils, and inked right off the bat. As Lee was fond of saying, "He could draw

Steve Ditko

THIS PAGE: A self-portrait of Steve Ditko "hard at work" from the featurette, "How Stan Lee and Steve Ditko Create Spider-Man!" (*The Amazing Spider-Man Annual* #1, October 1964). Script by Stan Lee. Art by Steve Ditko (pencils and inks).

OPOSITE PAGE: Artist Joe Maneely at the drawing board in San Francisco, California, 1945.

Captain America's
WEIRD TALES
THING
CHEST!

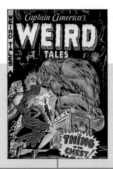

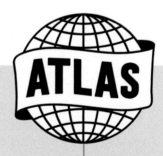

1950

FEBRUARY 1950

Captain America's Weird Tales #75 marks the end of the series dedicated to the Super Hero created by Joe Simon and Jack Kirby.

NOVEMBER 1951

The official debut of Atlas Comics, whose name was taken from Goodman's own distribution company. The name would change to Marvel Comics in 1961.

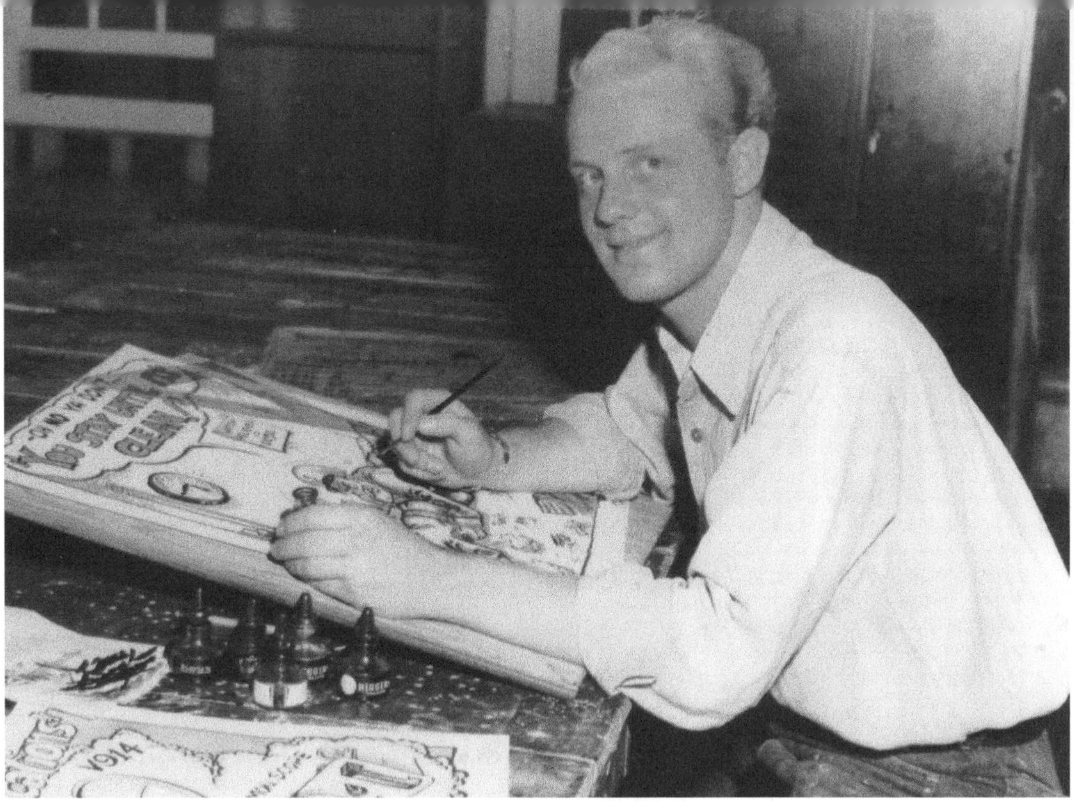

Artist Joe Maneely was one of Stan Lee's favorite collaborators.

anything." With Maneely's fine lines, speed, and versatility, he might very well have gone on to become a key member in the Super Hero boom of the 1960s. Sadly, a tragic accident ended his young life at the age of 32. While returning to New Jersey after a dinner in Manhattan with fellow artists on the night of June 7, 1958, Maneely was struck by a commuter train, and was killed.

Other artists worked with Lee as well. They included Bill Everett, who returned to work on horror comics and the Sub-Mariner following the glory days of the Golden Age, as well as Wally Wood, Syd Shores, Paul Reinman, Dick Ayers, Larry Lieber (Stan's younger brother), Don Heck, George Tuska, and Gene Colan, who were all future stars of the Marvel Age.

By the late 1950s, Atlas Comics was in trouble. Comic book sales across the board had dropped. Martin Goodman had shut down his distributorship in 1956, and struck a deal with the American News Company, which, however, soon closed its doors. The upshot: Goodman was forced to sign a distribution deal with the "Distinguished Competition," rival National Periodical Publications (the future DC Comics), which drastically cut the number of Goodman's monthly comic book releases. Ultimately, Goodman would opt to sift through the Atlas archives and use the wealth of heretofore unpublished stories and artwork he found there, ordering Lee to hold off on buying any new material. Staff were laid off. Disheartened, Lee was left to hold down the fort.

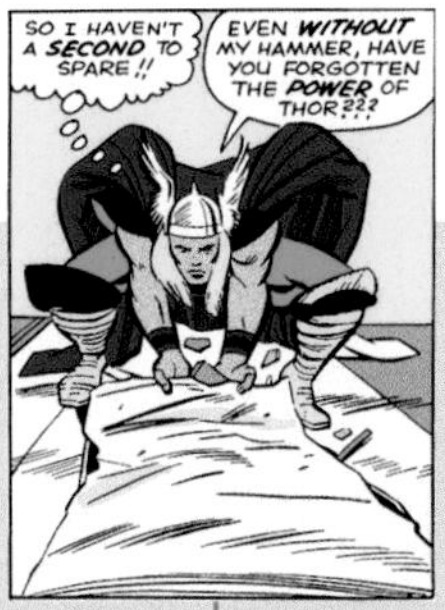
SO I HAVEN'T A SECOND TO SPARE!!
EVEN WITHOUT MY HAMMER, HAVE YOU FORGOTTEN THE POWER OF THOR???

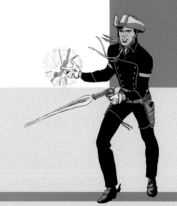

JUNE 1952

The horror and suspense series *Journey into Mystery* is released, following 1951's *Strange Tales*. Thor would make his first appearance in the August 1962 issue.

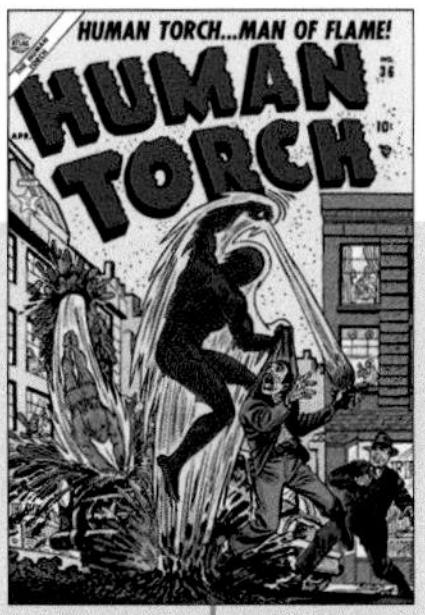
HUMAN TORCH...MAN OF FLAME!
HUMAN TORCH

APRIL 1954

The Human Torch, the Sub-Mariner and Captain America returned in *Young Men #24* (December 1953). The heroes would appear in their own short-lived titles as well.

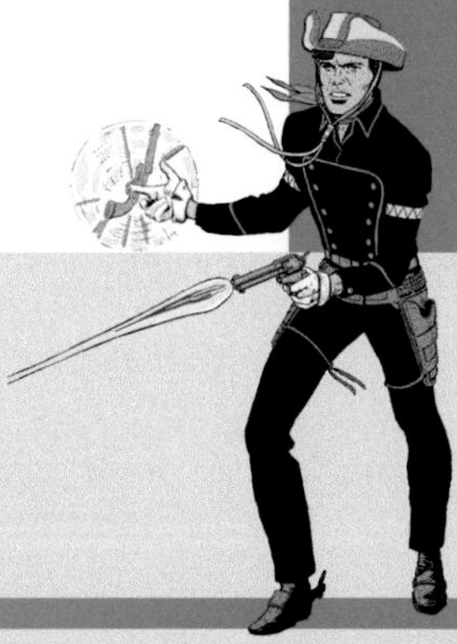

SPRING 1955

Rawhide Kid, one of Marvel's most celebrated western heroes, debuts. The series would become even more popular in the 1960s, along with other western heroes like Kid Colt.

U.S. VS. THE COMICS INDUSTRY

In the 1950s, comics came to symbolize a new type of menace for some—but how would comics respond to this attack?

The 1950s would also go down in history as the era of McCarthyism, a term denoting the witch hunt led by Republican senator Joseph McCarthy that targeted so-called communist sympathizers, who were considered a threat to national security at a time of all-out opposition to the Soviet Union. Accusations roiled politics, the motion picture industry, literature, and even everyday life, as many wound up paying the price for what were, in numerous instances, false allegations. A similar bane would plague the world of comic books.

Psychiatrist Fredric Wertham claimed that comics exerted a deleterious influence over the youth of America. According to Wertham, kids who read

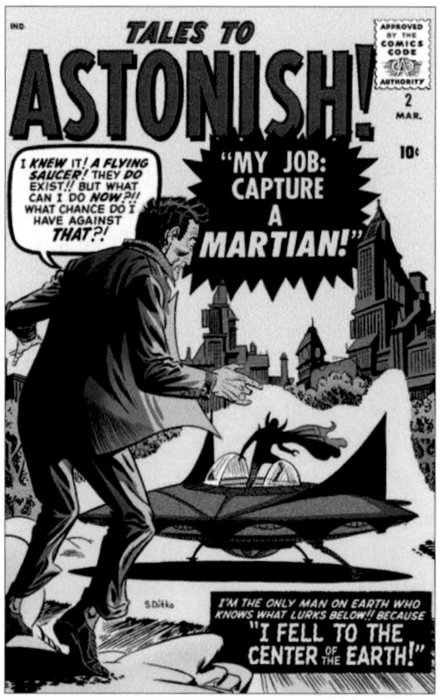
TALES TO
ASTONISH!
APPROVED BY THE COMICS CODE AUTHORITY
2 MAR.
10¢
I KNEW IT! A FLYING SAUCER! THEY DO EXIST!! BUT WHAT CAN I DO NOW?!! WHAT CHANCE DO I HAVE AGAINST THAT?!
"MY JOB: CAPTURE A MARTIAN!"
I'M THE ONLY MAN ON EARTH WHO KNOWS WHAT LURKS BELOW!! BECAUSE
"I FELL TO THE CENTER OF THE EARTH!"

comic books—which at that time sold millions of copies each month—ran serious risks of becoming criminals. There was no scientific proof behind such claims, which, nonetheless, took hold among certain segments of society at that time. The consequences proved devastating—from the burning of comic books in town squares, to investigations carried out against newspapers, magazines, and television broadcasters.

The frenzy reached its height on June 4, 1954 when Bill Gaines, owner of EC Comics, appeared before a U.S. Senate subcommittee at a hearing broadcast on live TV. His publishing outfit, famous for its unconventional, cutting-edge tales of horror steeped in violence, was at the eye of the storm of accusations. Gaines found himself

THIS PAGE: *Tales to Astonish #2* (March 1959). Art by Steve Ditko and Stan Goldberg. Letters by Artie Simek.

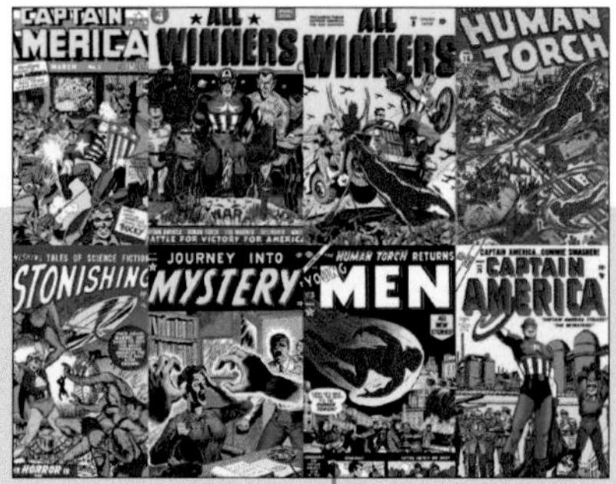
CAPTAIN AMERICA
ALL WINNERS
ALL WINNERS
HUMAN TORCH
ASTONISHING
JOURNEY INTO MYSTERY
MEN
CAPTAIN AMERICA

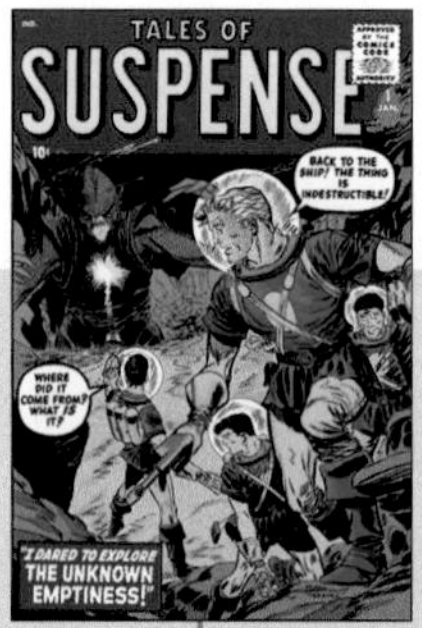
TALES OF
SUSPENSE
BACK TO THE SHIP! THE THING IS INDESTRUCTIBLE!
WHERE DID IT COME FROM? WHAT IS IT?
I DARED TO EXPLORE THE UNKNOWN EMPTINESS!

1960

1957

Goodman had made a deal with the distributor American News, but it shut down in May. Which meant he would have to come to terms with DC-owned Independent News.

1959

Atlas launches *Tales of Suspense* and *Tales to Astonish* in January, featuring monster stories drawn by Jack Kirby. Both titles would feature Super Heroes in the 1960s.

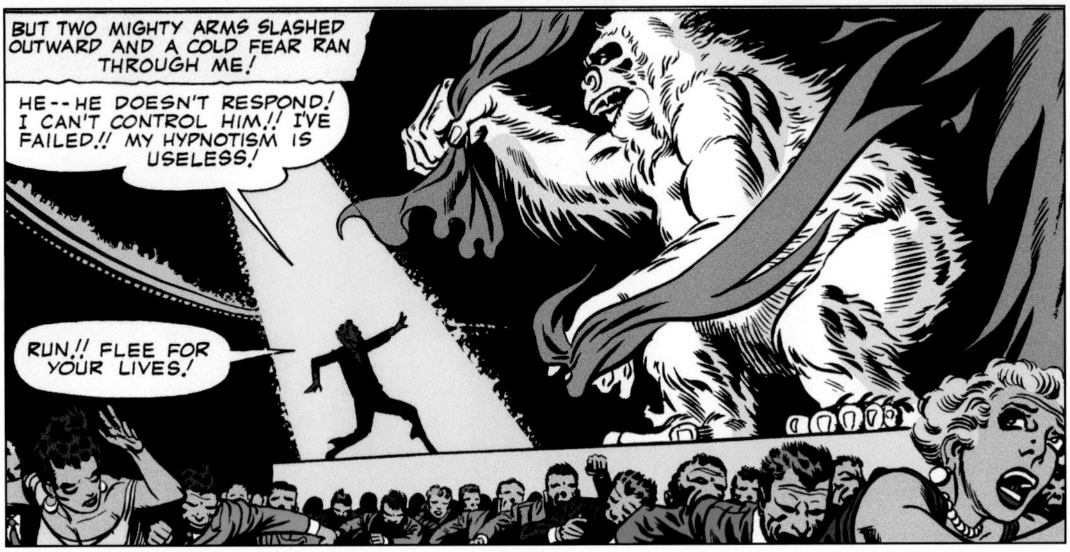
BUT TWO MIGHTY ARMS SLASHED OUTWARD AND A COLD FEAR RAN THROUGH ME!
HE--HE DOESN'T RESPOND! I CAN'T CONTROL HIM!! I'VE FAILED!! MY HYPNOTISM IS USELESS!
RUN!! FLEE FOR YOUR LIVES!

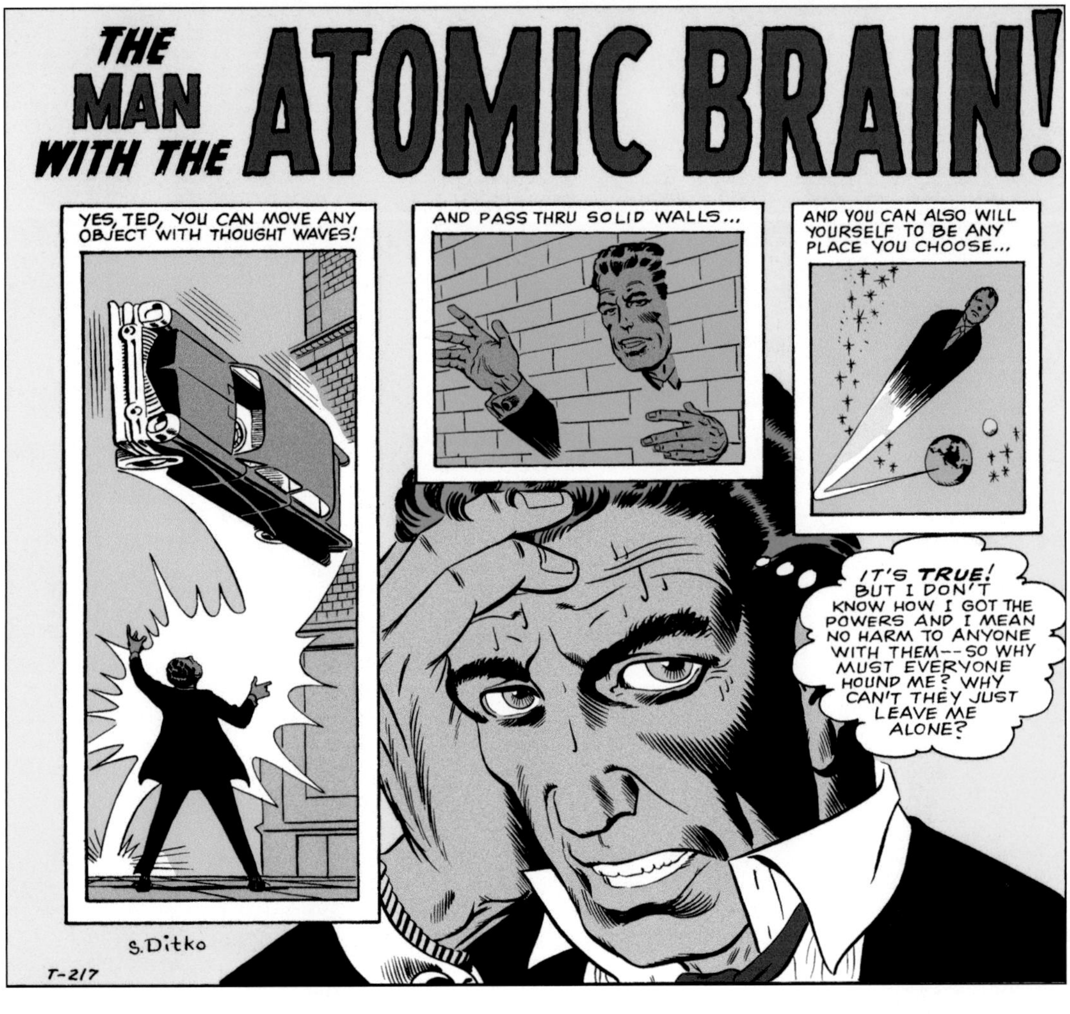
THE MAN WITH THE ATOMIC BRAIN!
YES, TED, YOU CAN MOVE ANY OBJECT WITH THOUGHT WAVES!
AND PASS THRU SOLID WALLS...
AND YOU CAN ALSO WILL YOURSELF TO BE ANY PLACE YOU CHOOSE...
IT'S TRUE! BUT I DON'T KNOW HOW I GOT THE POWERS AND I MEAN NO HARM TO ANYONE WITH THEM--SO WHY MUST EVERYONE HOUND ME? WHY CAN'T THEY JUST LEAVE ME ALONE?
S. Ditko
T-217

APPROVED BY THE COMICS CODE AUTHORITY

at a loss when it came to defending his brand in the face of Senator Estes Kefauver's baited questioning, and, in fact, his answers served to make things worse. Subsequently, comic book publishers banded together to self-regulate the industry, tantamount to censorship, in order to placate public opinion. The Comics Code Authority, established in 1954, set strict limits on comic book content: no blood, no positive representation of evil, no more vampires and zombies, and so on. To be sure, the police would be depicted as good guys, always on the winning side.

This sanitization of comic book stories and artwork would condition the work of the creators and force them to come up with new solutions. Naturally, Atlas was forced to comply and, as a result, began publishing stories and series that featured monsters from outer space, menaces from other planets, and forays into bygone eras like the Middle Ages, the Wild West, and the days when pirates roamed the seas. But the revolution that would change comic book culture the world over was within sight, and Goodman's publishing house, soon to be known as Marvel Comics, would lead the charge. ■

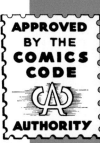

ABOVE: The seal of the "Comics Code Authority," part of the Comics Magazine Association of America formed in 1954.

TOP: Panel detail from "I Unleashed Monstro on the World!" *Journey Into Mystery* #54 (September 1959). Script by Stan Lee. Art by Steve Ditko (pencils, inks).

LEFT: "The Man With the Atomic Brain!" from *Journey Into Mystery #52* (May 1959). Script by Stan Lee. Art by Steve Ditko (pencils, inks), Stan Goldberg (colors).

THE 1960s

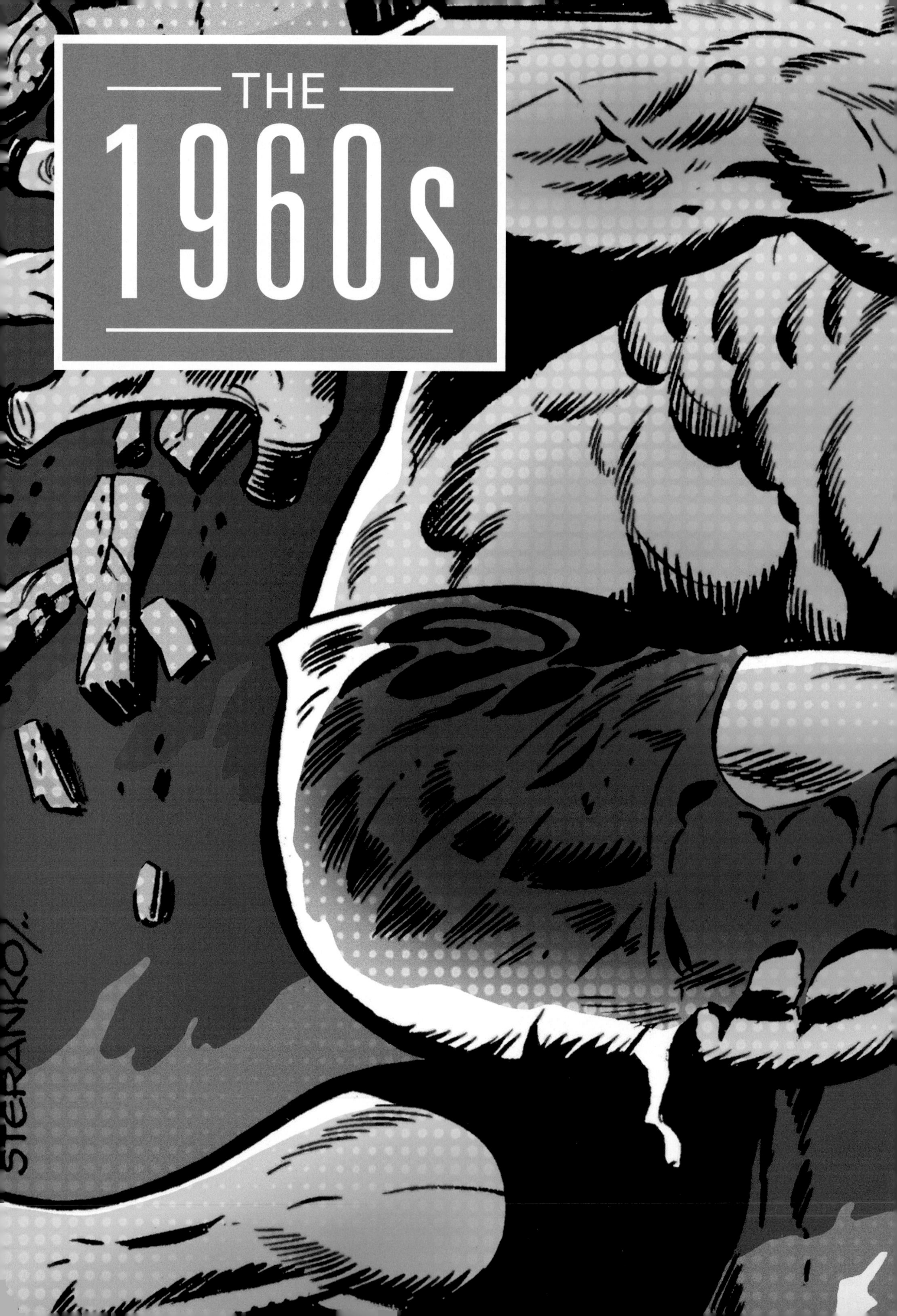
STERANKO

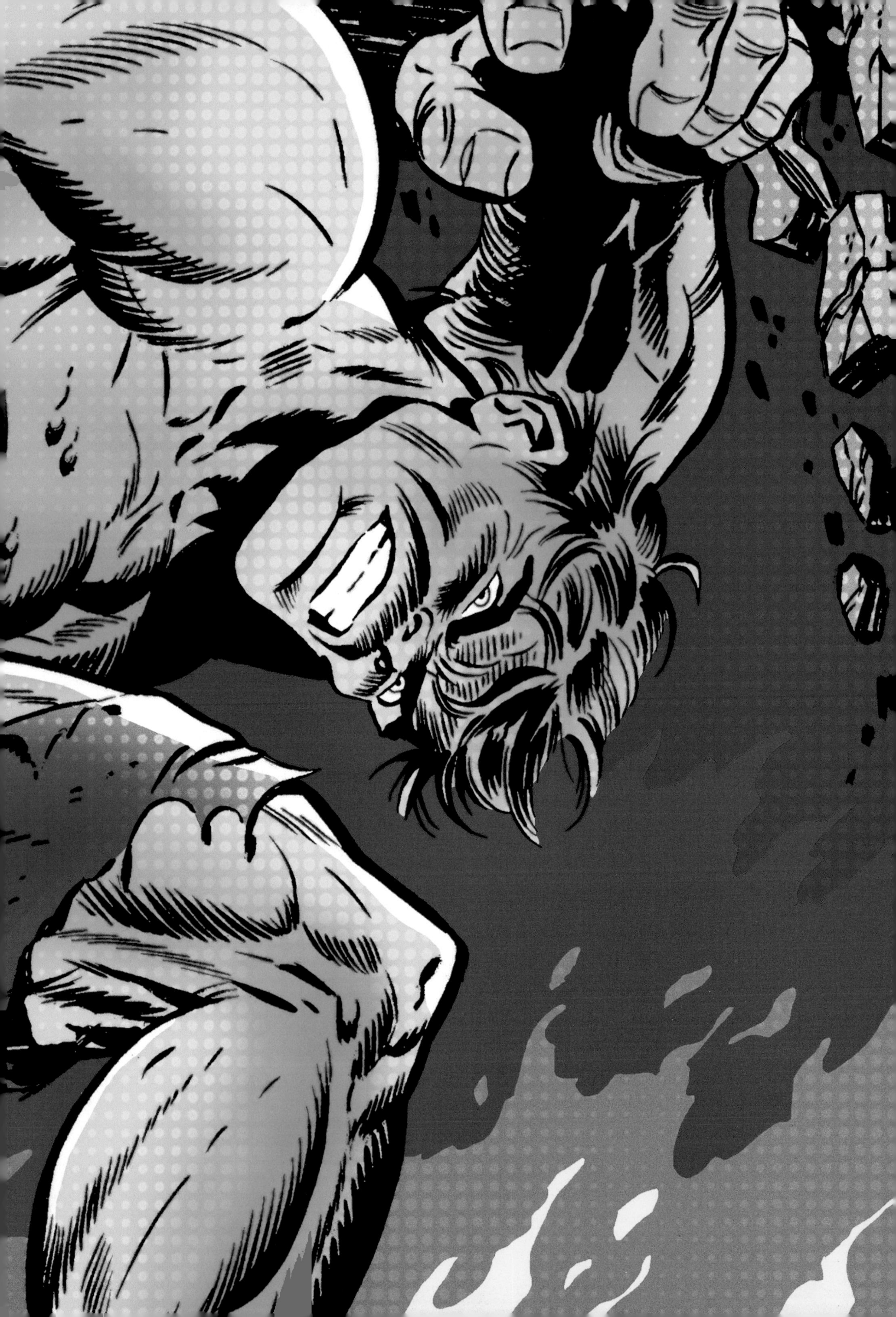

THE COMING OF THE MARVEL AGE

The 1960s would see a real atomic explosion of creativity from the mighty halls of Marvel.

The new frontier, the civil rights struggle, the conquest of space, the collapse of the myth of invincibility. The stage was set for the creation of the greatest comic book universe ever.

Comic book creator Stan Lee was fed up with the old routine. He'd been working for Timely/Atlas for over twenty years, joining when he was just 17, and was appointed editor shortly thereafter. He had a knack for handling writers and artists, choosing covers, assigning stories and, most of all, for writing stories in an incredibly wide range of genres. He had no problem typing out an episode about a Wild West gunslinger and a few minutes later detail the invasion of monsters from outer space. But he was burned out. He felt as though his dreams were slipping away, and that he might not ever write that great American novel he'd been saving his real last name for. So he thought about walking into publisher Martin Goodman's office, and telling him he'd be moving on in search of a new path in life. But before he could do that, something...happened.

In 1956, National Comics (soon to be called DC) published their first story starring a new version of the 1940s character the Flash. National was hoping to bring back the glory days of their first Super Heroes (Superman, Batman, Wonder Woman, and others). Legend has it, National publisher Jack Liebowitz and Martin Goodman played golf together one morning. Liebowitz had been bragging about skyrocketing sales of the *Justice League*, a new series that teamed up his company's greatest Super Heroes. Goodman returned to his office, and called in Lee, asking him to devise a series featuring a team of Super Heroes.

Lee had a dilemma. He went home and talked with his wife Joan. She had a good head on her shoulders and was able to view the situation from a more

NOSTALGIC NOTE: WE INTERRUPT THIS MAG TO BRING YOU--FOR THE FIRST TIME ANYWHERE--A PANARAMIC PIN-UP OF EVERY SINGLE SUPERHERO WHO HAS EVER BEEN A FULL-FLEDGED AVENGER! ENJOY, PILGRIM!

detached perspective. Her advice? Why not put all his creative energy into this assignment, just to see what he could really do?

Stan took those words to heart, and immediately began exploring ideas for a new story that would be completely different and original. One that featured Super Heroes, only not in the classic mold, not the invincible, perfect kind. Not the ones who encountered their enemies at the start of a story, wound up defeating them over the course of twenty pages, and stood there all smiles in the final panel. No. Lee was after a story about real people. They would have super-powers, yes, but they would also be vulnerable, subject to disappointments, losers even. Then Lee worked out the story with Jack Kirby.

Kirby had made his way back to Goodman's fold in the late 1950s, where he, Steve Ditko, and a few other artists drew the short stories—mainly thrillers and horror—which filled Atlas comic books at that time. And truth be told, there weren't all that many comic books coming out.

After the decision to shut down Atlas's own distribution company and put distribution in the hands of the American News Company, which soon folded, Goodman was forced to strike a deal with National's distributor to get his comic books to newsstands—a deal that allowed for no more than eight comics a month. To get around this snag, Goodman began putting out bi-monthly issues, which allowed him to have sixteen different comic books on newsstands in any given month.

Lee and Kirby worked out a plot featuring the new Super Heroes. It detailed their origins and main characteristics. There was the scientist, the girlfriend, the "hot-headed" brother, the grumpy pilot friend. The four of them would challenge destiny and set out for space, on a mission to beat the Soviet Union, who at that time was leading the United States in the space

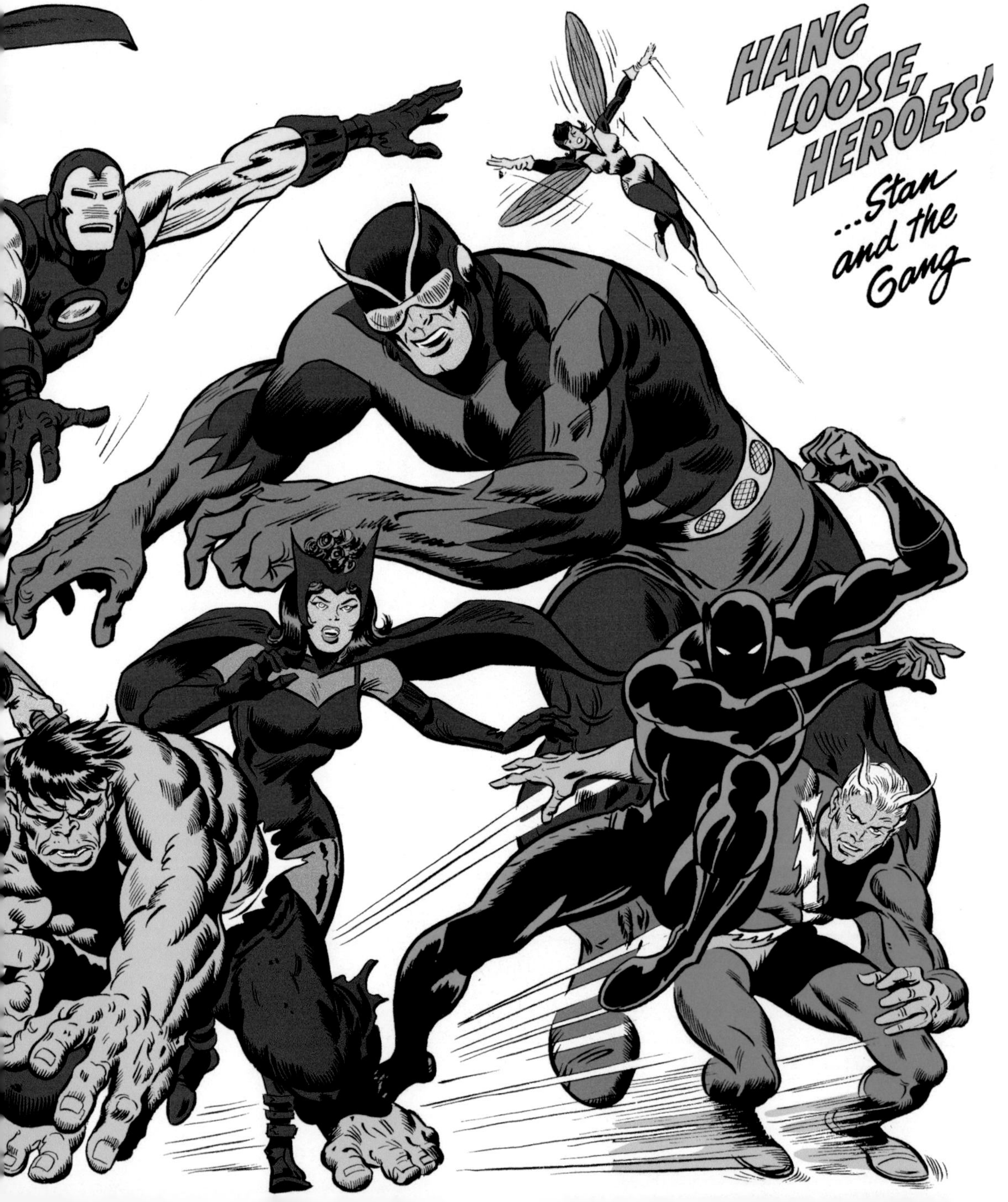
HANG LOOSE, HEROES!
...Stan and the Gang

THIS SPREAD: Pin-up from The Avengers Annual #2 (Sept. 1968). Art by John Buscema (pencils), Bill Everett (inks), Joe Roseqn (letters).

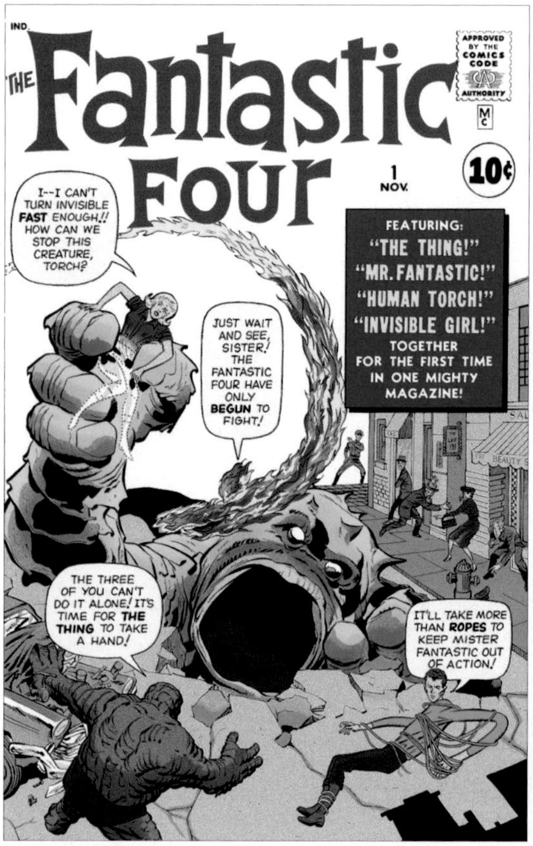
IND.
THE Fantastic Four
APPROVED BY THE COMICS CODE AUTHORITY
MC
1 NOV.
10¢
I--I CAN'T TURN INVISIBLE FAST ENOUGH!! HOW CAN WE STOP THIS CREATURE, TORCH?
FEATURING: "THE THING!" "MR. FANTASTIC!" "HUMAN TORCH!" "INVISIBLE GIRL!" TOGETHER FOR THE FIRST TIME IN ONE MIGHTY MAGAZINE!
JUST WAIT AND SEE, SISTER! THE FANTASTIC FOUR HAVE ONLY BEGUN TO FIGHT!
THE THREE OF YOU CAN'T DO IT ALONE! IT'S TIME FOR THE THING TO TAKE A HAND!
IT'LL TAKE MORE THAN ROPES TO KEEP MISTER FANTASTIC OUT OF ACTION!

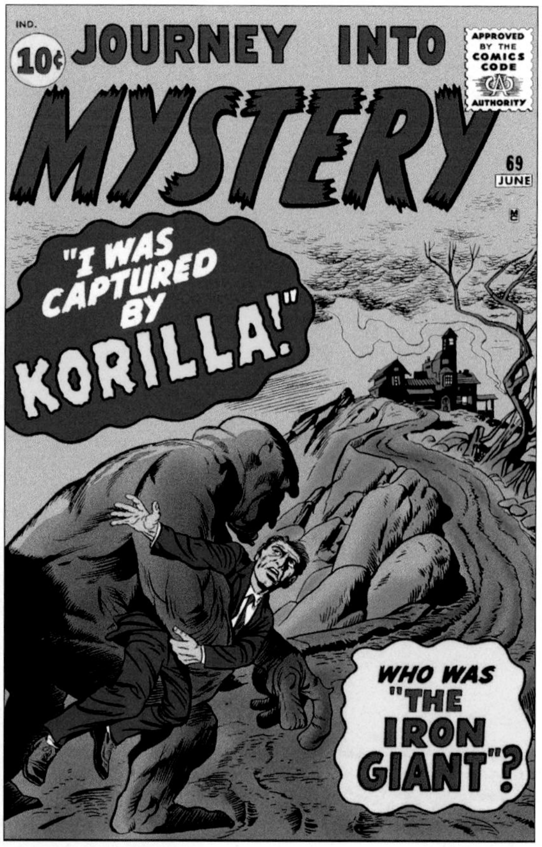
IND.
10¢ JOURNEY INTO MYSTERY
APPROVED BY THE COMICS CODE AUTHORITY
69 JUNE
"I WAS CAPTURED BY KORILLA!"
WHO WAS "THE IRON GIANT"?

ABOVE LEFT: *The Fantastic Four* #1 (November 1961). Cover art by Jack Kirby (pencils) and Dick Ayers (inks).

ABOVE RIGHT: At the dawn of the decade, the company was producing monster stories like "I Was Captured By Korilla!" (*Journey into Mystery* #69, June 1961).

RIGHT: House ad heralding the arrival of the 1966 animated series Marvel Super Heroes.

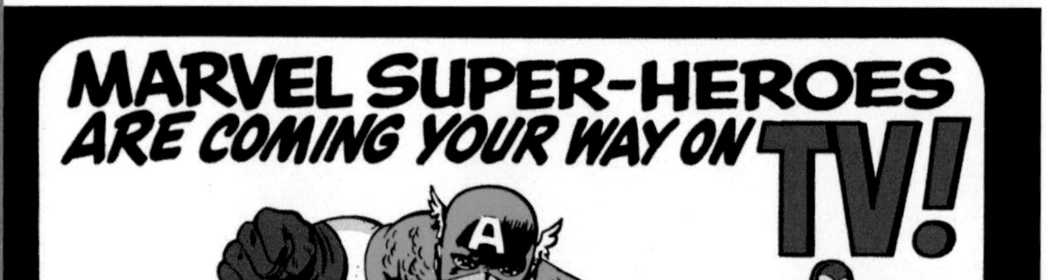
MARVEL SUPER-HEROES
ARE COMING YOUR WAY ON TV!
© MARVEL COMICS GROUP
CAPTAIN AMERICA! THE SUB-MARINER!
IRON MAN! THE MIGHTY THOR!
THE INCREDIBLE HULK!
LOOK FOR THEM ON THE FOLLOWING TELEVISION STATIONS!

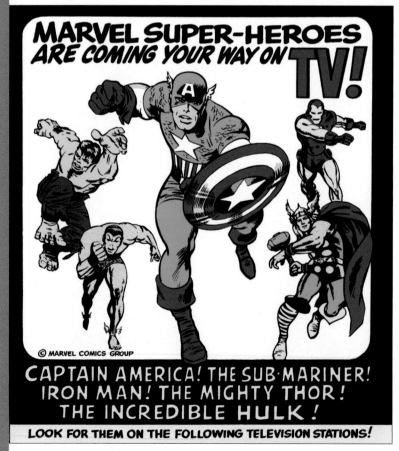

race. Only these Americans hadn't taken into account the cosmic rays that would zap them as soon as they left Earth's atmosphere. A dose of radiation that would change not only their lives, but the lives of Marvel fans as well. Lee would script over Kirby's art.

The *Fantastic Four* #1 (cover-dated November 1961) hit newsstands on August 8, 1961. Nothing quite like it had ever been published. Its release marked the start of the Marvel Age in comics—a period when the creators would become as famous as the Super Heroes they wrote about and drew. Now characters would be loved more for the human adventures they embarked upon, their romances, the drama and tragedy in their personal lives, than the battles against their foes.

Lee, Kirby, Ditko, and later on John Buscema, John Romita, Sr., Bill Everett, Larry Lieber (Stan's brother), Gene Colan, Don Heck, Dick Ayers, Roy Thomas, Jim Steranko, and others worked as if they'd been possessed by the demon of creativity. It was a decade that saw the birth of Spider-Man and Thor, Ant-Man and the Avengers, Daredevil and the X-Men, Iron Man and the Hulk, Black Panther and the Silver Surfer, while Super Heroes like Captain America and the Sub-Mariner would be reborn.

THE MARVEL SUPER HEROES HAVE ARRIVED

From 1961 through 1964, Marvel brought some of the most beloved Super Heroes to life.

With the release of The *Fantastic Four* #1 in 1961, through April 1964 (the cover date for *Daredevil* #1), Lee and his team created some of the greatest characters of all time— fueled in part by the daunting competition from Batman and Superman, and distribution constraints that plagued Atlas (which would soon become Marvel, taken from the title of the first Timely comic book to feature Super Heroes way back in 1939).

The success of the Fantastic Four was unexpected. Mister Fantastic, the Invisible Girl (later known as the Invisible Woman), the Human Torch (a tribute to the Golden Age Super Hero of the same name), and the Thing all spoke the same language as their readers, so it was easy to identify with them. Goodman wasted no time in ordering Lee to forge ahead.

Cover-dated May 1962—but released on March 1—*The Incredible Hulk* #1 marked the introduction of a monstrous creature. Initially gray in color, later green, possessed of uncontrollable brute strength, the Hulk was the scientist Bruce Banner, victim of a gamma-ray accident. The series, created by Lee and Kirby, was soon folded into the anthology title *Tales to Astonish*, a comic book series with no fixed main character and focused on horror and suspense. Before that, issue #35 (cover-dated September 1962) had featured another new, highly original Super Hero: Ant-Man (created by Lee, Lieber, and Kirby), whose alter ego was again a scientist, Hank Pym, who devised a formula that allowed him to shrink to

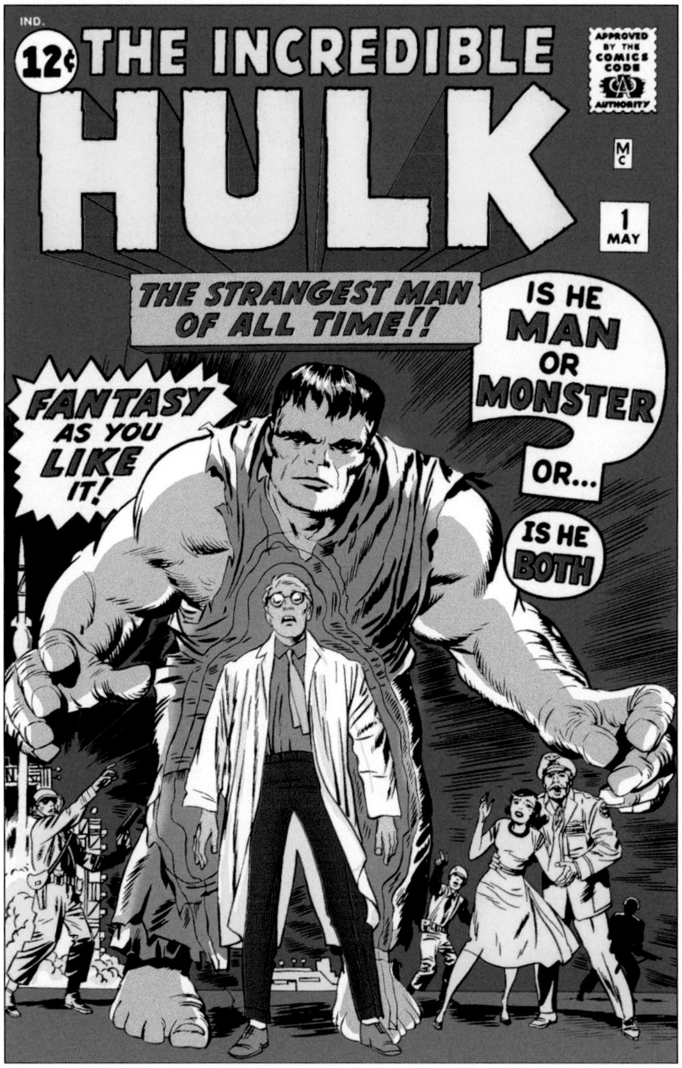
IND.
12¢
THE INCREDIBLE
HULK
APPROVED BY THE COMICS CODE AUTHORITY
MC
1 MAY
THE STRANGEST MAN OF ALL TIME!!
IS HE MAN OR MONSTER OR... IS HE BOTH
FANTASY AS YOU LIKE IT!

THIS PAGE: *The Incredible Hulk* #1 (May 1962). Cover art by Jack Kirby (pencils) and George Roussos (inks).

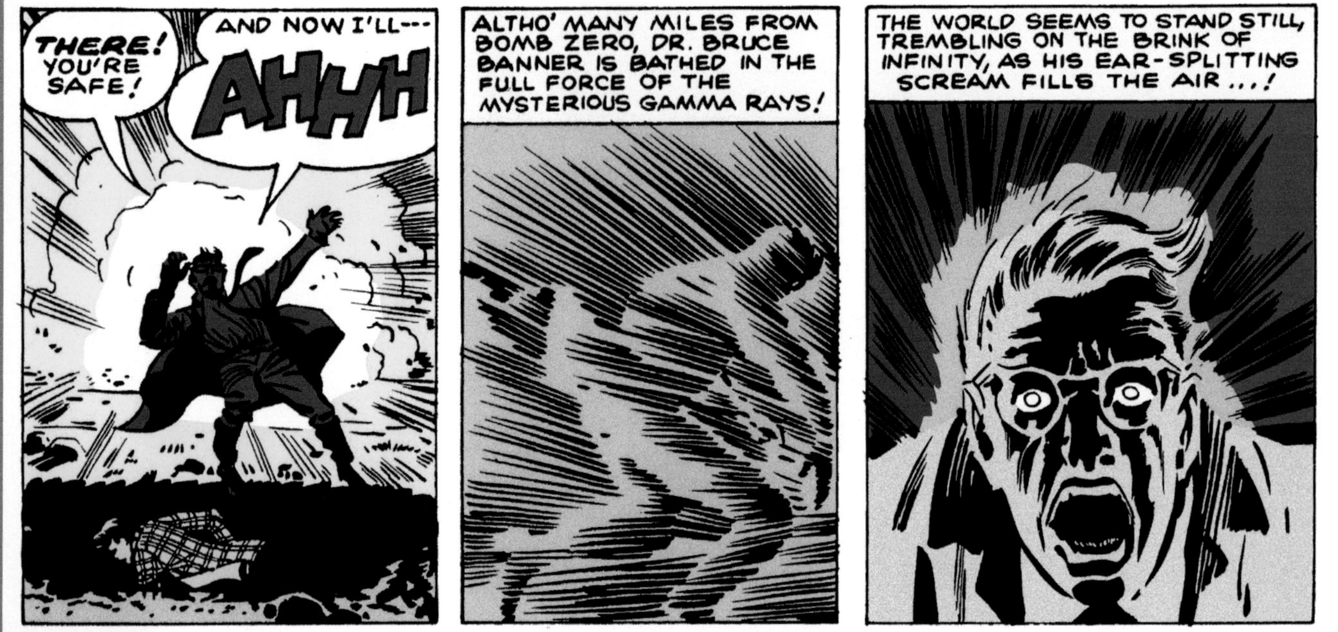
THERE! YOU'RE SAFE!
AND NOW I'LL---
AHHH
ALTHO' MANY MILES FROM BOMB ZERO, DR. BRUCE BANNER IS BATHED IN THE FULL FORCE OF THE MYSTERIOUS GAMMA RAYS!
THE WORLD SEEMS TO STAND STILL, TREMBLING ON THE BRINK OF INFINITY, AS HIS EAR-SPLITTING SCREAM FILLS THE AIR ...!

TOP: Bruce Banner is caught in the blast of the gamma bomb in *The Incredible Hulk* #1. Script by Stan Lee. Art by Jack Kirby (pencils), Paul Reinman (inks), and Artie Simek (letters).

the size of an insect and communicate with ants. Two more all-time greats were on their way: Thor and Spider-Man. Their respective first appearances were made in comic books cover-dated August 1962, but they must certainly have been released before that. Spider-Man made his first appearance in *Amazing Fantasy* #15, the last issue in an anthology series. It contained an unforgettable 11-page story, written by Lee and drawn by Steve Ditko, starring a high-school kid from Queens, New York, who gets bitten by a radioactive spider. He would receive astonishing powers. However, tragedy would strike, and young Peter Parker's life would never be the same.

But getting that first Spider-Man story published was no easy task. Lee has said that Goodman reacted poorly to the idea. "People don't like spiders!" he commented drily. Lee wound up including the story in the last issue of a series that was headed for cancellation. But lo and behold, that issue turned out to be a big seller, and Marvel received lots of letters from fans overflowing with praise. With *Amazing Fantasy* out of the picture, the only viable solution was... *The Amazing Spider-Man* #1 (cover-dated March 1963), the first comic book centered around the wall-crawler.

The other momentous debut saw Thor springing into action in *Journey into Mystery* #83, another anthology series without a fixed protagonist, which was mostly focused on mystery and suspense. Lee, Lieber, Kirby, and inker Joe Sinnott came up with the 13-page adventure that laid the foundations for the comic book version of the god of thunder, an immortal from Asgard who was cast among mankind by his father as punishment for his youthful arrogance. With issue #126, the series was renamed *The Mighty Thor*.

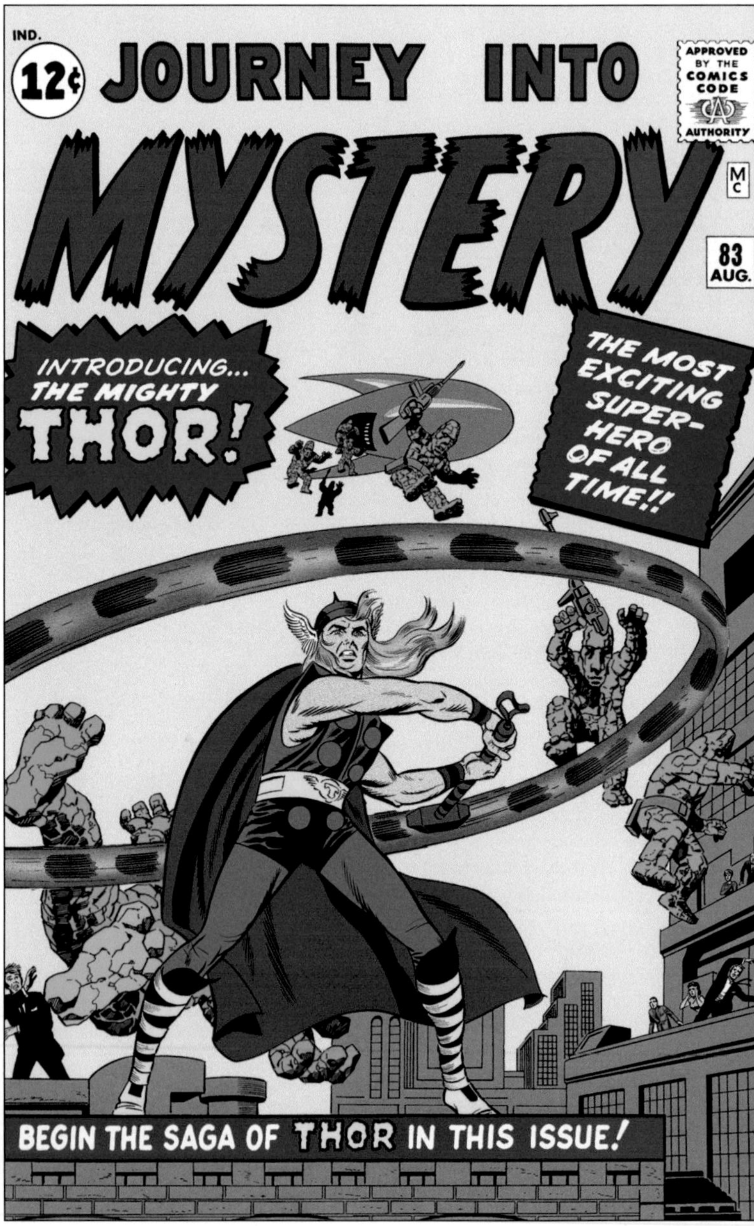
IND.
12¢
JOURNEY INTO MYSTERY
APPROVED BY THE COMICS CODE AUTHORITY
MC
83 AUG.
INTRODUCING... THE MIGHTY THOR!
THE MOST EXCITING SUPER-HERO OF ALL TIME!!
BEGIN THE SAGA OF THOR IN THIS ISSUE!

RIGHT: *Journey Into Mystery* #83 (August 1962). Art by Jack Kirby (pencils) and Joe Sinnott (inks).

OPPOSITE PAGE: *Amazing Fantasy* #15 (August 1962). Art by Jack Kirby (pencils) and Steve Ditko (inks).

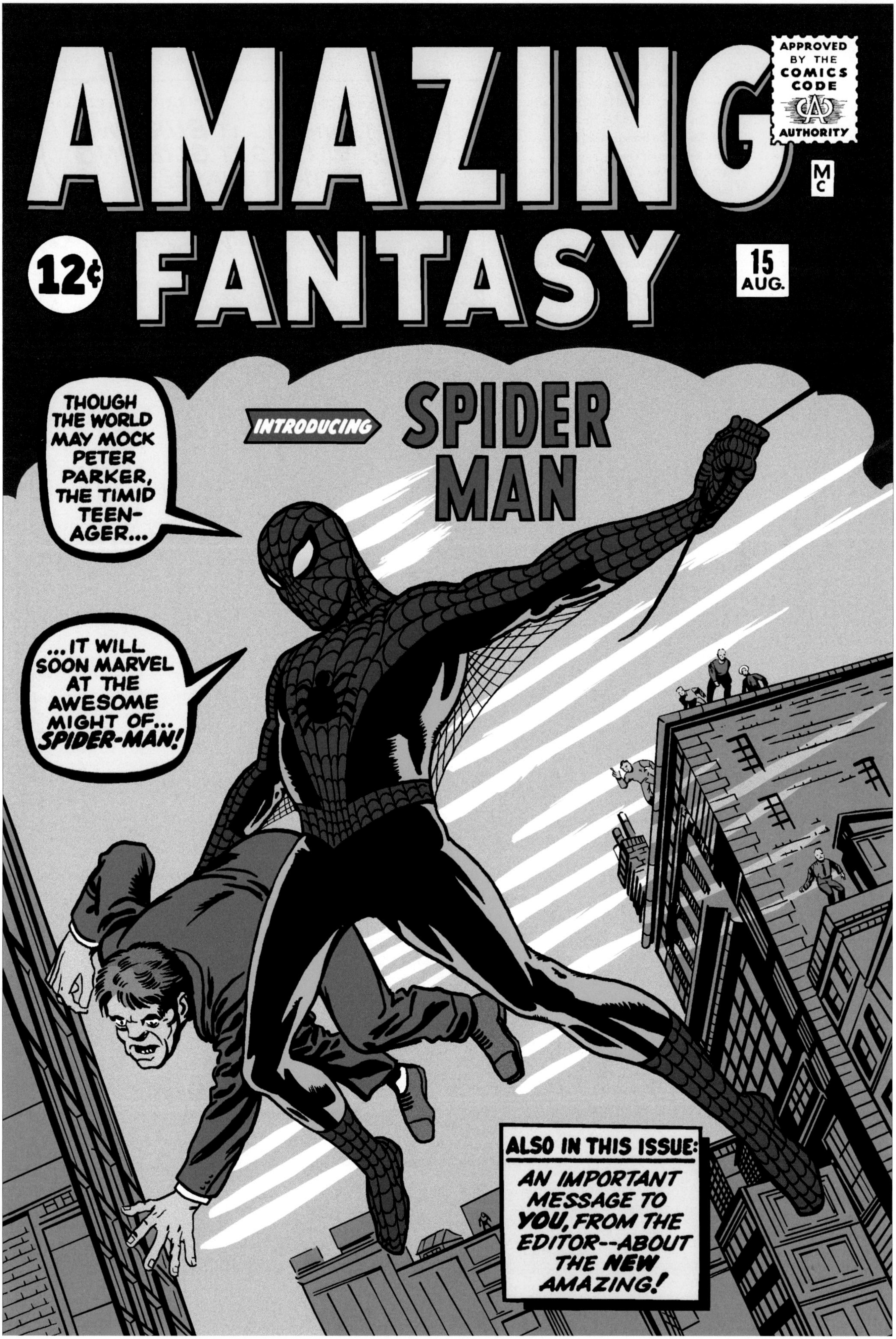
APPROVED BY THE COMICS CODE AUTHORITY
AMAZING FANTASY
MC
12¢
15 AUG.
INTRODUCING SPIDER MAN
THOUGH THE WORLD MAY MOCK PETER PARKER, THE TIMID TEEN-AGER...
...IT WILL SOON MARVEL AT THE AWESOME MIGHT OF... SPIDER-MAN!
ALSO IN THIS ISSUE:
AN IMPORTANT MESSAGE TO YOU, FROM THE EDITOR--ABOUT THE NEW AMAZING!

Intent on launching more new Super Heroes, Lee and his brother Larry, this time along with Don Heck, created Iron Man, who first appeared in the science-fiction and horror anthology series *Tales of Suspense* #39 (March 1963, with a cover by Jack Kirby). His alter ego was the billionaire industrialist Tony Stark, who during the Vietnam War donned a suit of iron armor in order to fend off a life-threatening piece of shrapnel lodged near his heart.

The Avengers #1 (cover-dated September 1963) marked the start of a new comic book series featuring a second supergroup. Thor, Iron Man, Ant-Man, the Wasp, and the Hulk were the founding members. It was clear from the start that Marvel wasn't going to rest on its laurels. In issue #2, the Hulk left the team, and became their enemy. Then, in issue #4, Captain America returned to the modern world, found frozen in the North Atlantic and brought back to life from a state of suspended animation.

September 1963 witnessed the arrival of a unique supergroup—a bizarre collection of individuals called the X-Men. Another product of Lee's and Kirby's fervid imaginations, the series featured a cast of young Super Heroes born with genetic mutations and trained by their mentor Charles Xavier, A.K.A. Professor X.

And then came Daredevil, A.K.A. young Matt Murdock, who'd gone blind following an act of heroism, acquiring a "radar sense" that allowed him to envision his surroundings. Daredevil was the creation of Stan Lee and Bill Everett, the artist behind the Sub-Mariner for Timely Publications back in the Golden Age. *Daredevil* #1 was cover-dated April 1964.

And the new characters kept on coming. In another anthology series, *Strange Tales*, the Human Torch appeared in solo stories, followed by the appearance of the Master of the Mystic Arts, Doctor Strange, and Nick Fury, agent of S.H.I.E.L.D. Then there were all-new protagonists introduced within the pages of *The Fantastic Four*, like the cosmic Silver Surfer, the incredible Inhumans, and the ground-breaking Black Panther, adding to the ever-expanding Marvel Comics universe that told the story of 1960s America.

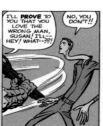

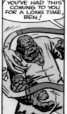

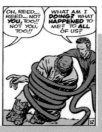

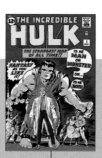

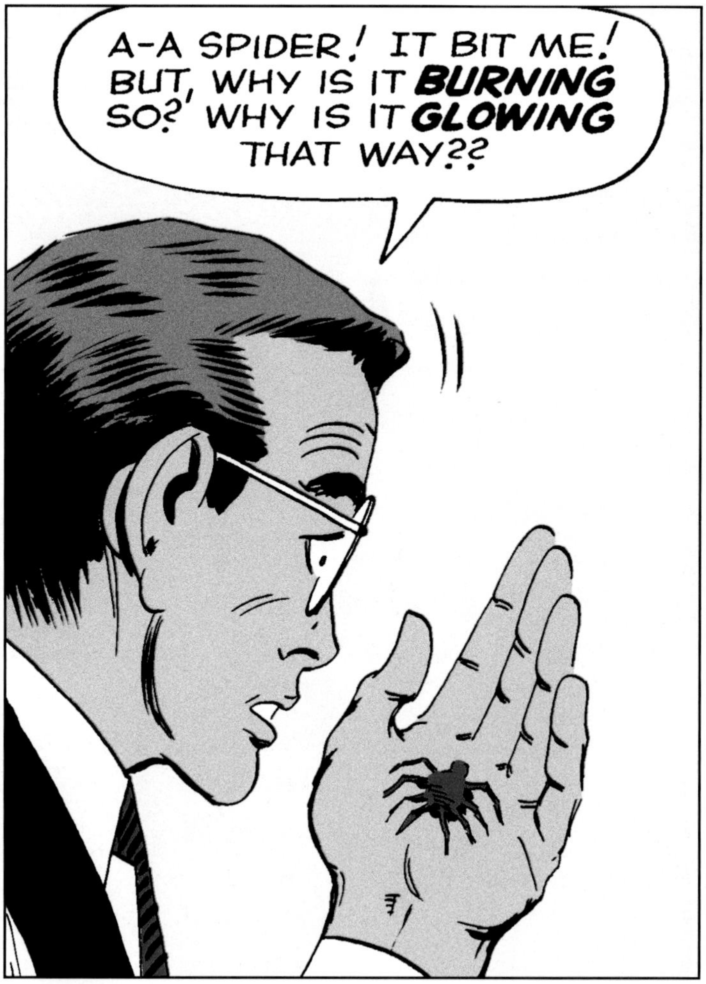

A-A SPIDER! IT BIT ME! BUT, WHY IS IT BURNING SO? WHY IS IT GLOWING THAT WAY??

THIS PAGE: Peter Parker is bitten by a radioactive spider in *Amazing Fantasy* #15. Script by Stan Lee. Art by Steve Ditko (pencils, inks), Stan Goldberg (colors), Artie Simek (letters).

OPPOSITE PAGE: *The Avengers* #1 (September 1963). Art by Jack Kirby (pencils) and Dick Ayers (inks).

1960

I'LL PROVE TO YOU THAT YOU LOVE THE WRONG MAN, SUSAN! I'LL-- HEY! WHAT--??!
NO, YOU DON'T!!
YOU'VE HAD THIS COMING TO YOU FOR A LONG TIME, BEN!
OH, REED... REED... NOT YOU, TOO!! NOT YOU, TOO!!
WHAT AM I DOING? WHAT HAPPENED TO ME? TO ALL OF US?
12

AUGUST 8, 1961

Although the cover date says November, historians date the start of the Marvel Age as August 8, 1961, with the release of *The Fantastic Four #1* by Lee and Kirby.

THE INCREDIBLE HULK

MAY 1962

The Incredible Hulk #1 hits the newsstands. This was the second big gun for the Marvel Universe, featuring Kirby's beautiful cover, inked by George Roussos.

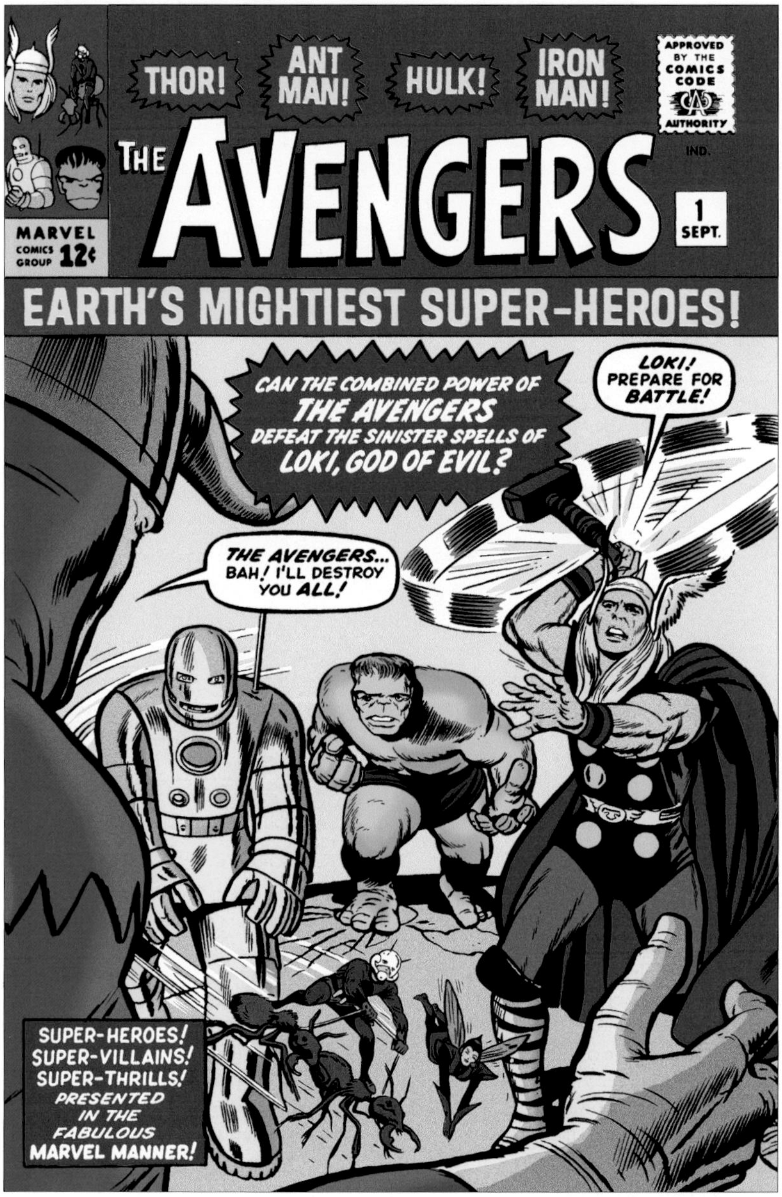
THOR!
ANT MAN!
HULK!
IRON MAN!
APPROVED BY THE COMICS CODE AUTHORITY
IND.
THE AVENGERS
1 SEPT.
MARVEL COMICS GROUP 12¢
EARTH'S MIGHTIEST SUPER-HEROES!
CAN THE COMBINED POWER OF THE AVENGERS DEFEAT THE SINISTER SPELLS OF LOKI, GOD OF EVIL?
LOKI! PREPARE FOR BATTLE!
THE AVENGERS... BAH! I'LL DESTROY YOU ALL!
SUPER-HEROES! SUPER-VILLAINS! SUPER-THRILLS! PRESENTED IN THE FABULOUS MARVEL MANNER!

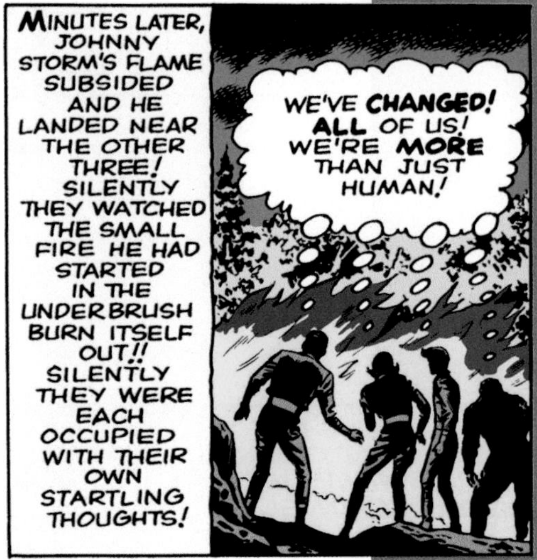
MINUTES LATER, JOHNNY STORM'S FLAME SUBSIDED AND HE LANDED NEAR THE OTHER THREE! SILENTLY THEY WATCHED THE SMALL FIRE HE HAD STARTED IN THE UNDERBRUSH BURN ITSELF OUT!! SILENTLY THEY WERE EACH OCCUPIED WITH THEIR OWN STARTLING THOUGHTS!
WE'VE CHANGED! ALL OF US! WE'RE MORE THAN JUST HUMAN!

ABOVE: The Fantastic Four are born, *The Fantastic Four* #1. Script by Stan Lee. Art by Jack Kirby (pencils), George Klein/ Christopher Rule (inks), Stan Goldberg (colors), Artie Simek (letters).

Marvel's new breed of Super Heroes had quirks and problems to spare—just like their readership.

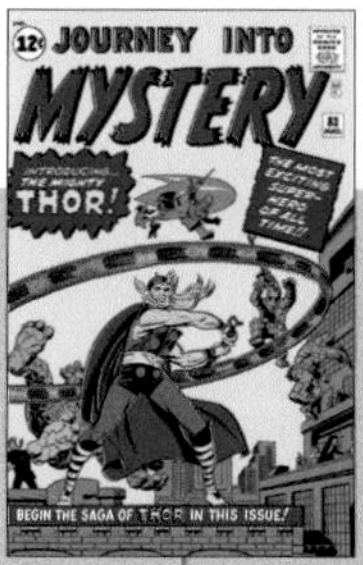
12¢
JOURNEY INTO MYSTERY
THOR!
BEGIN THE SAGA OF THOR IN THIS ISSUE!

JUNE 5, 1962

June 1962 marked the debut of two Marvel mainstays. *Amazing Fantasy #15* featured the origin of Spider-Man, while *Journey into Mystery #83* saw the first appearance of Thor.

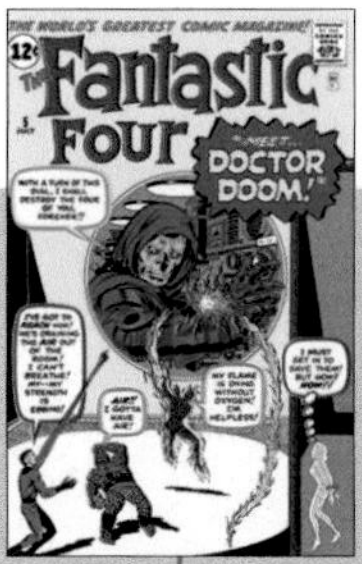
12¢
Fantastic Four
DOCTOR DOOM!

JULY 1962

Doctor Doom made his debut in *The Fantastic Four #5*. The FF's worst enemy, Doom, went to college with Mr. Fantastic, then went on to rule the tiny nation of Latveria.

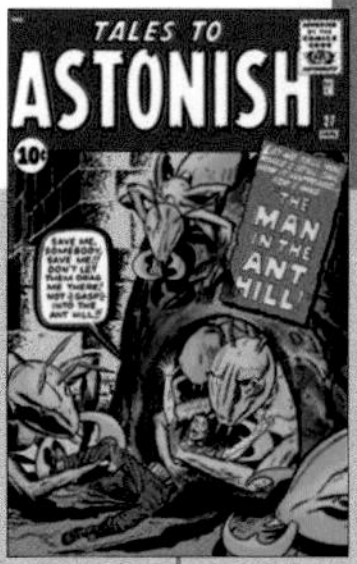
TALES TO
ASTONISH
10¢
THE MAN IN THE ANT HILL

SEPTEMBER 1962

Following his appearance in a self-contained story in *Tales to Astonish #27*, by the time #35 rolled around Ant-Man had become a full-fledged member of the Marvel Universe.

FLAWS AND ALL

Driven by endless creative fury, Stan Lee—with Jack Kirby, Steve Ditko, and a host of others—really was writing the Great American Novel.

BEN, WE'VE GOT TO TAKE THAT CHANCE... UNLESS WE WANT THE COMMIES TO BEAT US TO IT!
I-- I NEVER THOUGHT THAT YOU WOULD BE A COWARD!
A COWARD!! NOBODY CALLS ME A COWARD! GET THE SHIP! I'LL FLY HER NO MATTER WHAT HAPPENS!!

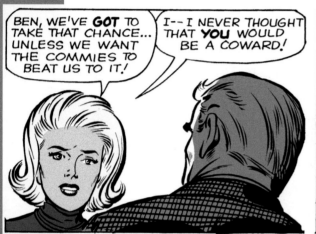

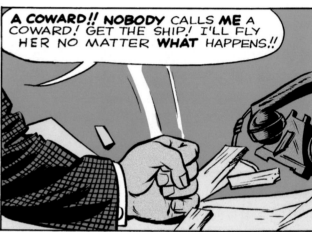

Only this story wasn't told in prose, but in comic books. A long coming-of-age novel in which characters are born, evolve, change, die...and along the way they argue, fight, lie, cheat, and let the insults fly. They seemed to be people just like us, hardly specimens of perfection that could do no wrong. That was the kind of stuff Lee had always wanted to write about. It was also the kind of material that series after series, origin after origin, won over readers across the globe.

Marvel characters could lose even when they won. They were constantly faced with trying dilemmas, forever forced to cope with the latest tragedy. Wasn't it that way for the Fantastic Four? True, they may have been a family, but a dysfunctional one, not the kind they showed in TV commercials. They bickered from the very first panels. They arranged a trip to the Moon and would waste no time getting there—after all, the United States ran the risk of being overtaken by the Soviet Union. And when they set out, they broke the rules—ultimately to their own detriment, since they had not taken into account a host of variables and wound up paying the price.

TALES OF SUSPENSE
IRON MAN!

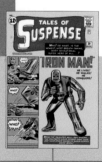

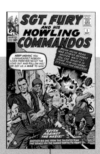

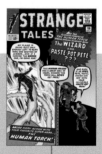

MARCH 1963

Tales of Suspense #39 unveils Iron Man, A.K.A. industrialist Tony Stark, an arms dealer who sells weaponry to the U.S. government.

SGT. FURY AND HIS HOWLING COMMANDOS

MAY 1963

Lee and Kirby come out with *Sgt. Fury and His Howling Commandos*. The war is on, and Fury would see continued action in the Marvel Universe as head of S.H.I.E.L.D.

STRANGE TALES
The WIZARD AND PASTE POT PETE ???
HUMAN TORCH!

JULY 1963

Strange Tales #110 sees the debut of the counterculture hero, Doctor Strange. Stan Lee and Steve Ditko came up with the character and wrote and drew the character's early stories.

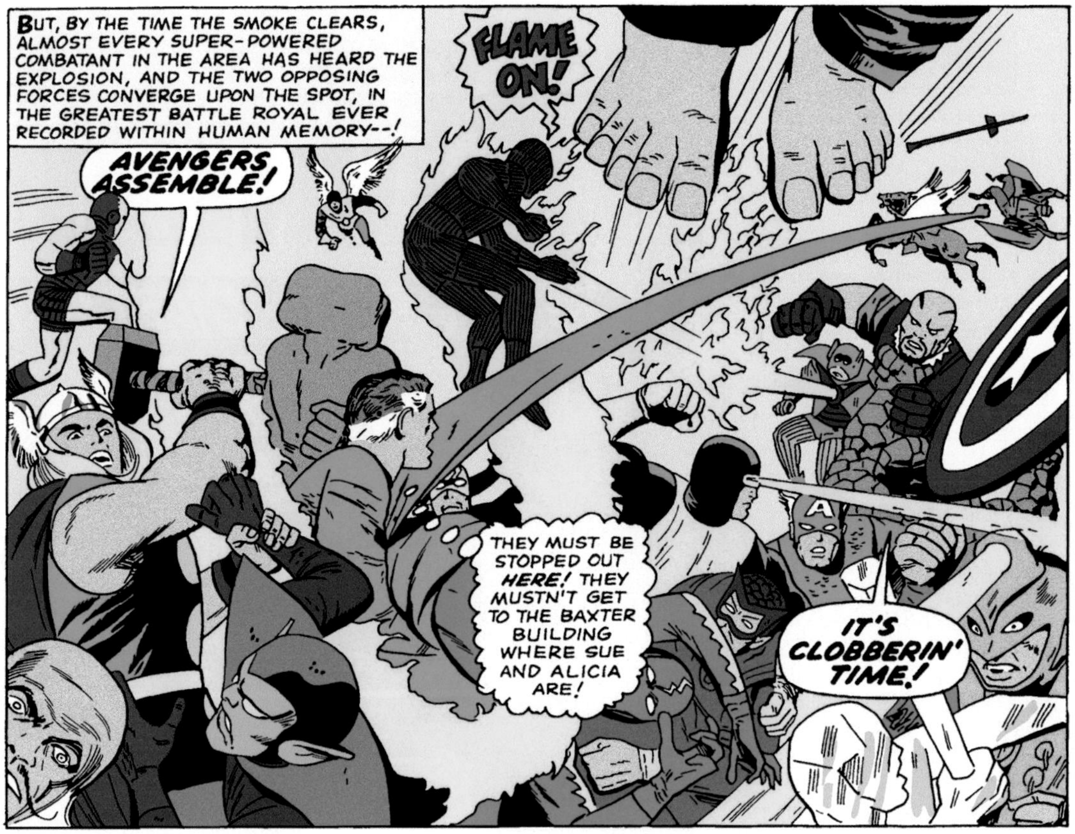
BUT, BY THE TIME THE SMOKE CLEARS, ALMOST EVERY SUPER-POWERED COMBATANT IN THE AREA HAS HEARD THE EXPLOSION, AND THE TWO OPPOSING FORCES CONVERGE UPON THE SPOT, IN THE GREATEST BATTLE ROYAL EVER RECORDED WITHIN HUMAN MEMORY--!
FLAME ON!
AVENGERS, ASSEMBLE!
THEY MUST BE STOPPED OUT HERE! THEY MUSTN'T GET TO THE BAXTER BUILDING WHERE SUE AND ALICIA ARE!
IT'S CLOBBERIN' TIME!

OPPOSITE PAGE: The space race between the U.S. and the U.S.S.R. is highlighted in *The Fantastic Four* #1. Script by Stan Lee. Art by Jack Kirby (pencils), George Klein/Christopher Rule (inks), Stan Goldberg (colors), Artie Simek (letters).

THIS PAGE: Reed Richard and Sue Storm fight off a host of Marvel villains before they can tie the knot in *The Fantastic Four Annual* #3 (October 1965). Script by Stan Lee. Art by Jack Kirby (pencils), Vince Colletta (inks), Stan Goldberg (colors), Artie Simek (letters).

Sue Storm criticized Ben Grimm for being a coward because he was afraid something bad might happen on their flight into the unknown—of course, he was right. Their leader, the scientist Reed Richards, who was Sue's boyfriend and Ben's pal, put new conquests and discoveries above all else—an attitude that would cost him dearly. Then there was Johnny Storm, Sue's little brother, who was fiery and impulsive. Cosmic rays turned the four of them into "elemental" characters: Johnny became the Human Torch (fire); Ben morphed into the Thing (earth, which is to say, rock); Reed would be Mister Fantastic, so stretchable that he appeared to be almost liquid (water); and Sue turned into the Invisible Girl (air). A sense of guilt would loom large over the scenario, beginning with the first Fantastic Four story. Ben, the most tortured and best-loved character among readers, who wound up paying more dearly than anyone when he became more monster than man, would be a constant reminder for Reed of the mistake he made. And there was no lack of awesome Super Villains in their epic adventures, with Doctor Doom and Galactus standing out among them.

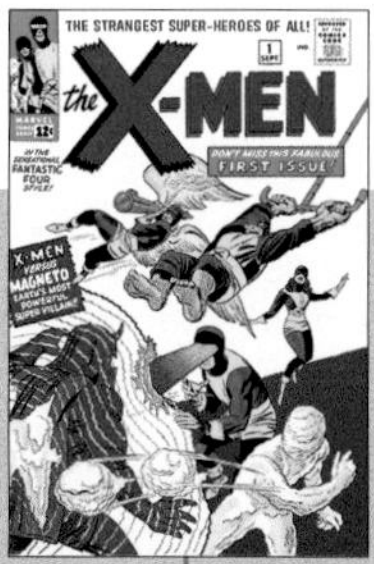
THE STRANGEST SUPER-HEROES OF ALL!
the X-MEN
FIRST ISSUE

SEPTEMBER 1963

The Avengers and the X-Men, both by Lee and Kirby, make the scene. The former assembled a team of preexisting heroes; the latter showcased a new concept: mutants.

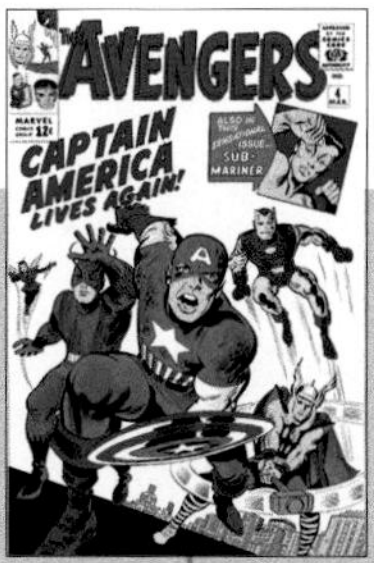
AVENGERS
CAPTAIN AMERICA LIVES AGAIN!

MARCH 1964

A flashback from the Golden Age: In *The Avengers* #4 Lee and Kirby bring back Captain America, who had been frozen in the North Atlantic Ocean since World War II. A new Avenger!

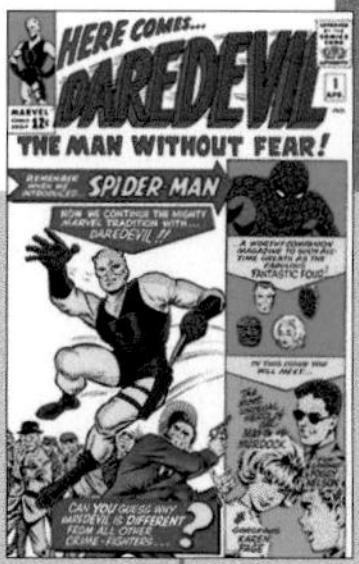
HERE COMES...
DAREDEVIL
THE MAN WITHOUT FEAR!
SPIDER MAN

APRIL 1964

The dynamic Daredevil made his debut in his own series, written by Lee and illustrated by Bill Everett (of Sub-Mariner fame). Note Daredevil's original red-and-yellow costume.

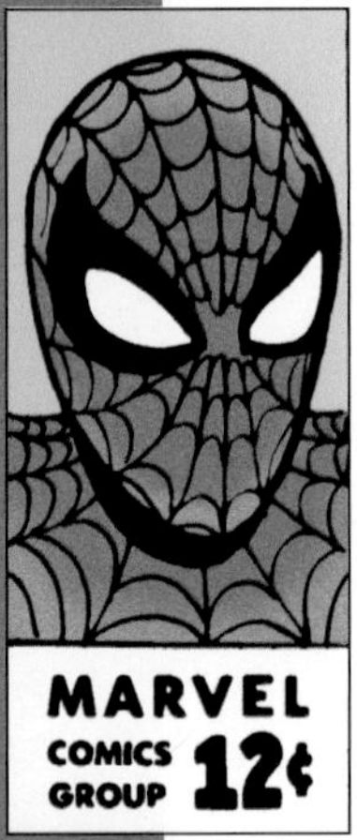
MARVEL
COMICS GROUP
12¢

While the Fantastic Four laid the foundations for what would become known as the Marvel Universe, the most popular Super Hero of all—the very symbol of Marvel Comics—would be Spider-Man. Perhaps no other character could claim origins as poetic and intense.

Peter Parker was a nerdy high school kid. An ace science student, he never fit in and had no friends. His classmates considered him a bookworm, and on top of it all, his parents had died and he lived with his aunt and uncle, his elderly guardians Ben and May. Peter got his superpowers during an experiment, from the bite of a radioactive spider. Peter's new powers were proportional to those of a spider, and like any teenager, he thought only of taking advantage of his "good luck" and sought to parlay it into some cash in order to help out his poor aunt and uncle. His hubris would cost him dearly, however. Cynical and indifferent, Peter let a thief get away from the scene of a crime he witnessed—little knowing that the same man would wind up killing his uncle during another robbery.

That proved to be Spider-Man's original sin, responsible for the feelings of guilt that would haunt Peter for the rest of his days. Lesson learned, as Lee wrote in the last panel, "With great power there must also come—great responsibility!" Those words summed up the philosophy of a comic book series that would go on to become a cartoon, a TV series, a live-action movie, an animated movie, a Broadway musical, and an eternal icon of the tragic, losing hero.

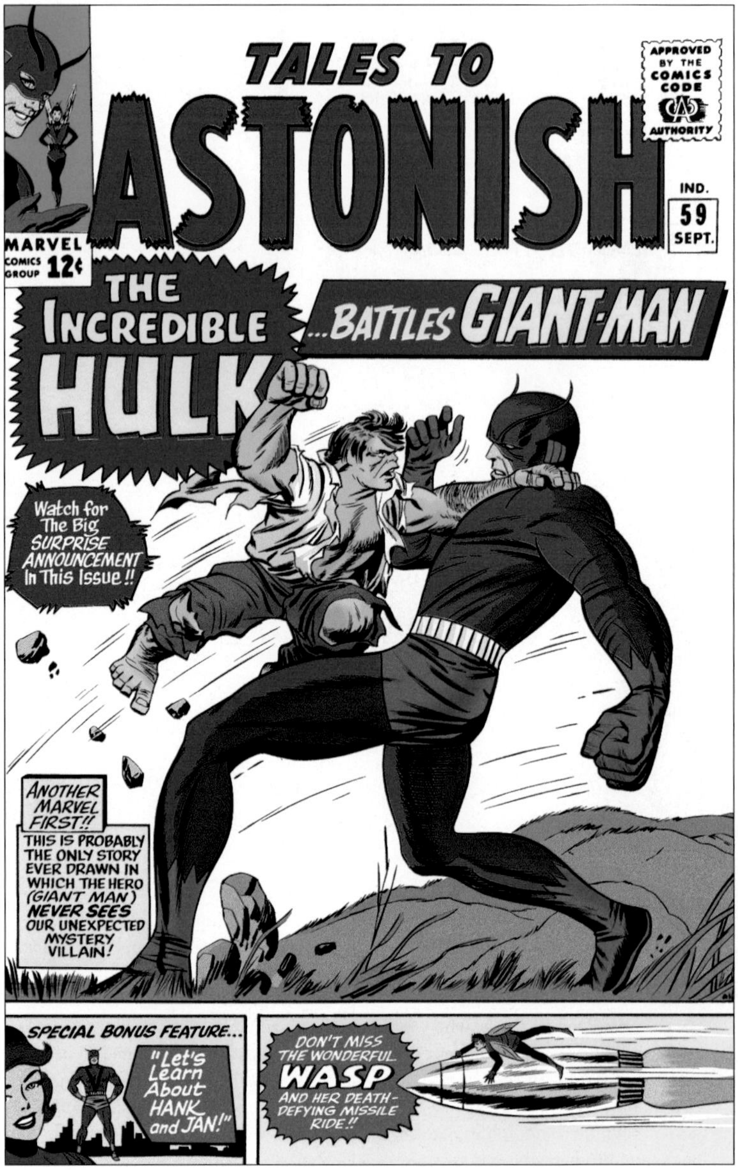
TALES TO ASTONISH
APPROVED BY THE COMICS CODE AUTHORITY
IND.
59
SEPT.
MARVEL COMICS GROUP 12¢
THE INCREDIBLE HULK
...BATTLES GIANT-MAN
Watch for The Big SURPRISE ANNOUNCEMENT In This Issue!!
ANOTHER MARVEL FIRST!!
THIS IS PROBABLY THE ONLY STORY EVER DRAWN IN WHICH THE HERO (GIANT MAN) NEVER SEES OUR UNEXPECTED MYSTERY VILLAIN!
SPECIAL BONUS FEATURE...
"Let's Learn About HANK and JAN!"
DON'T MISS THE WONDERFUL WASP AND HER DEATH-DEFYING MISSILE RIDE!!

ABOVE:
One of the corner boxes that adorned Marvel covers throughout the 1960s. Art by Steve Ditko.

THIS PAGE:
Tales to Astonish #59 (September 1964). Art by Jack Kirby.

OPPOSITE PAGE:
Tales to Astonish #44 (June 1963). Art by Jack Kirby (pencils), Don Heck (inks), Stan Goldberg (colors).

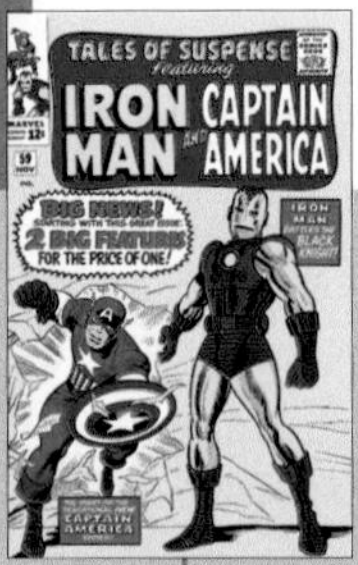
TALES OF SUSPENSE
IRON MAN CAPTAIN AMERICA

NOVEMBER 1964

Captain America gets his own series, which was actually *Tales of Suspense*, beginning with issue #59, in tandem with Iron Man. Soon each would be headliners.

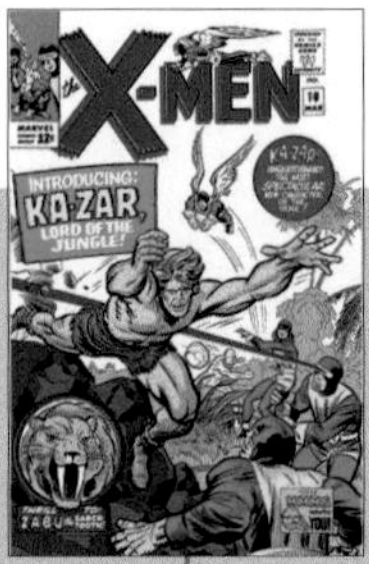
X-MEN
KA-ZAR

MARCH 1965

Ka-Zar returns from the Golden Age in *X-Men* #10. In the 1930s, this pulp creation appeared in *Marvel Comics* #1 with the Human Torch and the Sub-Mariner.

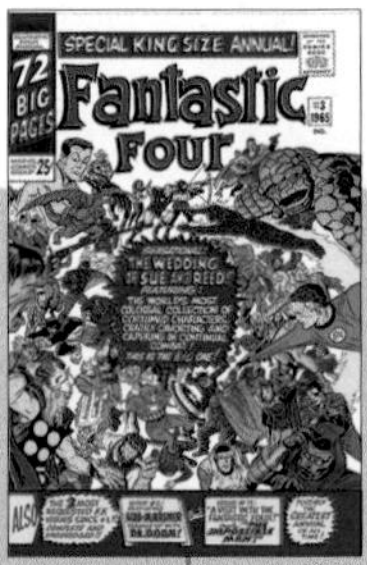
SPECIAL KING SIZE ANNUAL!
Fantastic Four

NOVEMBER 1965

In *Fantastic Four Annual* #3 Marvel celebrates Reed and Sue's wedding. The happy couple is cheered on by plenty of heroes, but sinister Super Villains also lurk in their midst.

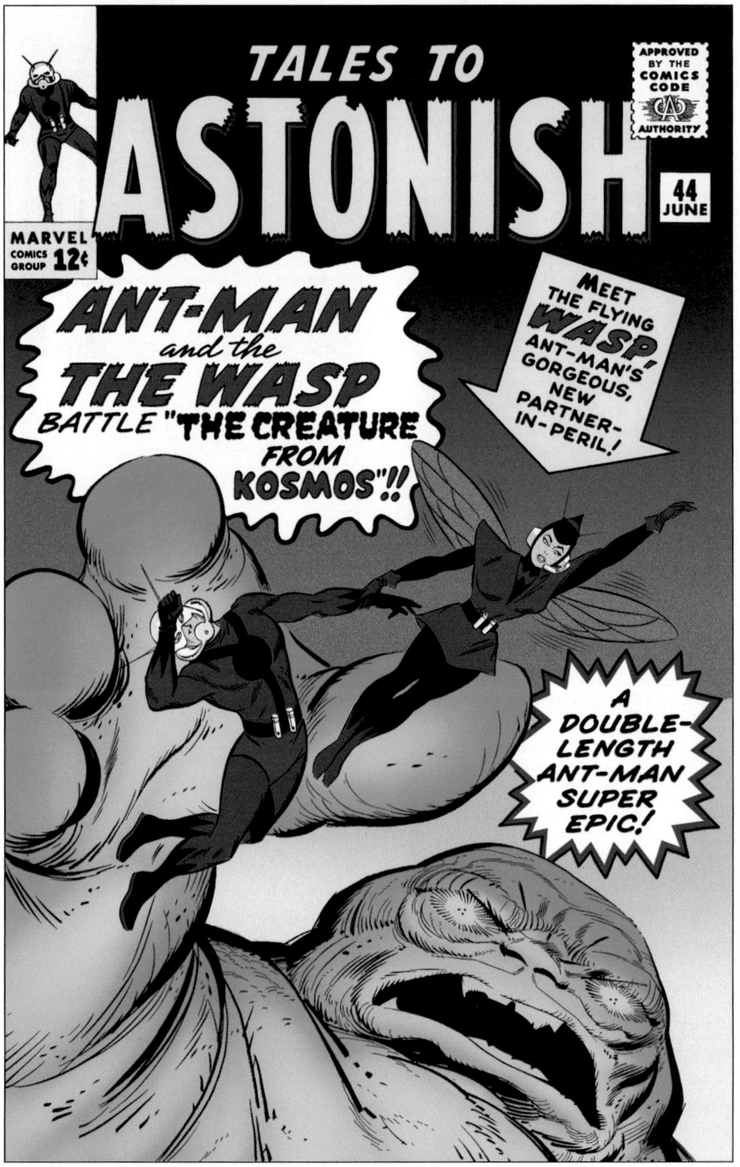
TALES TO ASTONISH
APPROVED BY THE COMICS CODE AUTHORITY
44 JUNE
MARVEL COMICS GROUP 12¢
ANT-MAN and the THE WASP BATTLE "THE CREATURE FROM KOSMOS"!!
MEET THE FLYING WASP! ANT-MAN'S GORGEOUS, NEW PARTNER-IN-PERIL!
A DOUBLE-LENGTH ANT-MAN SUPER EPIC!

The Peter Parker/Spider-Man saga would count on a cast of unparalleled supporting characters. Like J.J. Jameson, publisher of the Daily Bugle, who despises Spidey, but buys photos of the hero taken by Parker himself. Then came his friends, like Betty Brant, Gwen Stacy, Mary Jane Watson, Flash Thompson, and Harry Osborn, a melodrama tinged with tragedy, where mourning someone's death turns into a lifelong dedication to helping others.

To some extent there is a focus on society's fear of the unpredictable developments in science, as symbolized by the appearance of the radioactive spider. Nuclear radiation would be found at the origin of another legendary Marvel character, the Hulk, along with Cold War and literary influences. Bruce Banner was the scientist who morphed into the musclebound green monster (who at first was gray, a color that in print did not do justice to this Super Hero, forcing a change). During a military experiment, which went awry thanks to Soviet spy Igor Starsky, Banner was caught in the blast of a gamma bomb while successfully rescuing Rick Jones, a distracted teenager wandering around the New Mexico desert. At night, he transformed into the ornery, super- strong creature known as the Hulk, in a tug of war between split personalities that recalled Robert Louis Stevenson's Dr. Jekyll and Mr. Hyde, with a dash of Boris Karloff's Frankenstein monster.

But science wasn't always to be feared. Dr. Henry "Hank" Pym's scientific experiments were portrayed in a positive light. The "Pym Particles" he discovered had the power to shrink

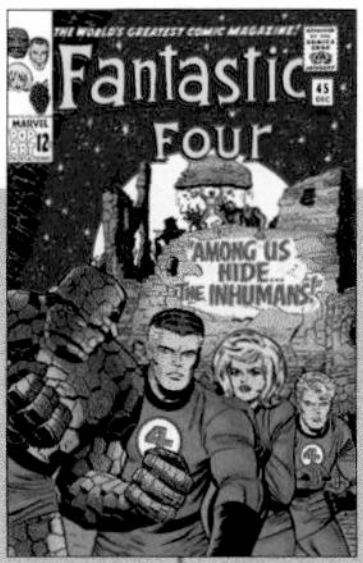
Fantastic Four
AMONG US HIDE... THE INHUMANS!

DECEMBER 1965

Month after month, Lee and Kirby continue to redefine comics and creativity with the *Fantastic Four*. Issue #45 saw the debut of the mysterious Inhumans.

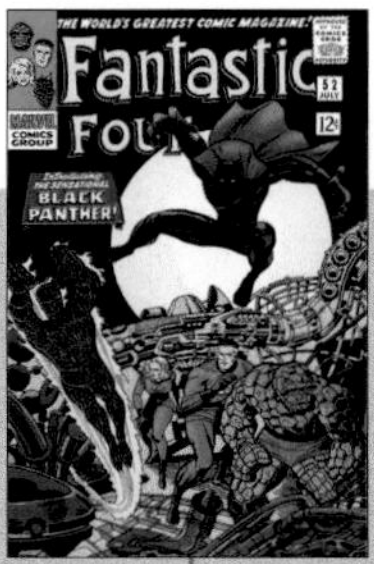
Fantastic Four
BLACK PANTHER!

MARCH–JULY 1966

Black Panther, Marvel's first black Super Hero, makes his debut in the pages of *Fantastic Four* #52. He would eventually join the Avengers, and star in his own solo series in the 1970s.

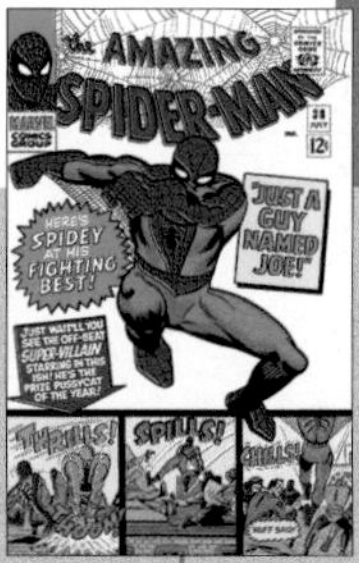
The AMAZING SPIDER-MAN
SPIDEY AT HIS FIGHTING BEST!
"JUST A GUY NAMED JOE!"

AUGUST 1966

Marvel Shakeup: Steve Ditko quits after issue #38 of *The Amazing Spider-Man*. John Romita, Sr. takes the reins with issue #39, ushering in a new era of creativity.

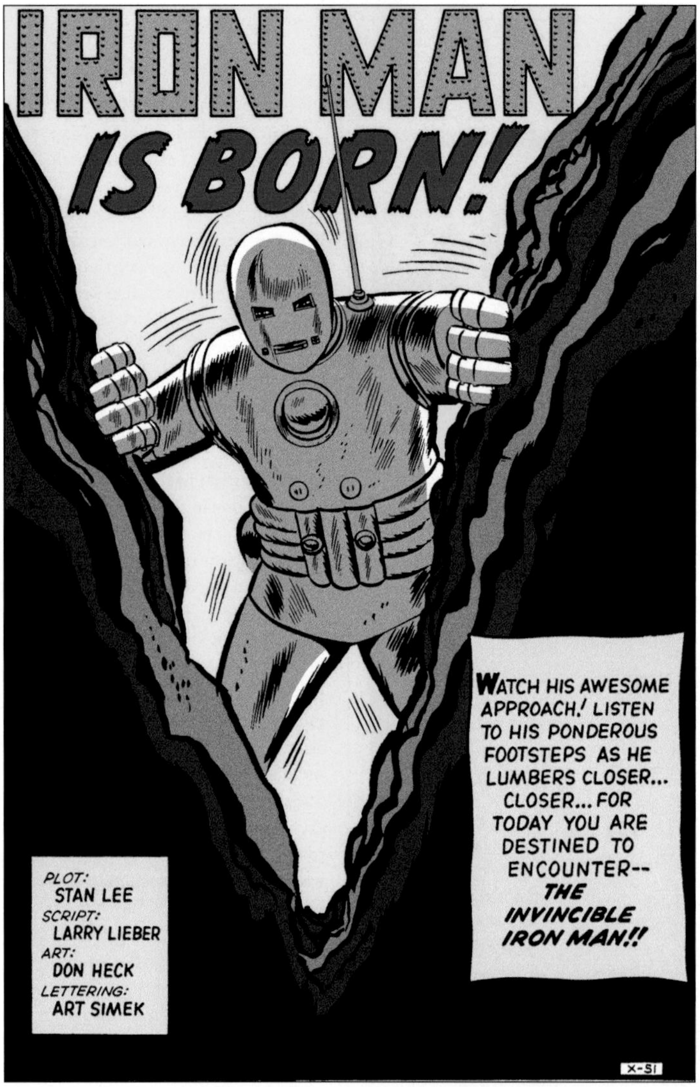
IRON MAN IS BORN!
WATCH HIS AWESOME APPROACH! LISTEN TO HIS PONDEROUS FOOTSTEPS AS HE LUMBERS CLOSER... CLOSER... FOR TODAY YOU ARE DESTINED TO ENCOUNTER-- THE INVINCIBLE IRON MAN!!
PLOT: STAN LEE SCRIPT: LARRY LIEBER ART: DON HECK LETTERING: ART SIMEK
X-51

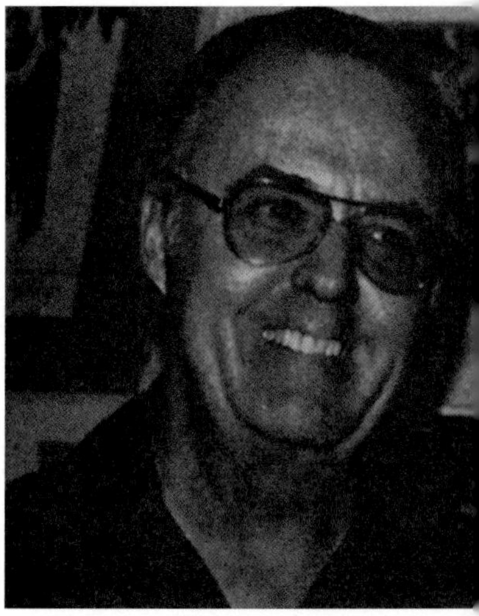

THIS PAGE: Splash page to *Tales of Suspense* #39 (March 1963), the first appearance of Iron Man. Script by Larry Lieber. Art by Don Heck (pencils and inks), Stan Goldberg (colors), and Art Simek (letters).

him to almost microscopic dimensions and, later on, to increase his size dramatically. Introducing: Ant-Man, the Super Hero who could "talk" to ants. Hank teamed up with a rich young heiress, Janet Van Dyne, who became his partner, the Wasp. But life for the scientific genius was torment that few Super Heroes are accustomed to. For one thing, he had a habit of changing identities—from Ant-Man to Giant-Man to Goliath to the Yellowjacket. He also involuntarily created his archnemesis Ultron, his "son" of sorts.

Ever in search of new scenarios and narrative angles, Lee and Kirby turned to the stuff of Norse legends to come up with another illustrious character, Thor. As in all of their creations, the main focus would be the human aspect. It all began in a cave in Norway, where American surgeon Don Blake comes across Thor's hammer, Mjolnir, in the guise of a walking stick. When he bangs it on a rock, Blake is transformed into the Asgardian god of thunder Thor, son of Odin. In reality, Don Blake never existed. He was only a fictional identity created by Odin as punishment for his son's arrogance, after the wayward lad had become overly powerful and lost all restraint. Odin wiped out his memory and relegated him to an existence that wasn't anything close to the one the blond-haired, invincible god had ever known—a healing man, one who tended to the sick and injured. He learned humility—a lesson Thor would never forget.

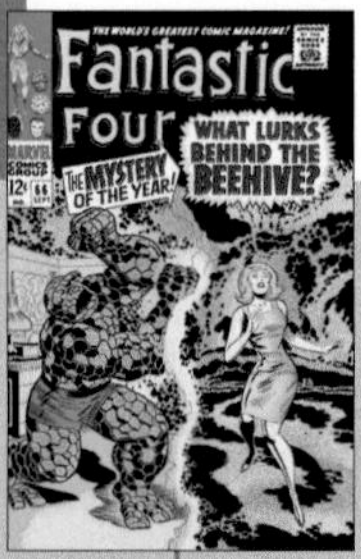
Fantastic Four
WHAT LURKS BEHIND THE BEEHIVE?
THE MYSTERY OF THE YEAR!

SEPTEMBER 1967

Lee and Kirby are unstoppable: for *Fantastic Four* #66 they create another extraordinary Super Hero, Adam Warlock, who was originally called Him.

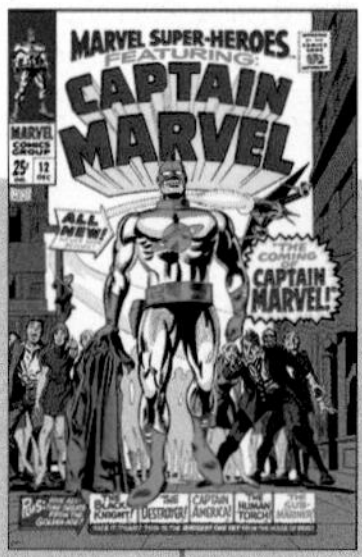
MARVEL SUPER-HEROES FEATURING CAPTAIN MARVEL
THE COMING OF CAPTAIN MARVEL!

DECEMBER 1967

An unlikely hero from space appears in *Marvel Super-Heroes* #12: Captain Marvel. Created by Lee and Gene Colan, Mar-Vell was a Kree warrior, fascinated by the people of Earth.

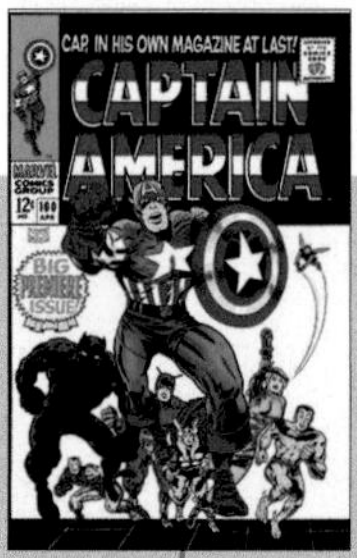
CAP. IN HIS OWN MAGAZINE AT LAST!
CAPTAIN AMERICA

APRIL 1968

Captain America receives his own title in *Captain America* #100 (April 1968), with a cover and story penciled by Jack Kirby.

If Thor's was the most symbolic and "moralistic" origin in Marvel history, then Iron Man's was no less intense and involved just as much commitment. Industrialist Tony Stark suffers a life-threatening wound in Vietnam, the brutal and widely unpopular conflict that gripped America throughout the 1960s and early '70s. Tony was cut in the mold of billionaire playboy Howard Hughes—rich, intelligent, good-looking, an incurable lady's man. In the Vietnamese jungle, Stark has an all-too-close encounter with a landmine and is subsequently taken prisoner by a local warlord bent on forcing him to build weapons for the enemy. But to save himself from the shrapnel lodged dangerously close to his heart, Tony, along with fellow prisoner and Vietnamese physicist Yinsen, secretly builds a magnetic chest plate to ward off the threat.

His first somewhat primitive suit of armor gives Stark the power he needs to escape. Later on, that first suit would be replaced by gold, then red-and-gold models that were increasingly high-tech. The stories featuring Tony Stark focused on adult themes. His heart problems remained a constant, his own mortality looming large. He was a truly unique Super Hero, and lived a tormented existence. He had to be super just to stay alive.

MIDDLE:
Joe Sinnott (left) and Jack Kirby, circa 1975.

THIS PAGE:
The Avengers meet Spider-Man (almost!) in *The Avengers* #11 (December 1964). Art by Jack Kirby (pencils) and Dick Ayers (inks).

1970

JULY 1968

Lee and Romita come up with a new magazine, *The Spectacular Spider-Man*. Giant-sized and black and white, only two issues were released.

OCTOBER 1968

Two new heroes appear in the pages of *The Avengers*: the Vision, an android with emotions, and Yellowjacket (A.K.A. Hank Pym, the former Ant-Man/Giant-Man).

MARION'S BRAINSTORM ABOUT TURNING *IRON MAN* INTO A KNIGHT IN SHINING ARMOR IS A HONEY! I'LL COAT EVERY VISIBLE PART OF MY COSTUME WITH UNTARNISHABLE *GOLD PAINT!*

hero's face. Though he lost his sight, Matt's other senses were amplified way beyond normal human capacity. Meanwhile, his father was murdered for not taking a dive in the ring. Out of all that wreckage, Daredevil was born. In time, the crime fighter's alter ego Matt would open a law practice with friend Franklin "Foggy" Nelson.

While Daredevil's ultrakeen senses were the result of an accident, the X-Men would be born with their superpowers—which is to say, the genetic mutations that made them "different." And there lies the greatness of the new supergroup, featuring team members Cyclops, Marvel Girl, Beast, Angel, and Iceman. Mutants were a metaphor of discrimination against anyone that might be different, and proved to be a profound and dramatic excursion into teenage angst. The X-Men took their name from their mentor, Professor Charles Xavier, the world's preeminent telepath.

Among the classic characters of the Silver Age, it's impossible to forget Doctor Strange, a practitioner of mystic arts who makes his home in Manhattan's Greenwich Village. His alter ego is one Stephen Strange, formerly a haughty, cynical world-class surgeon, whose career went down the drain after his hands were severely damaged in a car crash. Broke and depressed, Strange tries his luck at a monastery in the Himalayas, where he meets up with the Ancient One, a wise man who teaches him the secrets of mysticism and changes his life forever. Steve Ditko worked with Lee to come up with this unforgettable Super Hero.

Meanwhile, by 1963 Lee and

ABOVE:
Tony Stark decides on a gold paint job for his Iron Man armor in *Tales of Suspense* #40. Script by Stan Lee and Robert Bernstein. Art by Jack Kirby (pencils), Don Heck (inks), Stan Goldberg (colors), Artie Simek (letters).

RIGHT:
Captain America is revived in the then-modern 1960s in *The Avengers* #4 (March 1964). Script by Stan Lee. Art by Jack Kirby (pencils), George Roussos (inks), Stan Goldberg (colors), Artie Simek (letters).

But torment comes in many forms. Thanks to the Super-Soldier Serum, Steve Rogers—Captain America himself—survived 20 years of suspended animation to be revived in the 1960s. But he is a man out of time, a man guided by principles and passions that have more to do with the 1940s than the 1960s. He is haunted by the memory of his old sidekick, Bucky Barnes, whom he believed was killed on their last mission together, and was racked by feelings of guilt over his death. Of course, comic book readers and movie fans know that Bucky never died, but

wound up doing a stint as a secret agent for the Soviets as the Winter Soldier. He's since returned to Captain America's side, and we'll be talking more about him in the chapters to come.

Daredevil was another solitary Super Hero with a heart-rending, melodramatic past. Raised by his father, the hapless boxer, Battlin' Jack Murdock, Matt was blinded after he saved a blind man from an oncoming truck carrying barrels of a radioactive isotope (once again, the atomic menace). The truck crashed and spilled the toxic substance on the brave young

Kirby had created former World War II commando Nick Fury, now an eyepatch-wearing, cigar-smoking spy—a James Bond–type character who heads the fictional espionage organization known as S.H.I.E.L.D. (Supreme Headquarters International Espionage Law-Enforcement Division).

Kirby's far-reaching imagination and Lee's taste for dialogue proved to be an irresistible combination. Together, they created the Black Panther, one of the bravest and most well-known Super Heroes. Black and African, his character was born during the heyday of the American civil rights movement. His alter ego T'Challa was king of Wakanda, a tiny but highly developed country in the heart of Africa, where technology was more advanced than in the western world.

Lee and Kirby continued to take chances and amaze. The Inhumans were a group of human beings who possessed bizarre super-powers and lived hidden from the rest of mankind in the Himalayan city of Attilan. Inhumans like Black Bolt, Gorgon, Karnak, Triton, and Medusa would take part in the adventures of the Fantastic Four.

Then there was the ultra-intense, ultra-tragic Silver Surfer, A.K.A. Norrin Radd, from the planet Zenn-La, who made his first appearance in *Fantastic Four* #48. He traveled through space on a silver surfboard—taking his cue from the surf craze at that time—and sacrificed himself to save his people, who were threatened by Galactus, the "world devourer." The Silver Surfer serves as his herald until Galactus reaches Earth, where, won over by the humanity of the planet's inhabitants, the Silver Surfer rebels against him.

ABOVE:
The X-Men #1 (September 1963). Art by Jack Kirby (pencils), Sol Brodsky (inks).

LEFT:
The Silver Surfer appears for the first time in *Fantastic Four* #48 (March 1966). Script by Stan Lee. Art by Jack Kirby (pencils), Joe Sinnott (inks), Artie Simek (letters).

THE MERRY MARVEL BULLPEN

With the rise of the Marvel Universe came the legend
of the Marvel Bullpen—the men and women who created the stories the fans loved.

He came to symbolize Marvel Comics. The front man, the spokesman, the poster boy. He was but a teenager when he first set foot in the offices of Martin Goodman's Timely Publications, and for the rest of his life would remain a seminal figure in the world of comic books. Stan "the Man" Lee left us in 2018, but until the end, he reveled in making cameo appearances in the live-action movies that featured characters he had co-created, to the joy of fans old and new.

The perfection of Marvel's creations lies in the fact that the writers and artists were so willing to share their art, their genius, and their amazing skills. It was one of those situations where the whole is definitely greater than the sum of its parts. There's another comparison we might make in order to underscore that idea. Founding fathers Lee and Kirby were to Marvel what John Lennon and Paul McCartney were to the Beatles. Certain chords and sounds may be the hallmarks of either John or Paul, but the final products, true works of art and beauty, can only be attributed to the both of them.

However, there is one thing we can be sure of, and that is how irreplaceable Lee was in his role as editor. He was the one who chose the pencilers and inkers, his was the last word regarding which direction stories would take when he wrote the dialogue for panels whose artwork had already been completed. Lee himself invented an approach to working together that was on the surface chaos, but in reality harnessed the ultimate creativity of the artists. This was the so-called "Marvel Method," born out of the demands made by a particular publishing

THIS PAGE: Studio photo of Jack Kirby, circa 1969-1970.

OPPOSITE PAGE: The Silver Surfer appears on the cover of *Fantastic Four* #50 (May 1966). Art by Jack Kirby (pencils), Joe Sinnott (inks), and Stan Goldberg (colors).

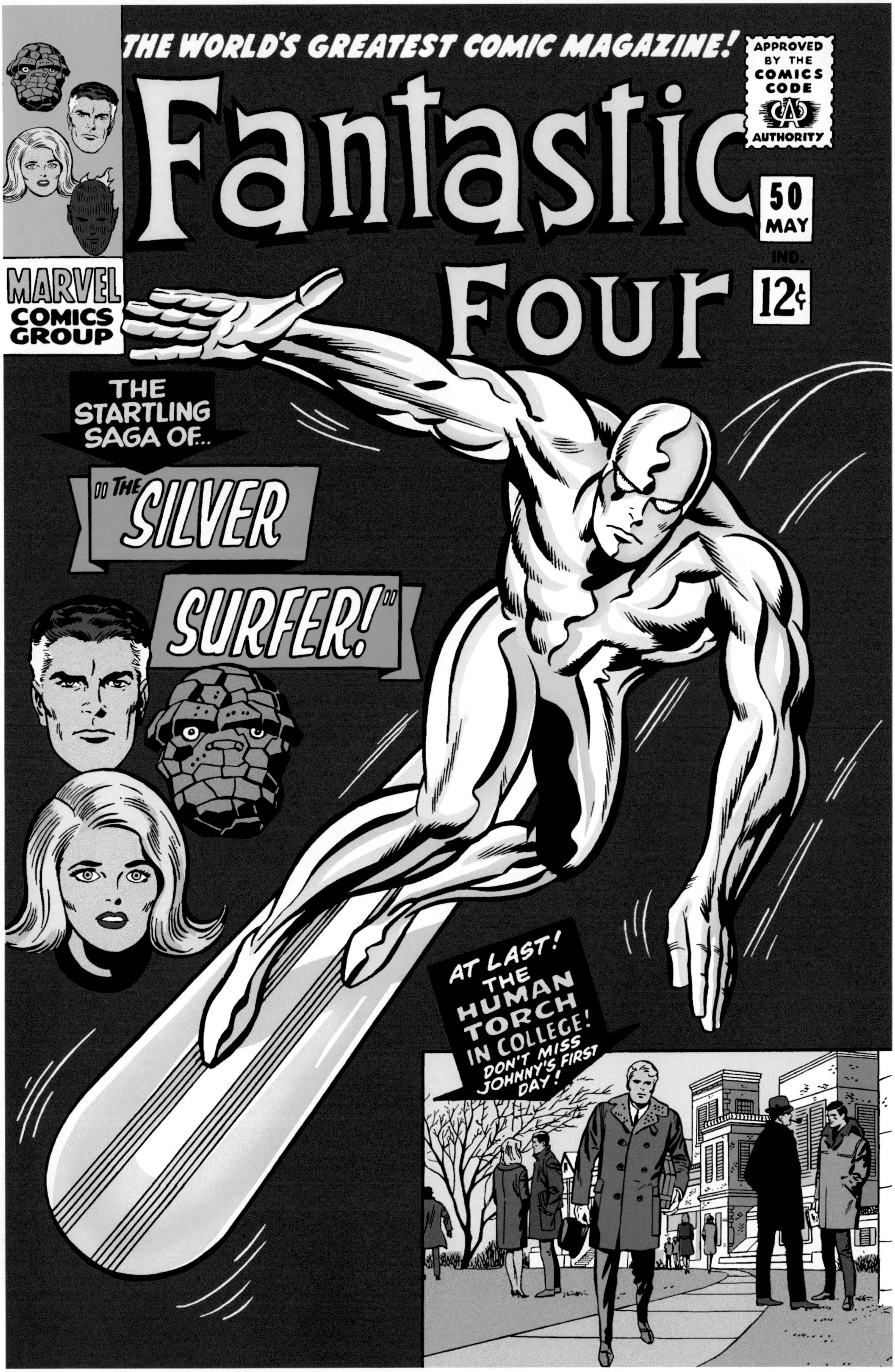
THE WORLD'S GREATEST COMIC MAGAZINE!
APPROVED BY THE COMICS CODE AUTHORITY
Fantastic Four
50 MAY
IND. 12¢
MARVEL COMICS GROUP
THE STARTLING SAGA OF...
"THE SILVER SURFER!"
AT LAST! THE HUMAN TORCH IN COLLEGE! DON'T MISS JOHNNY'S FIRST DAY!

situation. Marvel started out as a small publishing outfit, with a small staff. Nearly everything was written by Lee, including the synopses—plots—for his artists. If he had relied on traditional methods, which called for full scripts, deadlines would have been missed. There would have been no Marvel Comics at all.

This, of course, was possible because Lee's artists were the best in the business, capable of "writing" stories as they went along. And as those stories materialized, pencilers and inkers turned into something like movie directors. Lee would write a one- or two-page plot, or, if time was of the essence, might even convey the message over the phone, or act out a story in front of the artists right there in his office.

Artists would then expand upon the original idea, adding or subtracting scenes, perhaps scribbling notes for the dialogue in the margins, as they penciled stories of 20 or more pages. Once the artwork was finished, it would go back to Lee, who filled in the panels with dialogue like no one else could. The words he put in characters' mouths were brilliant, funny, emphatic, tragic, human, entertaining. This was the innovation that set Marvel apart. Stories were built in layers, freewheeling, one-of-a-kind masterpieces.

Lee worked as Marvel's Editor in Chief and main writer until 1972,

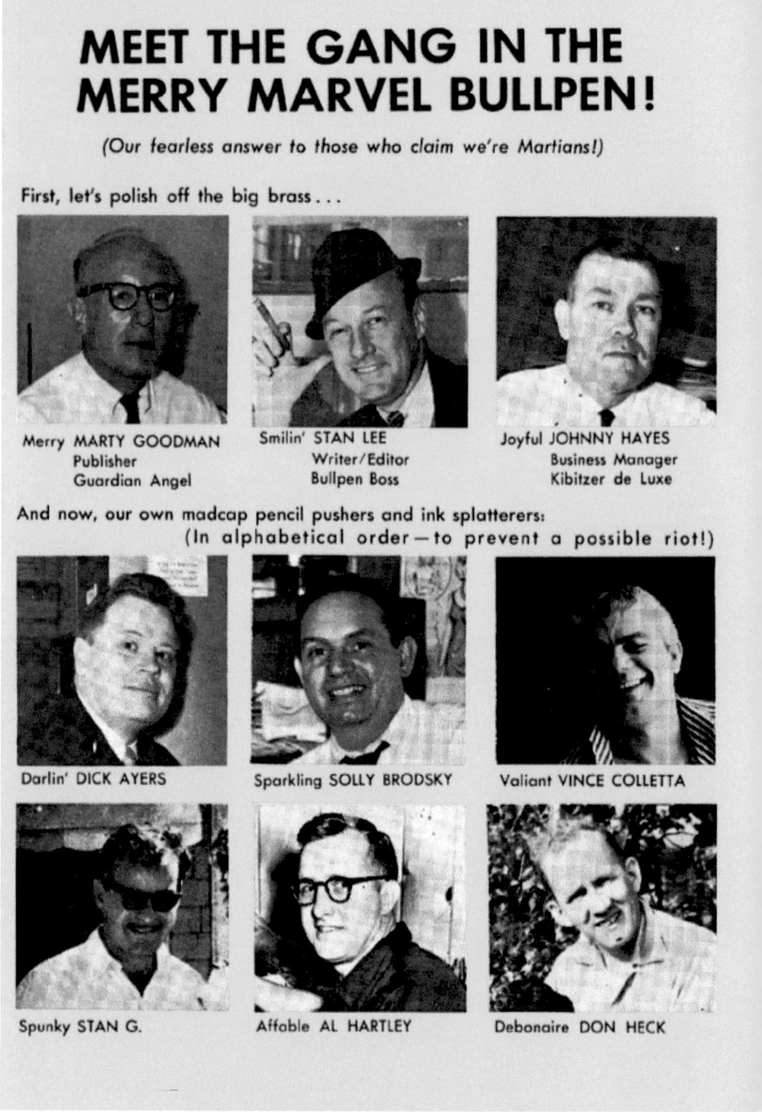
MEET THE GANG IN THE MERRY MARVEL BULLPEN!

(Our fearless answer to those who claim we're Martians!)

First, let's polish off the big brass . . .

Merry MARTY GOODMAN
Publisher
Guardian Angel

Smilin' STAN LEE
Writer/Editor
Bullpen Boss

Joyful JOHNNY HAYES
Business Manager
Kibitzer de Luxe

And now, our own madcap pencil pushers and ink splatterers:
(In alphabetical order—to prevent a possible riot!)

Darlin' DICK AYERS

Sparkling SOLLY BRODSKY

Valiant VINCE COLLETTA

Spunky STAN G.

Affable AL HARTLEY

Debonaire DON HECK

BELOW: The Marvel Bullpen in the mid-1960s: (from left to right) Stan Lee, Marie Severin, John Romita, Sr., and Roy Thomas (as Spider-Man).

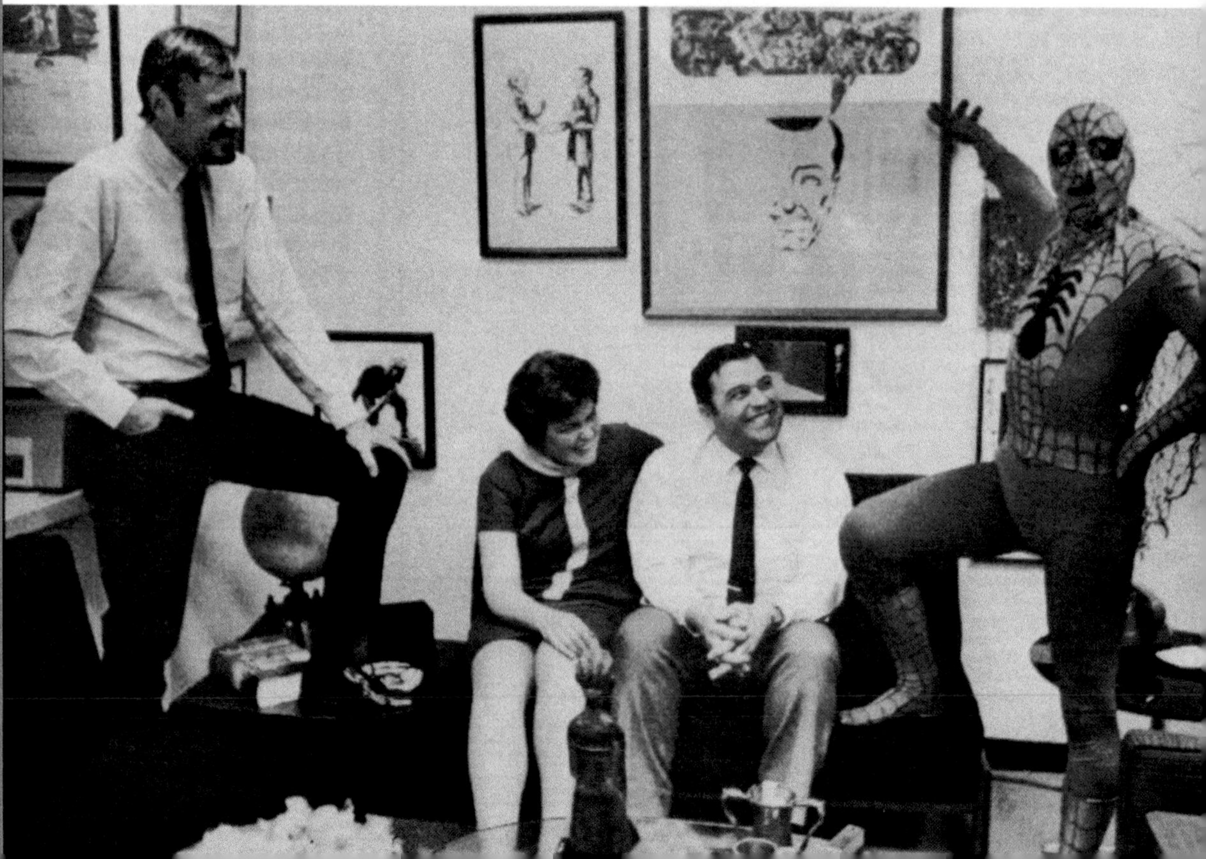

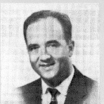

oyful JACK KELLER
Jolly ol' JACK KIRBY
Laughin' LARRY LIEBER
ıvial JOE ORLANDO
Peerless PAUL REINMAN
Sprightly SAM ROSEN
dorable ARTIE SIMEK
Cheerful CHIC STONE
A few of our bullpen buddies were out of town when these pix were taken—so we'll try to print their pans later on. (A sneaky way to coax you to read all our future issues!)
ınd now, we present our ever-lovin' glamor department...
ıbulous FLO STEINBERG Corresponding Secy. Gal Friday
Nifty NANCY MURPHY Subscriptions Overseas Mailings
Dazzling DEBBY ACKERMAN Campus Rep. Student Surveys

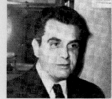

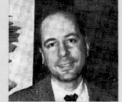

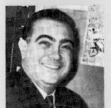

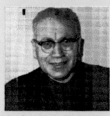

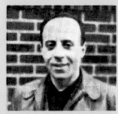

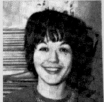

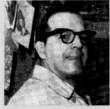

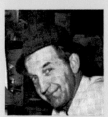

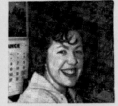

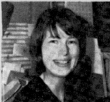

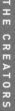

LEFT: The Marvel Bullpen from the pages of Marvel Comics.

CORNER BOXES

A few months earlier, on the already dazzling, modern covers, so dynamic and action packed that they practically told entire stories by themselves, something new appeared in the upper left corner box. For the very first time, that little rectangle contained the faces of the Super Heroes featured in that issue. Lee attributed the concept of the corner boxes to Steve Ditko. A reader from Ohio sent congratulations for that corner box, to which letter Lee replied, "Steve was the one who came up with that, and we're grateful to him for it." For decades, these corner boxes would be associated with the covers of Marvel Comics.

when the new ownership promoted him to publisher. But in the meantime, he had hired his right-hand man, young Roy Thomas, an English teacher from Missouri—not to mention a big comics fan, well-versed in the Golden Age, with literary aspirations of his own. Thomas had come to New York to work for the Distinguished Competition, but after spending a harrowing week under Mort Weisinger, the Superman editor who was notoriously difficult to work with, he wrote Lee asking if they could meet. Lee wasted no time in replying. The two met, and Lee, after testing out Thomas's writing skills, offered him a job on his staff. Thomas would go on to become Lee's most in-synch collaborator, and took up Lee's work on projects involving the Fantastic Four, Spider-Man, the Avengers, and other characters.

For the first time, comic book writers and artists had achieved celebrity status. Up till then, their names were practically unknown to fans. In the 1950s, EC Comics had made some strides with regard to informing readers as to the artistic components involved, but Lee ushered in the concept of turning artists and authors into stars, with their names appearing on opening splash pages, oftentimes with amusing nicknames: Jack "the King" Kirby, "Rascally" Roy Thomas, Gene "the Dean" Colan, "Jazzy" John Romita, "Sturdy" Steve Ditko, Stan "the Man" Lee…

Jack Kirby and Steve Ditko were Marvel's big guns. Kirby was considered a model to follow, known for his cinematographic imagery and larger-than-life portrayals, an emphatic expressionism that reveled in large-size panels, muscular bodies, and kinetic lines. With his cigar, his smile, and his Lower East Side spontaneity, Kirby could very well have been one of his own characters—Ben Grimm and the Thing might be considered his comic book counterparts. Ditko, on the other hand, was introverted, refined, a fan of Ayn Rand—the author who, to put it very succinctly, shunned nuances and viewed things pretty much in black and white. Indeed, his Spider-Man character reflects those trademarks.

At least in Spidey's first 38 stories. After which, Ditko packed up and left Marvel (though he would return in the 1970s, and continued working for Marvel through the 1990s). Ditko was considered a master storyteller. His pages typically contained nine panels, three to a row, treating readers to unsurpassed readability. Ditko's departure could have spelled disaster for Marvel. Spider-Man had probably become its best-loved character—how would readers take it? Fortunately, Lee was ready for anything. He had recently hired John Romita, Sr., who had cut his teeth on romance comics and knew how to draw pretty women and magnetizing men. Although Romita had begged Stan to limit his duties to inking, he was called on to pencil Daredevil—the urban-set stepping- stone to Spider-Man. Under Romita, the wall-crawler took on a

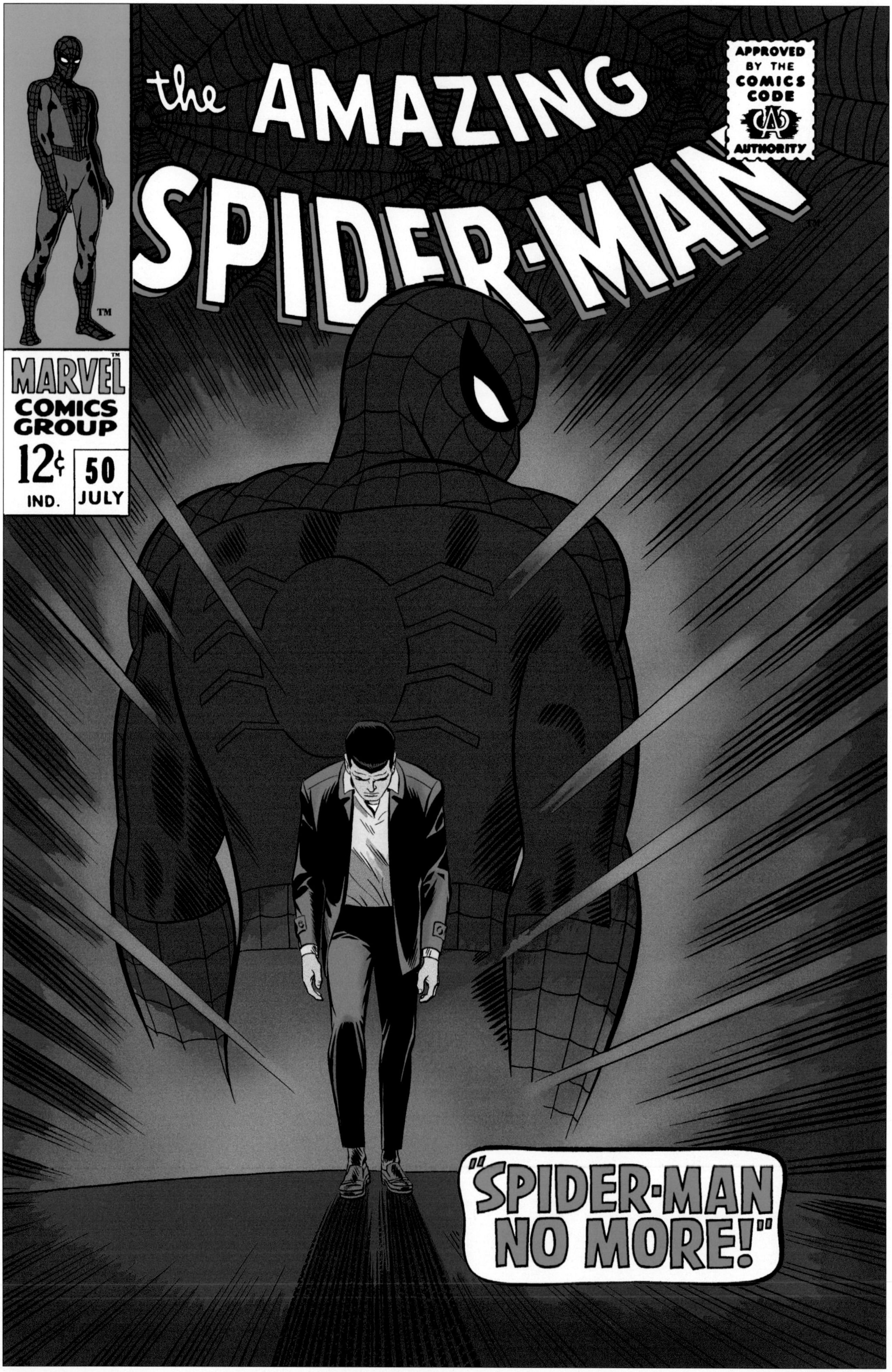
the AMAZING
SPIDER-MAN™
APPROVED BY THE COMICS CODE AUTHORITY
MARVEL™
COMICS GROUP
12¢
IND.
50
JULY
"SPIDER-MAN NO MORE!"

more glamorous and pleasing appeal. Gone was Peter Parker's awkwardness , and Spider-Man soon became Marvel's best-selling Super Hero.

Year after year, the House of Ideas, as Marvel came to be known, edged ever closer to the sales figures achieved by the Distinguished Competition, until Marvel finally took the lead in 1972. DC was puzzled over the secret behind Marvel's success, and in vain they tried to imitate their compelling graphics and storytelling. They never realized that it was the complexity of Marvel's characters that made the difference. They weren't the kind of Super Heroes who hid behind detached alter egos to conceal their identities. Rather, they were real people who, caught up in exceptional circumstances, became Super Heroes despite themselves. The key, then, to Marvel's success was its characters and the people who told their stories.

Two of the biggest stars at this time had to have been John Buscema and Gene Colan. Buscema was a refined artist skilled in depicting anatomy. Known as the Michelangelo of comic book art, his mark became Marvel's mark. He and Lee eventually

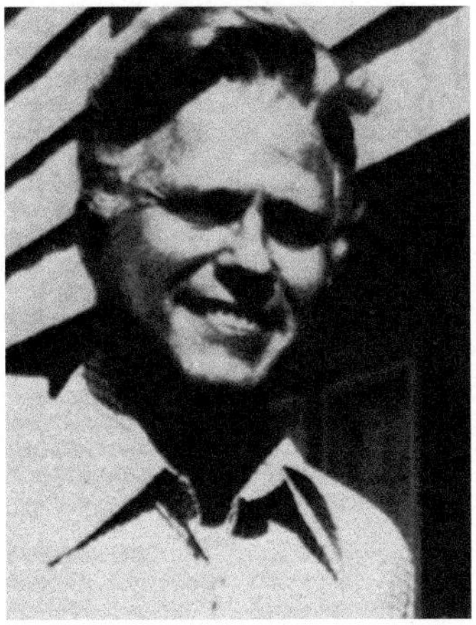

collaborated on the book *How to Draw Comics the Marvel Way*—written by Lee, artwork by Buscema. From Thor to the Fantastic Four to the Avengers, Buscema's touch became a hallmark of greatness. In the 1970s he'd conquer the world with his interpretation of Conan the Barbarian. His approach contrasted with the classic style of Gene Colan, the artist behind the beloved *Daredevil* series. He was known for his fleeting, ethereal touch, where shadows and movement reigned. Considering how far apart their styles were, Colan was among a select group of artists that Lee kept from basing his work on Kirby's.

Jim Steranko was yet another world-class comic book artist at Marvel. He hailed from a rough-and-tumble background in Reading, Pennsylvania, and had spent his early days working any number of odd jobs to get by—he is even said to have earned a living as a fire eater and a magician. Steranko had a psychedelic style and preferred futuristic layouts. He was a visionary whose work on Nick Fury stories (in *Strange Tales*, and the *Nick Fury, Agent of S.H.I.E.L.D.* series) broke new ground.

Then came a slew of indispensable behind-the-scenes figures, such as Larry Lieber, the writer who helped create Iron Man and Thor; artist Don Heck; Joe Sinnott, the master inker who handled Kirby's *Fantastic Four* panels; and people like Dick Ayers, Wally Wood, Paul Reinman, Werner Roth, Herb Trimpe (his *Hulk* series remains a classic), and John Severin, a superbly sleek artist who had previously worked for EC, and his sister, Marie, known for her eye-catching covers and extraordinary sense of humor.

OPPOSITE PAGE: *The Amazing Spider-Man* #50 (July 1967). Art by John Romita, Sr. (pencils and inks), Stan Goldberg (colors).

LEFT: Artist Gene Colan.

BELOW: Featurette from *Marvel Treasury Edition* #1: *The Spectacular Spider-Man* (1974). Gerry Conway (writer), Marie Severin (art).

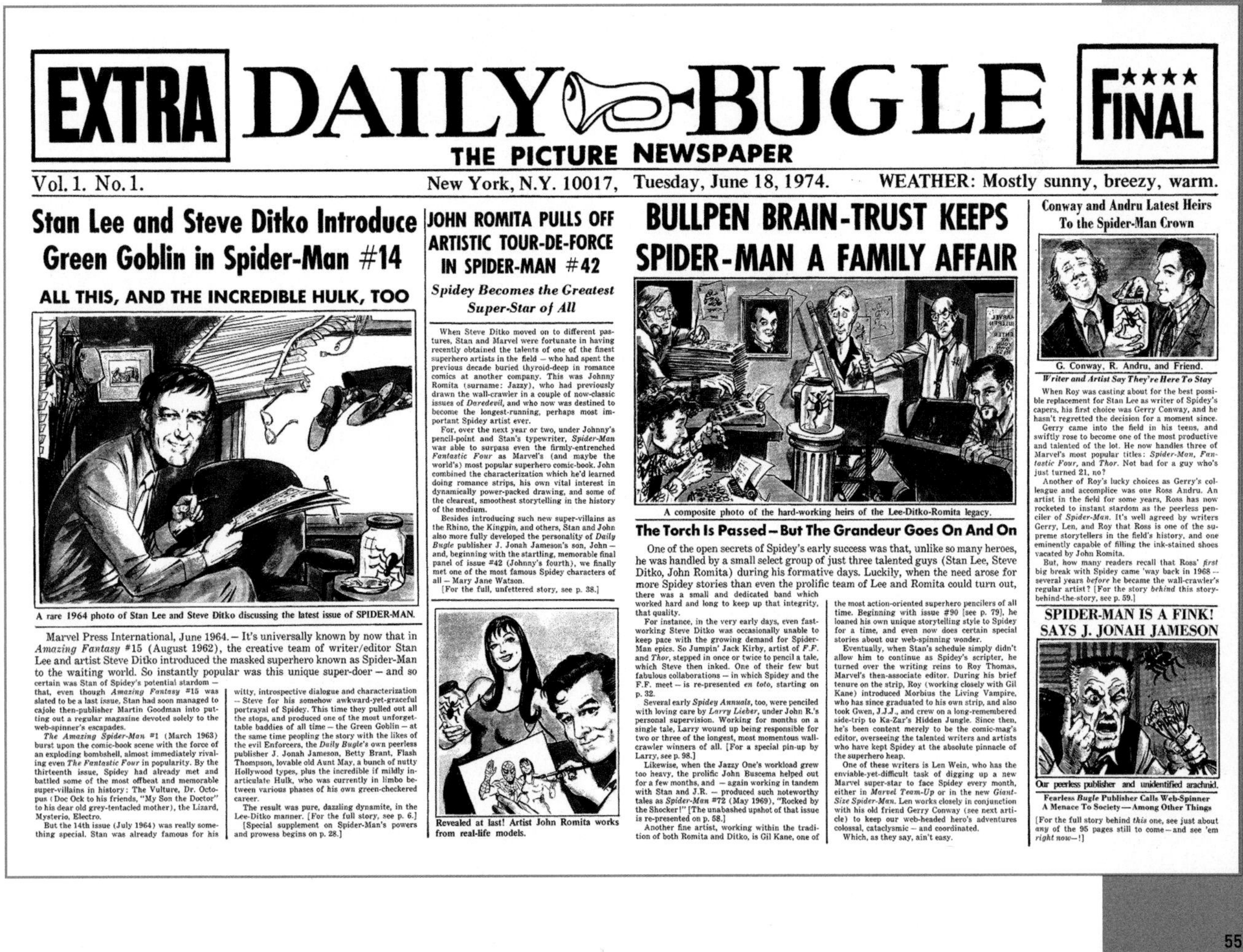

EXTRA DAILY BUGLE FINAL ★★★★

THE PICTURE NEWSPAPER

Vol. 1. No. 1. New York, N.Y. 10017, Tuesday, June 18, 1974. WEATHER: Mostly sunny, breezy, warm.

Stan Lee and Steve Ditko Introduce Green Goblin in Spider-Man #14

ALL THIS, AND THE INCREDIBLE HULK, TOO

A rare 1964 photo of Stan Lee and Steve Ditko discussing the latest issue of SPIDER-MAN.

Marvel Press International, June 1964. – It's universally known by now that in *Amazing Fantasy* #15 (August 1962), the creative team of writer/editor Stan Lee and artist Steve Ditko introduced the masked superhero known as Spider-Man to the waiting world. So instantly popular was this unique super-doer – and so certain was Stan of Spidey's potential stardom – that, even though *Amazing Fantasy* #15 was slated to be a last issue, Stan had soon managed to cajole then-publisher Martin Goodman into putting out a regular magazine devoted solely to the web-spinner's escapades.

The Amazing Spider-Man #1 (March 1963) burst upon the comic-book scene with the force of an exploding bombshell, almost immediately rivaling even *The Fantastic Four* in popularity. By the thirteenth issue, Spidey had already met and battled some of the most offbeat and memorable super-villains in history: The Vulture, Dr. Octopus (Doc Ock to his friends, "My Son the Doctor" to his dear old grey-tentacled mother), the Lizard, Mysterio, Electro.

But the 14th issue (July 1964) was really something special. Stan was already famous for his witty, introspective dialogue and characterization – Steve for his somehow awkward-yet-graceful portrayal of Spidey. This time they pulled out all the stops, and produced one of the most unforgettable baddies of all time – the Green Goblin – at the same time peopling the story with the likes of the evil Enforcers, the *Daily Bugle's* own peerless publisher J. Jonah Jameson, Betty Brant, Flash Thompson, lovable old Aunt May, a bunch of nutty Hollywood types, plus the incredible if mildly inarticulate Hulk, who was currently in limbo between various phases of his own green-checkered career.

The result was pure, dazzling dynamite, in the Lee-Ditko manner. [For the full story, see p. 6.]

[Special supplement on Spider-Man's powers and prowess begins on p. 28.]

JOHN ROMITA PULLS OFF ARTISTIC TOUR-DE-FORCE IN SPIDER-MAN #42

Spidey Becomes the Greatest Super-Star of All

When Steve Ditko moved on to different pastures, Stan and Marvel were fortunate in having recently obtained the talents of one of the finest superhero artists in the field – who had spent the previous decade buried thyroid-deep in romance comics at another company. This was Johnny Romita (surname: Jazzy), who had previously drawn the wall-crawler in a couple of now-classic issues of *Daredevil*, and who now was destined to become the longest-running, perhaps most important Spidey artist ever.

For, over the next year or two, under Johnny's pencil-point and Stan's typewriter, *Spider-Man* was able to surpass even the firmly-entrenched *Fantastic Four* as Marvel's (and maybe the world's) most popular superhero comic-book. John combined the characterization which he'd learned doing romance strips, his own vital interest in dynamically power-packed drawing, and some of the clearest, smoothest storytelling in the history of the medium.

Besides introducing such new super-villains as the Rhino, the Kingpin, and others, Stan and John also more fully developed the personality of *Daily Bugle* publisher J. Jonah Jameson's son, John – and, beginning with the startling, memorable final panel of issue #42 (Johnny's fourth), we finally met one of the most famous Spidey characters of all – Mary Jane Watson.

[For the full, unfettered story, see p. 38.]

Revealed at last! Artist John Romita works from real-life models.

BULLPEN BRAIN-TRUST KEEPS SPIDER-MAN A FAMILY AFFAIR

A composite photo of the hard-working heirs of the Lee-Ditko-Romita legacy.

The Torch Is Passed – But The Grandeur Goes On And On

One of the open secrets of Spidey's early success was that, unlike so many heroes, he was handled by a small select group of just three talented guys (Stan Lee, Steve Ditko, John Romita) during his formative days. Luckily, when the need arose for more Spidey stories than even the prolific team of Lee and Romita could turn out, there was a small and dedicated band which worked hard and long to keep up that integrity, that quality.

For instance, in the very early days, even fast-working Steve Ditko was occasionally unable to keep pace with the growing demand for Spider-Man epics. So Jumpin' Jack Kirby, artist of *F.F.* and *Thor*, stepped in once or twice to pencil a tale, which Steve then inked. One of their few but fabulous collaborations – in which Spidey and the F.F. meet – is re-presented *en toto*, starting on p. 32.

Several early *Spidey Annuals*, too, were penciled with loving care by *Larry Lieber*, under John R.'s personal supervision. Working for months on a single tale, Larry wound up being responsible for two or three of the longest, most momentous wall-crawler winners of all. [For a special pin-up by Larry, see p. 98.]

Likewise, when the Jazzy One's workload grew too heavy, the prolific John Buscema helped out for a few months, and – again working in tandem with Stan and J.R. – produced such noteworthy tales as *Spider-Man* #72 (May 1969), "Rocked by the Shocker!" [The unabashed upshot of that issue is re-presented on p. 58.]

Another fine artist, working within the tradition of both Romita and Ditko, is Gil Kane, one of the most action-oriented superhero pencilers of all time. Beginning with issue #90 [see p. 79], he loaned his own unique storytelling style to Spidey for a time, and even now does certain special stories about our web-spinning wonder.

Eventually, when Stan's schedule simply didn't allow him to continue as Spidey's scripter, he turned over the writing reins to Roy Thomas, Marvel's then-associate editor. During his brief tenure on the strip, Roy (working closely with Gil Kane) introduced Morbius the Living Vampire, who has since graduated to his own strip, and also took Gwen, J.J.J., and crew on a long-remembered side-trip to Ka-Zar's Hidden Jungle. Since then, he's been content merely to be the comic-mag's editor, overseeing the talented writers and artists who have kept Spidey at the absolute pinnacle of the superhero heap.

One of these writers is Len Wein, who has the enviable-yet-difficult task of digging up a new Marvel super-star to face Spidey every month, either in *Marvel Team-Up* or in the new *Giant-Size Spider-Man*. Len works closely in conjunction with his old friend Gerry Conway (see next article) to keep our web-headed hero's adventures colossal, cataclysmic – and coordinated.

Which, as they say, ain't easy.

Conway and Andru Latest Heirs To the Spider-Man Crown

G. Conway, R. Andru, and Friend.

Writer and Artist Say They're Here To Stay

When Roy was casting about for the best possible replacement for Stan Lee as writer of Spidey's capers, his first choice was Gerry Conway, and he hasn't regretted the decision for a moment since.

Gerry came into the field in his teens, and swiftly rose to become one of the most productive and talented of the lot. He now handles three of Marvel's most popular titles: *Spider-Man*, *Fantastic Four*, and *Thor*. Not bad for a guy who's just turned 21, no?

Another of Roy's lucky choices as Gerry's colleague and accomplice was one Ross Andru. An artist in the field for some years, Ross has now rocketed to instant stardom as the peerless penciler of *Spider-Man*. It's well agreed by writers Gerry, Len, and Roy that Ross is one of the supreme storytellers in the field's history, and one eminently capable of filling the ink-stained shoes vacated by John Romita.

But, how many readers recall that Ross' *first* big break with Spidey came 'way back in 1968 – several years *before* he became the wall-crawler's regular artist? [For the story *behind* this story-behind-the-story, see p. 59.]

SPIDER-MAN IS A FINK! SAYS J. JONAH JAMESON

Our peerless publisher and unidentified arachnid.

Fearless *Bugle* Publisher Calls Web-Spinner A Menace To Society — Among Other Things

[For the full story behind *this* one, see just about *any* of the 95 pages still to come – and see 'em *right now* –!]

THE SPIRIT OF THE 1960S

In the Marvel Age, inspiration comes from the real world—and the real world sees a need for this new mythology.

IT WILL NOT BE ALL! I SHALL NOW DE-MATERIALIZE AND INTRODUCE MYSELF TO THE PRESIDENT!
GREAT SCOTT! H-HE'S VANISHING BEFORE OUR VERY EYES!
HE MUST REALLY BE MERLIN, THE ONE WHO VANISHED FROM THE CRYPT-- IMPOSSIBLE AS IT SEEMS! WE-WE'VE GOT TO NOTIFY THE F.B.I.! AND ---SEND FOR THOR!
SOON, IN A WHITE HOUSE CORRIDOR...
ALL RIGHT, DEAR... I'LL TAKE YOU TO YOUR MOTHER AND TELL HER TO LET YOU RIDE "MACARONI"!
PERHAPS THAT MAN WITH HIS DAUGHTER IS-- NO! HE LOOKS TOO YOUNG! I'LL HAVE TO SEARCH FURTHER TILL I FIND THE PRESIDENT!

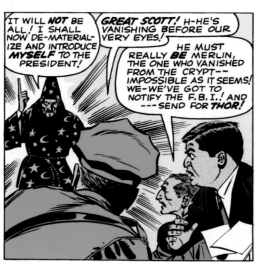

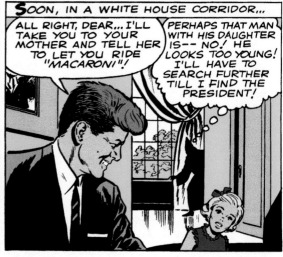

THIS PAGE: Real-world figures (like U.S. Press Secretary Pierre Salinger in panel 1, and John F. Kennedy in panel 2) appeared in the Marvel Universe. *Journey into Mystery* #96 (September 1963). Script by Stan Lee. Art by Larry Lieber (pencils, inks), Artie Simek (letters).

OPPOSITE PAGE: Black Panther appears in *Fantastic Four* #52 (July 1966). Art by Jack Kirby (pencils), Joe Sinnott (inks).

Marvel characters do not live in nonexistent fairy-tale worlds, but in places like the boroughs of New York City—their homes may be in Queens or in some Manhattan skyscraper. The president of the United States could very well be John F. Kennedy. Enemy number one? The Soviet Union. The Cold War is in full swing, with all its repercussions on everyday life, and the fear of an all-out war around the corner is palpable. Readers realize that the world portrayed by Marvel is the world they themselves live in; it's not life on some other planet, or set in a fictional city like Metropolis or Gotham. Marvel stories are awash in all the problems and anxiety of the times. Topping the list is the dread of a nuclear holocaust in the wake of Hiroshima and Nagasaki.

Science opens up new cans of worms every day—do the benefits outweigh the dangers? People were worried about what tomorrow would bring. Back in the 1960s, folks wondered where destiny was leading them. So did the fragile Super Heroes that Marvel created.

Those days, the vision of the future also comprised the conquest of space. President John F. Kennedy was eager to expand the space program in 1961, so the U.S. could catch up—and surpass—the Soviet Union. That's why the Fantastic Four risked everything to get into orbit, and why the theme of space travel became a recurrent theme—beginning with John Jameson, the son of Spider-Man's foe at the Daily Bugle, who eventually found a rock on the moon that wound up turning him into the Man-Wolf.

If patriotism—i.e., the U.S. vs. the Soviet Union—was considered a given in some earlier stories, Marvel's position on domestic issues remained more nuanced. But Lee's liberal spirit would shape stories whose tones became more progressive and in step with modern times. Lee approved of student protests against the war in Vietnam, and was in favor of civil rights. College campuses became settings for his stories, and college kids would be among the first to recognize him as a champion for peace and equality. Marvel Comics would be considered a friendly island in touch with the changing times, driven by the wave of reformism sweeping the country. John F. Kennedy, Martin Luther King, the Black Panthers and Beat generation authors had all left their mark. Lee began getting invitations to speak at universities and conferences where he outlined Marvel's philosophy—a school of thought very much appreciated by young people and the 1960s counterculture (Doctor Strange and the Silver Surfer were considered symbols of the times). Stan Lee had become Marvel's "public persona."

While other comic book publishers didn't dare touch upon issues regarding racial equality, whose few characters of color were only included for comic relief, black characters in Marvel stories

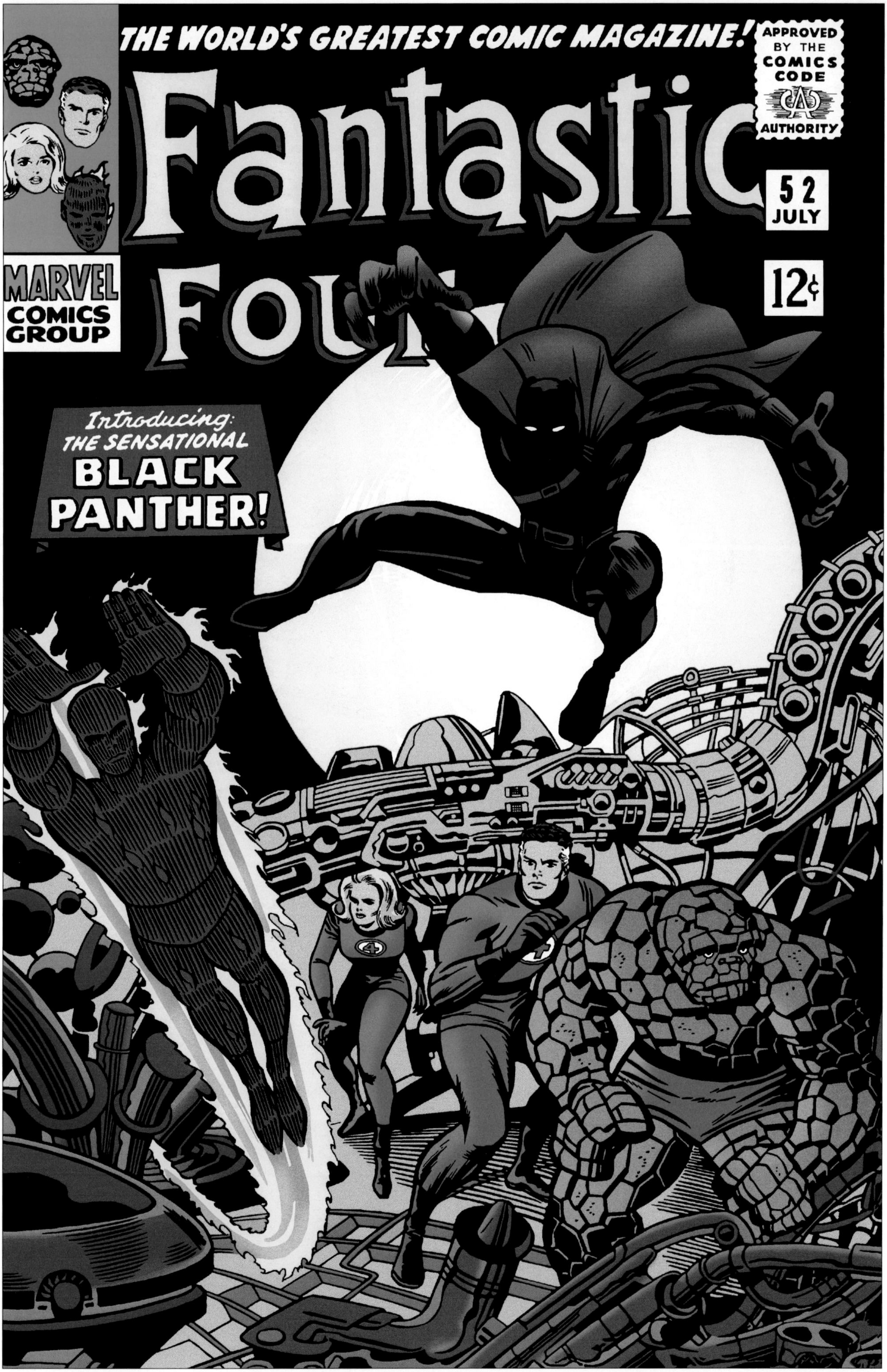
THE WORLD'S GREATEST COMIC MAGAZINE!
APPROVED BY THE COMICS CODE AUTHORITY
Fantastic Four
52
JULY
12¢
MARVEL COMICS GROUP
Introducing: THE SENSATIONAL BLACK PANTHER!

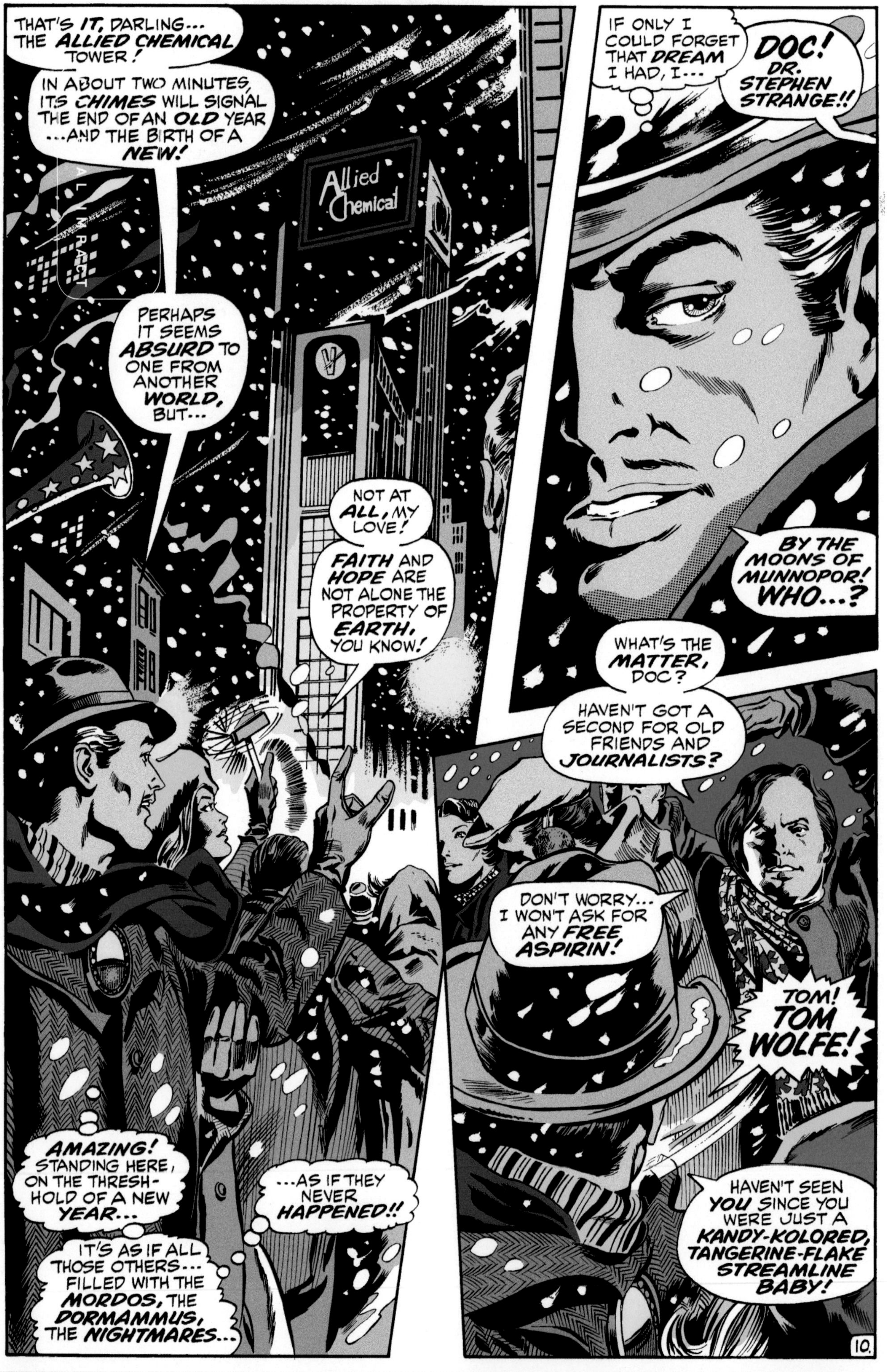

THAT'S IT, DARLING... THE ALLIED CHEMICAL TOWER!
IN ABOUT TWO MINUTES, IT'S CHIMES WILL SIGNAL THE END OF AN OLD YEAR ...AND THE BIRTH OF A NEW!
Allied Chemical
PERHAPS IT SEEMS ABSURD TO ONE FROM ANOTHER WORLD, BUT...
NOT AT ALL, MY LOVE!
FAITH AND HOPE ARE NOT ALONE THE PROPERTY OF EARTH, YOU KNOW!
AMAZING! STANDING HERE, ON THE THRESH-HOLD OF A NEW YEAR...
IT'S AS IF ALL THOSE OTHERS... FILLED WITH THE MORDOS, THE DORMAMMUS, THE NIGHTMARES...
...AS IF THEY NEVER HAPPENED!!
IF ONLY I COULD FORGET THAT DREAM I HAD, I...
DOC! DR. STEPHEN STRANGE!!
BY THE MOONS OF MUNNOPOR! WHO...?
WHAT'S THE MATTER, DOC?
HAVEN'T GOT A SECOND FOR OLD FRIENDS AND JOURNALISTS?
DON'T WORRY... I WON'T ASK FOR ANY FREE ASPIRIN!
TOM! TOM WOLFE!
HAVEN'T SEEN YOU SINCE YOU WERE JUST A KANDY-KOLORED, TANGERINE-FLAKE STREAMLINE BABY!
10.

STAN'S SOAPBOX

Let's lay it right on the line. Bigotry and racism are among the deadliest social ills plaguing the world today. But, unlike a team of costumed super-villains, they can't be halted with a punch in the snoot, or a zap from a ray gun. The only way to destroy them is to expose them — to reveal them for the insidious evils they really are. The bigot is an unreasoning hater — one who hates blindly, fanatically, indiscriminately. If his hang-up is black men, he hates ALL black men. If a redhead once offended him, he hates ALL redheads. If some foreigner beat him to a job, he's down on ALL foreigners. He hates people he's never seen — people he's never known — with equal intensity — with equal venom. Now, we're not trying to say it's unreasonable for one human being to bug another. But, although anyone has the right to dislike another individual, it's totally irrational, patently insane to condemn an entire race — to despise an entire nation — to vilify an entire religion. Sooner or later, we must learn to judge each other on our own merits. Sooner or later, if man is ever to be worthy of his destiny, we must fill our hearts with tolerance. For then, and only then, will we be truly worthy of the concept that man was created in the image of God — a God who calls us ALL — His children.

Pax et Justitia,
Stan.

THE AVENGERS
APPROVED BY THE COMICS CODE AUTHORITY
MARVEL COMICS GROUP
12¢ IND.
43 AUG
THE RED GUARDIAN!
HERE HE IS..!
DESTINED TO BE THE MOST TALKED ABOUT SUPER-VILLAIN OF THE YEAR!
(AND WAIT'LL YOU LEARN HIS STARTLING SECRET IDENTITY!)

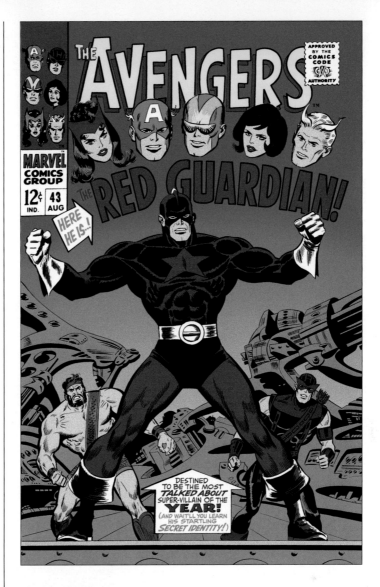

were portrayed with dignity and power. Black Panther was the first black Super Hero in comic book history, and in the 1970s was followed by Falcon, Captain America's new partner, and Luke Cage, the wrongly accused "Hero for Hire" out of Harlem. But even in the 1960s, the House of Ideas had taken on the issue of racism with courage and foresight, introducing irresistible supporting characters like Joe "Robbie" Robertson, city editor at the Daily Bugle and perhaps Peter Parker's closest friend.

Marvel's antiwar stance was even more clear-cut and resolute. The threat of Nazism was long gone, but by the 1960s new dangers had appeared, and antiwar themes began to appear in the books regularly. From the advent of the Hulk onward, antiwar themes became the watchword. People everywhere began to take note of the nonconformist, liberal tide. Even intellectuals now admitted they were Marvel fans. Author and journalist Tom Wolfe, one of the founders of New Journalism, was among the admirers of the Marvel style and its all-too-human, tridimensional characters, just like the ones that inhabit great novels.

The Italian filmmaker Federico Fellini loved the far-sightedness of the stories concocted by Lee, Kirby, and Ditko—he must have felt a certain kinship there, and one day even showed up unannounced at the Marvel offices for a surprise visit. The story Lee told about that fabled encounter, with Fellini and two other gentlemen in black suits and hats walking through the door in single file, was absolutely charming. Alain Resnais, a director from France, was another big fan and even became friends with Lee.

I BELONG
THE MERRY MARVEL MARCHING SOCIETY
THE MMMS WANTS YOU!
BE BRAVE! BUY BRAND ECHH!
THOU SHALT FIGHT DANDRUFF!
MAKE MINE MARVEL
SUPPORT BROTHERHOOD WEEK!
HELP RESIST RUST!
BE A BIG BROTHER TO AN AMPHIBIAN!
BANISH TIGHT MASKS!
DOWN WITH COOL!
STAMP OUT YANCY STREET!
CONGRATULATIONS!
THIS ENVELOPE CONTAINS A GENUINE MARVEL COMICS NO-PRIZE WHICH YOU HAVE JUST WON!
HANDLE WITH CARE

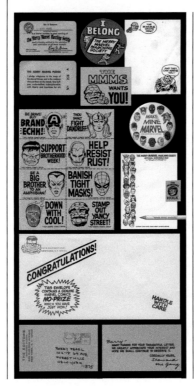

Lee was extremely active when it came to international P.R., and instilled a warm relationship with Marvel readers across the globe, creating an inchoate virtual community. He hit the mark when he started answering fans' letters, because young Americans couldn't wait to get serious feedback from an editor like Lee, whose tone was always upbeat and playful, and he was always glad to provide info on Marvel's writers, artists, and publishing strategy. Lee even started the Merry Marvel Marching Society, a fan club which counted thousands of members and contributed to the creation of a generation of responsible readers and collectors who would be tomorrow's critical minds.

A Marvel comic book wasn't simply read—it was analyzed, commented on, and critiqued from literary and artistic perspectives. A new way of creating and appreciating comic books had been born—an exquisite blend of high and popular culture. The 1960s were drawing to a close, and Marvel had become a cultural phenomenon that was poised to conquer the world. ■

OPPOSITE PAGE: Doctor Strange meets author Tom Wolfe in *Doctor Strange* #180 (May 1969). Script by Roy Thomas. Art by Gene Colan (pencils), Tom Palmer (inks), Sam Rosen (letters).

TOP LEFT: Regularly featured in each issue of Marvel Comics of the 1960s and 1970s, "Stan's Soapbox" presented Lee's thoughts to the readers.

ABOVE: Marvel introduces a Soviet Super Hero in the form of the Red Guardian, *The Avengers* #43 (August 1967). Art by John Buscema (pencils), George Bell (inks).

LEFT: The Merry Marvel Marching Society fan club kit, circa 1967.

THE 1970s

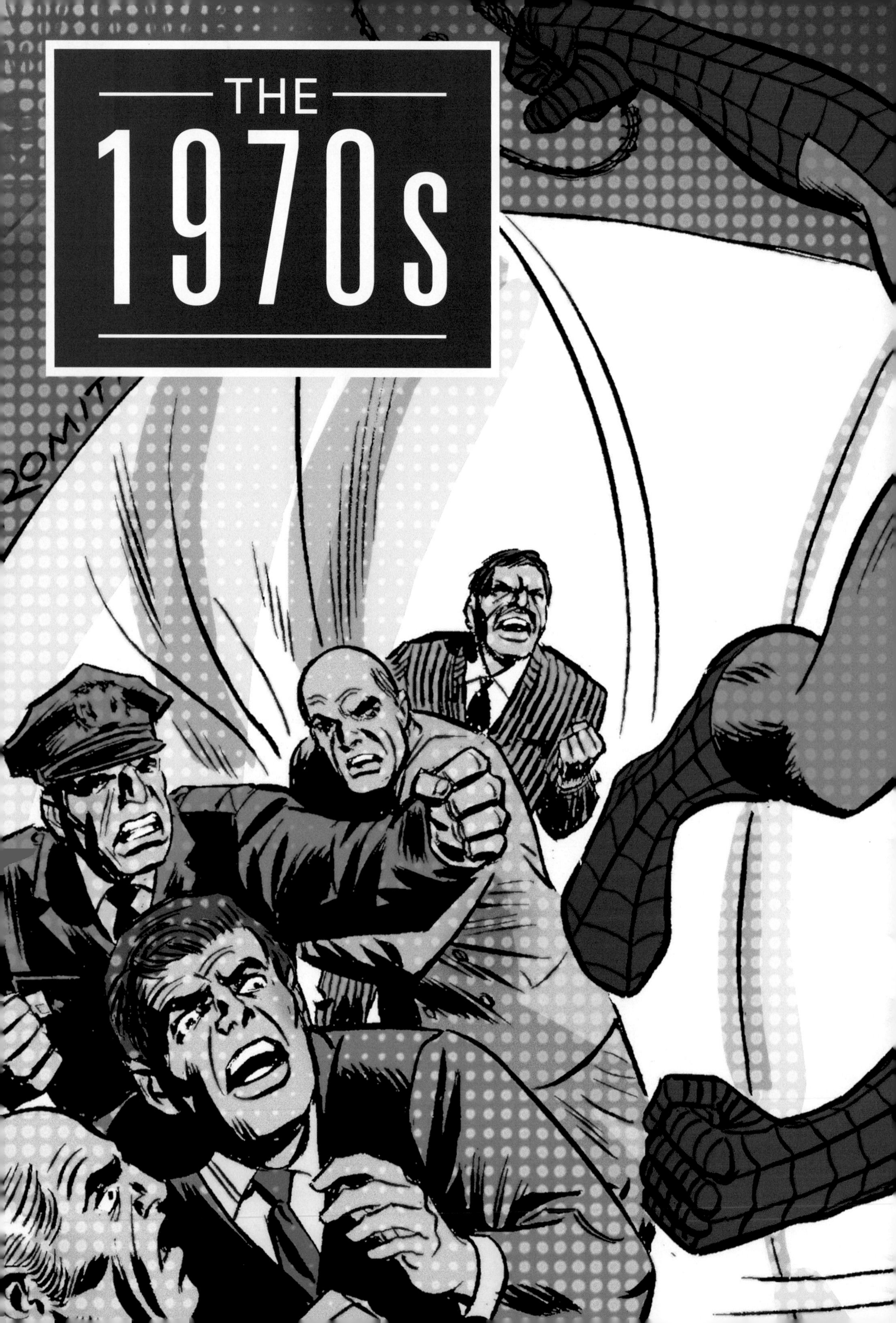

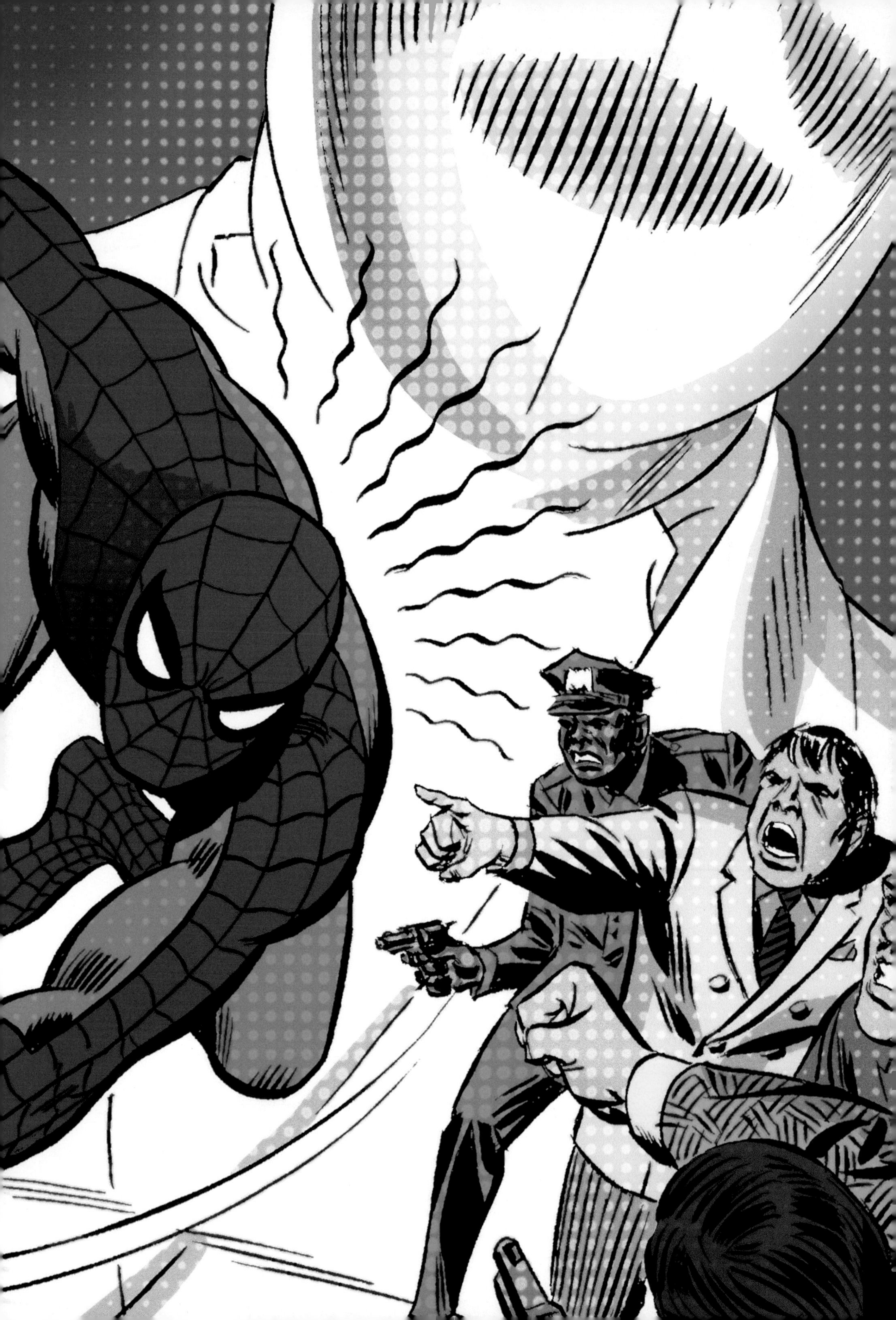

AN ERA OF IMAGINATION AND INNOVATION

"The Night Gwen Stacy Died" was the night innocence came to an end, too. It marked the passage to adulthood. Nothing would ever be the same after that Spider-Man story. Marvel had made its way into the new decade.

If the 1960s had been characterized by Marvel's pursuit of the Distinguished Competition—thanks to a cast of more human, three-dimensional characters, stories based on lots of melodrama and realism, artwork that was visionary and spectacular, writers that revolutionized the genre, a solid, two-way relationship with the cultural backdrop of the times, and the creation of a virtual community—the following decade witnessed a development that no one would have thought possible: Marvel outdid its rival not only in terms of quality, but in terms of sales as well. That supremacy, apart from brief, disconnected intervals along the way, has continued to this day.

It didn't matter that Jack Kirby had quit, or that Lee, as we shall see, would do less comic writing as the years went by. The new writers and artists had grown up reading the classic Marvel stories, and embarked upon careers in comic books not out of necessity, but because it was a future they'd always dreamed of. They had learned their lessons from the masters to perfection. The big standout among the latest generation of creators was Roy Thomas, whose publishing acumen proved matchless. A tireless reader possessed of great curiosity, he was the one who suggested introducing an old pulp hero into the comic book format—a hero who lived in some other undefinable dimension in space and time. One armed with only his brawn, his sword and his courage. A guy surrounded by women to seduce and enemies to kill.

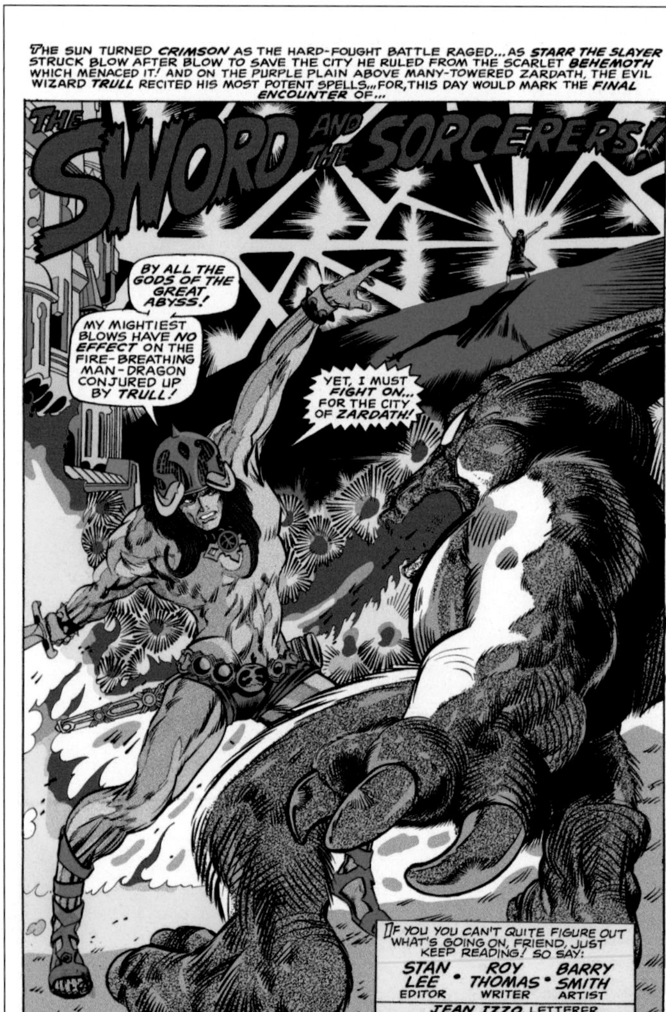
THE SUN TURNED CRIMSON AS THE HARD-FOUGHT BATTLE RAGED... AS STARR THE SLAYER STRUCK BLOW AFTER BLOW TO SAVE THE CITY HE RULED FROM THE SCARLET BEHEMOTH WHICH MENACED IT! AND ON THE PURPLE PLAIN ABOVE MANY-TOWERED ZARDATH, THE EVIL WIZARD TRULL RECITED HIS MOST POTENT SPELLS... FOR, THIS DAY WOULD MARK THE FINAL ENCOUNTER OF...
THE SWORD AND THE SORCERERS!
BY ALL THE GODS OF THE GREAT ABYSS!
MY MIGHTIEST BLOWS HAVE NO EFFECT ON THE FIRE-BREATHING MAN-DRAGON CONJURED UP BY TRULL!
YET, I MUST FIGHT ON... FOR THE CITY OF ZARDATH!
IF YOU YOU CAN'T QUITE FIGURE OUT WHAT'S GOING ON, FRIEND, JUST KEEP READING! SO SAY:
STAN LEE EDITOR • ROY THOMAS WRITER • BARRY SMITH ARTIST
JEAN IZZO, LETTERER

THIS PAGE: Roy Thomas and Barry Smith featured their proto-Conan character, Starr the Slayer, in *Chamber of Darkness* #4 (April 1970). Script by Roy Thomas. Art by Barry Smith (pencils, inks), Jean Izzo (letters).

OPPOSITE PAGE: *Conan the Barbarian* #1 (October 1970). Art by Barry Smith (pencils).

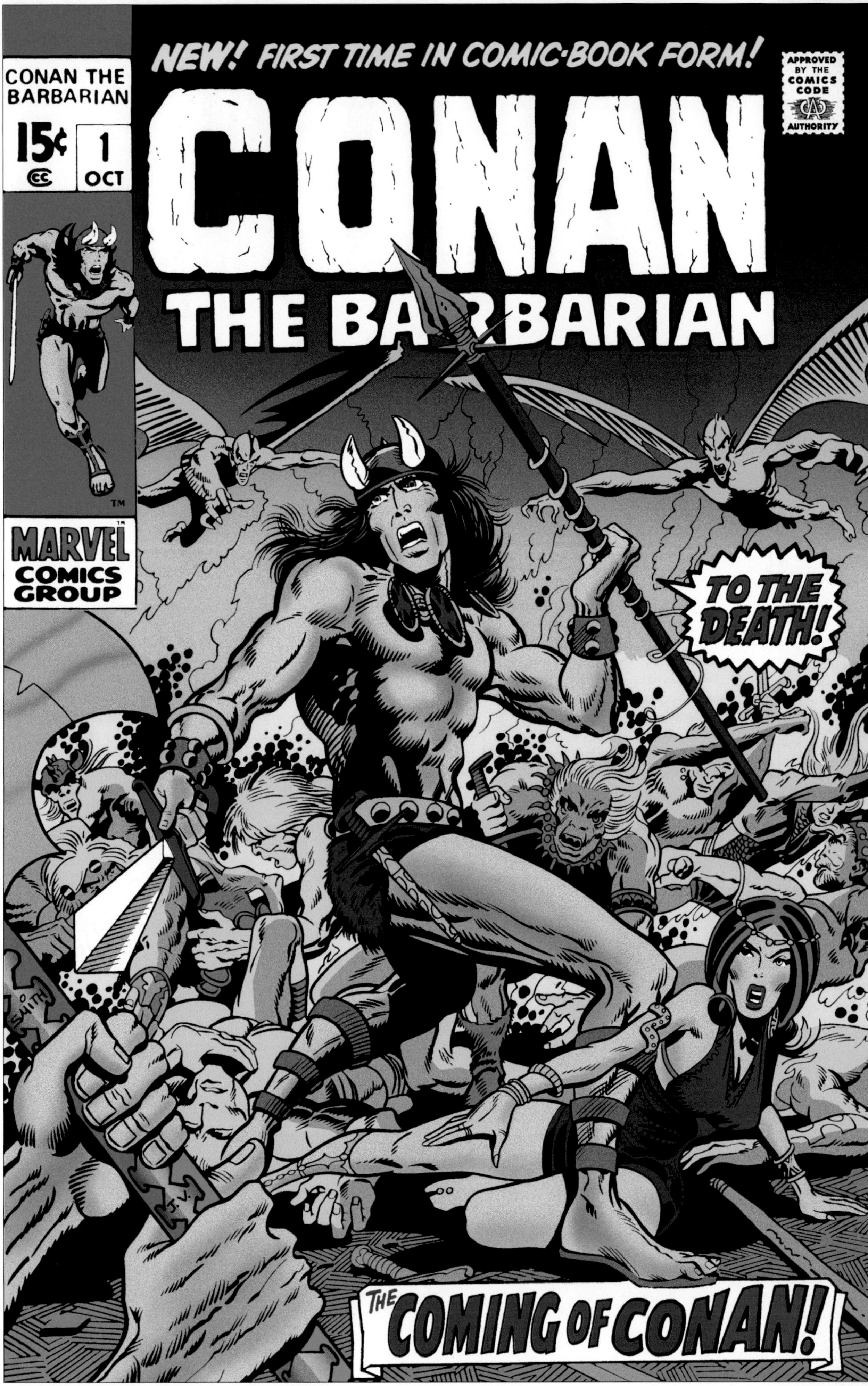
NEW! FIRST TIME IN COMIC·BOOK FORM!
CONAN THE BARBARIAN
15¢
1
OCT
APPROVED BY THE COMICS CODE AUTHORITY
CONAN
THE BARBARIAN
MARVEL COMICS GROUP
TO THE DEATH!
THE COMING OF CONAN!

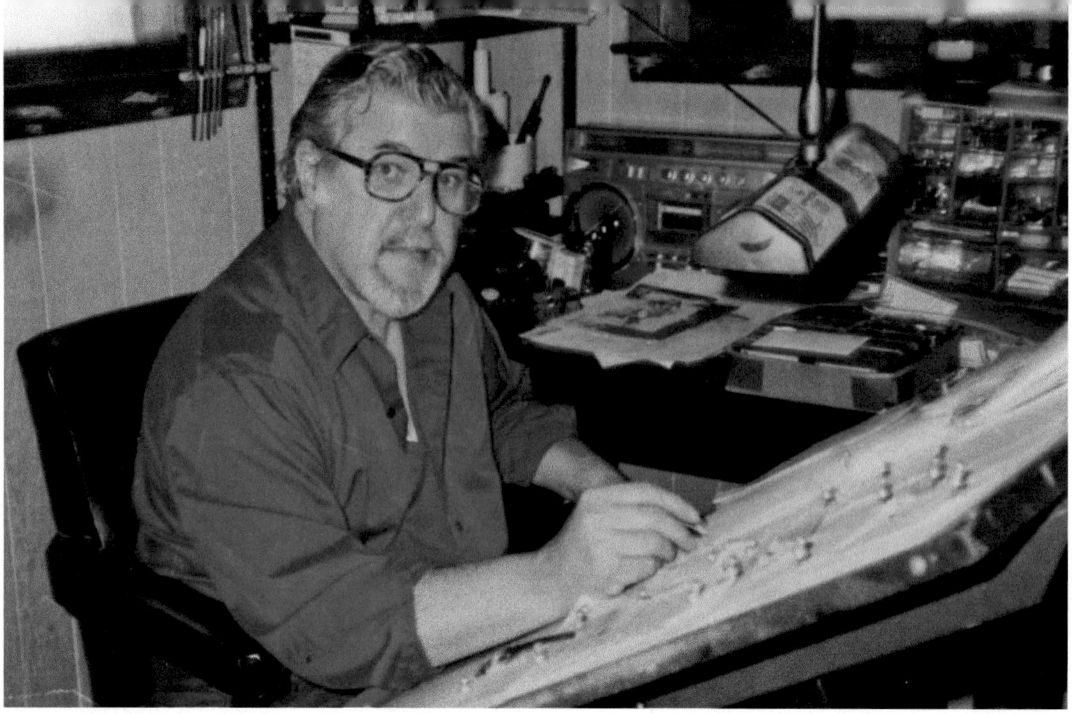

ABOVE:
Artist John Buscema at work in his home studio.

BELOW:
The three issues of *The Amazing Spider-Man* published without the approval of the Comics Code Authority.

Lee took a liking to the idea, and was especially pleased with the character's name—Thongor—which sounded just right for a comic book. But negotiations with the author, Lin Carter, got nowhere. From there, Thomas contacted Robert E. Howard's agents. Howard had been a pulp fiction writer in the 1930s, best known as the creator of Conan the Barbarian, until he committed suicide in 1936. His novels were a goldmine of ideas and adventures that Thomas would adapt with the help of Barry Smith, a young British artist who, to complicate matters, had trouble obtaining a work visa for the United States and was often forced to return to the U.K., where he lived in a London suburb. Interestingly enough, his smooth and elegant touch was just right when it came to creating the harsh, wild settings of Conan's fictional homeland, Cimmeria. This marked the start of Smith's extraordinary career.

Conan turned out to be a success right off the bat, with fans and critics alike. But once the first series had run its course—22 stories in all—Smith was out and John Buscema was in. Buscema focused on bringing out Conan's physical prowess and an attitude that was violent and noble at the same time, even in black-and-white comic books where the tone was more adult-oriented. Conan would become an icon that transcended comics, and by the 1980s he had hit the silver screen, played by none other than Arnold Schwarzenegger.

While Conan was a revolution in publishing terms, an ideological development, masterminded by Lee himself, was about to send shock-waves through the American comic

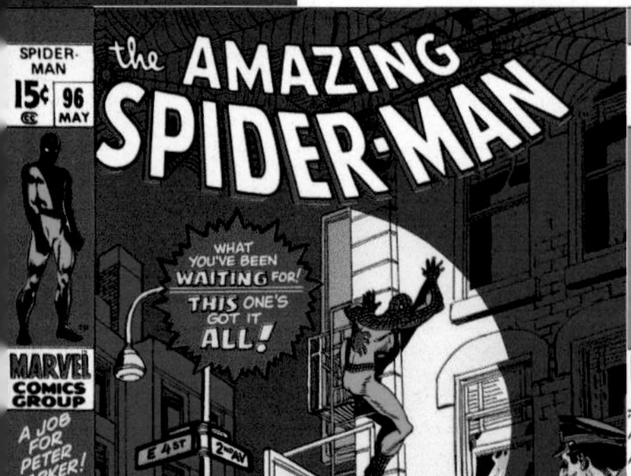
SPIDER-MAN 15¢ 96 MAY
the AMAZING SPIDER-MAN
WHAT YOU'VE BEEN WAITING FOR! THIS ONE'S GOT IT ALL!
MARVEL COMICS GROUP
A JOB FOR PETER PARKER!
THE LAST FATAL TRIP!
MARY JANE KNOCKS 'EM DEAD!
AND
THE GREEN GOBLIN RETURNS!
VILLAGE THEATER
SPIDER-MAN'S GETTING AWAY!

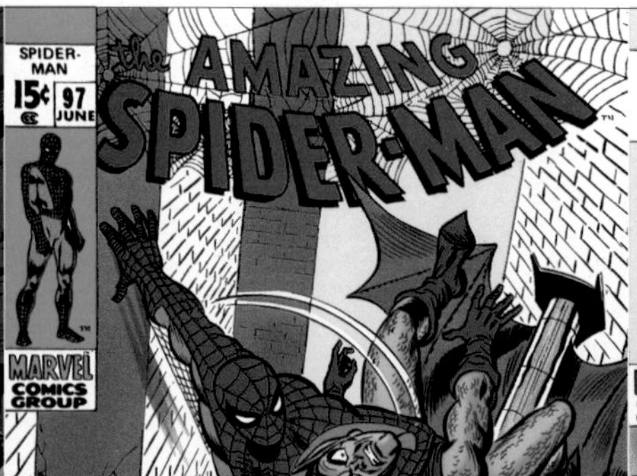
SPIDER-MAN 15¢ 97 JUNE
the AMAZING SPIDER-MAN
MARVEL COMICS GROUP
SPIDEY FIGHTS THE GOBLIN-- AND LOTS, LOTS MORE! 'NUFF SAID!

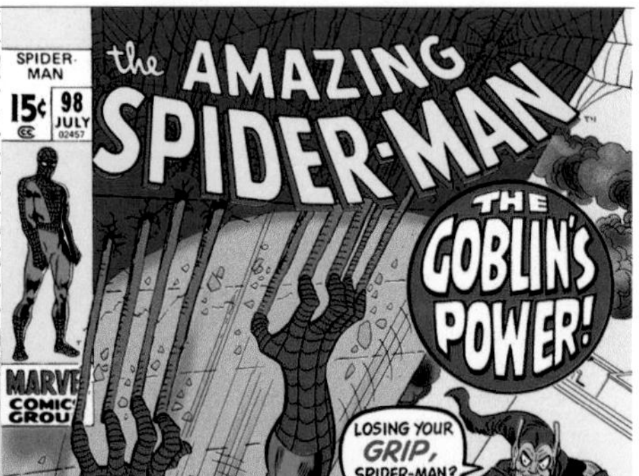
SPIDER-MAN 15¢ 98 JULY
the AMAZING SPIDER-MAN
THE GOBLIN'S POWER!
LOSING YOUR GRIP, SPIDER-MAN?
IT HAD TO HAPPEN-- I PLANNED IT THIS WAY!

...SULLEN EYELIDS OPEN NARROWLY...
...AND A LEATHERED HAND DARTS OUT...
...THOUGH, SO DOES A HARD-SOLED BOOT!
RRFF

TOP: Panels from *Conan the Barbarian* #44 (November 1974). Script by Roy Thomas. Art by John Buscema (pencils), Crusty Bunkers, Neal Adams, Dick Giordano, Larry Hama, Ralph Reese (inks), Glynis Wein (colors), John Costanza (letters).

book industry. For the time being, the Comics Code Authority still imposed strict limits on content. With Marvel's success and its influence over the country's youth in mind, in 1971 the U.S. Department of Health, Education and Welfare asked Marvel to come up with a story that put the spotlight on the evils of drug abuse, which at that time was growing rampant. Lee seized the opportunity to script what would become a classic three-part story that appeared in *The Amazing Spider-Man* (issues #96–98). Snared by the web of addiction would be Peter Parker's best friend, Harry Osborn, the son of Norman Osborn, A.K.A. the Super Villain Green Goblin. The Comics Code Authority rejected the story because it did not meet their strict guidelines, despite its important message. Lee, however, refused to give

LEFT: Writer-turned-Editor-in-Chief Roy Thomas in 1973.

up, and sent the trilogy to print without the Authority's seal of approval on the front cover. It turned out to be a smash hit and led to the revision of the Code.

It was no fluke, then, that by the 1970s Marvel had become America's leading publisher of comic books. Nor was it a coincidence that the business community had begun courting Marvel, a company that had practically started from nothing and was now a major focus of the mass media. In 1968 a large conglomerate, the Perfect Film & Chemical Corporation (which would soon become Cadence Industries), bought Marvel from Martin Goodman for about $15 million. Goodman, however, remained Marvel's de facto publisher until 1972, when he finally left. The move from being a family business to one run by a multinational corporation was not exactly painless

OH, BY THE WAY-- THE OUT-OF-TOWNERS DRESSED AS SPIDER-MAN AND MRS. FANTASTIC ARE ROY AND JEANIE THOMAS!
THEY CAME ALL THE WAY FROM FROM THE BIG BAD CITY FOR RUTLAND'S ELEVENTH HALLOWEEN PARADE!
THE AVENGERS! OH WOW!
WHICH ONE OF YOU IS MRS. PEEL?
COOL IT, KID!
I'M ONLY SORRY, TOM, THAT WE'RE NOT HERE FOR PURELY SOCIAL REASONS!
STILL, I HOPE THE RUMORS WE HEARD CONCERNING A KIDNAP PLOT WERE UNFOUNDED!
I'LL DRINK TO THAT! NOW WE'D BETTER GET CRACKING--!

BELOW: Roy Thomas (first panel, left) and wife Jean made a cameo appearance in the pages of *The Avengers* #83 (December 1970). Script by Roy Thomas. Art by John Buscema (pencils), Tom Palmer (inks), Herb Cooper (letters).

RIGHT:
Daredevil #161 (November 1979). Art by Frank Miller and Klaus Janson.

INCREDIBLE HULK
MARVEL COMICS GROUP
25¢ 181 NOV
THE INCREDIBLE HULK
AND NOW... the WOLVERINE!
HE'S HERE! THE WORLD'S FIRST AND GREATEST CANADIAN SUPER HERO!
AND THE SURVIVOR OF THEIR EPIC BATTLE MUST FACE— the WENDIGO!

BELOW:
The full-blown first appearance of Wolverine in *The Incredible Hulk* #181 (November 1974). Art by Herb Trimpe (pencils), John Romita, Sr. (inks).

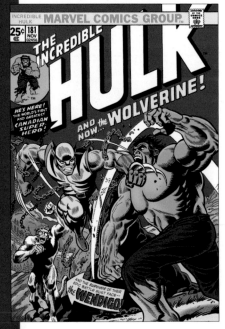

and it didn't happen overnight. The company's structure underwent a thorough reorganization. Lee was promoted to publisher and sent to work developing multimedia projects for television and the movies. However, the dream of Hollywood incarnations of Marvel characters would come true only with the spread of 21st-century digital culture.

Roy Thomas, Lee's right-hand man and heir to the throne, became Marvel's Editor in Chief—but Thomas was more interested in writing, and left that role in 1974. This turn of events marked the start of one of the most chaotic, albeit also one of the most creative, periods in Marvel history. With an increased number of monthly releases, centralized control became more and more difficult. This meant that writers of each individual series would, in practical terms, often be their own editors. The unbridled creativity of Marvel's writers, who had never experienced so much freedom, was able to generate a slew of high-power series and characters.

Meanwhile, the successors to Lee and Thomas came and went at a stunning rate, and some lasted for no more than a few days. People like Marv Wolfman, Len Wein, Gerry Conway, and Archie Goodwin were Editors in Chief. It would not be until Jim Shooter came along in 1978, who was in for a nearly 10-year run as Editor in Chief, that things stabilized. Under his reign, series and characters would be revised and revamped, leading to classic runs such as Frank Miller's *Daredevil* and Walter Simonson's *Thor*. Marvel remained in step with the times, and American sociopolitical realities would continue to influence its creators, as seen in comic book stories that showed increasing commitment to and relevance regarding the issues at hand.

MARVEL'S MIGHTY MUTANT REVOLUTION

A series that went from running reprints catapults to the top of the charts with the introduction of some offbeat, amazing mutants.

In terms of comic book thrills and spills, arguably the high point of the '70s came with the 1973 release of the story "The Night Gwen Stacy Died" in *The Amazing Spider-Man* (#121). In it, Spider-Man tries to rescue Peter Parker's girlfriend Gwen Stacy after she has been abducted by the Green Goblin—who, of course, knows the identity of his adversary's alter ego. In the ensuing battle, the Green Goblin hurls Gwen from the Brooklyn Bridge. But Spider-Man is the one who actually causes Gwen's death, when her neck is broken in the webbing that catches her as she falls. A moving story indeed, with dialogue and characters that flaunted all-new heights in realism, which literally jettisoned readers—many of whom must have considered the blonde bombshell their girlfriend—into mourning. Some even mailed death threats to writer Gerry Conway for having sent Gwen to an early grave. In truth, having her die was a group decision approved by Lee—the idea was to kill off an important supporting character in order to shake things up. At first, it looked like Aunt May would be the victim. But then Romita suggested Gwen…

From an artistic perspective, there may have been one story that could compete with the greatness of that chapter in the annals of Spider-Man. It involved the revival of the X-Men, whose series had stopped publishing new stories, before starting up again with *Giant-Size X-Men* #1. Marvel's new ownership wanted a new supergroup made up of characters from different countries in order to broaden its sales base. In 1975, writer Len Wein and artist Dave Cockrum revived two of the original X-Men, Cyclops and Marvel Girl, along with Professor X, and teamed them up with a crew of young mutants in the Marvel milestone *Giant-Size X-Men* #1. That marked the start of an epic series

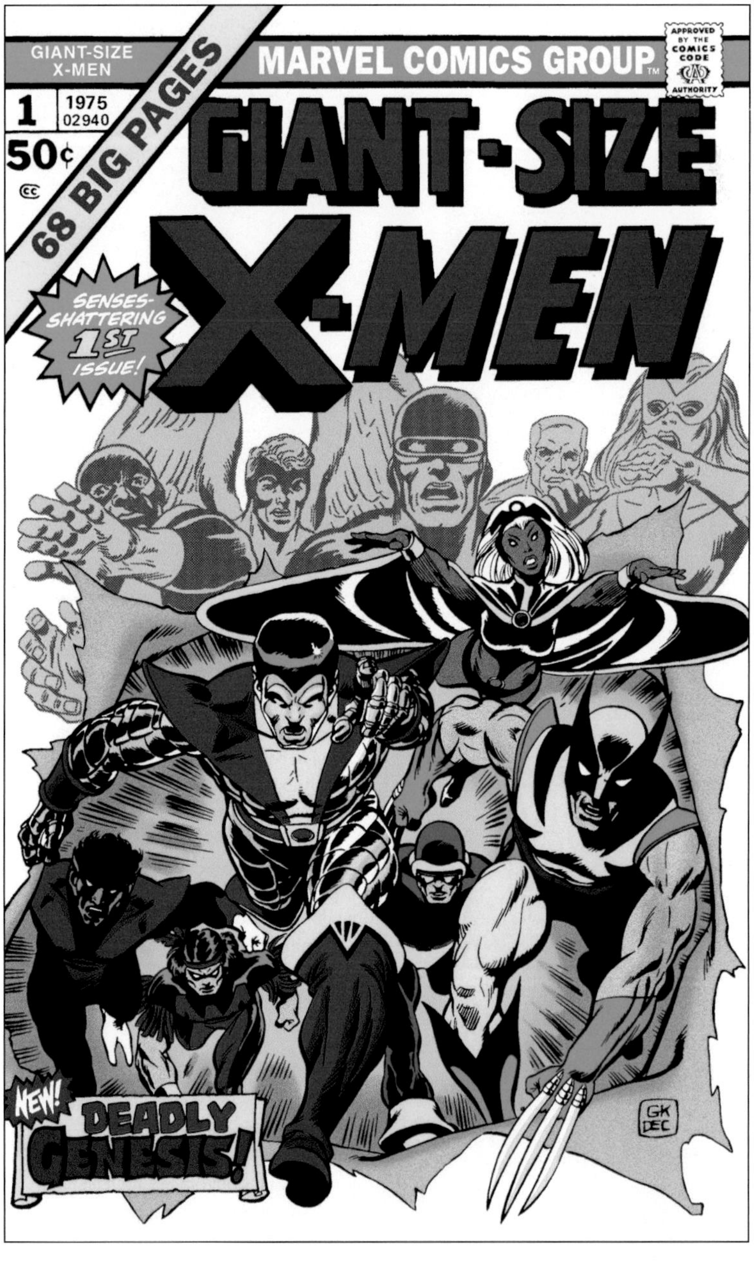
GIANT-SIZE X-MEN
68 BIG PAGES
MARVEL COMICS GROUP
APPROVED BY THE COMICS CODE AUTHORITY
1
1975
02940
50¢
GIANT-SIZE
X-MEN
SENSES-SHATTERING 1ST ISSUE!
NEW!
DEADLY GENESIS!
GK DEC

LEFT: Giant-Size X-Men #1 (May 1975). Art by Gil Kane (pencils) and Dave Cockrum (inks).

TOP:
The last page of *The Amazing Spider-Man* #121 (June 1973), featuring the death of Gwen Stacy. Script by Gerry Conway. Art by Gil Kane (pencils), John Romita, Sr. and Tony Mortellaro (inks), Dave Hunt (colors), Artie Simek (letters).

OPPOSITE PAGE:
The pencils and inks for page 32 of *The Incredible Hulk* #180 (October 1974), marking the first appearance of Wolverine. Script by Len Wein. Art by Herb Trimpe (pencils), Jack Abel (inks), ChristieScheele (colors), Artie Simek (letters).

YOU'RE THE CREEP WHO'S GOING TO PAY!
I'M GOING TO GET YOU, GOBLIN! I'M GOING TO DESTROY YOU SLOWLY-- AND WHEN YOU START BEGGING FOR ME TO END IT--
--I'M GOING TO REMIND YOU OF ONE THING--
--YOU KILLED THE WOMAN I LOVE--
AND FOR THAT, YOU'RE GOING TO DIE!
AT LAST, WE CAN TELL YOU THE TITLE TO OUR TALE, THOUGH IT'S ONE TITLE WE'D HOPED WE'D NEVER SEE. WE CALL IT--
THE NIGHT GWEN STACY DIED
--AND YOU CAN BE SURE THE STORY DOESN'T END HERE!
TO BE CONTINUED!

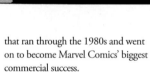

STAR WARS

One of Marvel's biggest hits in the 1970s was the comic book version of *Star Wars*. Oddly enough, it was Lucasfilm that approached Marvel about making a deal, but at first Stan Lee turned them down. Roy Thomas, however, convinced him to change his mind. The first *Star Wars* comic book, written by Thomas and featuring artwork by Howard Chaykin, hit newsstands in March 1977, before the release of the movie, and sold millions of copies.

STAR WARS
MARVEL COMICS GROUP
30¢
4
OCT
02817
THE GREATEST SPACE-FANTASY FILM OF ALL!
STAR WARS
AT LAST! THE BATTLE WITH DARTH VADER! TO THE DEATH!!
NO, LUKE!
HERE I STAND-- THOUGH I MAY DIE!

that ran through the 1980s and went on to become Marvel Comics' biggest commercial success.

Such an accomplishment was mostly thanks to writer Chris Claremont, who replaced Wein, whose duties as Editor in Chief took up most of his time. British-born Claremont might be described as an author with a penchant for soap opera–style comic book stories. He would later be joined by artist/writer John Byrne to create some of the greatest moments in X-Men history.

The new team of mutants also happened to include Wolverine, the Canadian Super Hero with retractable claws who would soon have the honor of being the most famous among the second generation of Marvel characters. Wolverine had made his debut in 1974, in *The Incredible Hulk* #180–181. Based on an initial suggestion by Roy Thomas, Wolverine was designed by John Romita, Sr., and brought fully to life by writer Len Wein and artist Herb Trimpe.

Readers were immediately mesmerized by this muscle-bound maniac in yellow and black, but no one ever imagined he'd become a superstar the world over. One of the reasons must have been the decades-long secrecy regarding his origins—he had been kidnapped and forced to undergo experiments involving Adamantium implants that reinforced his bones and claws, and gave him regenerative powers, otherwise known as the healing factor, which for all practical purposes made him immortal.

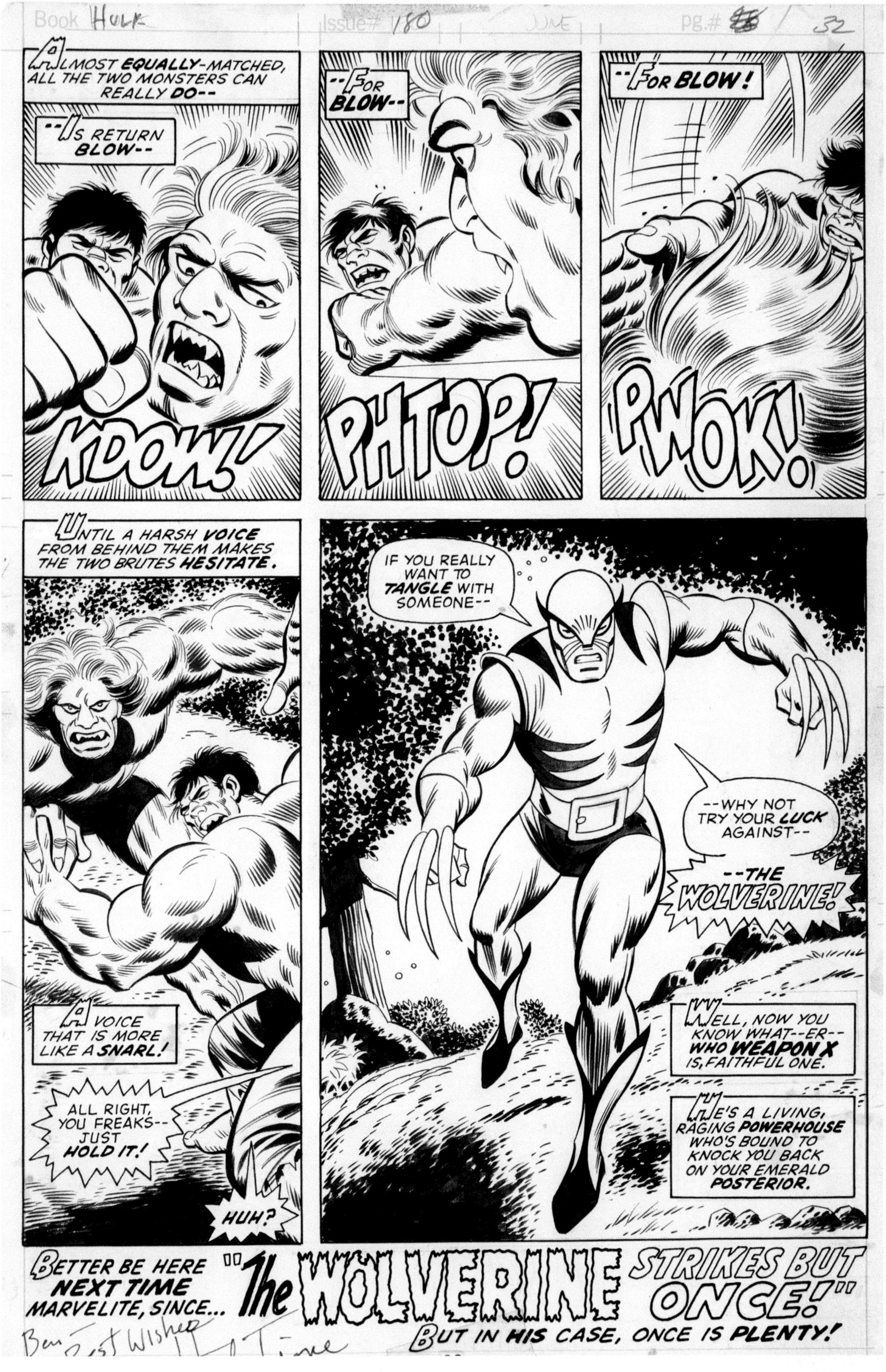
Book HULK Issue# 180 JUNE pg.# 32
ALMOST EQUALLY-MATCHED, ALL THE TWO MONSTERS CAN REALLY DO--
--IS RETURN BLOW--
KDOW!
--FOR BLOW--
PHTOP!
--FOR BLOW!
PWOK!
UNTIL A HARSH VOICE FROM BEHIND THEM MAKES THE TWO BRUTES HESITATE.
A VOICE THAT IS MORE LIKE A SNARL!
ALL RIGHT, YOU FREAKS-- JUST HOLD IT!
HUH?
IF YOU REALLY WANT TO TANGLE WITH SOMEONE--
--WHY NOT TRY YOUR LUCK AGAINST--
--THE WOLVERINE!
WELL, NOW YOU KNOW WHAT--ER-- WHO WEAPON X IS, FAITHFUL ONE.
HE'S A LIVING, RAGING POWERHOUSE WHO'S BOUND TO KNOCK YOU BACK ON YOUR EMERALD POSTERIOR.
BETTER BE HERE NEXT TIME MARVELITE, SINCE... "The WOLVERINE STRIKES BUT ONCE!"
BUT IN HIS CASE, ONCE IS PLENTY!

COSMIC ADVENTURES AND HORRIBLE HORRORS

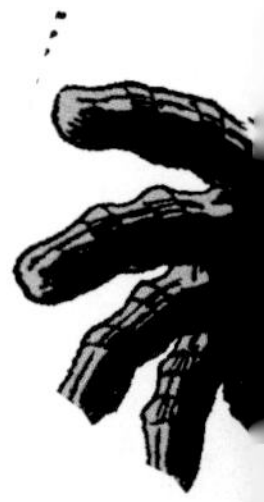

The Comics Code relaxes its restrictions, as Marvel returns to the horror fold. Meanwhile, new talent takes the Super Heroes into the depths of space—and beyond.

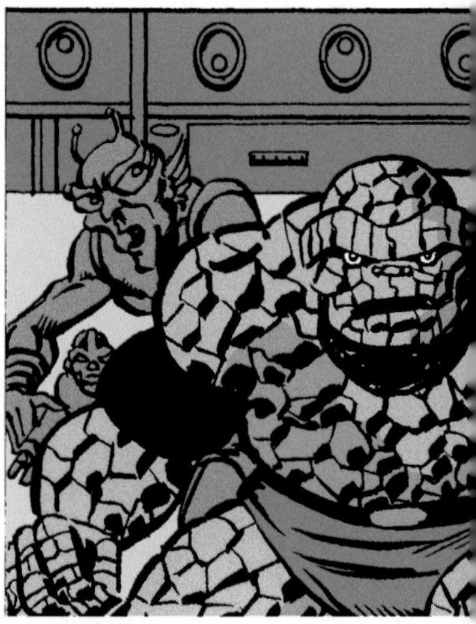

Lee's "rebellion" against the Comics Code Authority helped usher in a new era for comic book genres like horror and suspense. As of 1971, publishing stories featuring zombies, werewolves, vampires, and bloodbaths no longer breached CCA regulations. Marvel took advantage of this development to launch a new line of comic books in color and in black-and-white, which to this day retain their cult following. The best-known and best-selling was probably *The Tomb of Dracula* series. Writer Marv Wolfman, penciler Gene Colan, and inker Tom Palmer worked together to come up with their own original, up-to-date version of Bram Stoker's creation, whose facial features were based on the actor Jack Palance's physiognomy. The series racked up some 70 issues and introduced successful new characters like Blade, who starred in his own three-film franchise, launched in the 1990s.

Dracula wasn't the only new Marvel Super Hero that struck fear in the hearts of fans and foes alike. Other scary creations included Werewolf by Night, afflicted by the curse of lycanthropy, which in his family went back many a generation; Ghost Rider, a biker who

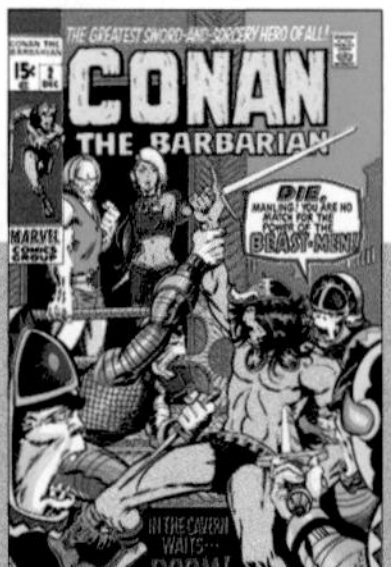
CONAN
THE BARBARIAN
IN THE CAVERN WAITS— DOOM!

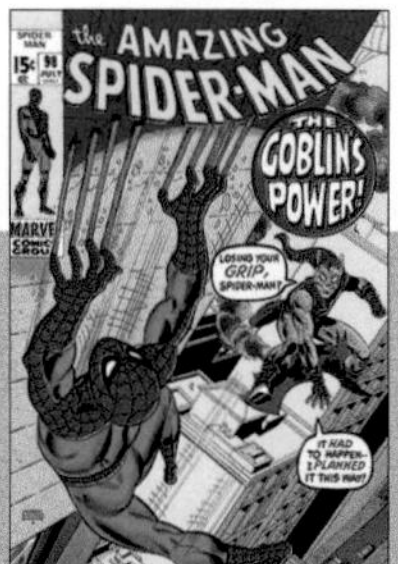
the AMAZING SPIDER-MAN
THE GOBLIN'S POWER!

1970

FALL 1970

The decade opens with the successful *Conan the Barbarian*, Marvel's adaptation of Robert E. Howard's pulp hero, by writer Roy Thomas and artist Barry Smith.

MAY–JULY 1971

The U.S. Department of Health, Education, and Welfare asks Stan Lee to publish a story about drug abuse—which appears in *The Amazing Spider-Man* without the approval of the Comics Code.

sold his soul in a futile attempt to save his girlfriend's father; Brother Voodoo; Frankenstein's Monster, another spectacular literary classic redux; Morbius, the Living Vampire, A.K.A. Dr. Michael Morbius, who made his debut in *The Amazing Spider-Man #101* as an incurable blood-drinker afflicted by leukemia; Man-Wolf, A.K.A. the astronaut John Jameson, son of the ornery publisher of the *Daily Bugle*, who was transformed by the Godstone he found on the moon; and the Son of Satan, A.K.A. Daimon Hellstrom, who waged war against the forces of evil for humanity's sake. Just to name a few.

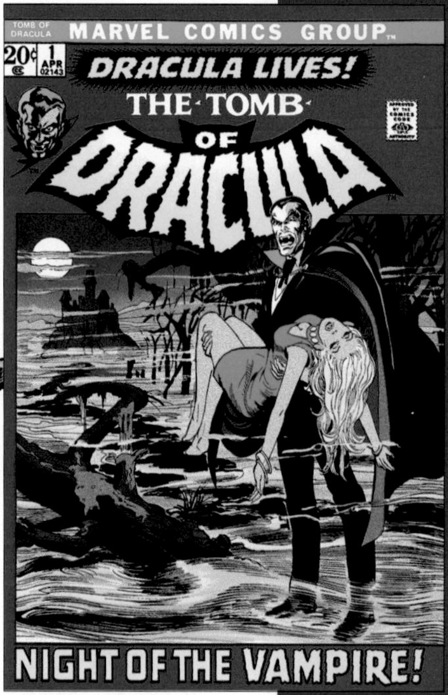
MARVEL COMICS GROUP
DRACULA LIVES!
THE TOMB OF DRACULA
NIGHT OF THE VAMPIRE!

ABOVE: *The Tomb of Dracula #1 (April 1972).* Art by Neal Adams.

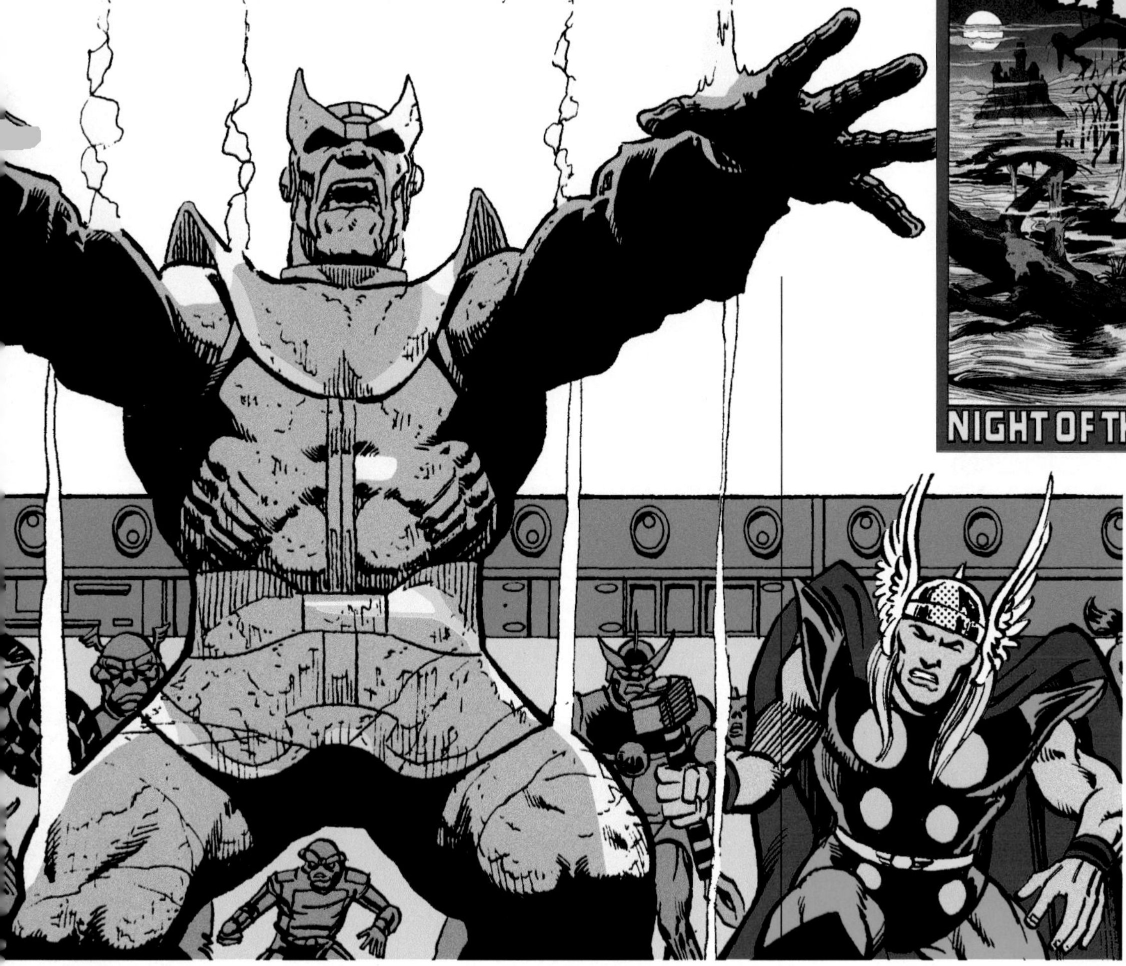

LEFT: Thanos is turned to stone in the pages of *Marvel Two-In-One Annual #2* (December 1977). Art by Jim Starlin (pencils), Joe Rubinstein (inks), Petra Goldberg (colors).

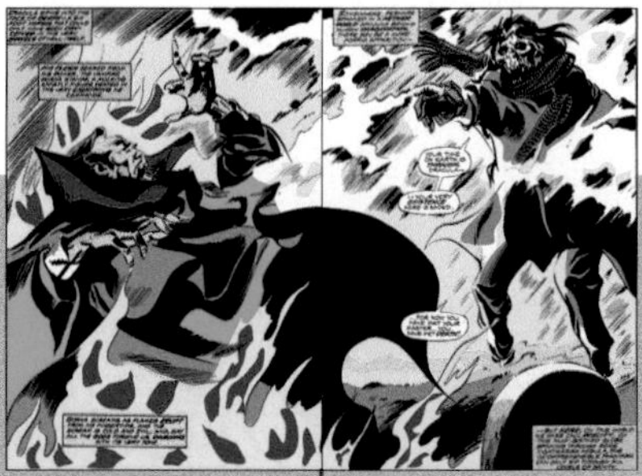

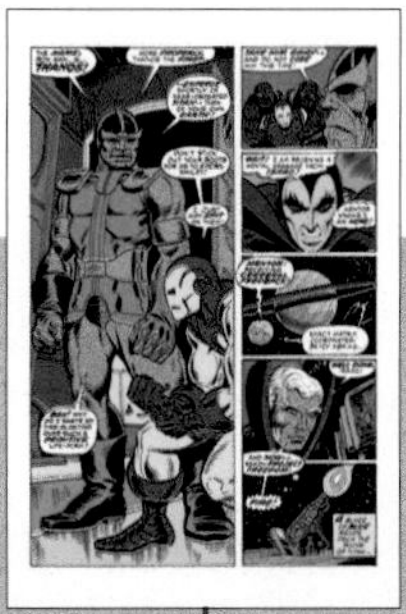

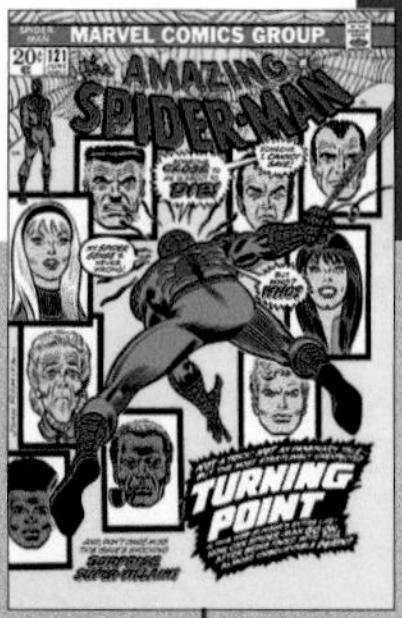
MARVEL COMICS GROUP
THE AMAZING SPIDER-MAN
TURNING POINT

1972–1973

The latest trends are horror and the martial arts. Marvel responds with *The Tomb of Dracula* in April 1972, and *Shang-Chi, Master of Kung Fu*, in December 1973.

FEBRUARY 1973

Thanos, created by Jim Starlin, makes his first appearance in the pages of *The Invincible Iron Man #55* (February 1973).

JUNE 1973

Marvel rocks fandom in the pages of *The Amazing Spider-Man #121* with the death of Gwen Stacy at the hands of the Green Goblin.

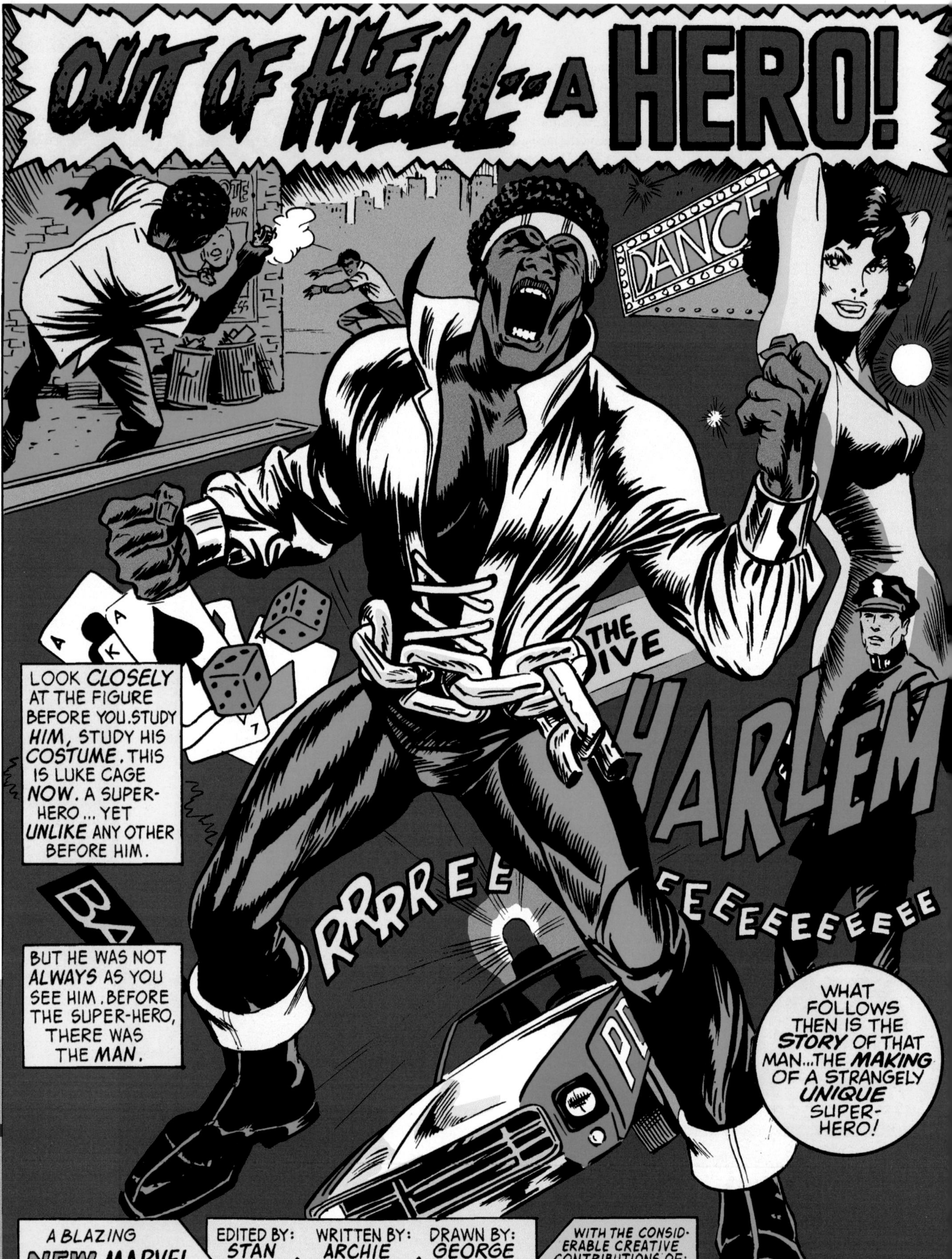
OUT OF HELL--A HERO!
DANCE
THE DIVE
HARLEM
LOOK CLOSELY AT THE FIGURE BEFORE YOU. STUDY HIM, STUDY HIS COSTUME. THIS IS LUKE CAGE NOW. A SUPER-HERO ... YET UNLIKE ANY OTHER BEFORE HIM.
RRRREEE EEEEEEEEEEE
BUT HE WAS NOT ALWAYS AS YOU SEE HIM. BEFORE THE SUPER-HERO, THERE WAS THE MAN.
WHAT FOLLOWS THEN IS THE STORY OF THAT MAN...THE MAKING OF A STRANGELY UNIQUE SUPER-HERO!
A BLAZING NEW MARVEL MILESTONE!
EDITED BY: STAN LEE · WRITTEN BY: ARCHIE GOODWIN · DRAWN BY: GEORGE TUSKA
BILLY GRAHAM INKER · SKIP KOHLOFF LETTERER
WITH THE CONSIDERABLE CREATIVE CONTRIBUTIONS OF: ROY THOMAS AND JOHN ROMITA

GHOST RIDER
MARVEL COMICS GROUP
20¢
1 SEPT 02900
THE MOST SUPERNATURAL SUPERHERO OF ALL!
GHOST RIDER
FEARSOME FIRST ISSUE! NOW IN HIS OWN MIND-BENDING MAG—BECAUSE YOU DEMANDED IT!
DO NOT CROS
POLICE
WANTED: DEAD AND ALIVE!

GIANT SIZE MASTER OF KUNG FU
MARVEL COMICS GROUP
1 SEPT 02927
50¢
68 BIG PAGES
GIANT-SIZE
MASTER OF KUNG FU
5 ALL-NEW STEEL-SMASHING SAGAS STARRING THE ONE AND ONLY SHANG-CHI!
BIGGEST MARTIAL ARTS ACTION ISSUE EVER!

The space-based Super Heroes were yet another avenue that spelled success for Marvel. It all began with Jim Starlin's revamped version of Captain Marvel, a Lee-Colan creation from the 1960s. Starlin was a young writer fascinated by the counterculture and alternative themes. His Captain Marvel—a Kree warrior who fought for the survival of mankind, donned a sleek red and yellow costume featuring an eight-pointed star on his chest, and was not immune to tragedy—was another Marvel highpoint of the 1970s.

Starlin also revised Warlock, a character originally created by Lee and Kirby, and later developed for a series by Thomas and Kane. Starlin transformed him into an enigmatic, almost lysergic hero from outer space, and a sacrificial one at that. Last but not least, Starlin introduced Thanos, the most feared of all supervillains in the Marvel Universe. His appearances at this time would lead to the limited series *Infinity Gauntlet*.

The 1970s also played host to the martial arts and Blaxploitation—two incredibly fascinating subgenres—and Marvel couldn't help but join the bandwagon. New arrivals on the scene included Shang-Chi, Master of Kung Fu (1973), rebel son of the lethal Fu Manchu. Created by Steve Englehart and Jim Starlin, Shang-Chi owes his status as Marvel mainstay largely to the long run by writer Doug Moench and artist Paul Gulacy. Also introduced were the Sons of the Tiger (1974); and the big performer Iron Fist (1974), whose martial arts skills were enhanced by the powers of K'un-L'un, the ancient mystical city of the Orient where young heir-to-a-fortune Danny Rand attains the power of the Iron Fist after the deaths of his parents.

At the same time, hero for hire Luke Cage opens an office in Times Square. A black ex-con who did time in prison after being framed, Cage got his super-powers while in the pen, courtesy of a cellular regeneration experiment gone haywire. A.K.A. Power Man, he was the latest Super Hero of color to hit the spotlight, after Black Panther and the Falcon, and the very first with his own comic book series.

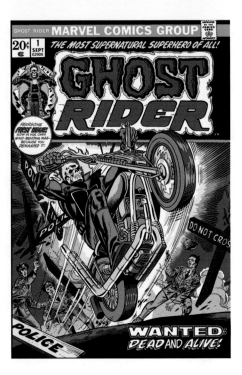

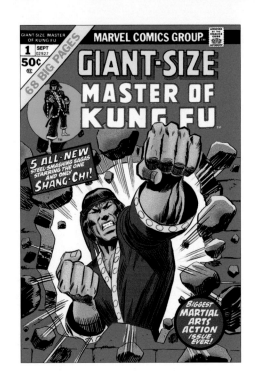

OPPOSITE PAGE: Splash page from *Luke Cage, Hero for Hire #1* (June 1972). Script by Archie Goodwin. Art by George Tuska (pencils), Billy Graham (inks), Skip Kohloff (letters).

ABOVE LEFT: *Ghost Rider #1* (September 1973). Art by Gil Kane (pencils) and Joe Sinnott (inks).

ABOVE RIGHT: *Giant-Size Master of Kung Fu #1* (September 1974). Art by Ron Wilson (pencils), Mike Esposito (inks).

MARVEL COMICS GROUP
THE INCREDIBLE HULK
AND NOW THE WOLVERINE!

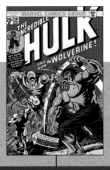

FALL 1974

Conan is followed by another seminal Marvel character of the 1970s, Wolverine, who made his first appearance in *The Incredible Hulk #180–181*.

MARVEL COMICS GROUP
THE AMAZING SPIDER-MAN
THE PUNISHER!
THE JACKAL!

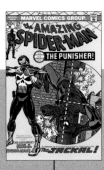

WINTER 1974

Inspired by turbulent times and such films as *Death Wish* starring Charles Bronson, the Punisher, a Vietnam vet-turned-vigilante, debuts in *The Amazing Spider-Man #129*.

MARVEL COMICS GROUP
68 BIG PAGES
GIANT-SIZE X-MEN

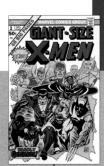

JULY 1975

Giant-Size X-Men #1 ushers in an all-new era with the debut of a team of international mutants. The series would grow in popularity throughout the 1970s.

ALL THE MAN'S MEN

As Stan Lee moves Marvel into the media spotlight, new faces come aboard to guide the comics to new heights.

As Lee became more and more involved in projects outside the realm of publishing, his attention was moved away from comics. His work with Kirby on *The Fantastic Four* series came to an end with issue #114; *The Amazing Spider-Man* wound up in the hands of Thomas and Conway. Meanwhile up-and-coming writers and artists breathed new life into a host of other well-known characters. Come to think of it, Lee's true heir may have been Conway. He'd joined Marvel as a young man and soon got the nod to write for *Spider-Man*. It seemed the perfect choice—at the tender age of 19 he could definitely relate to the issues that roiled the wall-crawler and his peers. Conway brought out the soap-opera aspect of the series starring Lee and Ditko's most famous creation, giving the world a Spider-Man in step with the times, surrounded by a slew of revamped supporting characters.

While Starlin focused on outer space scenarios, and Trimpe carried on with antimilitarist sentiment in the Hulk's realm, Sal Buscema, John's younger brother, stepped onto the scene. Sal was a true craftsman of comic book art, an artist so talented he

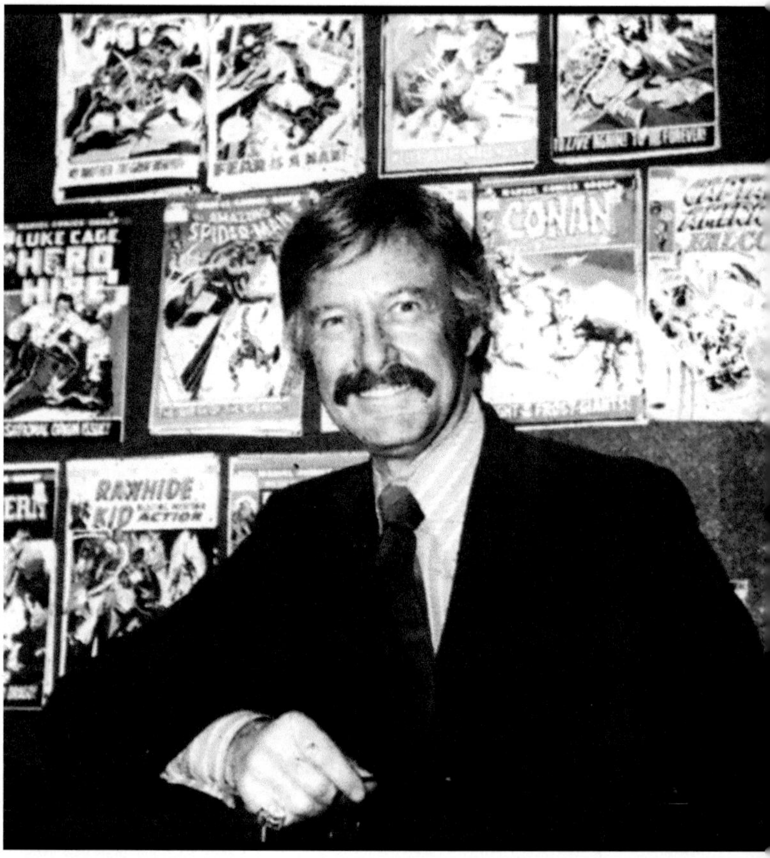

THIS PAGE: Stan Lee in the Marvel offices, with the latest comic book offerings behind him.

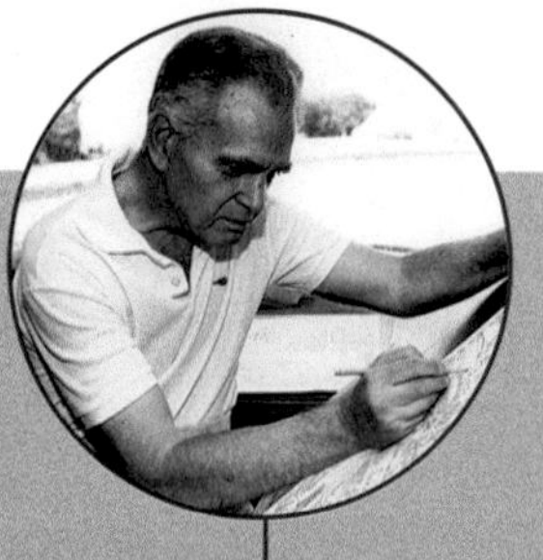

1975

Jack "the King" Kirby is back at Marvel after a five-year absence. He would create new hits like the Eternals, and tell new adventures of Captain America and Black Panther.

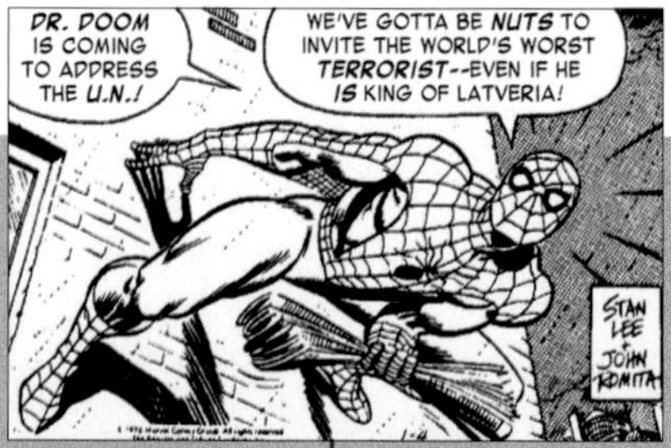
DR. DOOM IS COMING TO ADDRESS THE U.N.!
WE'VE GOTTA BE NUTS TO INVITE THE WORLD'S WORST TERRORIST--EVEN IF HE IS KING OF LATVERIA!
STAN LEE JOHN ROMITA

JANUARY 1977

January 3, 1977, sees the launch of the syndicated *Spider-Man* comic strip by Stan Lee and John Romita, Sr.

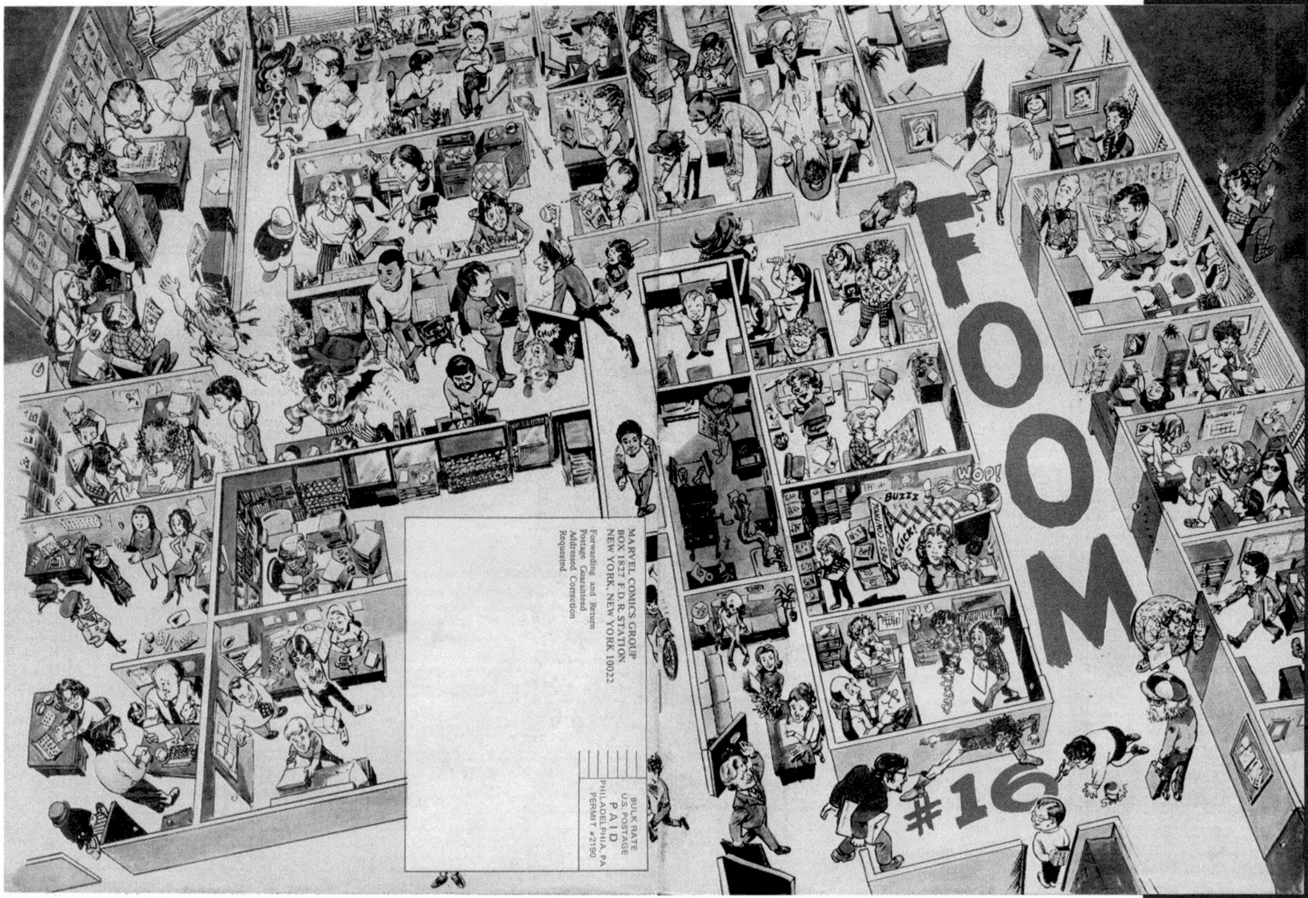
FOOM
#16
WOP!
BUZZ
MARVEL COMICS GROUP
BOX 1827 F.D.R. STATION
NEW YORK, NEW YORK 10022
Forwarding and Return
Postage Guaranteed
Addressed Correction
Requested
BULK RATE
U.S. POSTAGE
PAID
PHILADELPHIA, PA
PERMIT #2190

could draw any Marvel character you happened to pull out of the hat—at the drop of a hat. He and a handful of others were the go-to guys when editors needed to make up for lost time and get their panels to print. Sal Buscema and Bob Brown penciled one of Marvel's first crossover events, *The Avengers vs. The Defenders*, the latter comprising a "non-team" of characters we might call anarchic outsiders that included Dr. Strange, Namor, the Silver Surfer, the Hulk, and Valkyrie, who would take on the classic Avengers lineup led by Thor and Captain America.

British-born writer and artist John Byrne definitely left his mark on the history of Marvel Comics. Before teaming up with Claremont on the *X-Men* series, he helped develop characters like Iron Fist and Star-Lord, and in the 1980s worked on memorable runs featuring the Fantastic

ABOVE: A map of the mighty Marvel bullpen from the pages of *FOOM #16*. Art by Marie Severin.

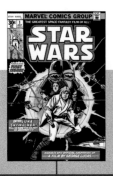

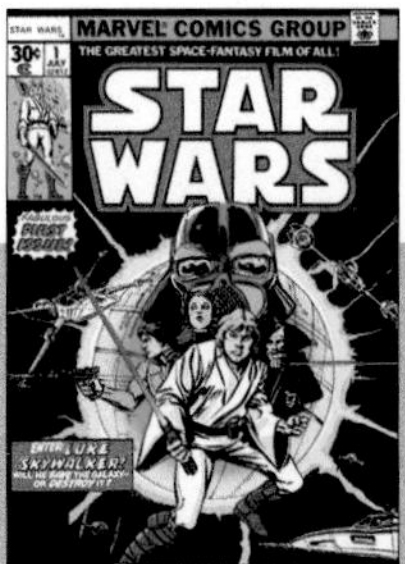
MARVEL COMICS GROUP
30¢
THE GREATEST SPACE-FANTASY FILM OF ALL!
STAR WARS
A FILM BY GEORGE LUCAS

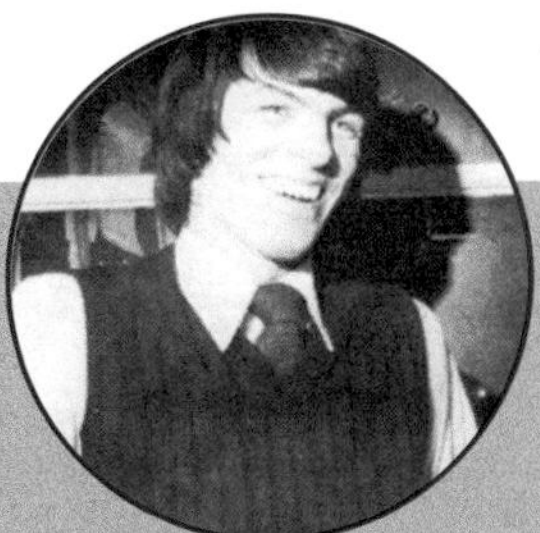

SPRING 1977

Lucasfilm approaches Marvel, pitching a comic book version of the soon-to-be released film *Star Wars*. Thomas convinces a reluctant Lee to agree. The series is an immediate success..

1978

Following Lee's promotion to publisher, several individuals held the title Editor in Chief. In 1978, Jim Shooter was named to the position, where he would remain until 1987.

1980

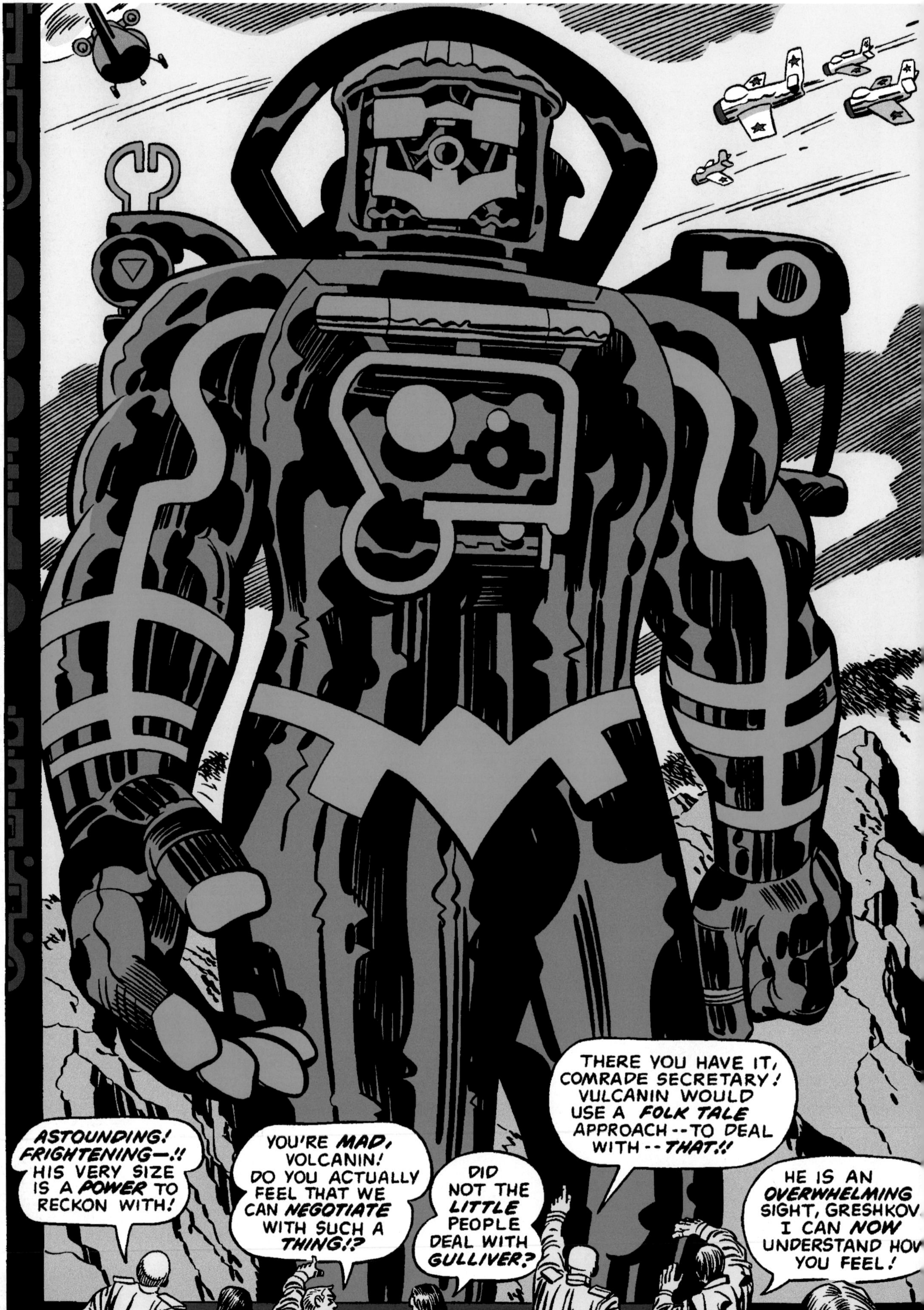
ASTOUNDING! FRIGHTENING—!! HIS VERY SIZE IS A POWER TO RECKON WITH!
YOU'RE MAD, VOLCANIN! DO YOU ACTUALLY FEEL THAT WE CAN NEGOTIATE WITH SUCH A THING!?
DID NOT THE LITTLE PEOPLE DEAL WITH GULLIVER?
THERE YOU HAVE IT, COMRADE SECRETARY! VULCANIN WOULD USE A FOLK TALE APPROACH--TO DEAL WITH--THAT!!
HE IS AN OVERWHELMING SIGHT, GRESHKOV I CAN NOW UNDERSTAND HOV YOU FEEL!

Four and Captain America. But in all probability, at that time the main man on the scene was Frank Miller, a young visionary embarking on what would be an extraordinary career as comic book artist. Enthralled by inner-city settings and noir fiction, in the late '70s he reinvented Daredevil, transforming him into a dark, tormented hero, a character imbued with strong religious connotations.

Shock waves: Jack "the King" Kirby left the Distinguished Competition in 1975 and made his way back to Marvel, where no one had forgotten him. He was given absolute artistic freedom and set about writing, drawing, and editing his own work. His unbounded imagination gave us the saga *The Eternals*, featuring off-shoots of humanity who received their powers from genetic experiments conducted by the intergalactic Celestials and wound up siding with Marvel's pantheon of Super Heroes Kirby also recouped two classic characters, Captain America and Black Panther, to write and draw them in their very own series. Also worth remembering are Kirby's Devil Dinosaur, Machine Man and his extraordinary comic book adaptation of Stanley Kubrick's *2001: A Space Odyssey.*

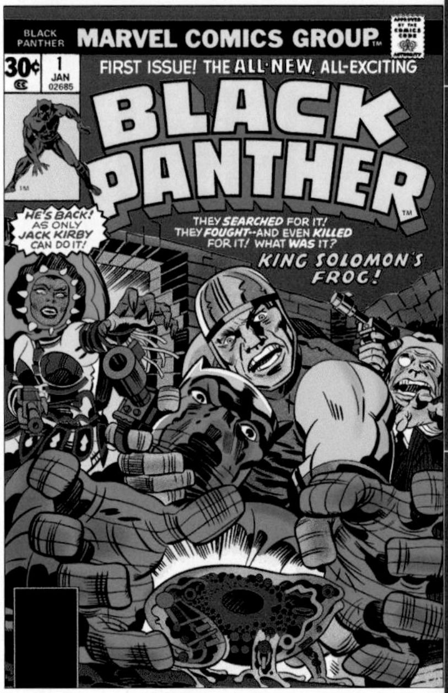
BLACK PANTHER
MARVEL COMICS GROUP
30¢
1 JAN 02685
FIRST ISSUE! THE ALL-NEW, ALL-EXCITING
BLACK PANTHER
HE'S BACK! AS ONLY JACK KIRBY CAN DO IT!
THEY SEARCHED FOR IT! THEY FOUGHT--AND EVEN KILLED FOR IT! WHAT WAS IT?
KING SOLOMON'S FROG!

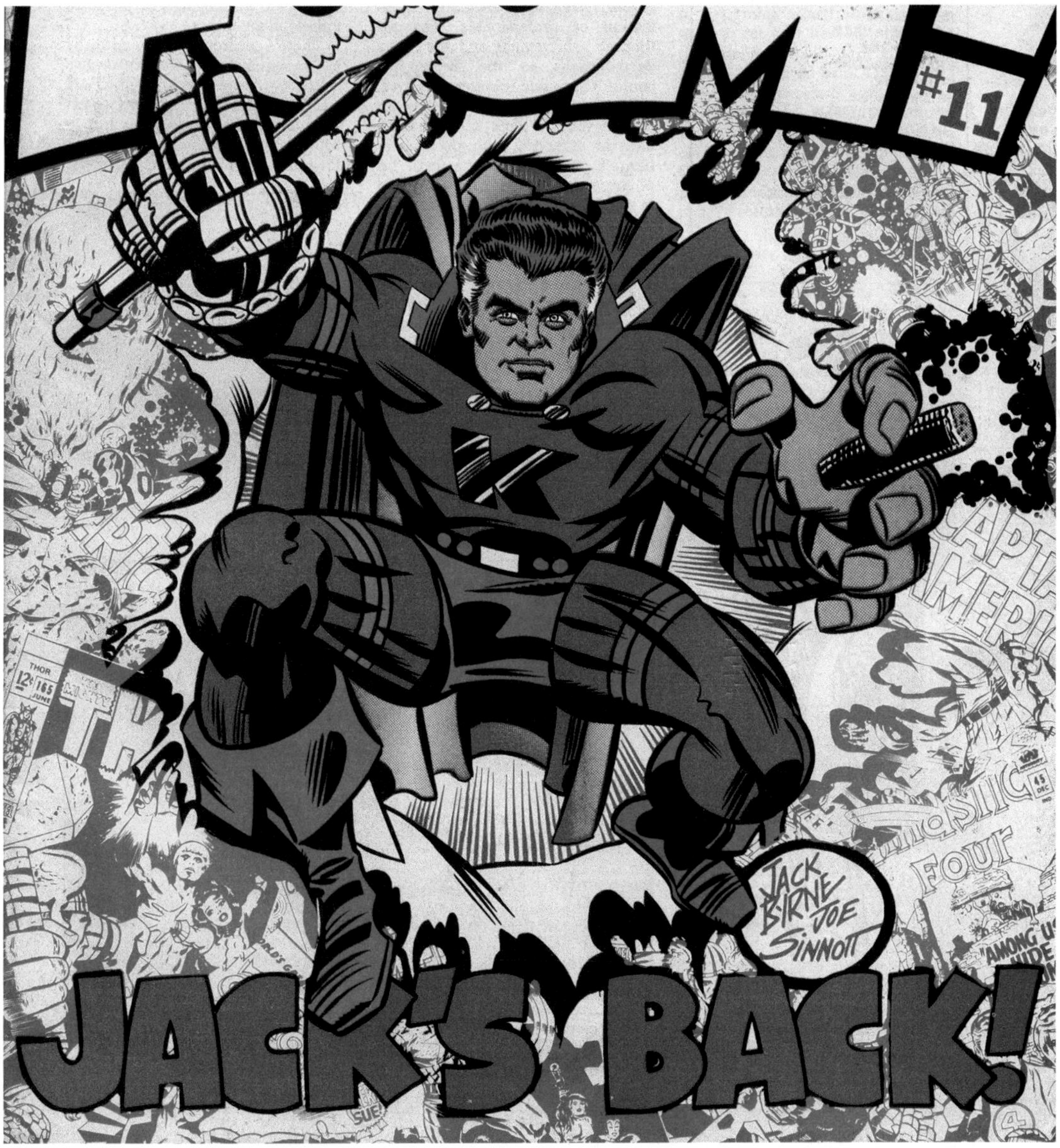
#11
JACK BYRNE JOE SINNOTT
JACK'S BACK!

OPPOSITE PAGE: The U.S.S.R. attacks the Celestial Nezarr in *The Eternals #11* (May 1977). Script by Jack Kirby. Art by Jack Kirby (pencils), Mike Royer (inks, letters), Glynis Wein (colors).

ABOVE *Black Panther #1* (January 1977). Art by Jack Kirby (pencils), John Verpoorten (inks).

LEFT: The return of Jack Kirby to the Marvel fold is announced in *FOOM #11* (art by John Byrne and Joe Sinnott).

FROM STREET CRIME TO WATERGATE

The 1970s prove to be turbulent in all aspects, and Marvel reflects the changing times with gritty realism and stories pulled from the headlines.

In the 1940s, Marvel Super Heroes fought against the Nazis. The 1950s and '60s saw them Commie-bashing their way through the Cold War, and dealing with threats of nuclear war and the latest developments that science had to offer, not to mention post-1968 student protests and antiwar sentiment. But the 1970s ushered in a host of new problems for the average American. Political identity came under fire when the president himself turned out to be a crook and was forced to resign.

Another young, politically aware Marvel writer, Steve Englehart, was the genius behind the Secret Empire, about a government plot involving high-ranking officials in the ultimate power grab. Incredibly enough, the conspiracy is led by the President of the United States himself—although we only catch a glimpse of his silhouette—who in the end winds up committing suicide. It was a powerful story that dissected the political reality of the times, in the same way the Punisher provided a critique on a social level.

Life was rough-and-tumble on America's big city streets. Crime rates spiked, daily life was torn upside down by robberies, rapes, and murders. The police, like the citizens they were sworn to protect, appeared helpless. At the movies, people's longing for vigilante justice found expression in the 1974 classic *Death Wish*, starring Charles Bronson, which spawned four sequels. It portrayed an architect-turned-vigilante following the murder of his wife and the rape of his daughter, a man who took justice into his own hands after losing all faith in the authorities.

Marvel came out with its own version of a do-it-yourself crime-stopper that same year: the Punisher, a new character created by Conway, Romita, and Ross

I'VE GOT A SECRET TO TELL YOU, PAL--

RIGHT: The wall-crawler takes out the Punisher in *The Amazing Spider-Man #129* (February 1974). Script by Gerry Conway. Art by Ross Andru (pencils), Frank Giacoia and Dave Hunt (colors), John Costanza (letters).

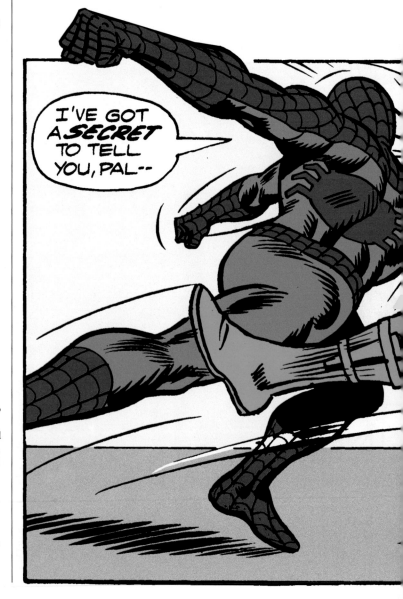

Andru, who debuted in *The Amazing Spider-Man #129*.

Frank Castle was a Vietnam vet whose wife and two small children were killed after they had by chance witnessed a mob killing in Central Park. Vowing revenge, Frank Castle dons a black costume emblazoned with a skull across the front, and becomes the Punisher. He takes to the streets, a one-man war machine targeting criminals of every sort.

The character is still popular today, and like Iron Fist and Luke Cage, has starred in his own series on Netflix (2017-2019). Whether right or wrong, he treats audiences to an expression of commonly felt sentiments. Antiheroes like the Punisher would give us a taste of things to come in a decade that promised to be grim and gritty, the perfect backdrop for what would be a revisionist overhaul of our favorite Super Heroes.

The time had come for Marvel characters to branch out, and the

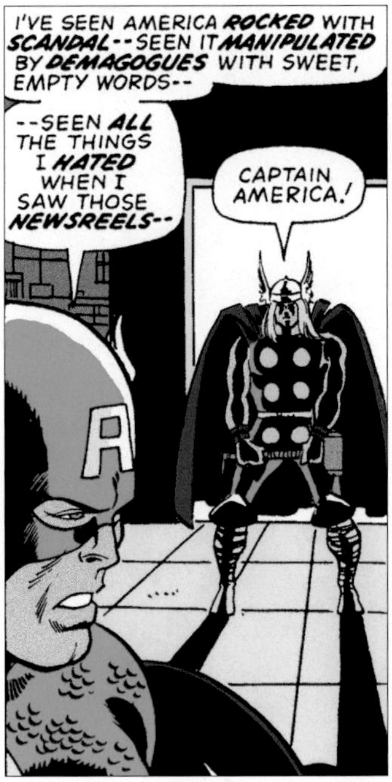
I'VE SEEN AMERICA ROCKED WITH SCANDAL--SEEN IT MANIPULATED BY DEMAGOGUES WITH SWEET, EMPTY WORDS--
--SEEN ALL THE THINGS I HATED WHEN I SAW THOSE NEWSREELS--
CAPTAIN AMERICA.!

company's top brass had their sights set on TV and the movies. The new owners put Stan Lee in charge of the mission, and he began traveling back and forth to Los Angeles to promote various projects.

Not an easy task at the time, since technology back then was hard put to recreate incredible comic book effects for film.

The first step would be cartoons. In 1966, the first Marvel cartoon series—*Marvel Super Heroes*—appeared, followed in 1967 by *Spider-Man* and *Fantastic Four*. In 1978, NBC came out with a *Fantastic Four* cartoon series, featuring Herbie the robot in place of the Human Torch. The following year, ABC ran a weekly cartoon series featuring one of the new Super Heroes from the 1970s, Spider-Woman, which was created by Archie Goodwin and Marie Severin.

As for live action on television and in the movies, things were somewhat more complicated. Spider-Man would be the character to focus on first. In

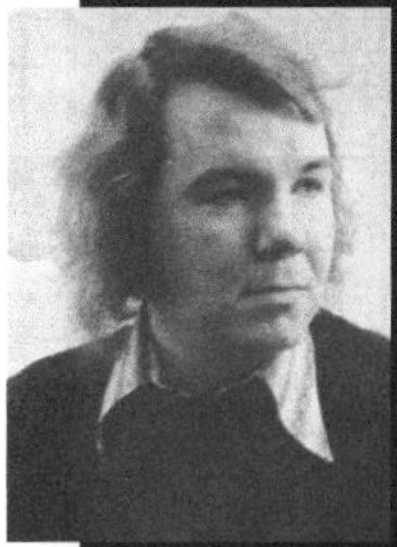

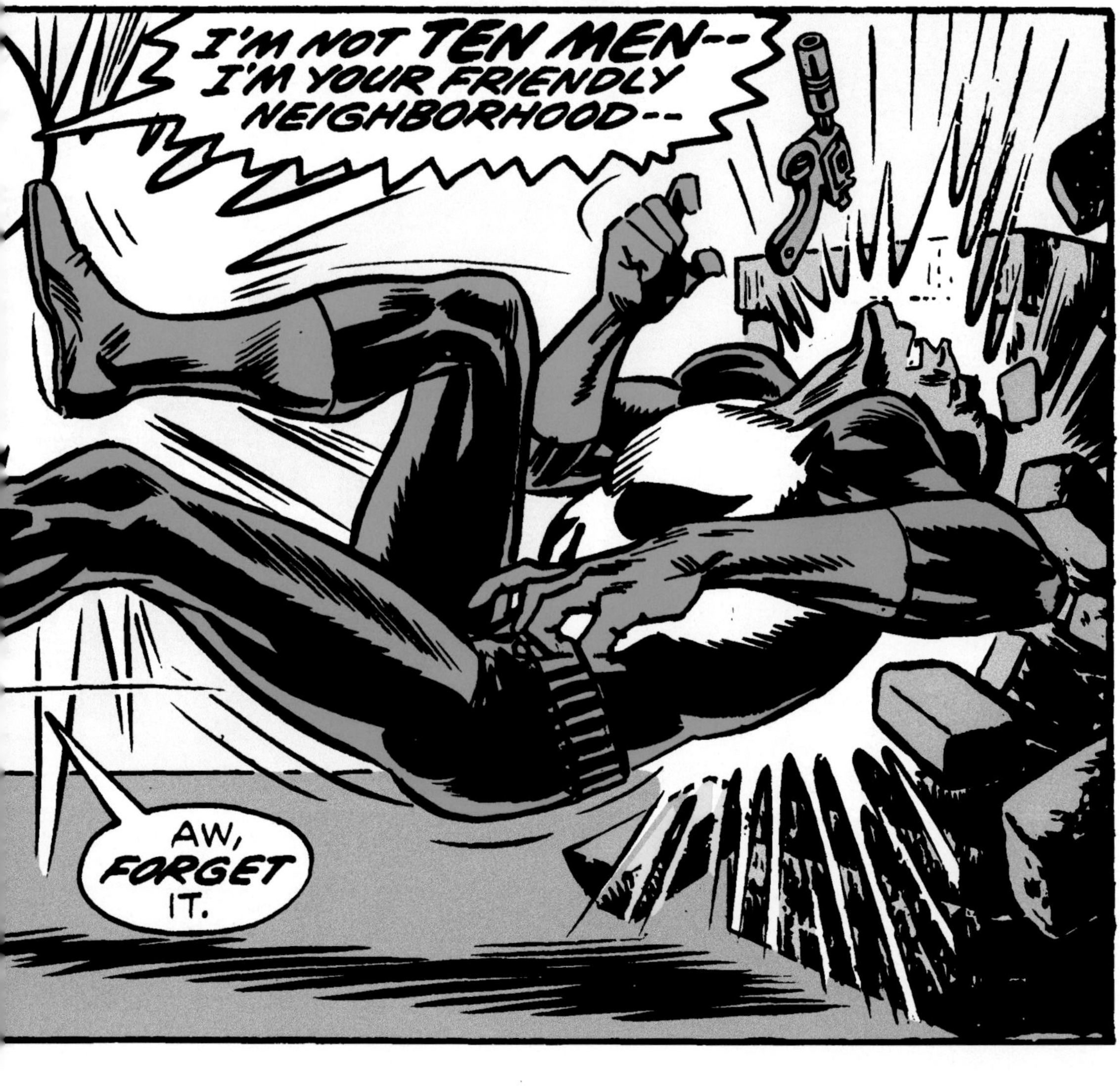
I'M NOT TEN MEN-- I'M YOUR FRIENDLY NEIGHBORHOOD--
AW, FORGET IT.

ABOVE: Writer Gerry Conway.

ABOVE LEFT: Captain America contemplates his future in *Captain America #176* (August 1974). Script by Steve Englehart. Art by Sal Buscema (pencils), Vince Colletta (inks), Linda Lessmann (colors), Artie Simek (letters).

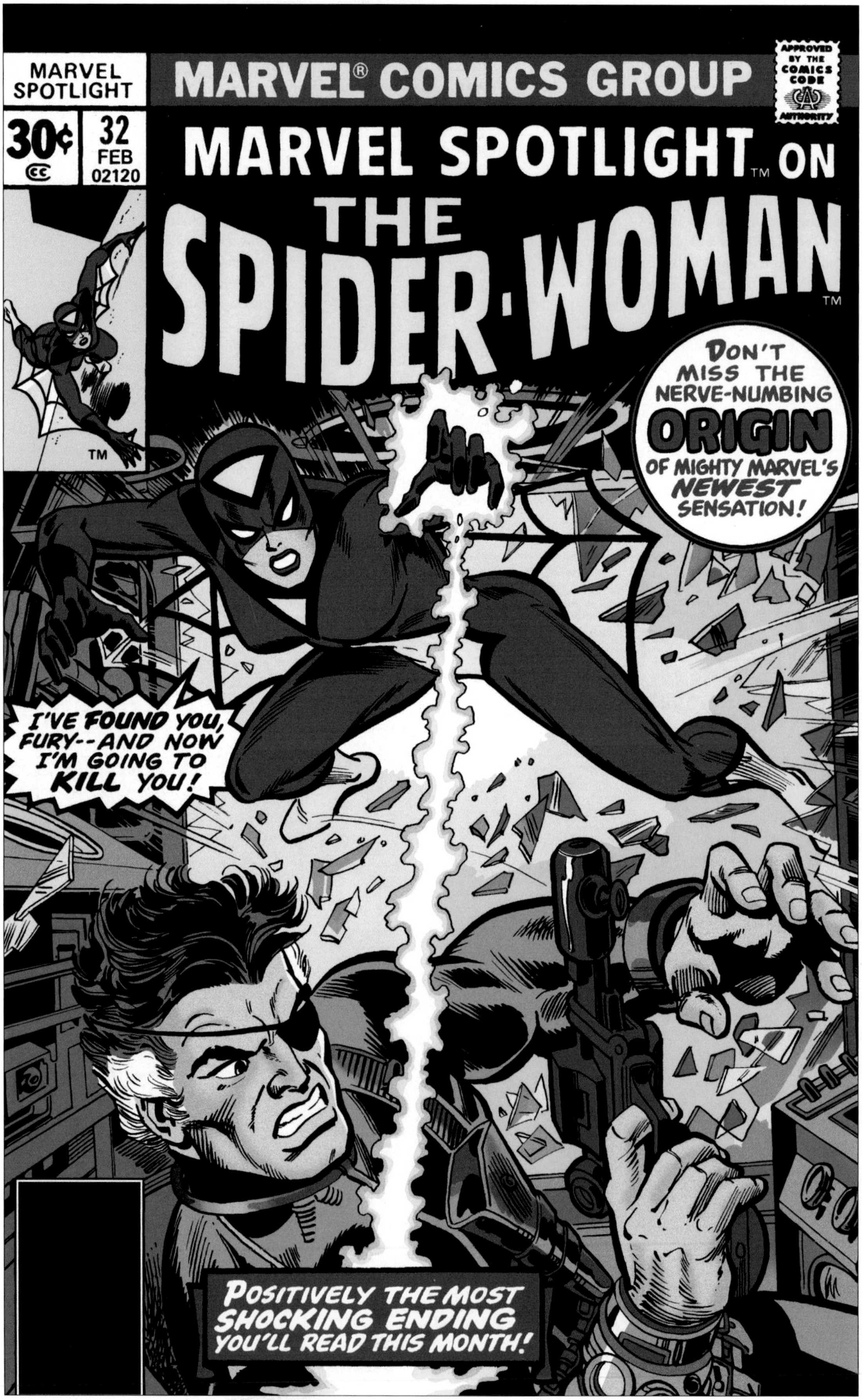
MARVEL SPOTLIGHT
MARVEL® COMICS GROUP
APPROVED BY THE COMICS CODE AUTHORITY
30¢
32 FEB 02120
MARVEL SPOTLIGHT™ ON
THE SPIDER-WOMAN™
DON'T MISS THE NERVE-NUMBING ORIGIN OF MIGHTY MARVEL'S NEWEST SENSATION!
I'VE FOUND YOU, FURY--AND NOW I'M GOING TO KILL YOU!
POSITIVELY THE MOST SHOCKING ENDING YOU'LL READ THIS MONTH!

RIGHT: The first appearance of Spider-Woman from *Marvel Spotlight #32* (February 1977). Art by Gil Kane (pencils), Dick Giordano and John Romita, Sr. (inks).

1977, CBS produced the TV series *The Amazing Spider-Man*, which was limited to just 13 episodes before it was canceled (1977–79).

The same network also came out with a TV movie, while some of the TV series episodes were pieced together and released as full-length motion pictures for distribution outside the United States. The series starred a fairly credible Nicholas Hammond as Peter Parker, but supporting characters were different from the ones comic book readers were accustomed to. Among fans, the series eventually achieved cult status.

The live-action TV series *The Incredible Hulk* (1977–82) proved to be of much higher production value, and achieved much greater success. It starred Bill Bixby as Dr. David Banner and body builder Lou Ferrigno as the Hulk, and featured the theme song, dripping with emotion, "The Lonely Man" by Joe Harnell. Banner grappled with his curse for 80 episodes, plus three made-for-TV movies.

While feature films for theater distribution were still beyond Marvel's reach, more TV movies were made. The best known of these was *Captain America* (1979), only loosely based on the comic book Super Hero. It featured a motorcycle-riding Cap who got his superpowers from a steroid called F.L.A.G., short for "full latent ability gain." Another was *Doctor Strange* (1978), which placed a psychiatrist in the lead role and veered significantly from the comic book version. It was produced by CBS as a pilot for a TV series that would never see the light of day. ■

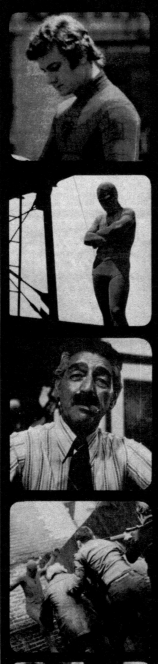

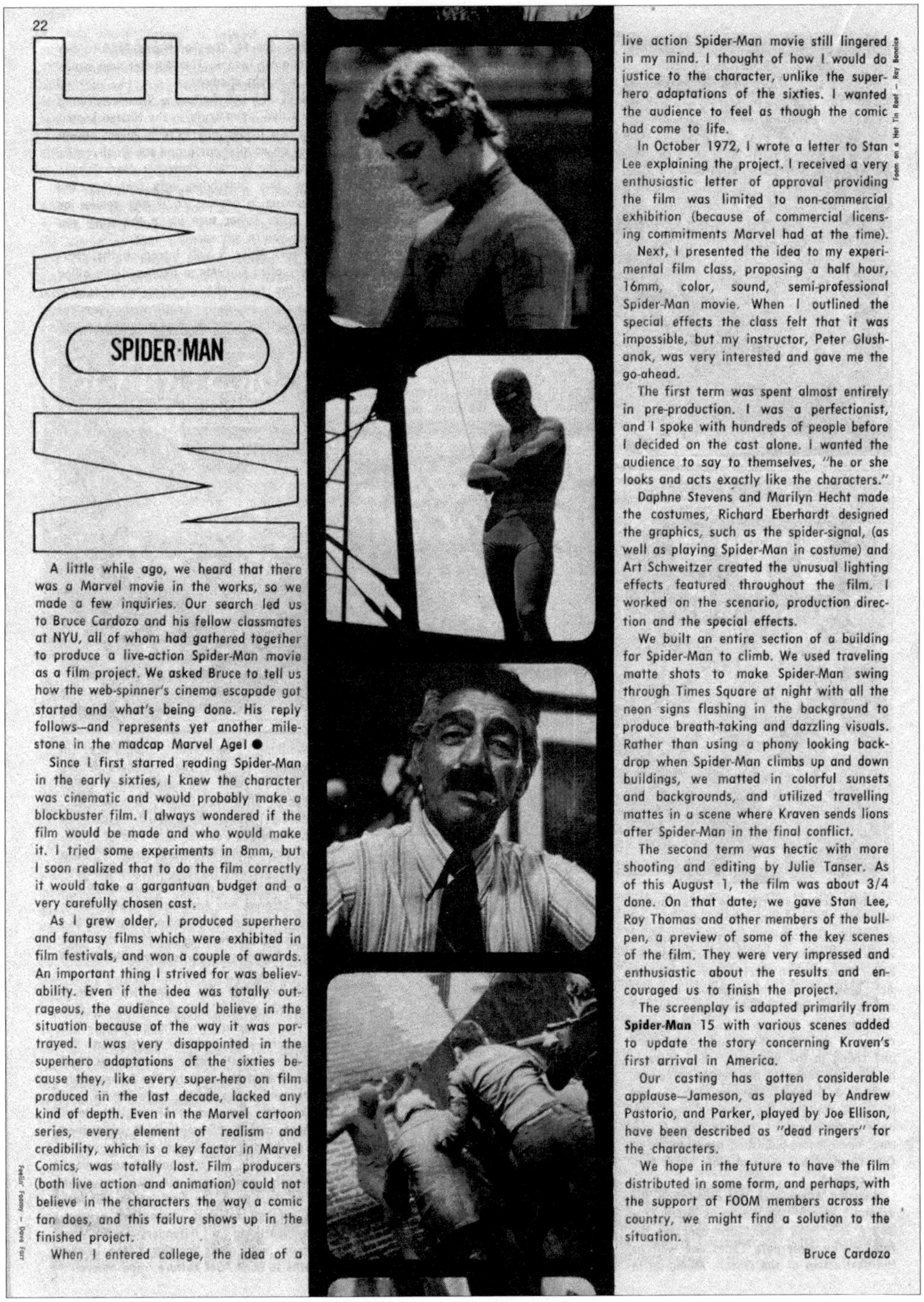

22

MOVIE

SPIDER-MAN

A little while ago, we heard that there was a Marvel movie in the works, so we made a few inquiries. Our search led us to Bruce Cardozo and his fellow classmates at NYU, all of whom had gathered together to produce a live-action Spider-Man movie as a film project. We asked Bruce to tell us how the web-spinner's cinema escapade got started and what's being done. His reply follows—and represents yet another milestone in the madcap Marvel Age! ●

Since I first starred reading Spider-Man in the early sixties, I knew the character was cinematic and would probably make a blockbuster film. I always wondered if the film would be made and who would make it. I tried some experiments in 8mm, but I soon realized that to do the film correctly it would take a gargantuan budget and a very carefully chosen cast.

As I grew older, I produced superhero and fantasy films which were exhibited in film festivals, and won a couple of awards. An important thing I strived for was believability. Even if the idea was totally outrageous, the audience could believe in the situation because of the way it was portrayed. I was very disappointed in the superhero adaptations of the sixties because they, like every super-hero on film produced in the last decade, lacked any kind of depth. Even in the Marvel cartoon series, every element of realism and credibility, which is a key factor in Marvel Comics, was totally lost. Film producers (both live action and animation) could not believe in the characters the way a comic fan does, and this failure shows up in the finished project.

When I entered college, the idea of a live action Spider-Man movie still lingered in my mind. I thought of how I would do justice to the character, unlike the super-hero adaptations of the sixties. I wanted the audience to feel as though the comic had come to life.

In October 1972, I wrote a letter to Stan Lee explaining the project. I received a very enthusiastic letter of approval providing the film was limited to non-commercial exhibition (because of commercial licensing commitments Marvel had at the time).

Next, I presented the idea to my experimental film class, proposing a half hour, 16mm, color, sound, semi-professional Spider-Man movie. When I outlined the special effects the class felt that it was impossible, but my instructor, Peter Glushanok, was very interested and gave me the go-ahead.

The first term was spent almost entirely in pre-production. I was a perfectionist, and I spoke with hundreds of people before I decided on the cast alone. I wanted the audience to say to themselves, "he or she looks and acts exactly like the characters."

Daphne Stevens and Marilyn Hecht made the costumes, Richard Eberhardt designed the graphics, such as the spider-signal, (as well as playing Spider-Man in costume) and Art Schweitzer created the unusual lighting effects featured throughout the film. I worked on the scenario, production direction and the special effects.

We built an entire section of a building for Spider-Man to climb. We used traveling matte shots to make Spider-Man swing through Times Square at night with all the neon signs flashing in the background to produce breath-taking and dazzling visuals. Rather than using a phony looking backdrop when Spider-Man climbs up and down buildings, we matted in colorful sunsets and backgrounds, and utilized travelling mattes in a scene where Kraven sends lions after Spider-Man in the final conflict.

The second term was hectic with more shooting and editing by Julie Tanser. As of this August 1, the film was about 3/4 done. On that date, we gave Stan Lee, Roy Thomas and other members of the bullpen, a preview of some of the key scenes of the film. They were very impressed and enthusiastic about the results and encouraged us to finish the project.

The screenplay is adapted primarily from **Spider-Man** 15 with various scenes added to update the story concerning Kraven's first arrival in America.

Our casting has gotten considerable applause—Jameson, as played by Andrew Pastorio, and Parker, played by Joe Ellison, have been described as "dead ringers" for the characters.

We hope in the future to have the film distributed in some form, and perhaps, with the support of FOOM members across the country, we might find a solution to the situation.

Bruce Cardozo

LEFT: *FOOM #4* (Winter 1973) took a look at a New York University student film based on Spider-Man.

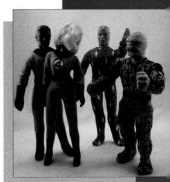

MEGO

With an ever-growing impact on popular culture in America and throughout the world, in the 1970s Marvel began a highly successful merchandising campaign. Its most famous characters soon appeared on an array of objects and clothing, and kids played with action figures that were destined to become collectors' items. In 1971 Mego, the leading manufacturer of action figures in those days, purchased the rights to make and market models based on Marvel characters. First off the assembly line were miniature versions of Spider-Man and the Hulk—toys that became best-sellers worldwide.

THE 1980s

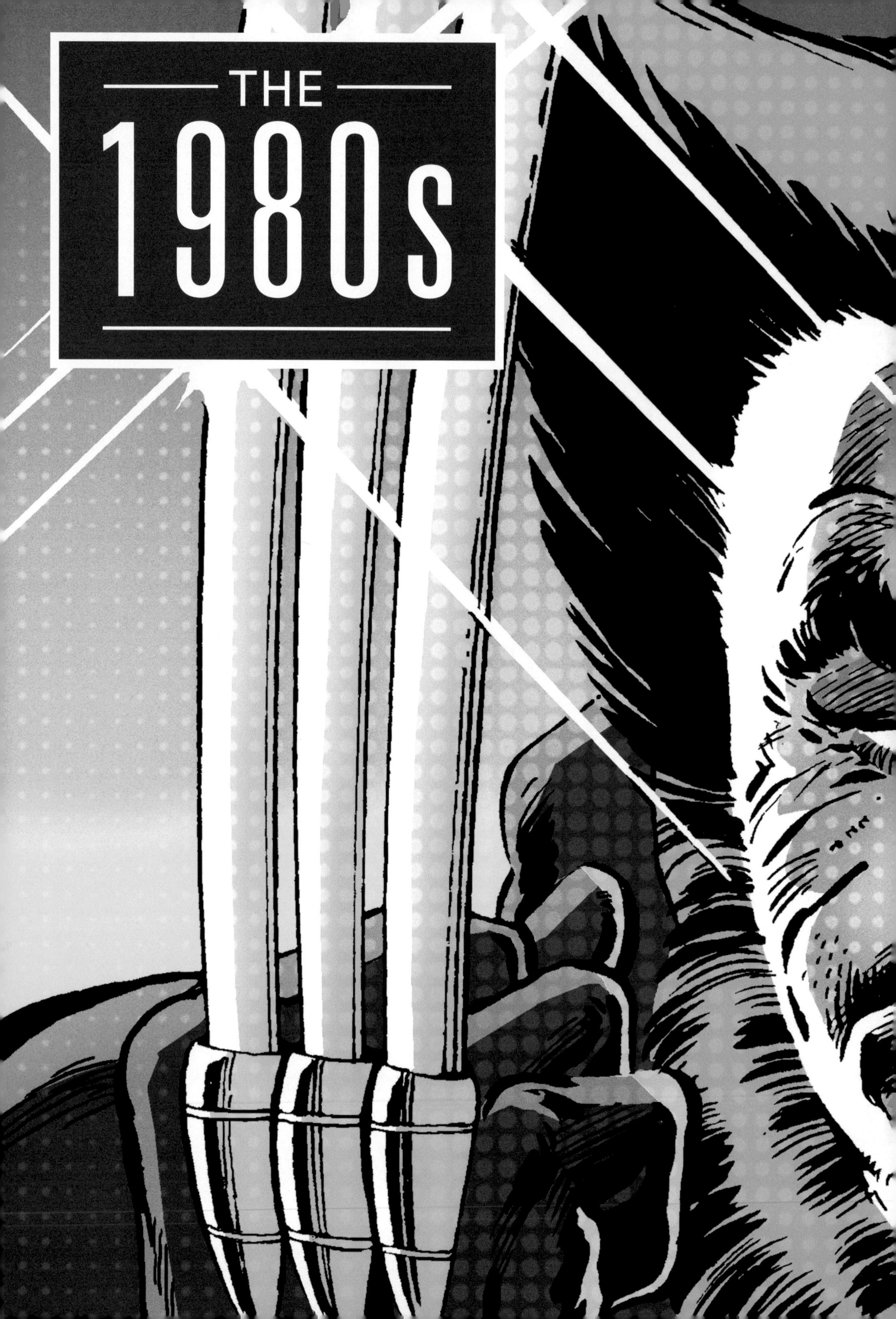

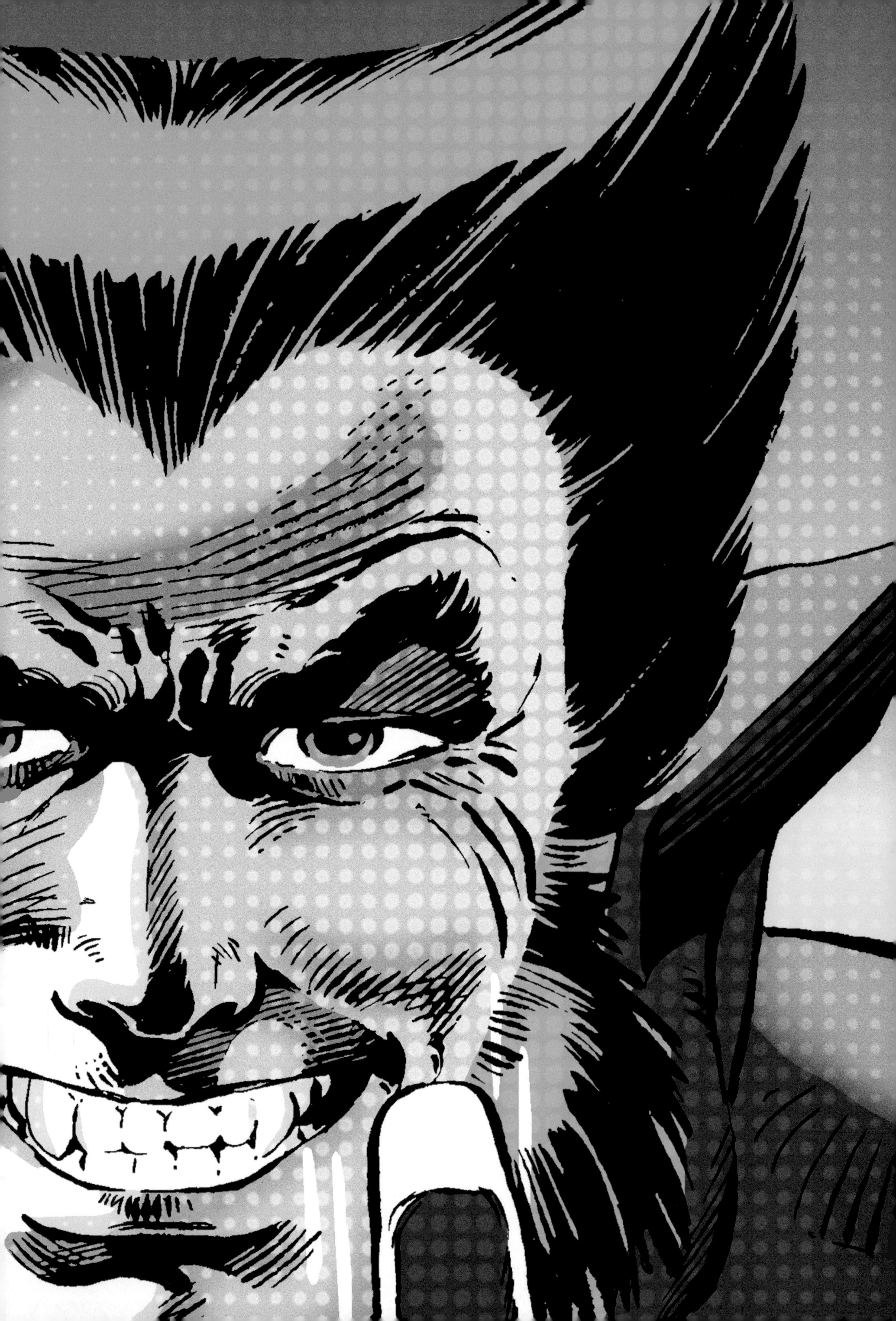

SECRET WARS AND NEW WORLDS

In the 1980s, Marvel celebrated the 25th anniversary of the Marvel Universe—but they refused to rest on their creative laurels.

The 1980s were all about innovation at Marvel, in terms of experimentation, quality, and new characters, approaches, and trends that would set the stage for future developments. A significant portion of the editorial decisions, including the key takes on the narrative end, would be guided by Editor in Chief Jim Shooter. Meanwhile, things began to change industry-wide. With the gradual disappearance of old sales channels and the rise of comic book shops and direct market sales, publishers set out to create projects that exclusively targeted specialty venues. It was a winning bet. The first issue of *Dazzler*, which featured a heroine that had originally been created for a cross-media project that never took off, sold 428,000 copies.

What drove commercial success were the publishing events, to the point where they began appearing annually. Event comics became the big sellers, bringing together the pantheon of Marvel characters in releases like *Contest of Champions*, which was the first limited series that appeared in this format, and others featuring tie-ins, like *Secret Wars* and *Secret Wars II*. The decade also saw the comics pushing into uncharted territory. It saw the first time that someone took the place of an iconic hero under the mask. Make that under the helmet.

In 1983's *Iron Man #170*, James Rhodes, Tony Stark's trusted pilot and friend, took Iron Man's place when the inventor endured a debilitating personal crisis. In *Captain America #333* (1987), Cap himself assumed the new identity of the Captain and found himself on a collision course with the U.S. government and a violent super-patriot John Walker, who became the "new" Captain America.

Then there was Thor, who, in the climax of the cycle scripted and drawn by Walt Simonson, and under a spell cast by the goddess of death Hela, wound up sporting new heavy armor. The sequence of stories was so innovative that at one point the God of Thunder relinquished his hammer to the horse-like alien Beta Ray Bill!

Spider-Man, too, would change his look in *The Amazing Spider-Man #252* and *Secret Wars #7*, and don a black costume for four years. In the late 1980s, Hulk became gray again and took on the clever Joe Fixit identity. The Avengers' latest lineup change saw the creation of the West Coast "branch," led by Hawkeye.

Many of these new developments were masterminded by Shooter, who, once the idea of doing away with the main heroes altogether was scrapped, launched the imprint New Universe, featuring a cast of all-new characters. But the series that bore more changes than any other starred a group of mutants known as the uncanny X-Men. Even after Shooter left in 1987 and Tom DeFalco became Editor in Chief, the uncanny X-Men's popularity continued to soar.

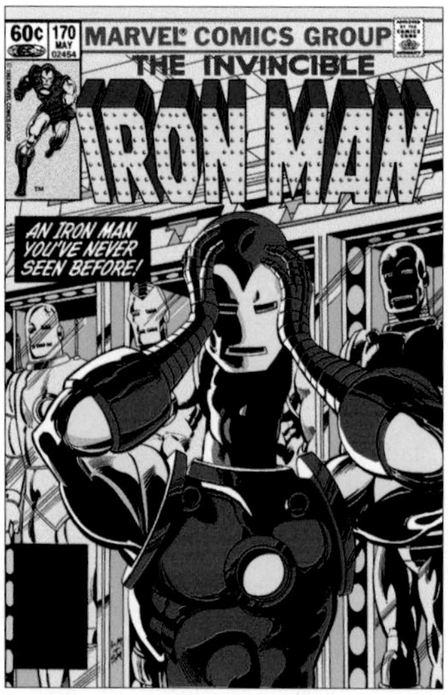
60¢ 170 MAY
MARVEL COMICS GROUP
THE INVINCIBLE
IRON MAN
AN IRON MAN YOU'VE NEVER SEEN BEFORE!

ABOVE: *The Invincible Iron Man #170* (May 1983). Art by Luke McDonnell (pencils), Steve Mitchell (inks), Bob Sharen (colors).

OPPOSITE PAGE: *The Amazing Spider-Man #252* (May 1984). Art by Ron Frenz (pencils), Klaus Janson (inks), Glynis Wein (colors).

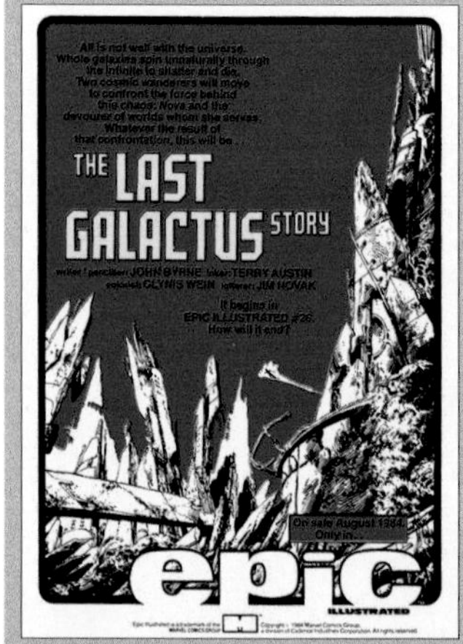
THE LAST GALACTUS STORY
epic

EPIC STORIES

Inspired by magazines like *Heavy Metal*, Marvel launched *Epic Illustrated* in 1980, aiming for an older audience. Epic occasionally presented adventure stories featuring Marvel Super Heroes. But it was more focused on stories that spanned a wide array of different genres, often by mainstream comic book writers and artists making their Marvel debuts, as well as talent from the independent press and the U.K. Cover paintings were created by the likes of Frank Frazetta, Richard Corben, and the Hildebrandt brothers, and the whole shebang was overseen by Archie Goodwin, a highly esteemed editor. *Epic Illustrated* would pave the way for an entire line of products brimming with masterpieces.

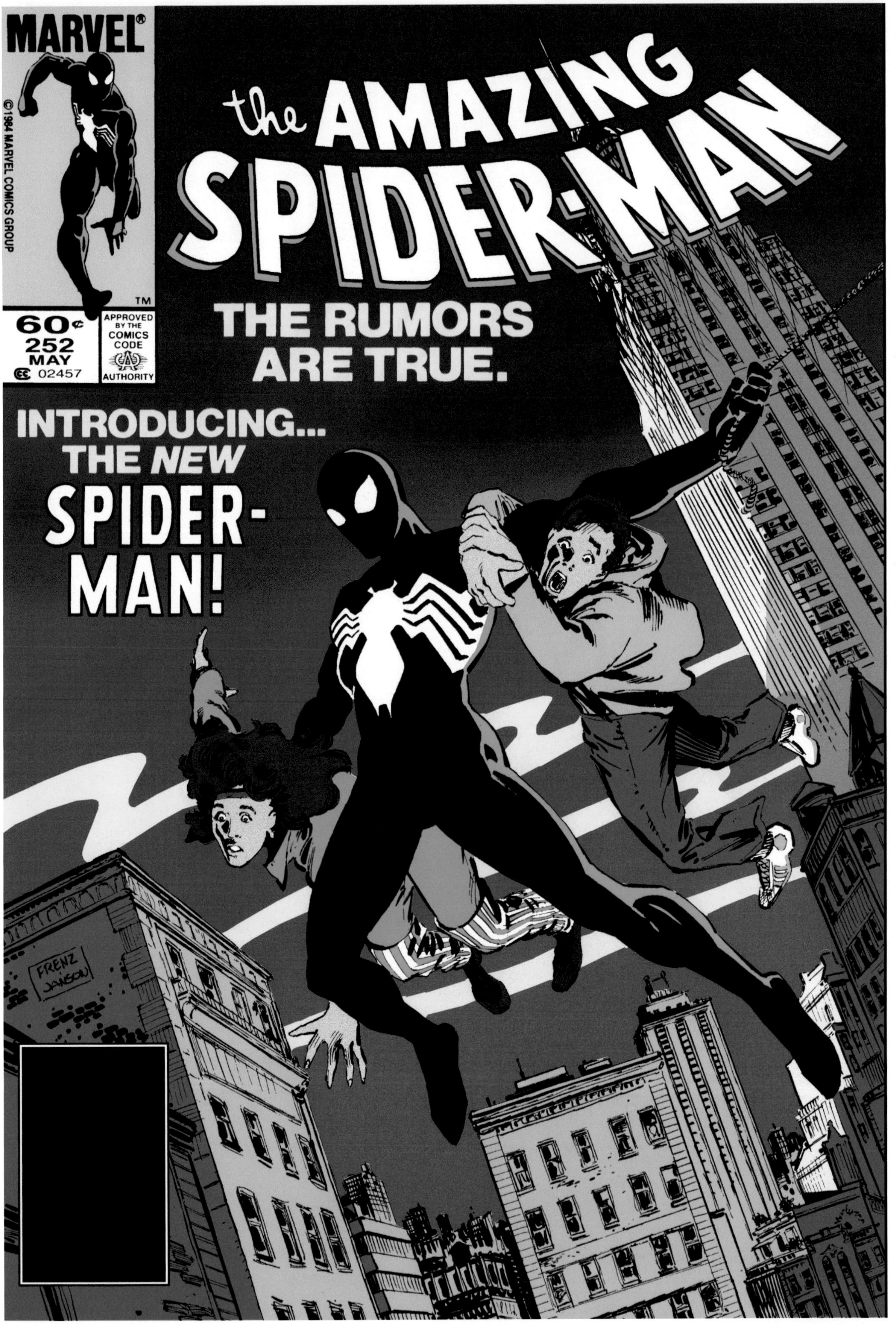
MARVEL®
©1984 MARVEL COMICS GROUP
60¢
252
MAY
02457
APPROVED BY THE COMICS CODE AUTHORITY
the AMAZING SPIDER-MAN™
THE RUMORS ARE TRUE.
INTRODUCING... THE NEW SPIDER-MAN!
FRENZ JANSON

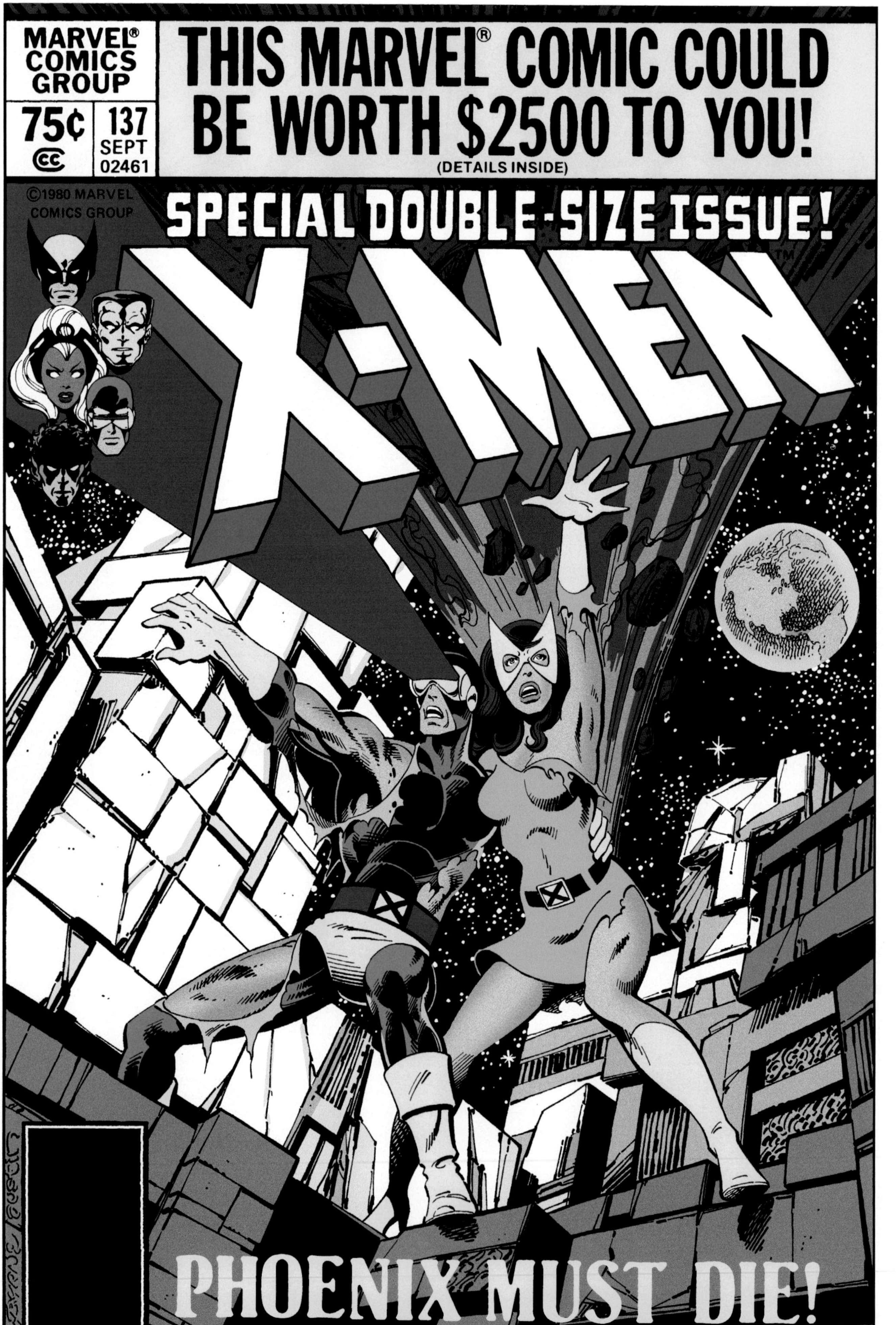
MARVEL® COMICS GROUP
75¢
137 SEPT 02461
THIS MARVEL® COMIC COULD BE WORTH $2500 TO YOU!
(DETAILS INSIDE)
©1980 MARVEL COMICS GROUP
SPECIAL DOUBLE-SIZE ISSUE!
X-MEN™
PHOENIX MUST DIE!

MUTANTS, NINJAS, AND BIG EVENTS

The 1980s saw the rise of the X-Men, Daredevil, and the Punisher, as Marvel embraced the changing tastes of its audience.

In *The Uncanny X-Men #137* (cover-dated September 1980) writer Chris Claremont and artist John Byrne, who often worked as a team, brought a long cycle, begun in 1976, to an end. Jean Grey, the former Marvel Girl who had assumed the powerful Phoenix identity under the watch of artist Dave Cockrum, was corrupted by an ambitious Super Villain, the mutant Mastermind, and became a force of evil. Power-crazed Dark Phoenix unleashed death and destruction on a rampage through the galaxies.

In a touching moment of lucidity, she ended her life in the arms of her beloved Cyclops on a desolate lunar landscape. Such a finale had a strong narrative and editorial impact—having the former heroine die was a big step for the creators, and for Shooter in particular.

A year later, Claremont and Byrne would go their separate ways, but not before creating another momentous saga: "Days of Future Past." After that, the title was illustrated by artists like Paul Smith, known for his humanizing touch, and the explosively talented John Romita, Jr. "Jazzy John's" son was one of his generation's most highly skilled and versatile artists (he also lent his prowess to artwork for *The Amazing Spider-Man* and, over the course of the '80s, *Iron Man* and *Daredevil*).

But even if Byrne had left the series to pursue other projects, throughout the years he spent working alongside Claremont, the two had laid the foundations for future decades of success for the X-Men, including the basis for film plots to come. And when a series is that successful, it's sure to spawn its share of spin-offs.

The first was *The New Mutants.* While everyone thought the X-Men were dead, Professor Xavier brought together a new team of teenage mutants from around the world to complete their training. The series debuted in 1983, and eventually racked up a hundred issues, with plenty of changes in squad lineups, leadership, and the artists and writers who created them. At one point, Professor X himself was replaced by his longtime nemesis, the reformed Magneto. One of the best-known cycles saw Claremont using the visionary artwork of Bill Sienkiewicz, which helped shift the series in a direction that incorporated horror atmospheres.

Another mutant spin-off marking the reunion of the original X-Men formation appeared in 1986. In *The Avengers* and the *Fantastic Four,* readers learned that Jean Grey was, in fact, still alive. In truth, she had never really died, in that the Phoenix Force had made a duplicate of her—it was this version who had turned into "Dark Phoenix," and who made the ultimate sacrifice.

Meanwhile, the real Jean was joined by her old teammates: Beast, Angel, Iceman, and, of course, Cyclops. The *X-Factor* series would soon come into its own thanks to the work of the husband-and-wife team of Walter and Louise Simonson—she wrote, he drew—who created, among other characters, the Super Villain Apocalypse.

In 1988, Chris Claremont and John Buscema introduced Logan's own personal series entitled *Wolverine,* which grew out of earlier adventures in a solo limited series of the same name created by Claremont and Frank Miller in 1982.

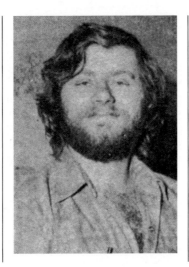

"As Dave [Cockrum] and I honed our craft, as individuals and a team, so did the characters make their initially halting and occasionally clumsy steps into becoming a team, and ultimately a family... The characters had only just met then, as opposed to having been together for longer than many readers' and some creators' lifetimes. There was the marvel of discovery to every aspect of the book."

—Chris Claremont

ABOVE: Writer Chris Claremont.

OPPOSITE PAGE *The Uncanny X-Men #137* (September 1980). Art by John Byrne (pencils), Terry Austin (inks), Glynis Wein (colors).

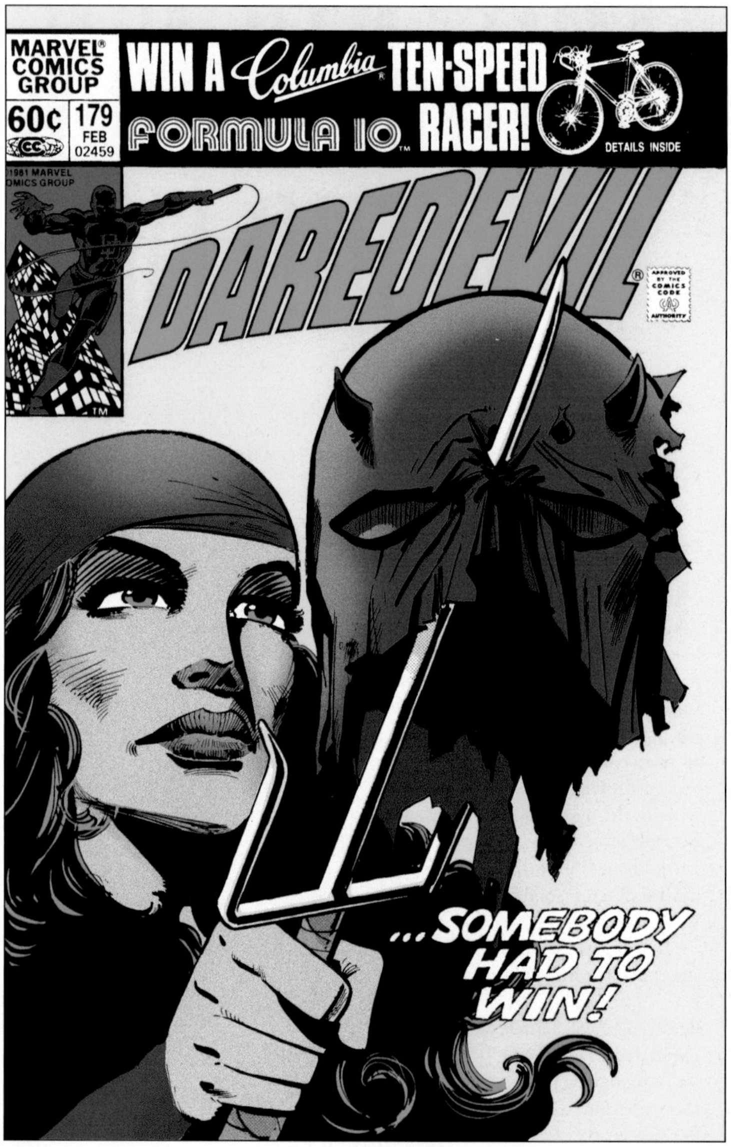
MARVEL COMICS GROUP
WIN A Columbia TEN-SPEED FORMULA 10 RACER!
60¢
179
FEB
02459
DETAILS INSIDE
DAREDEVIL
...SOMEBODY HAD TO WIN!

THIS PAGE: *Daredevil #179* (February 1982). Art by Frank Miller (pencils) and Klaus Janson (colors).

OPPOSITE PAGE: Detail from *The Marvel Fumetti Book* (April 1984), a humorous behind-the-scenes look at Marvel featuring photo comics. From left to right: Jim Shooter, Tom DeFalco, Mark Gruenwald, Ralph Macchio, Carl Potts.

In the years that followed, Logan would reappear in the anthology *Marvel Comics Presents*. In 1989 Claremont also teamed up with British writer and artist Alan Davis to launch a series set in the U.K., *Excalibur*, featuring X-Men characters alongside local Super Heroes like Captain Britain.

Meanwhile, a young writer who had debuted as an inker was poised to make his mark on comic book history when he turned his sights on a series that had been lagging in terms of sales. Frank Miller had honed his skills on *Marvel Team-Up* and a couple issues of *The Spectacular Spider-Man* guest-starring Daredevil.

Not long thereafter, Miller was assigned to *Daredevil* beginning with issue #158 (cover-dated May 1979), where he initially worked with writer Roger McKenzie. Ten issues later, Miller took over writing duties and began to develop the darker atmospheres that had already been a hallmark of his artwork. He was responsible for introducing characters like the sensei Stick and Elektra, a tormented ninja and Matt Murdock's former girlfriend; he also redefined supporting characters like crime boss Wilson "Kingpin" Fisk, the lethal assassin Bullseye, and investigative journalist Ben Urich.

1980

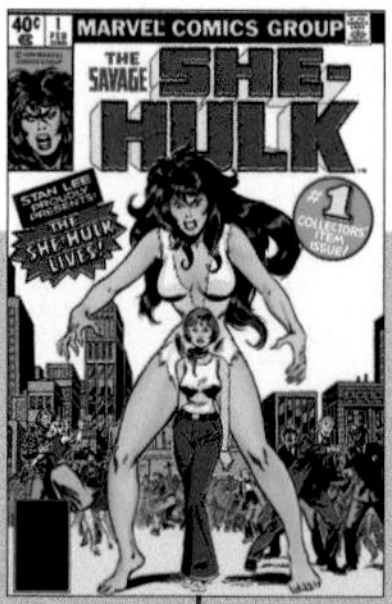
MARVEL COMICS GROUP
THE SAVAGE SHE-HULK

FEBRUARY 1980

Jen "She-Hulk" Walters, a Stan Lee and John Buscema creation, makes her debut in *The Savage She-Hulk #1*.

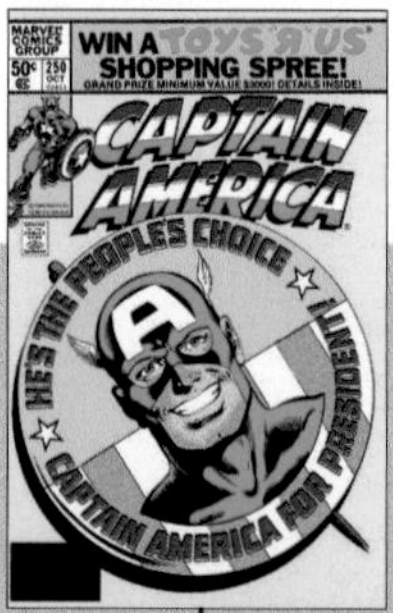
WIN A TOYS R US SHOPPING SPREE!
CAPTAIN AMERICA
HE'S THE PEOPLE'S CHOICE
CAPTAIN AMERICA FOR PRESIDENT!

OCTOBER 1980

Cap for President! In *Captain America #250*, by Roger Stern and John Byrne, Steve is asked to run for the country's highest office, but refuses.

THE MARVEL
FUMETTI
BOOK™

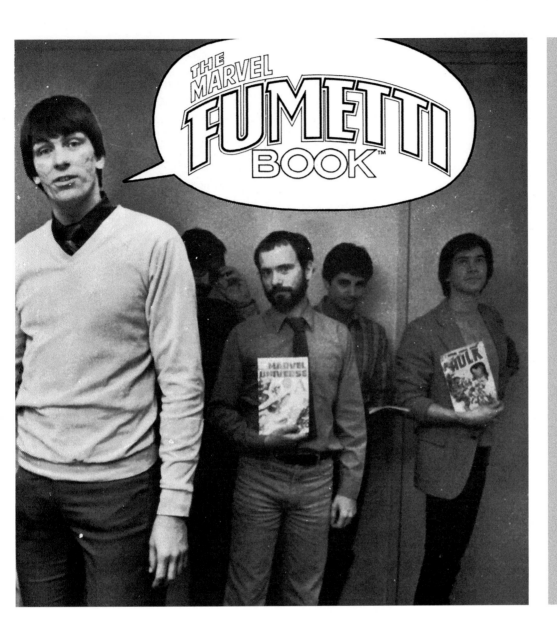

URBAN VIGILANTE

On the streets of New York, another Marvel Super Hero would rise to popularity in the 1980s: the Punisher. Vigilante Frank Castle made his debut in *The Amazing Spider-Man* #129 in 1974, and in the years that followed was relegated to bit parts. Marine veteran Castle had declared his own personal war on crime after his family was gunned down in a hail of crossfire in an exchange between rival mob factions. For years, the writer Steven Grant had tried proposing to Marvel a limited series based on the character. He finally got the green light for the project when artist Mike Zeck, riding the success of *Secret Wars*, signed on. The 1986 limited series *The Punisher* became an iconic hit and spawned more comics starring Castle in the years to come. In 1987, the ongoing series *The Punisher* made its debut, which ran all the way to 1995 and issue #104. Fans were also treated to *The Punisher War Journal* (80 issues, 1988–1995), *The Punisher War Zone* (41 issues, 1992–1995), and a slew of specials and graphic novels.

MARVEL COMICS GROUP
DAREDEVIL
THE MAN WITHOUT FEAR!
ELECKTRA

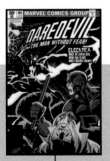

JANUARY 1981

Elektra makes her debut in *Daredevil #168*.

WIN A Columbia TEN-SPEED FORMULA 10 RACER!
KING-SIZE ANNUAL!
AVENGERS

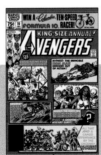

DECEMBER 1981

The Avengers Annual #10 features the first-ever appearance by Rogue, as a member of the Brotherhood of Evil Mutants.

MARVEL COMICS GROUP
PETER PARKER, THE SPECTACULAR
SPIDER-MAN
CLOAK
DAGGER

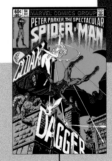

MARCH 1982

Vigilantes Cloak and Dagger make their debut in *The Spectacular Spider-Man #64*.

Over the course of a handful of issues, with the help of inker Klaus Janson, Miller would lay the foundation for Daredevil's most celebrated and imitated incarnation. The high point of Miller's first run on *Daredevil* was the death of Elektra in issue #181 (cover-dated April 1982).

Three years after leaving the series, Miller resumed writing for *Daredevil* in issue #227, in what was to be the start of yet another earth-shattering cycle: "Born Again." In this saga, illustrated by David Mazzucchelli, who was heavily influenced by Miller's dark themes, Matt's old flame and secretary Karen Page revealed Daredevil's secret identity to Kingpin. Thus began the fall and redemption/ rise of Matt Murdock.

Meanwhile, event comics featuring expanded casts of Super Heroes fulfilled every reader's question, "I wonder what would happen if X met Y and they fought Z?" The first of its kind, *Contest of Champions*, had originally been slated for publication as a limited series to be released in conjunction with the start of the 1980 Summer Olympics in Moscow. But the U.S. boycott following the Soviet invasion of Afghanistan led Marvel to delay the release and revise the project. As a result, it wasn't until 1982 that *Contest of Champions* reached fans.

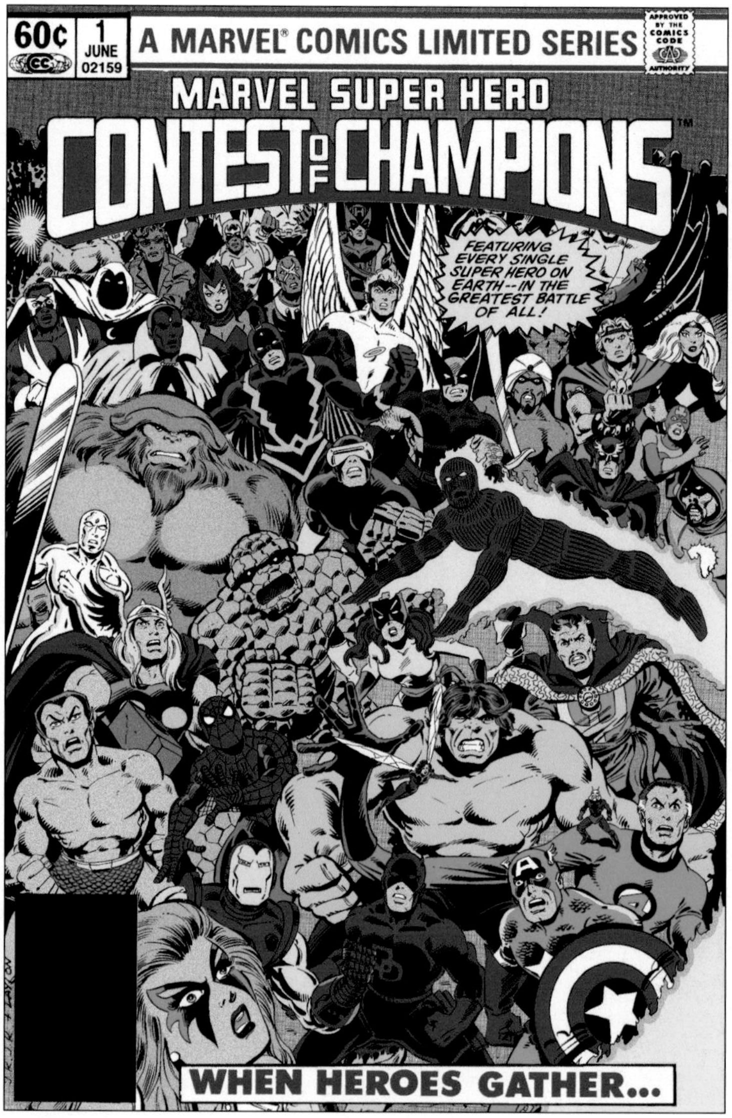
60¢
1 JUNE
02159
A MARVEL COMICS LIMITED SERIES
MARVEL SUPER HERO
CONTEST OF CHAMPIONS
FEATURING EVERY SINGLE SUPER HERO ON EARTH--IN THE GREATEST BATTLE OF ALL!
WHEN HEROES GATHER...

RIGHT: *Marvel Super Hero Contest of Champions #1* (June 1982). Art by John Romita, Jr. (pencils) and Bob Layton (inks).

OPOSITE PAGE: Cover detail from *Daredevil: Born Again* (1987), collecting the "Born Again" storyline from *Daredevil #227–231*. Cover by David Mazzucchelli.

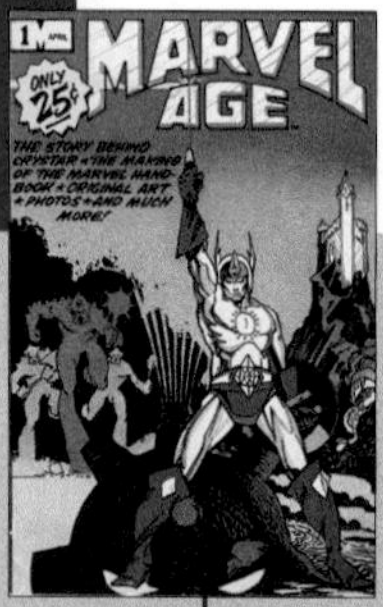
MARVEL AGE
ONLY 25¢

MARCH 1983

The first issue of *Marvel Age*, a long-running magazine featuring news and previews, hits the stores.

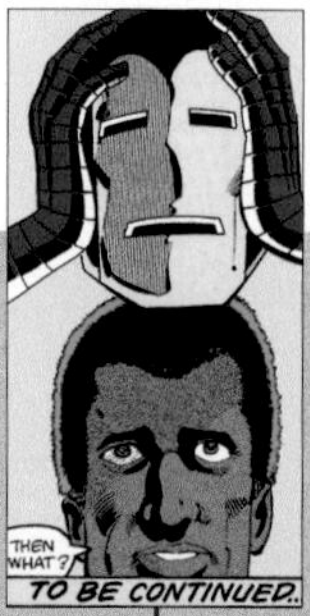
THEN WHAT?
TO BE CONTINUED.

APRIL 1983

African-American Marines pilot James Rhodes appears as Iron Man for the first time.

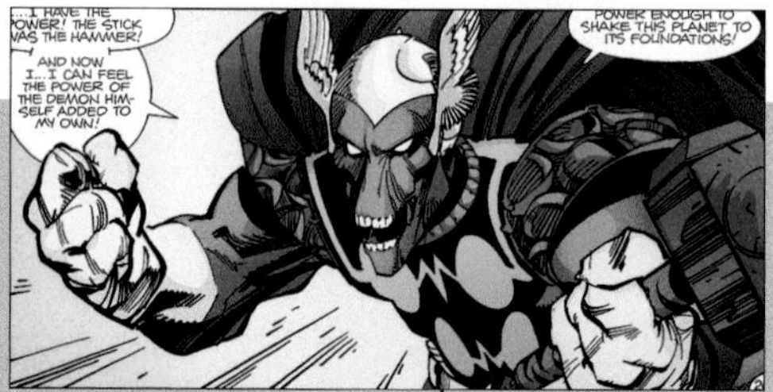
AND NOW I...I CAN FEEL THE POWER OF THE DEMON HIMSELF ADDED TO MY OWN!
POWER ENOUGH TO SHAKE THIS PLANET TO ITS FOUNDATIONS!

NOVEMBER 1983

Alien Beta-Ray Bill wields Thor's hammer for the first time.

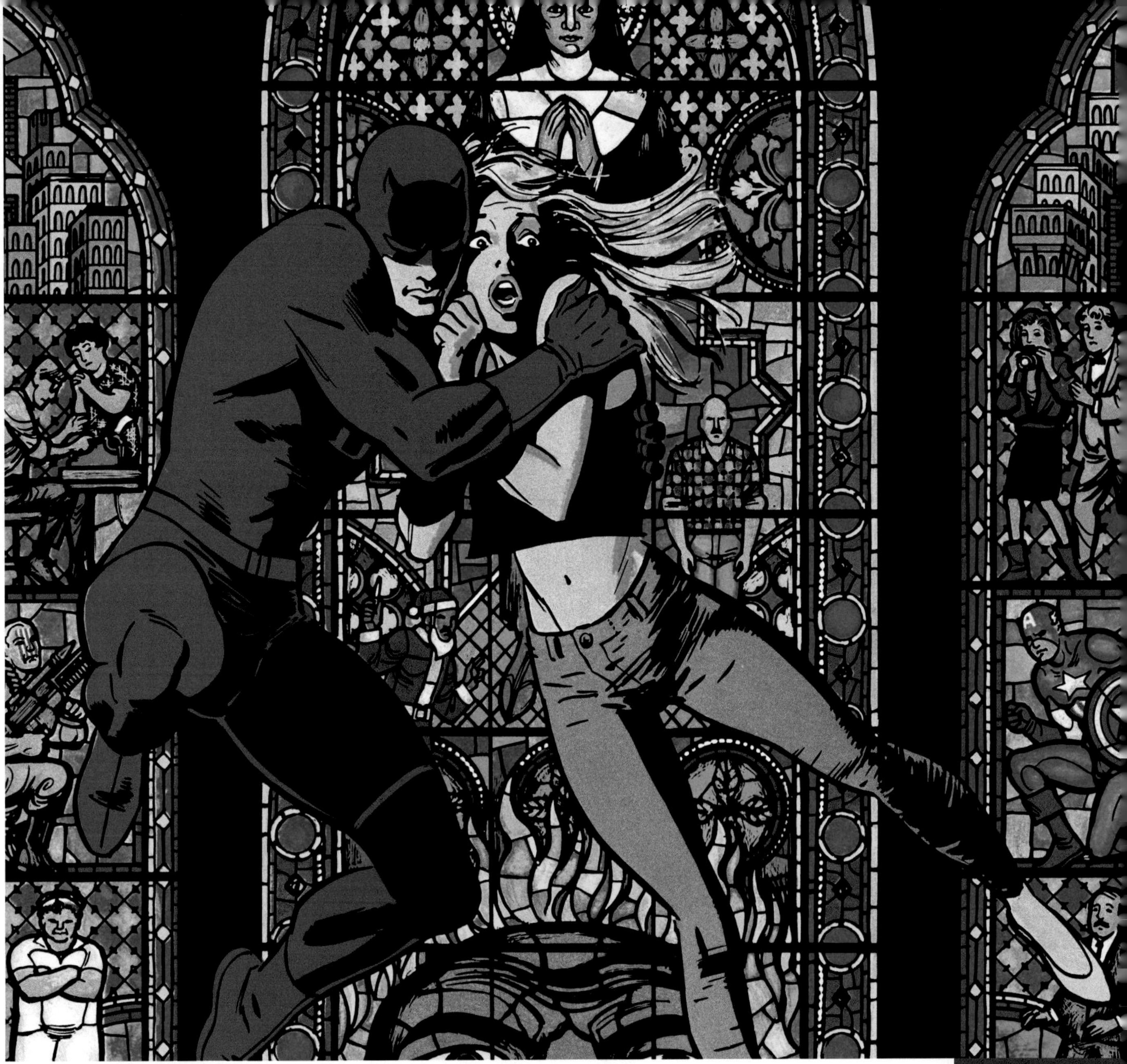

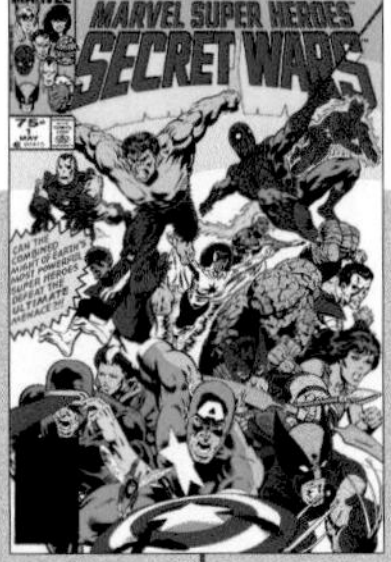
#1 IN A TWELVE-ISSUE LIMITED SERIES
MARVEL SUPER HEROES
SECRET WARS

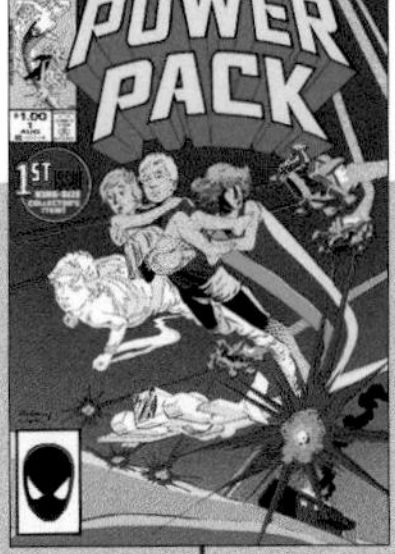
POWER
PACK

MAY 1984

Marvel Super Heroes Secret Wars #1 goes on sale.

AUGUST 1984

Writer Louise Simonson and artist June Brigman launch *Power Pack*, featuring a team of kid heroes.

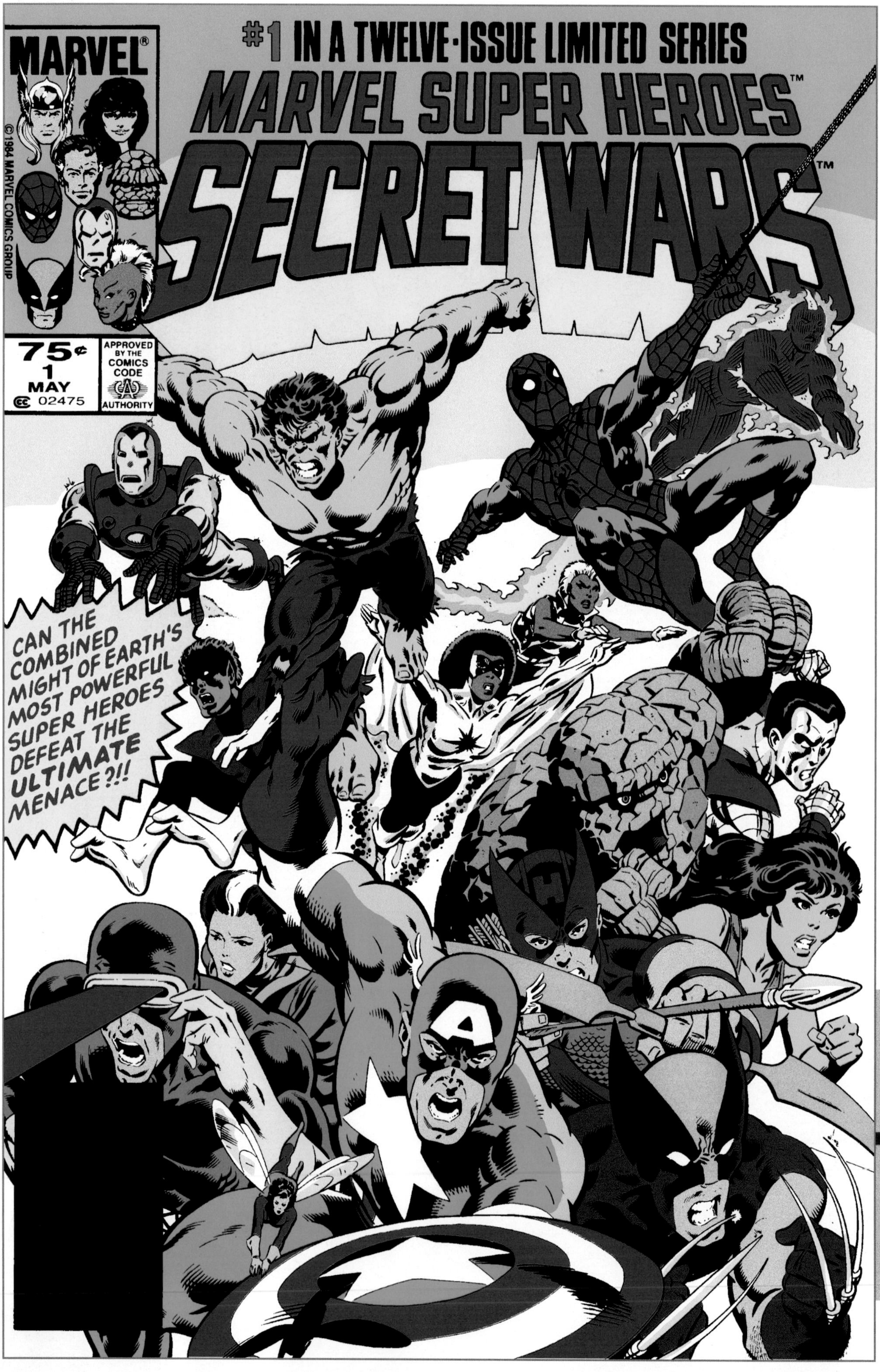
#1 IN A TWELVE-ISSUE LIMITED SERIES
MARVEL®
MARVEL SUPER HEROES™
SECRET WARS™
© 1984 MARVEL COMICS GROUP
75¢
1
MAY
02475
APPROVED BY THE COMICS CODE AUTHORITY
CAN THE COMBINED MIGHT OF EARTH'S MOST POWERFUL SUPER HEROES DEFEAT THE ULTIMATE MENACE?!!

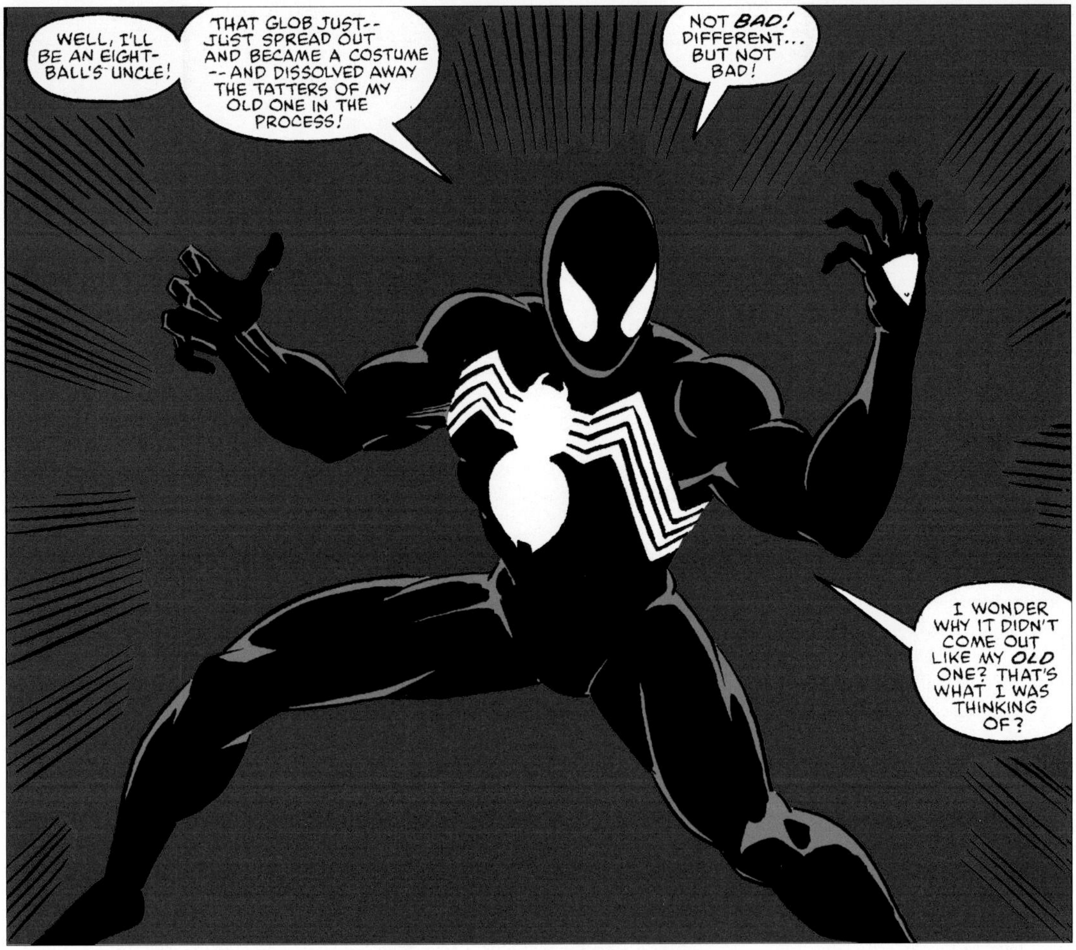
WELL, I'LL BE AN EIGHT-BALL'S UNCLE!
THAT GLOB JUST-- JUST SPREAD OUT AND BECAME A COSTUME --AND DISSOLVED AWAY THE TATTERS OF MY OLD ONE IN THE PROCESS!
NOT BAD! DIFFERENT... BUT NOT BAD!
I WONDER WHY IT DIDN'T COME OUT LIKE MY OLD ONE? THAT'S WHAT I WAS THINKING OF?

THIS PAGE: Spider-Man tries on his new costume for the first time in *Marvel Super Heroes Secret Wars* *#8* (December 1984). Script by Jim Shooter. Art by Mike Zeck (pencils), John Beatty, Jack Abel, Mike Esposito (inks), Christie Scheele (colors).

OPPOSITE PAGE: *Marvel Super Heroes Secret Wars #1* (May 1984). Art by Mike Zeck (pencils).

The three issues recount a cosmic game played by two powerful Super Villains who use Super Heroes from all over the world as pawns. A couple years down the road, Marvel raised the stakes when it released *Marvel Super Heroes Secret Wars*, a series written by Jim Shooter, with artwork by Mike Zeck. The 12-issue limited series featured all-time favorite Super Heroes and their most formidable Super Villains, locked in a fight to the finish staged by the almost omnipotent Beyonder on Battleworld, a planet he created in a far-off galaxy.

The project tied in with a successful toy line from Mattel. *Marvel Super Heroes Secret Wars* was such a big hit that the impact on the Marvel Universe was astounding. It wasn't long before work began on a sequel. Among the developments it sparked: a new costume for Spidey, a new lineup for the Fantastic Four, and the debut of the second Spider-Woman. A year later, Shooter wrote the scripts for *Secret Wars II*, whose plot wound up branching out to various monthly series.

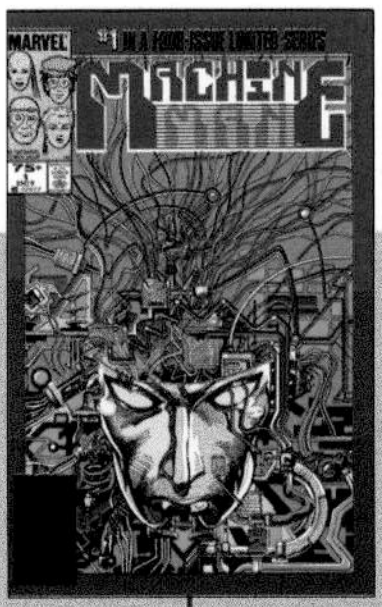

OCTOBER 1984

Barry Windsor-Smith illustrates the limited series starring Machine Man, the Super Hero created by Jack Kirby for the comic book adaptation of *2001: A Space Odyssey*.

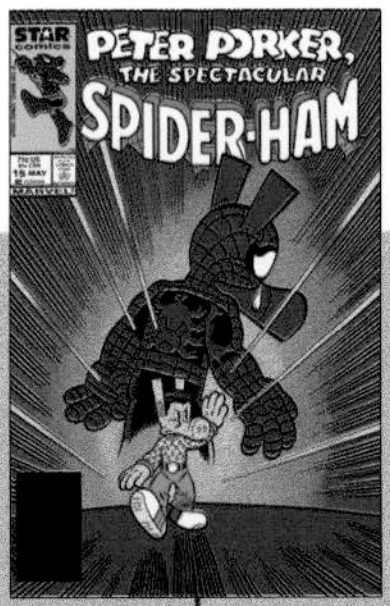
PETER PORKER, THE SPECTACULAR SPIDER-HAM

MAY 1985

The series *Peter Porker, the Spectacular Spider-Ham*, a Spider-Man parody, makes its debut under the newly born imprint for children Star Comics.

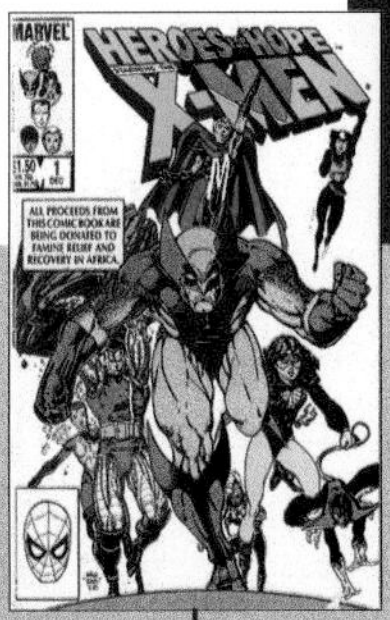
HEROES FOR HOPE
X-MEN

DECEMBER 1985

Marvel launches *Heroes for Hope*: Starring the X-Men, the comic book was designed to promote awaress of famine in Africa. Proceeds went to relief efforts.

MARVELOUS WOMEN

The 1980s saw the rise of heroes like Captain Marvel, She-Hulk, Elektra, and others who would change the face of the Marvel Universe.

The 1980s saw the rise of a new wave of female characters. When the Kree hero Mar-Vell was struck down by cancer (in the first Marvel Graphic Novel, Jim Starlin's *The Death of Captain Marvel*), the code name was inherited by a new heroine, Monica Rambeau. The new Captain Marvel made her debut in 1982 in *The Amazing Spider-Man Annual #16*. She would soon join the Avengers, and eventually became the team's leader.

Then there was She-Hulk, who got her superpowers through a blood transfusion from her cousin, Bruce Banner. She first appeared in *The Savage She-Hulk #1* (1980), a series launched by Stan Lee and John Buscema. Thanks to John Byrne, who had her take the Thing's place in the Fantastic Four, She-Hulk became more than just her cousin's female counterpart.

During Byrne's acclaimed tenure at the helm of *The Fantastic Four* (#232–293), he turned Susan Richards into an even more three-dimensional character, a far cry from the damsel in distress she'd been at the start. New arrival Elektra, despite her death in *Daredevil*, was a big hit with fans. She would soon be brought back to life and featured in memorable sagas and graphic novels, some of which were written by Frank Miller—like the limited series *Elektra: Assassin* (illustrated by Bill Sienkiewicz) and the 1990 graphic novel *Elektra Lives Again* (which was also illustrated by Miller).

Meanwhile, in *The Uncanny X-Men*, Chris Claremont was painstakingly developing the cast of female supporting characters, which included Rogue, who went from Super Villain to Super Hero; Storm, in search of redemption after temporarily losing her powers; teenager Kitty Pryde, who cut her teeth on the battlefield; and Carol Danvers, the former Ms. Marvel who morphed into the powerful Binary in *The Uncanny X-Men*.

The 1980s also ushered in some big changes for Spider-Man. There was his fiery relationship with reformed thief Black Cat; the death of his ally, N.Y.P.D. captain Jean DeWolff; the dramatic saga *Kraven's Last Hunt;* and, most notably, his marriage to Mary Jane Watson.

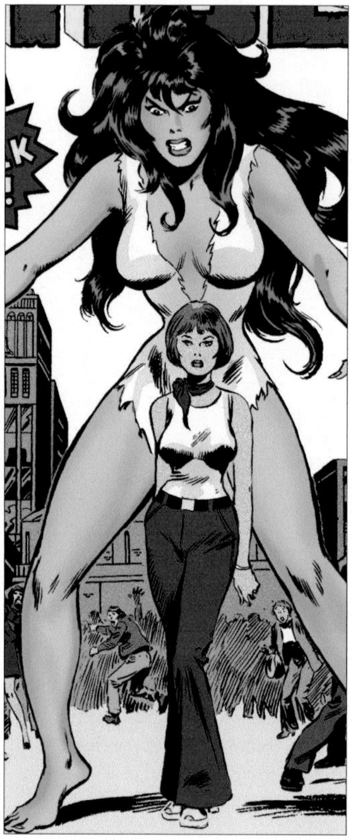

RIGHT: Cover detail from *The Savage She-Hulk #1* (February 1980). Art by John Buscema.

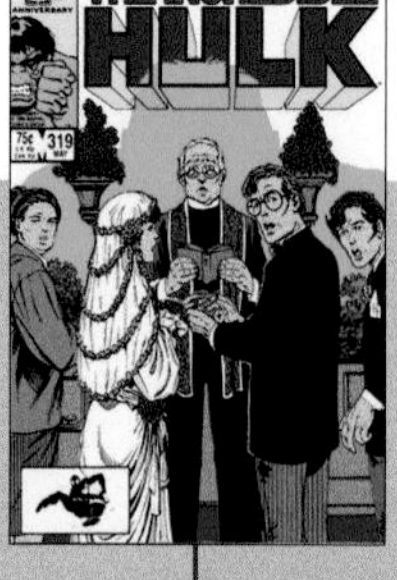
THE INCREDIBLE HULK
319

MAY 1986

Bruce Banner and Betty Ross are married in *The Incredible Hulk #319.*

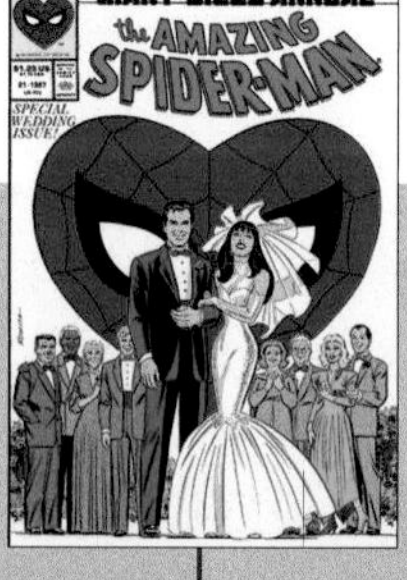
MARVEL
GIANT-SIZED ANNUAL
the AMAZING SPIDER-MAN
SPECIAL WEDDING ISSUE!

1987

Peter Parker and Mary Jane Watson tie the knot in *The Amazing Spider-Man Annual #21.*

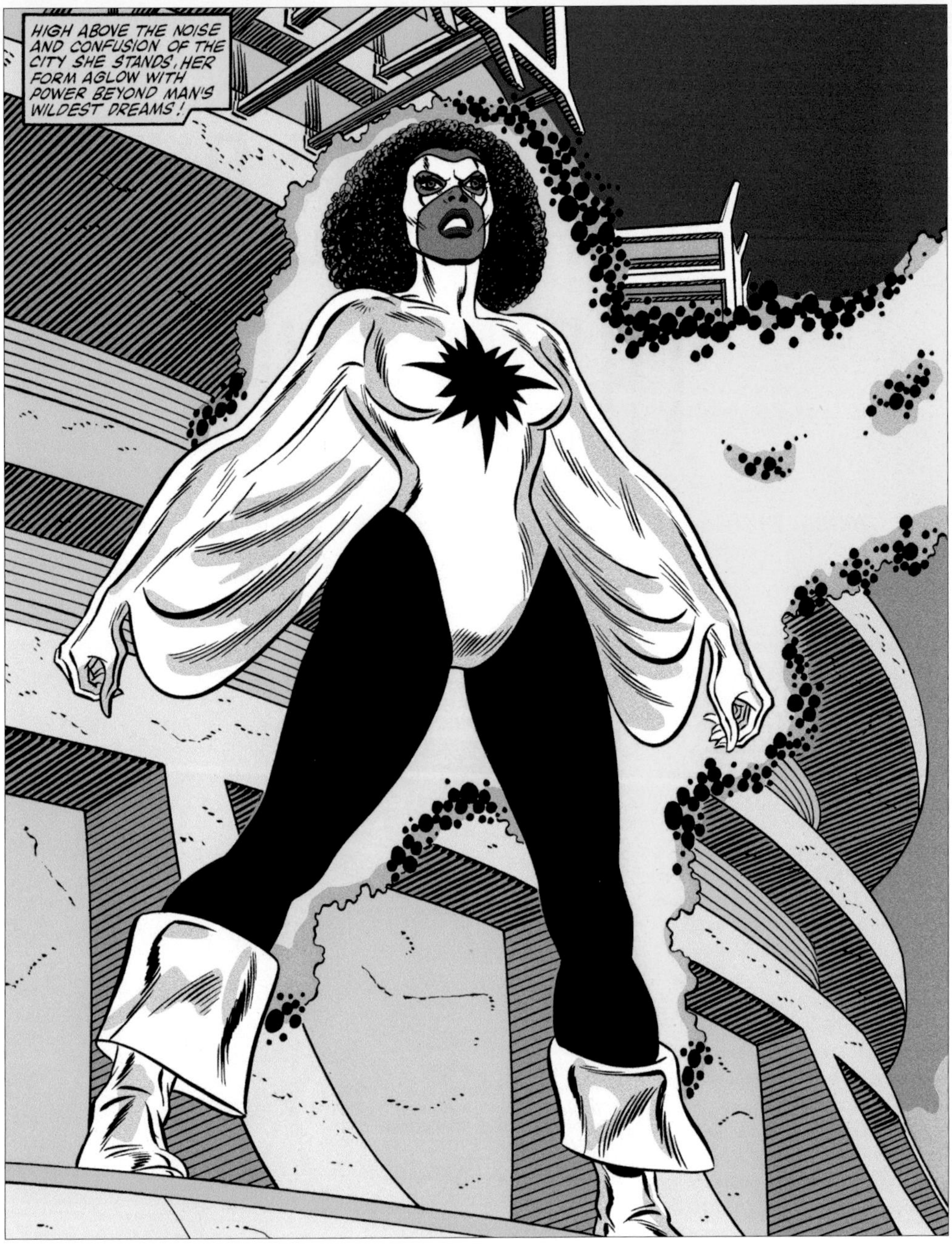
HIGH ABOVE THE NOISE AND CONFUSION OF THE CITY SHE STANDS, HER FORM AGLOW WITH POWER BEYOND MAN'S WILDEST DREAMS!

LEFT: Monica Rambeau makes her appearance as Captain Marvel from *The Amazing Spider-Man Annual #16* (October 1982). Script by Roger Stern. Art by John Romita, Jr. (pencils), John Romita, Sr. (inks), Stan Goldberg (colors), Jim Novak (letters).

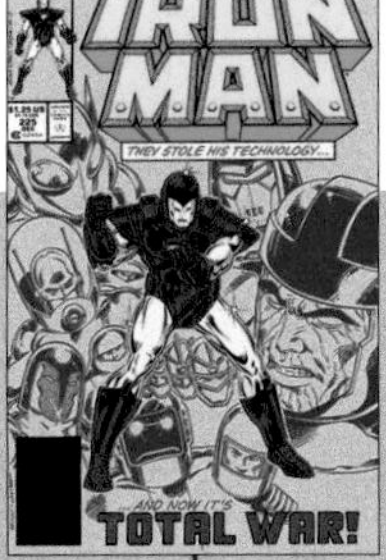
MARVEL
IRON MAN
THEY STOLE HIS TECHNOLOGY...
AND NOW IT'S TOTAL WAR!

DECEMBER 1987

The high-power saga Armor Wars gets underway in *Iron Man #225*.

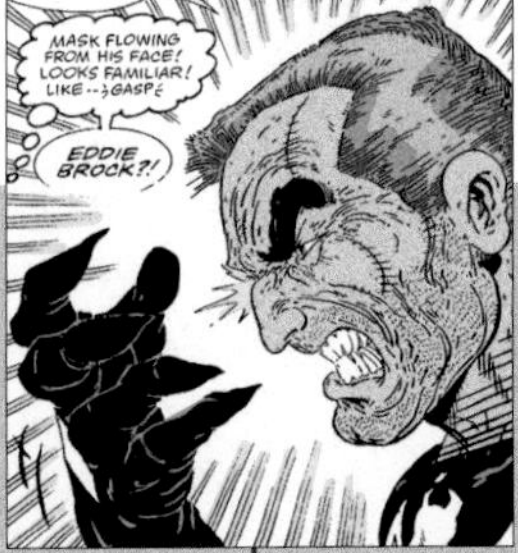
PERHAPS THIS WILL HELP!
MASK FLOWING FROM HIS FACE! LOOKS FAMILIAR! LIKE--¿GASP¿
EDDIE BROCK?!

MARCH 1988

Venom reveals himself to his nemesis Spider-Man in *The Amazing Spider-Man #300* by David Michelinie and Todd McFarlane.

IN A CLASS BY THEMSELVES

As the 1980s roared on, new artists arrived on the scene to take Marvel to even greater heights.

Frank Miller. John Byrne. Chris Claremont. Walt Simonson. Jim Lee. Rob Liefeld. Todd McFarlane. Mike Mignola. Arthur Adams. Peter David. An impressive array of talents who shaped the world of Marvel in the 1980s (and '90s). In a decade that proved crucial in the evolution of the medium, the Marvel talent roster was home to a bevy of masters of their crafts, par excellence. There was Byrne, who, following the success of *The Uncanny X-Men*, was known as the King Midas of Comics.

In those years, artists with a penchant for the classics consolidated their careers—people like Barry Windsor-Smith, who was the man behind some of the best-loved X-stories, and Bob Layton, who drew the definitive version of Iron Man, as well as several of that character's most important sagas. The masters

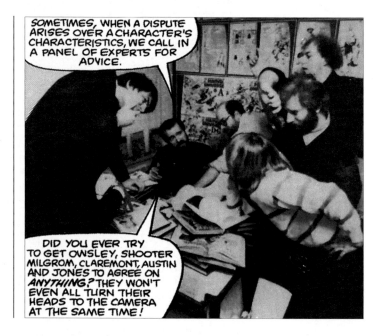

SOMETIMES, WHEN A DISPUTE ARISES OVER A CHARACTER'S CHARACTERISTICS, WE CALL IN A PANEL OF EXPERTS FOR ADVICE.
DID YOU EVER TRY TO GET OWSLEY, SHOOTER MILGROM, CLAREMONT, AUSTIN AND JONES TO AGREE ON ANYTHING? THEY WON'T EVEN ALL TURN THEIR HEADS TO THE CAMERA AT THE SAME TIME!

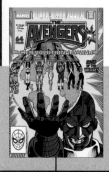

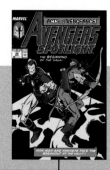

LEFT: Detail from *The Marvel Fumetti Book.*

AUGUST 1988

"The Evolutionary War" is the first of a new generation of crossover stories in annuals, linking various Marvel series together.

DECEMBER 1989

"Acts of Vengeance," an event that incorporated various series, featured Super Villains exchanging foes.

1990

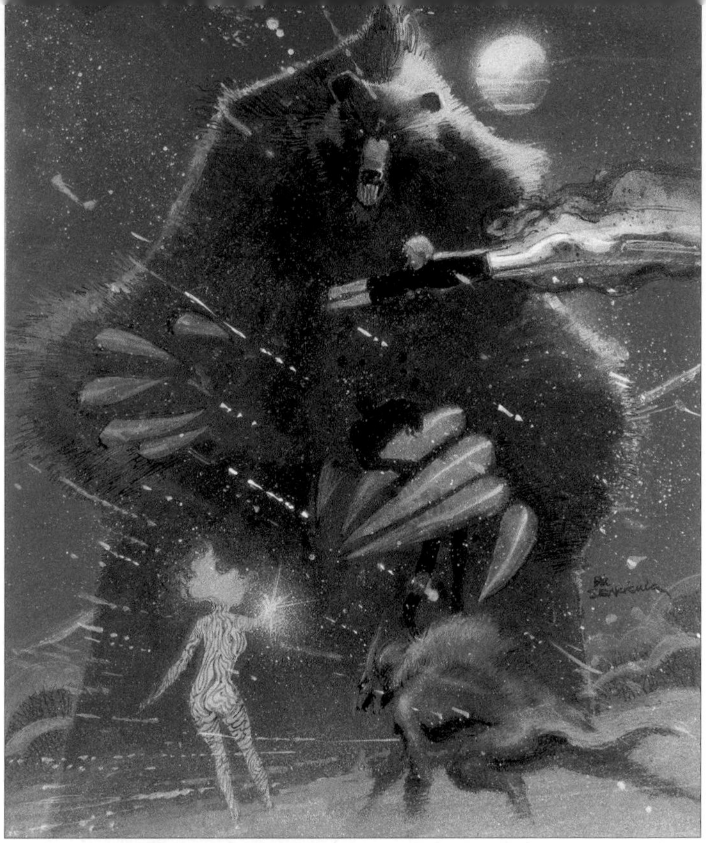

of the '60s and '70s made way for their most worthy heirs, including the aforementioned John Romita, Jr., who in his younger days incorporated much of his father's style, but went on to develop his own unique synthesis; and Bill Sienkiewicz, who experimented with oil painting, collages, and other unorthodox techniques.

Another revamping of Daredevil got underway in the late '80s thanks to writer Ann Nocenti, who, working with Romita, Jr., explored themes like environmental protection, religion, and women's rights through the mutant psychopath Typhoid Mary. Not lacking were writers and artists who exploited their in-depth knowledge of Marvel continuity to come up with memorable stories. Among them, Mark Gruenwald surely stood out. He created the young new Super Hero Quasar, and also penned long cycles for Captain America and Squadron Supreme, featuring a revisionist interpretation of the Avengers' old foes.

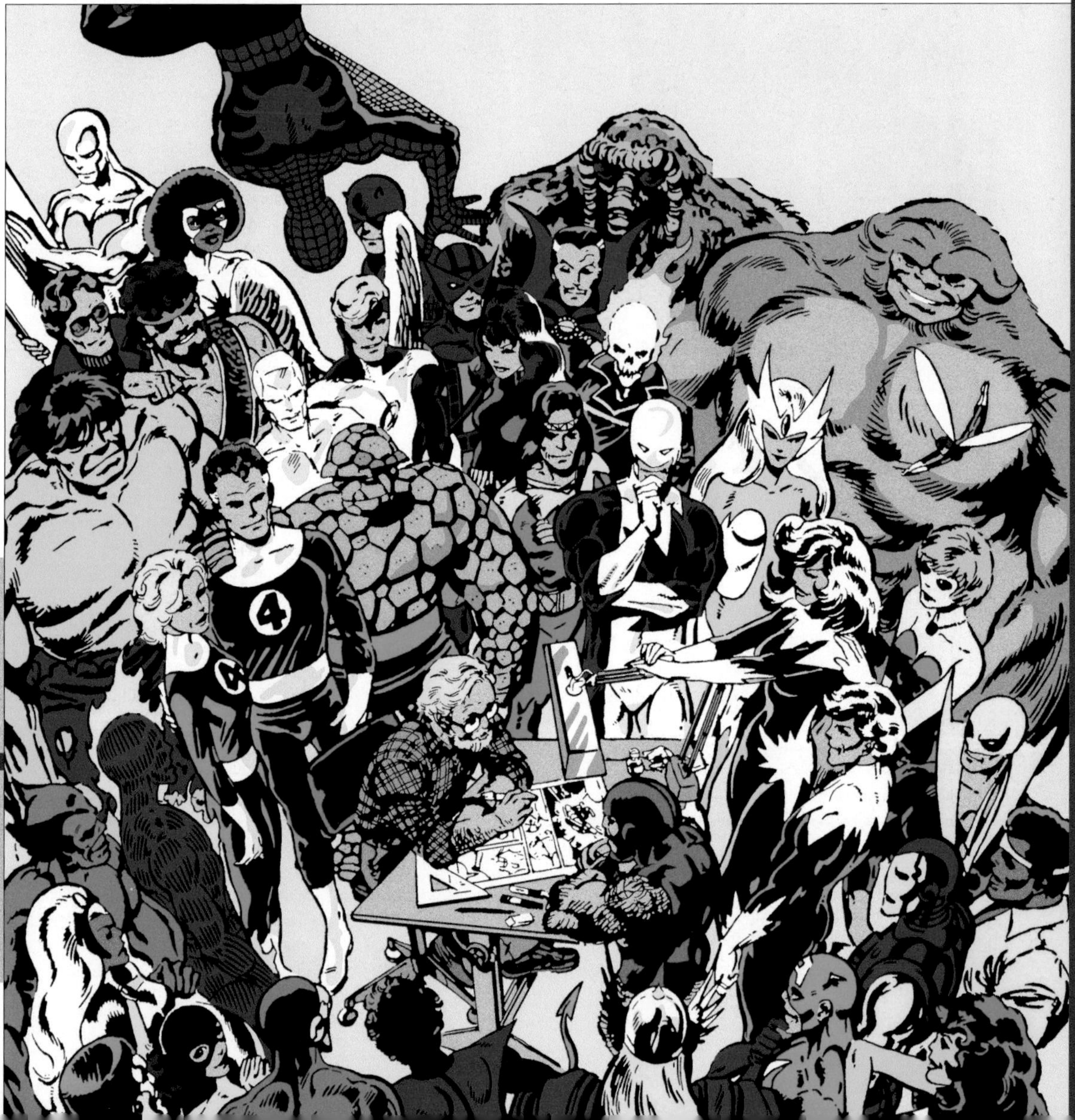

ABOVE: Artist Bill Sienkiewicz's *New Mutants #19* cover art (September 1984).

LEFT: Artist John Byrne with some heroic friends. Art by John Byrne.

MIGHTY MEDIA ON THE MOVE

Marvel continued to make a mark in popular culture, as it became a staple of one of the most beloved celebrations in the U.S.

ABOVE: The executives of Marvel Productions, Ltd. From left to right: Lee Gunther, David DePatie, Jim Galton, and Stan Lee.

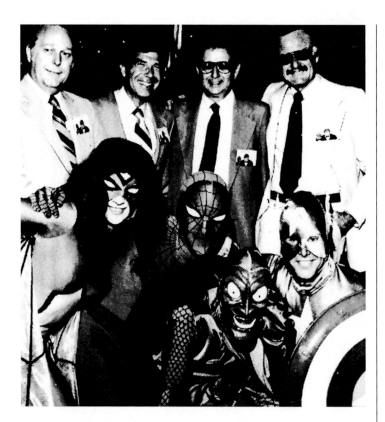

The popularity of Marvel characters continued to grow year after year. In part, this was due to their ever-expanding presence on TV. Newly founded, Hollywood-based Marvel Productions produced a pair of cartoon series destined to become classics. In 1981 the company simultaneously debuted *Spider-Man and His Amazing Friends* (which teamed Spidey up with Iceman and a new heroine, the flaming mutant Firestar) as well as the syndicated *Spider-Man*. They were joined in 1982 by *The Incredible Hulk*, which Stan Lee himself narrated.

Meanwhile, two of the most unlikely candidates from the Marvel pantheon would appear in live-action movies: *Howard the Duck* (1986, directed by Willard Huyck) and *The Punisher*, starring Dolph Lundgren (1989, directed by Mark Goldblatt).

The Incredible Hulk live-action series returned to the airwaves, spawning three made-for-TV movies: *The Incredible Hulk Returns* (1988), *The Trial of The Incredible Hulk* (1989) and *The Death of The Incredible Hulk* (1990). The first of these featured an appearance by a very loosely interpreted version of Thor, while Daredevil showed up in the latter—in the hopes that Matt Murdock's alter ego might get a TV series of his own if the movie proved successful enough.

If year in, year out comics stories gradually alluded to the end of the Cold War with the phasing out of once-frequent Soviet villains, wounds from the Vietnam War took a long time healing. Marvel explored that theme in *The 'Nam*, a war series based on the memories of writer Doug Murray and editor Larry Hama. Some characters featured in Super Hero series were still haunted by their experiences at the front, like Flash Thompson, an old acquaintance of Peter Parker's, and Daredevil's disturbed foe Nuke, another Frank Miller brainchild.

Meanwhile, children were playing with action figures from Mattel's *Marvel Super Heroes Secret Wars* collection, which took its cue from the comic book series created by Shooter and Zeck. G.I. Joe and the Transformers characters took the opposite route, beginning their lives as toy lines by Hasbro, with Marvel helping to develop the storylines and publishing two long-running comics series.

But it was Spider-Man who helped elevate Marvel to pop-culture immortality. To celebrate his and Mary Jane's wedding in 1987's *The Amazing Spider-Man Annual #21*, Marvel arranged a wedding ceremony at Shea Stadium in Queens, New York, where Peter Parker grew up. Prior to the Mets-Pirates game, with Stan Lee himself officiating, two actors dressed as Spidey and his beloved exchanged vows before a crowd of 45,000.

Later that year, a giant Spider-Man balloon made its debut in the Macy's Thanksgiving Day Parade—at long last, the web-slinger really was soaring amid the skyscrapers of New York! ■

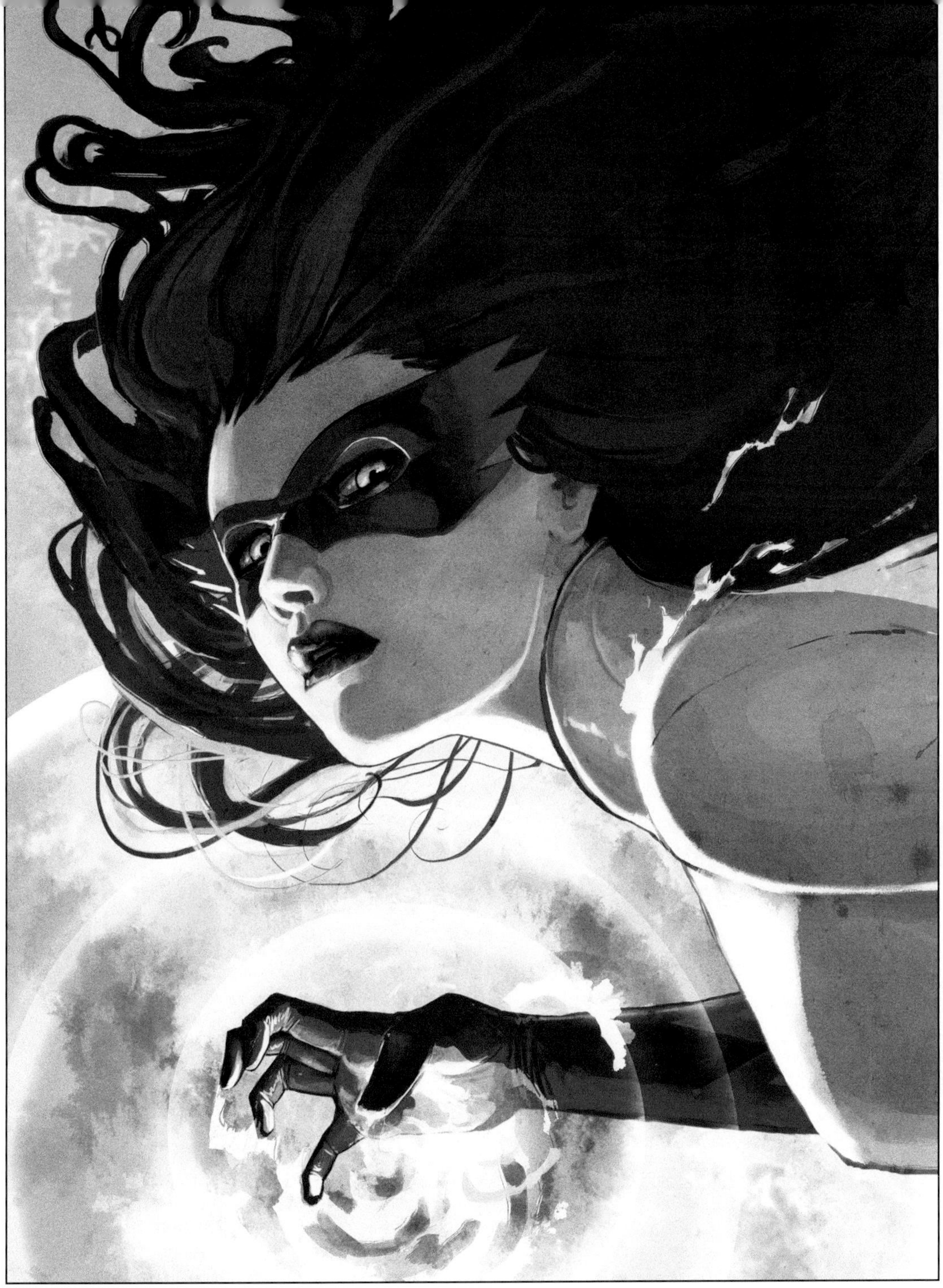

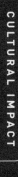

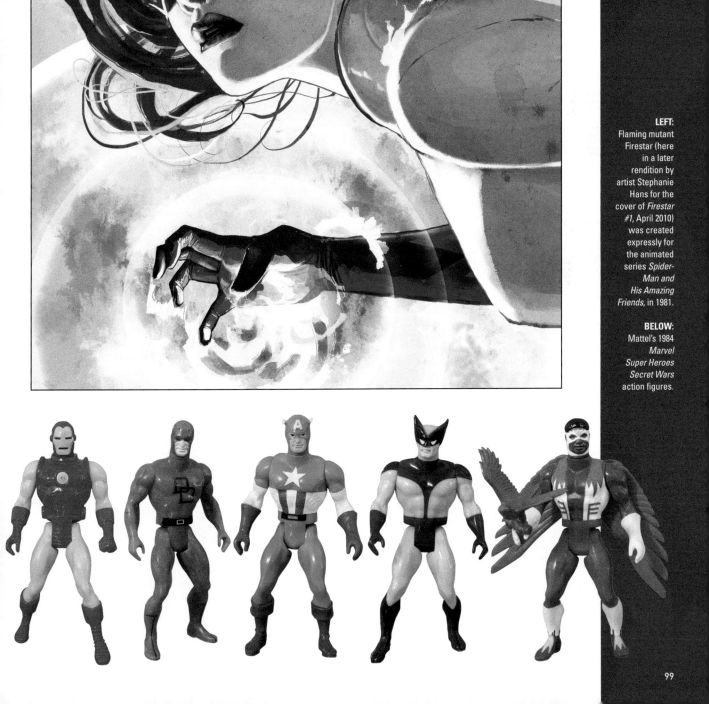

LEFT: Flaming mutant Firestar (here in a later rendition by artist Stephanie Hans for the cover of *Firestar #1*, April 2010) was created expressly for the animated series *Spider-Man and His Amazing Friends*, in 1981.

BELOW: Mattel's 1984 *Marvel Super Heroes Secret Wars* action figures.

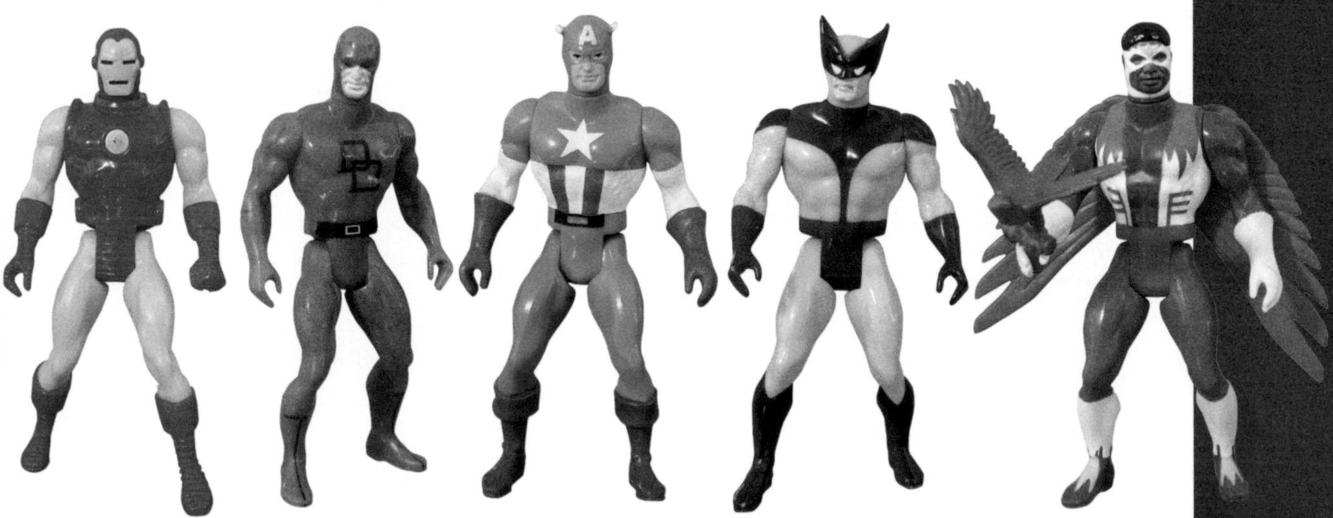

THE 1990s

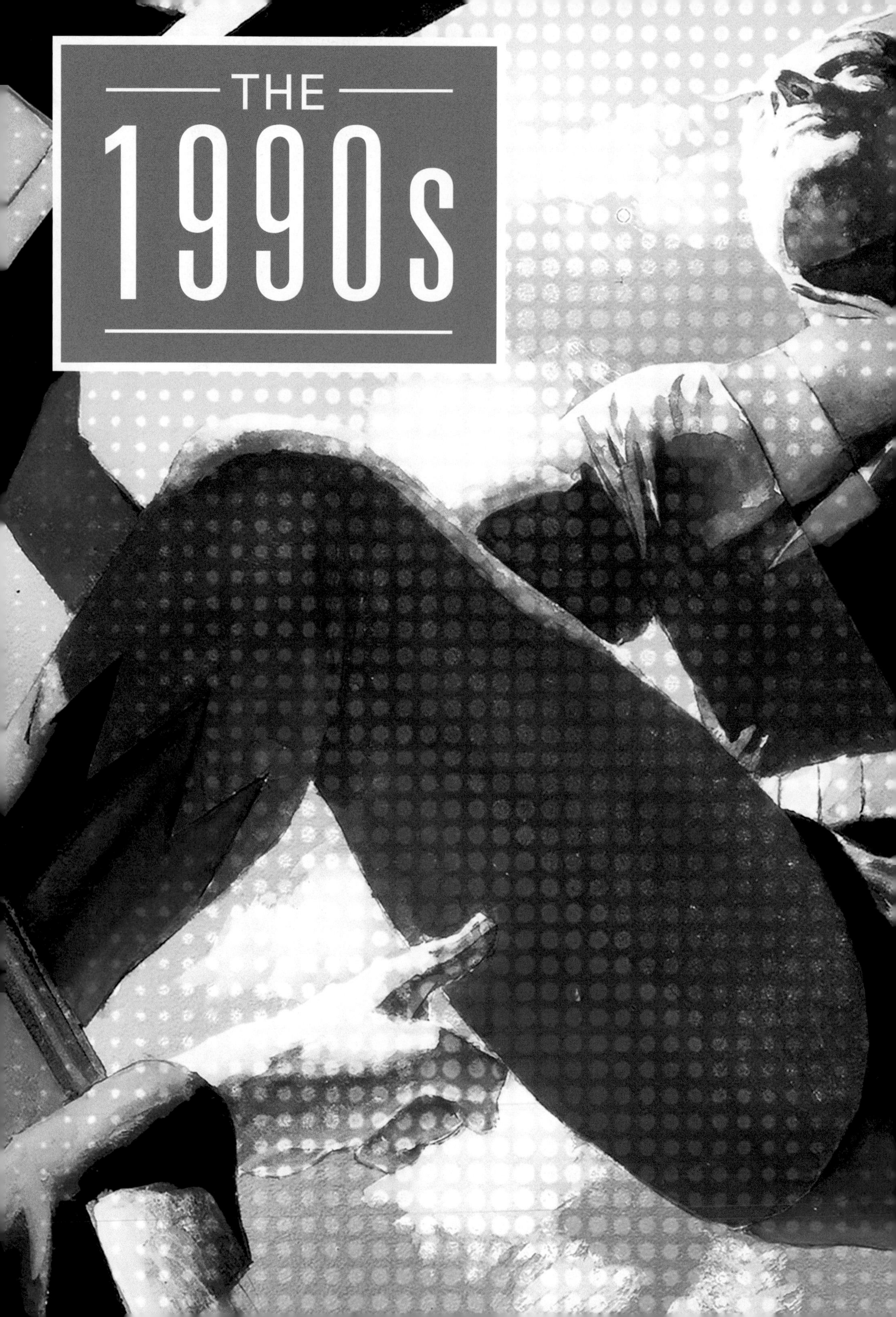

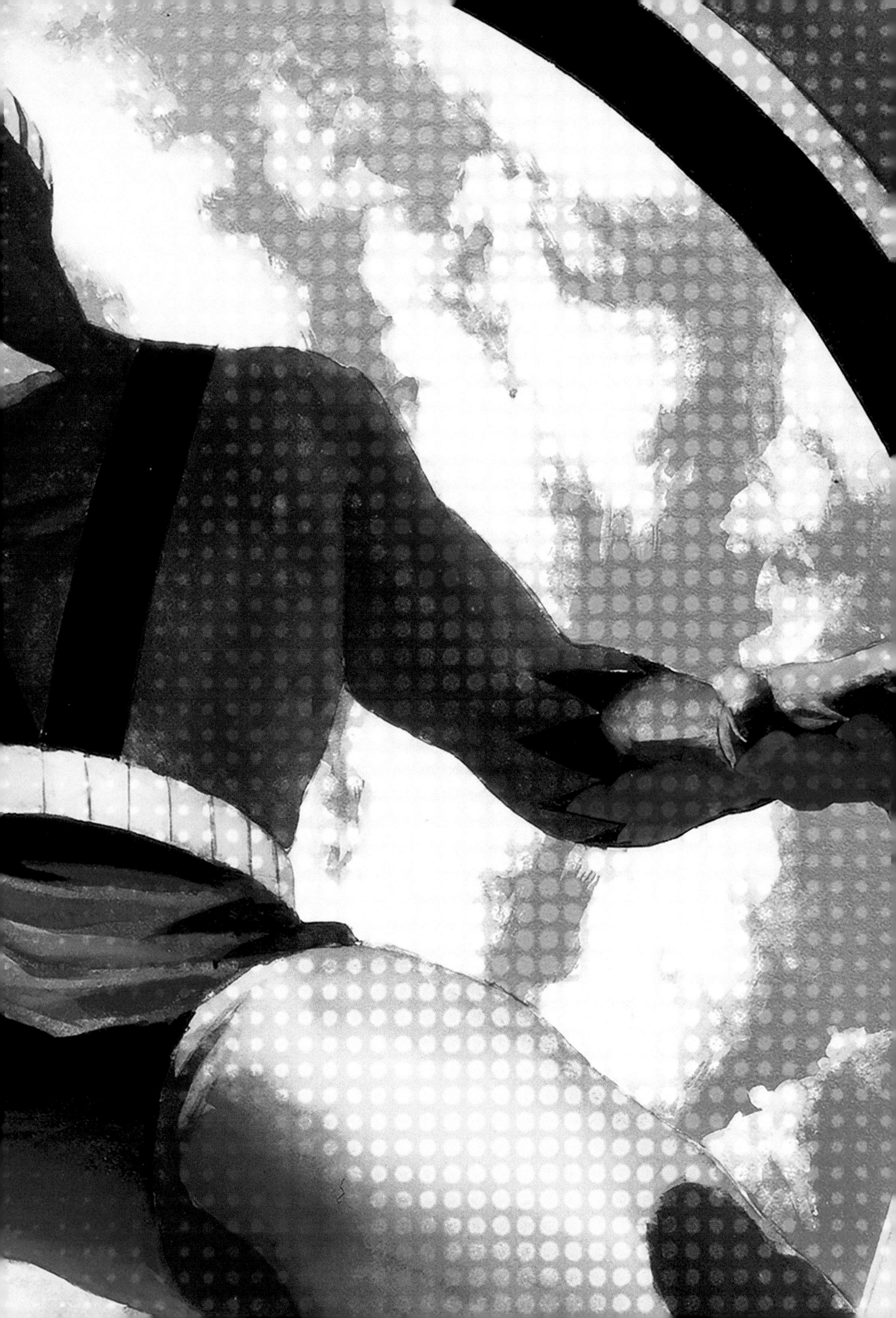

A GIANT STEP FORWARD

Spider-Man (August 1, 1990): 2 million copies sold. _X-Force_ (August 1, 1991): 4 million copies. _X-Men_ (October 1, 1991): 8 million copies. For Marvel the '90s rolled in with dizzying numbers.

Behind such extraordinary figures lay a series of unique coincidences. While they certainly had to do with the spirit of the times, there was also a wave of variant covers featuring incredible effects—many of which were interlocking—and fans who worshipped the new worldwide stars, the writers and artists behind the comics, and the spread of comic book stores and wholesale purchases by speculators. Of course, not every comic was a big hit, but sales were up even for series that had been less fortunate, and spin-offs and limited series events with connecting plots—the crossovers that had already been so successfully tried in the 1980s—came rolling off the presses in great quantities.

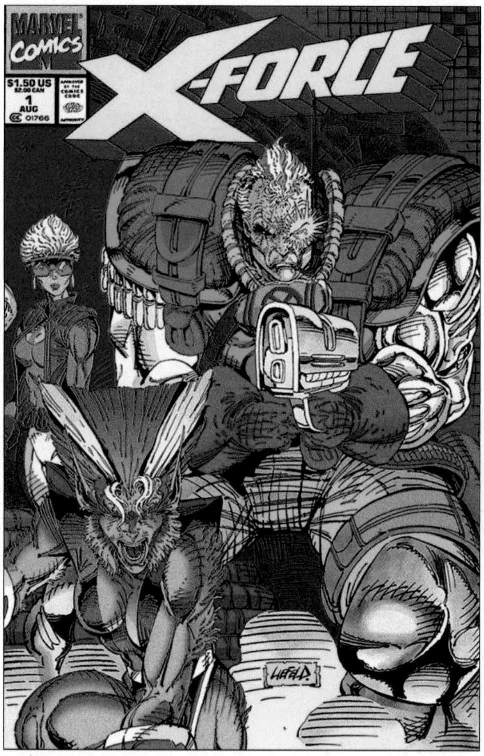
MARVEL COMICS
X-FORCE
$1.50 US
1
AUG
LIEFELD

ABOVE: Cable takes the reins of a new X-team in *X-Force #1* (August 1991). Art by Rob Liefeld.

The British imprint Marvel U.K. also introduced a host of new characters and series, which would later show up on the American market. The House of Ideas had begun giving room to young writers and artists with fresh ideas. Todd McFarlane, who had won the hearts of fans with his run in *The Amazing Spider-Man*, was given carte blanche for "his own" Spider-Man series.

Rob Liefeld, who did the artwork for the last issues of *New Mutants* to be written by Louise Simonson, and also contributed to the plots, transformed the team of young heroes into a hard-fighting posse, X-Force. And Jim Lee, who for a while had been doing the artwork for the famed series *The Uncanny X-Men*, with stories by Chris Claremont, would soon be heading the newly born *X-Men*, when "X-Chris" stepped down as the main mutant writer, his job since 1975. Super Heroes got fiercer and more weaponized; their looks mirrored the styles of the moment. Artists who used bold, vigorous lines replaced people with more classical approaches. Some series featured extended narratives that would go on for years, like the "Clone Saga" in various Spider-Man publications.

Of course, success wasn't just the result of the comics themselves and their creators, or the work of speculators. The world of comics had begun attracting audiences that feasted on new opportunities to get to know all those magnificent characters. Such as the first successful arcade video games featuring Marvel Super Heroes, and Saturday mornings with one of Marvel's most successful cartoons ever, *X-Men: The Animated Series*, which ran from 1992 to 1997. The characters' looks were taken right from the then-current looks of their comic book counterparts.

Growing commercial success meant that the company had to grow too. Marvel was no longer the tiny "Bullpen," as the staff was referred to in the 1960s, but a company listed on the stock exchange.

The move by new president Ron Perelman, who had bought Marvel from New World two years earlier, was officially announced to investors when an actor in a Spider-Man costume was featured in the opening ceremony at the New York Stock Exchange, alongside a smiling Stan Lee. But this wasn't the place where the seeds for a bright future would be planted. It wouldn't be long before Marvel characters caught the attention of that other temple of American power, Hollywood.

In those years, Marvel was publishing so many comics releases that in order to manage them, Editor in Chief Tom DeFalco broke them down into "families": Mutants, Heroes, Urban Heroes, Spider-Family, Cosmics. When Tom left the position in 1994, for a brief time the coordinators of the various families were basically the ones running the show at Marvel. The choice to fill the gap left by DeFalco fell upon Bob Harras, the editor who had

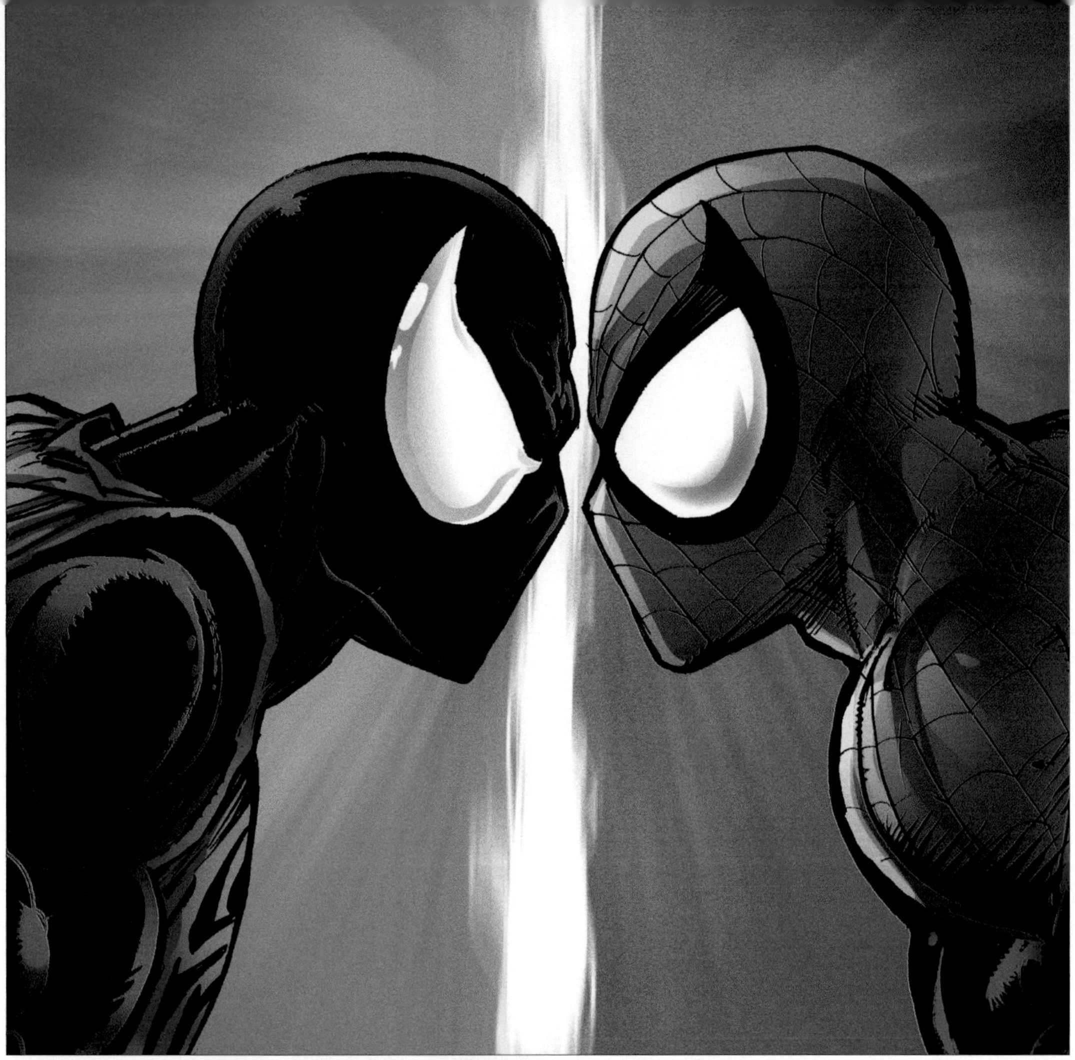

LEFT: Cover detail for *Spider-Man: Clone Saga Omnibus Volume 2* (November 2017). Art by Sal Buscema (pencils), Bill Sienkiewicz (inks).

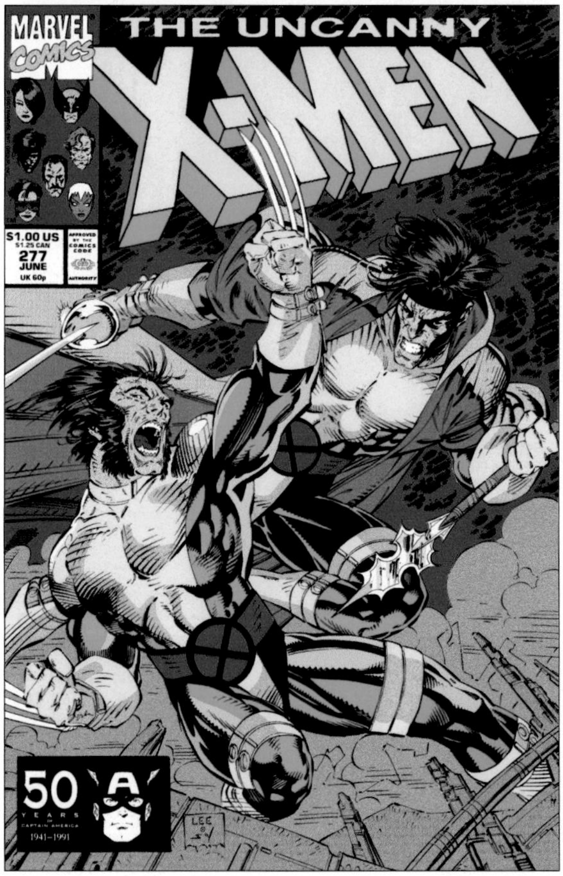
MARVEL COMICS
THE UNCANNY
X-MEN
$1.00 US
$1.25 CAN
277
JUNE
UK 60p
50 YEARS
CAPTAIN AMERICA
1941–1991

BELOW LEFT: *The Uncanny X-Men #277* (June 1991). Art by Jim Lee and Scott Williams

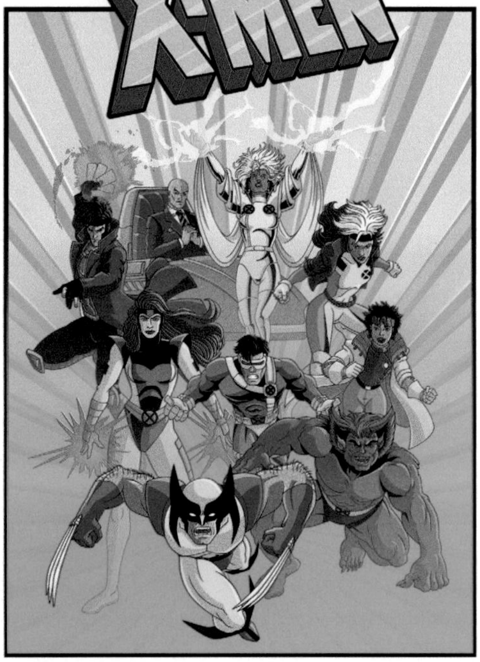
X-MEN

BELOW: A promotional image for the *X-Men* animated series that premiered on October 31, 1992.

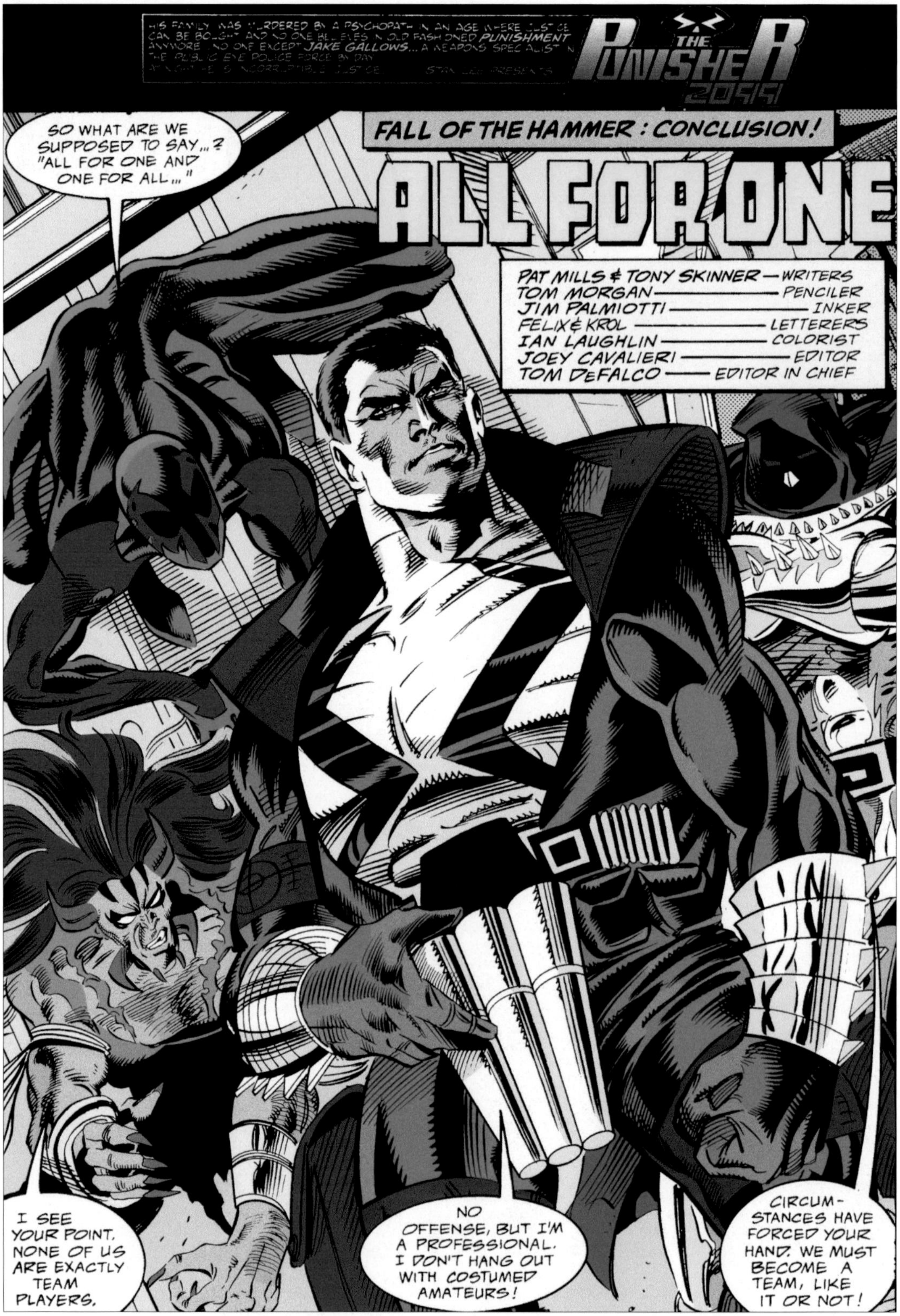
HIS FAMILY WAS MURDERED BY A PSYCHOPATH IN AN AGE WHERE JUSTICE CAN BE BOUGHT AND NO ONE BELIEVES IN OLD FASHIONED PUNISHMENT ANYMORE. NO ONE EXCEPT JAKE GALLOWS... A WEAPONS SPECIALIST IN THE PUBLIC EYE POLICE FORCE BY DAY
THE PUNISHER 2099
SO WHAT ARE WE SUPPOSED TO SAY...? "ALL FOR ONE AND ONE FOR ALL..."
FALL OF THE HAMMER: CONCLUSION!
ALL FOR ONE
PAT MILLS & TONY SKINNER—WRITERS
TOM MORGAN—PENCILER
JIM PALMIOTTI—INKER
FELIX & KROL—LETTERERS
IAN LAUGHLIN—COLORIST
JOEY CAVALIERI—EDITOR
TOM DEFALCO—EDITOR IN CHIEF
I SEE YOUR POINT. NONE OF US ARE EXACTLY TEAM PLAYERS.
NO OFFENSE, BUT I'M A PROFESSIONAL. I DON'T HANG OUT WITH COSTUMED AMATEURS!
CIRCUM-STANCES HAVE FORCED YOUR HAND. WE MUST BECOME A TEAM, LIKE IT OR NOT!

RIGHT: The future Punisher, from *Punisher 2099 #13* (February 1994). Script by Pat Mills and Tony Skinner. Art by Tom Morgan (pencils), Jimmy Palmiotti (inks), Ian Laughlin (colors), Phil Felix and Loretta Krol (letters).

led the X-Men to stratospheric heights of popularity. A good portion of that success had certainly come thanks to creators McFarlane, Lee, and Liefeld. Aware of their own potential strength on the market, they left Marvel in 1992 to seek new inroads. The three of them, along with other young, well-respected contemporary creators—Jim Valentino, Erik Larsen, and Marc Silvestri—soon founded Image Comics. But in 1996 Lee and Liefeld returned to Marvel when it was decided to launch new series based on classics like the Avengers, the Fantastic Four, Captain America, and Iron Man.

The Heroes Reborn project gave creators total artistic freedom—which meant resorting to a simple ploy. *Onslaught*, the saga that reunited the greatest Marvel Super Heroes, wound up stuck in a parallel dimension with the Avengers and the Fantastic Four—a narrative twist that allowed Lee and Liefeld to redevelop those characters from scratch. They were thus able to update their origins to meet modern demands, without having to worry about the burden of decades of continuity.

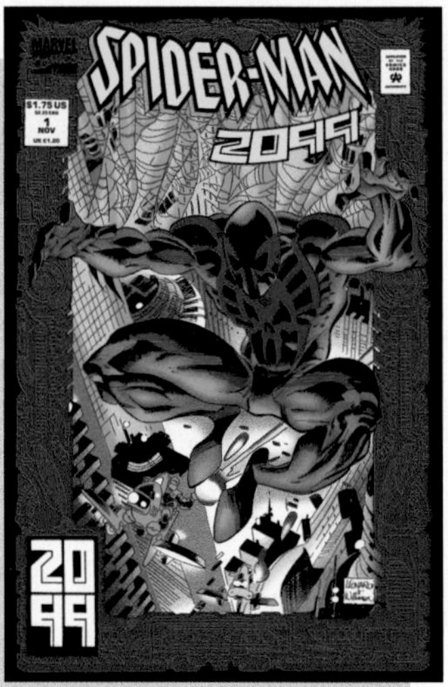
SPIDER-MAN
2099
$1.75 US
NOV
2099

2099

What would Marvel Super Heroes look like 100 years into the future? Who would be wearing the Spider-Man outfit? Would there be anyone left to fight for Xavier's dream? Would the Hulk still be around? Initially, Stan Lee and John Byrne were supposed to answer those questions in what would have been the special one-shot event entitled *The Marvel World of Tomorrow*, announced by Lee in one of the 1990 Stan's Soapbox columns. Over the next few years, however, the project underwent significant changes and was eventually transformed into the Marvel 2099 imprint. It kicked off in November 1992 with *Spider-Man 2099*. After the release of the other series in the hopper—*Punisher 2099*, *Doom 2099*, and *Ravage 2099* (written by Stan Lee)—more were added. They included *X-Men 2099* and *Ghost Rider 2099*, featuring the artwork of Chris Bachalo and Ashley Wood.

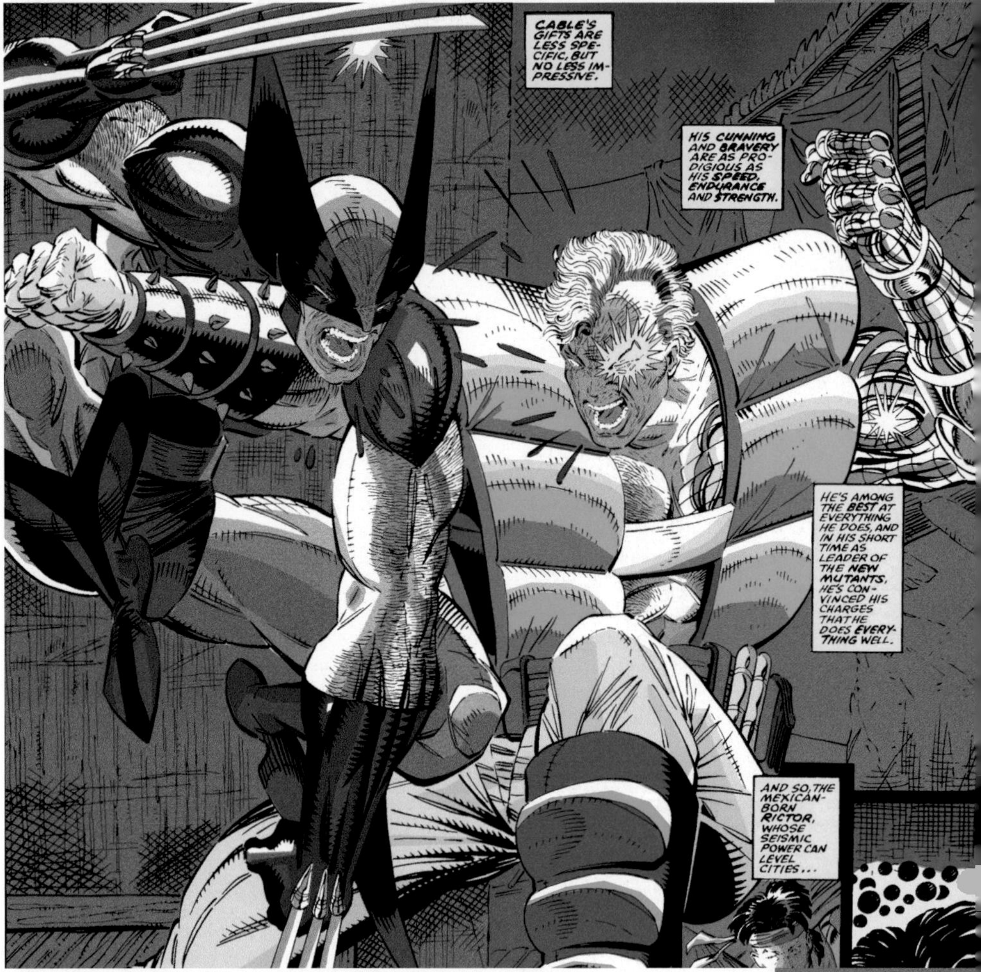
CABLE'S GIFTS ARE LESS SPECIFIC, BUT NO LESS IMPRESSIVE.
HIS CUNNING AND BRAVERY ARE AS PRODIGIOUS AS HIS SPEED, ENDURANCE AND STRENGTH.
HE'S AMONG THE BEST AT EVERYTHING HE DOES, AND IN HIS SHORT TIME AS LEADER OF THE NEW MUTANTS, HE'S CONVINCED HIS CHARGES THAT HE DOES EVERYTHING WELL.
AND SO, THE MEXICAN-BORN RICTOR, WHOSE SEISMIC POWER CAN LEVEL CITIES...

ABOVE: Wolverine battles Cable in *The New Mutants #94* (October 1990). Art by Rob Liefeld (pencils), Hilary Barta (inks), Brad Vancata (colors).

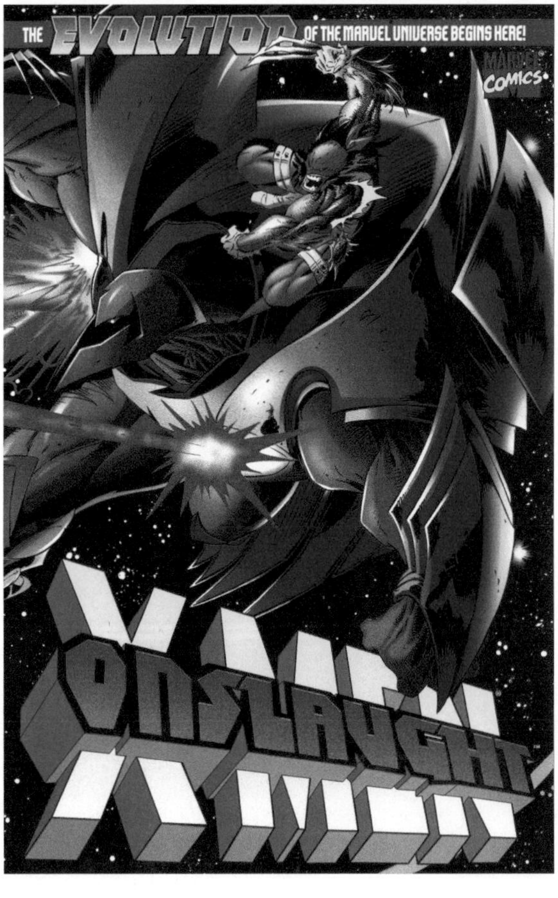
THE EVOLUTION OF THE MARVEL UNIVERSE BEGINS HERE!
MARVEL COMICS
ONSLAUGHT

LEFT: *X-Men: Onslaught #1* (August 1996). Art by Adam Kubert.

Marvel continued to trust their writers and artists with characters old and new, giving them free rein to develop the Super Heroes and Super Villains in new ways. It was fitting, then, that one of these artists—Joe Quesada—would go on to be named Editor in Chief of Marvel Comics as the new century dawned. Known for his expressive, personal style, Quesada would lead Marvel into the 2000s, leaving his mark as the company's longest-reigning Editor in Chief since Stan Lee himself.

INFINITE BATTLES

The *X-Men* and *Spider-Man* unveil epic story lines, as Elektra returns, and the Marvel Universe makes some big changes.

In the 1990s everything was spectacular and hyperbolic: the weapons characters wielded, their bulky armor, the spikes on their epaulets, their costumes, poses and proportions. Along with their brightly colored spandex suits, Super Heroes often sported leather jackets, long overcoats, and various details and accessories like pockets and belts, a likely nod to street fashion of the period. Each and every panel had to be breathtaking, and sagas tended to be very long, containing numerous crossovers.

Events like “The Crossing” (Avengers), “X-Cutioner’s Song” and “Fatal Attractions” (X-Men) and “Maximum Carnage” (the Spider-Man “family”) promised to change the status quo of Super Heroes over the course of many chapters and countless plot twists. Tony Stark was replaced by a teenage version of himself; the X-Men had to deal with the appearance of the Legacy Virus, which infected only mutants; Wolverine lost his Adamantium skeleton, revealing his bony claws; Spider-Man found an ally in Venom and a new enemy in Venom’s offspring, Carnage. But none of these events was comparable to the “Clone Saga,” which for four years ruled the roost, outselling all other Spider-Man comics.

BELOW: The hologram cover for *X-Factor #92* (July 1993). Art by Joe Quesada and Al Milgrom.

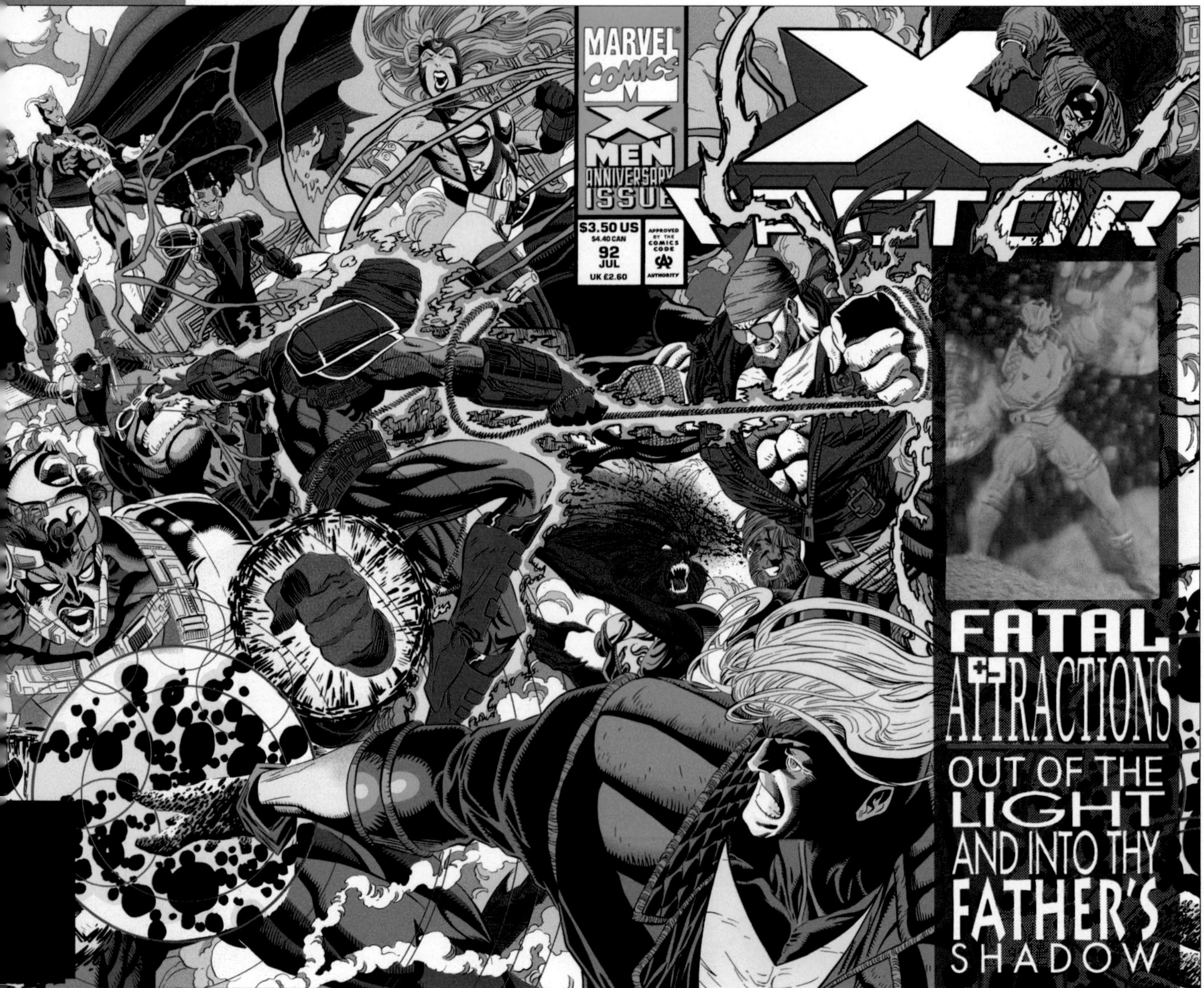
MARVEL COMICS
X MEN
ANNIVERSARY ISSUE
$3.50 US
$4.40 CAN
92
JUL
UK £2.60
APPROVED BY THE COMICS CODE AUTHORITY
X-FACTOR
FATAL
ATTRACTIONS
OUT OF THE
LIGHT
AND INTO THY
FATHER'S
SHADOW

PROFESSOR XAVIER'S SCHOOL FOR GIFTED YOUNGSTERS.

SALEM CENTER.

WESTCHESTER COUNTY.

NEW YORK.

THERE WAS A TIME WHEN THIS MANSION SERVED AS A TRAINING FACILITY FOR THE YOUNG MUTANTS KNOWN AS THE UNCANNY X-MEN.

SOMETIME BETWEEN THEN AND NOW, IT BECAME THEIR HOME.

I'LL CONFESS, CHARLES, I DIDNA KNOW THIS "READY ROOM" OF YUIR'S EVEN EXISTED. AND I POSED AS YUIR HOUSEKEEPER FOR NOT A SHORT AMOUNT O' TIME.

UNTIL RECENTLY, I DEEMED THIS ROOM OFF-LIMITS TO EVERYONE BUT MYSELF -- JUSTIFIED, I BELIEVED, BY THE OCCASIONAL NEED TO ESCAPE.

AT JUBILEE'S INSISTENCE I BECOME -- AS SHE PUT IT "MORE NINETIES"... I'M TRYING TO MAKE MYSELF MORE ACCESSIBLE.

I'M IMPRESSED -- EVEN MORE SO BY THIS SHI'AR TECHNOLOGY YE HAVE AT YUIR DISPOSAL.

BY INPUTTING ALL THE PERTINENT DATA ON THE ANOMALY... WE'VE MANAGED TO PIECE TOGETHER FROM THE MEDICAL REPORTS AND EXAMS ON VICTIMS OF THIS GENETIC DISORDER --

-- WE'VE COME UP WITH AN AMALGAMATED-HOLOGRAPHIC PROJECTION OF AN AFFLICTED DNA HELIX.

COMPUTER: OVERLAY MUTAGENIC ANOMALY.

THE COMICS

LEFT: Professor X and Dr. Moira MacTaggert analyze the Legacy Virus. *The Uncanny X-Men #300* (May 1993). Script by Scott Lobdell. Art by Brandon Peterson (pencils), Dan Green, Dan Panosian, Al Milgrom (inks), Steve Buccellato, Glynis Oliver (colors), Chris Eliopoulos (letters).

Taking its cue from a series of stories first published in 1975, in which Jackal created a Peter Parker clone, the creators brought back Peter's clone and led us to believe that the adventures over the past 19 years starring Peter Parker had actually involved his clone! The real Peter now called himself Ben Reilly, and assumed the identity of Scarlet Spider, fighting side by side with Spider-Man.

At one point, he even took his place, wearing a new costume designed by Mark Bagley. When Peter temporarily

chose to retire from the Super Hero life, he left Reilly with the responsibility of being Spider-Man. After numerous adventures featuring the new Spidey, the truth was finally revealed in *The Amazing Spider-Man #418* (cover-dated December 1996): Ben was the clone, Peter was the original.

This sensational story, written by Howard Mackie and illustrated by John Romita, Jr., also saw Norman Osborn, the first Green Goblin, back from the dead. Upon his return, Norman sets out

to become Spider-Man's worst enemy out of the many aspiring Goblins who in the past tried to take his place. For his part, Venom would star in a string of limited series releases, and along the way became one of Marvel's best-loved characters.

The early 1990s output, however, was not limited to long-running series and sagas, Super Heroes toting giant guns, and grim, gloomy tales. Amid so many products of this kind, one can't help but recall that in those years Marvel published some truly immortal gems. For

107

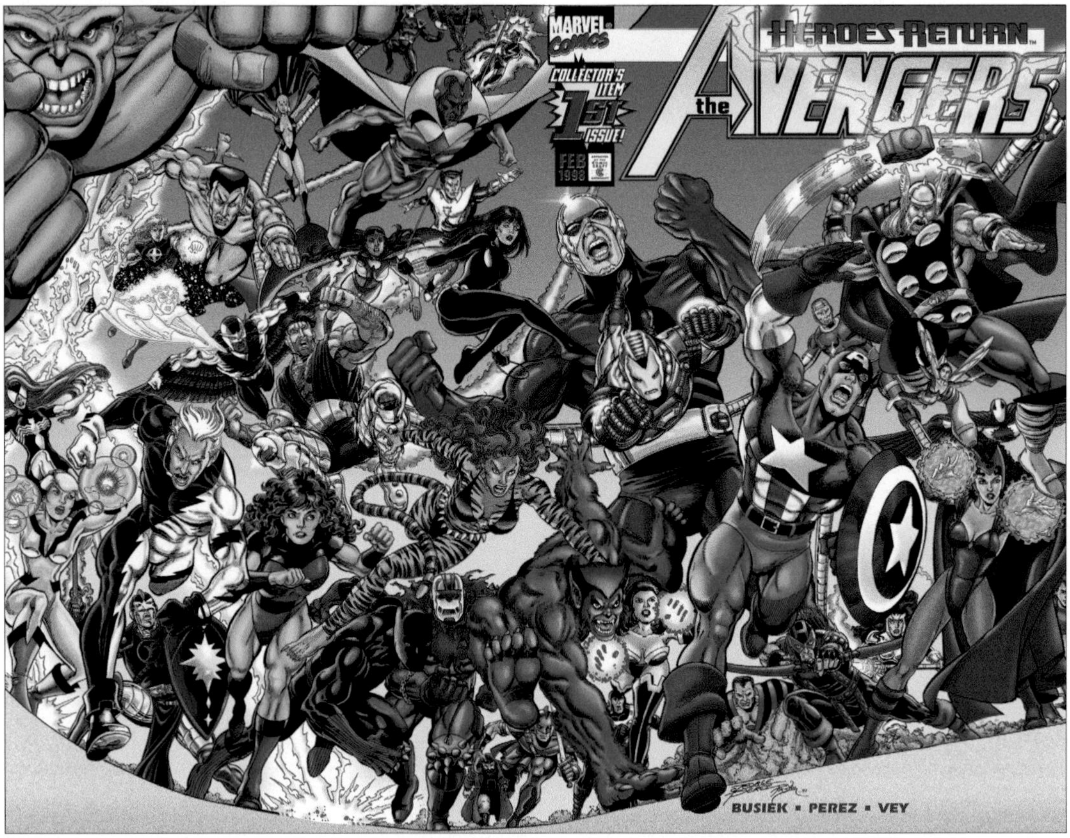
MARVEL COMICS
HEROES RETURN
the AVENGERS
COLLECTOR'S ITEM 1st ISSUE!
FEB 1998
BUSIEK • PEREZ • VEY

instance, in 1991 Frank Miller returned to "his" Elektra and wrote and illustrated the graphic novel *Elektra Lives Again*. That same year the acclaimed artist Barry Windsor-Smith wrote and illustrated the story "Weapon X," unveiling a crucial moment in Wolverine's past, which was published in the anthology series *Marvel Comics Presents* and soon followed by the trade paperback collection.

Miller came back to *Daredevil* in 1993, giving readers a glimpse of Matt Murdock's earliest experiences as a vigilante. Qualitatively, one of the high points of those years, and perhaps in the entire history of Marvel, was the four-issue series *Marvels*, released in a prestige format. Written by Kurt Busiek, an expert on Marvel continuity, and painted in its entirety in a hyperrealistic style by Alex Ross, it told the story of the Marvel Universe's early years from the point of view of the man on the street, news photographer Phil Sheldon. *Marvels* was a critical and commercial success and generated a slew of imitations and spin-offs.

In 1999 Alex Ross made his return to Marvel, this time as writer and cover artist. With another writer, Jim Krueger,

1990

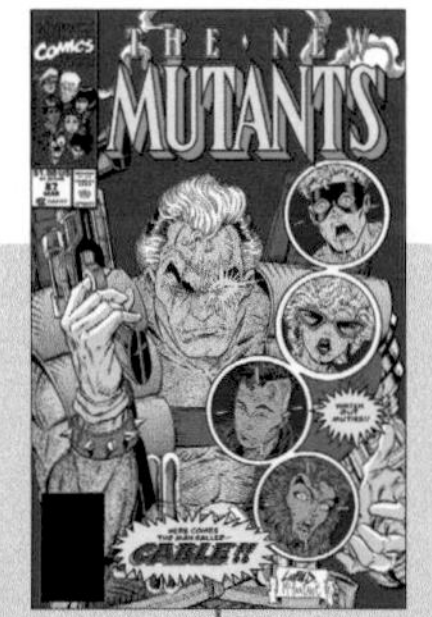
THE NEW MUTANTS

MARCH 1990

A future star of the '90s makes his debut in *The New Mutants* #87: Cable.

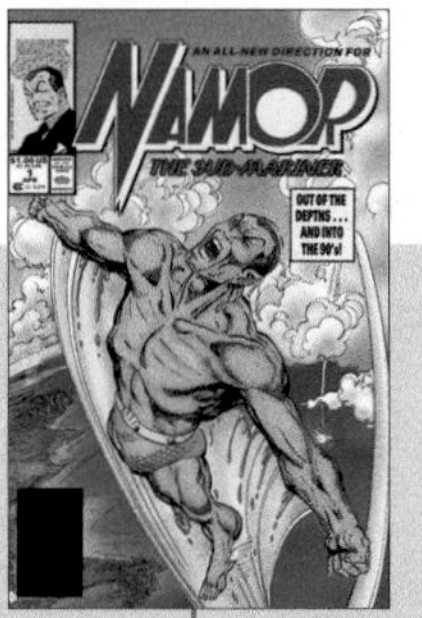
NAMOR
THE SUB-MARINER

APRIL 1990

Namor is back in a new series, written and illustrated by John Byrne, who has made his return to Marvel in 1989.

THE INFINITY GAUNTLET
THE END BEGINS HERE!

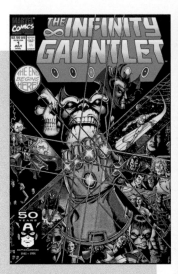

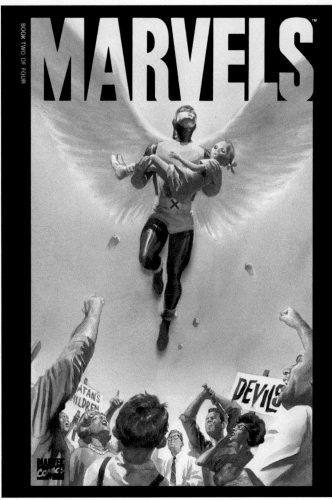

THE INFINITY SAGA

After bringing his creation Thanos back to the pages of the monthly *Silver Surfer* title and in the limited series *The Thanos Quest*, Jim Starlin, now in the role of writer, teamed up with artists George Perez and Ron Lim on a limited series that was a huge success. In *The Infinity Gauntlet*, Thanos places all six Infinity Gems on his gauntlet, and with a snap of his fingers wipes out half the life in the universe. *The Infinity Gauntlet* proved such a hit that it immediately spawned two sequels, *Infinity War* (1992) and *Infinity Crusade* (1993), both by the team of Starlin and Lim. The *Infinity* saga is known for its wide-ranging cast.

BOOK TWO OF FOUR
MARVELS
DEVILS

ABOVE: *Marvels #2* (February 1994). Art by Alex Ross.

OPPOSITE PAGE: Earth's mightiest heroes return to the Marvel Universe in *The Avengers #1* (February 1998). Art by George Pérez (pencils), Tom Smith (colors).

and artist John Paul Leon alongside, he laid the groundwork for the big 12-issue saga entitled *Earth X*, which debuted in 1999. This time around, readers got to check out what the Marvel Universe might end up looking like in the future, as told by a cold, distant observer, the android Machine Man.

In the second half of the 1990s, after *Heroes Reborn* came *Heroes Return*. These crossovers starring the Avengers were created by people who did not gravitate toward current trends, but were more firmly entrenched in

GHOST RIDER
A SPIRIT REBORN!

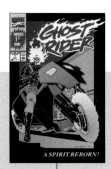

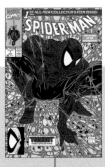

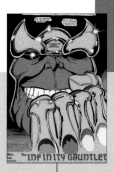

MAY 1990

A new Spirit of Vengeance appears in *Ghost Rider #1*: Danny Ketch takes the place of Johnny Blaze.

SPIDER-MAN

AUGUST 1990

Spider-Man #1 hits the stores—and what a hit it was! Written and illustrated by Todd McFarlane.

THE INFINITY GAUNTLET

JULY 1991

The Infinity Gauntlet and *X-Force* make their respective debuts.

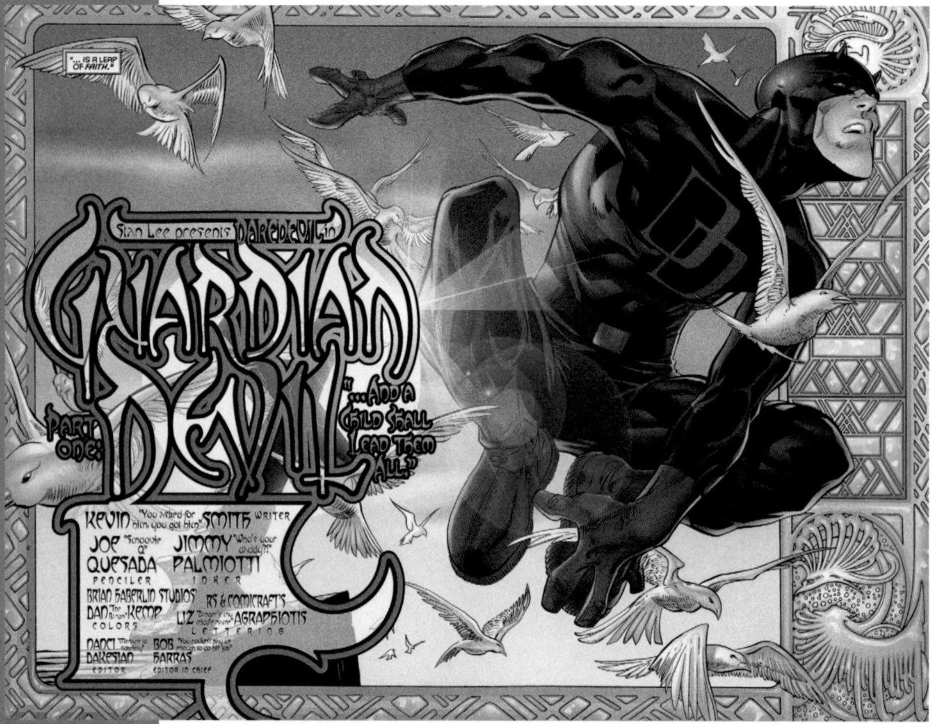
"...IS A LEAP OF FAITH."
Stan Lee presents Daredevil in
Guardian Devil
Part one:
"...And a child shall lead them all."
Kevin Smith Writer
Joe Quesada Penciler
Jimmy Palmiotti Inker
Brian Haberlin Studios
RS & Comicraft's
Dan Kemp Colors
Liz Agraphiotis Lettering
Nanci Dakesian Editor
Bob Harras Editor in Chief

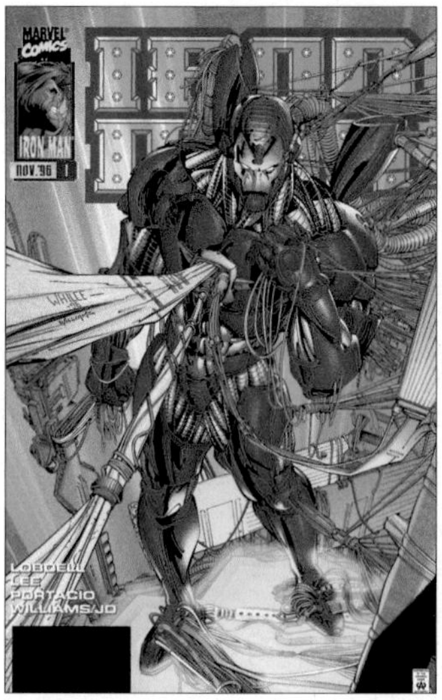
MARVEL COMICS
IRON MAN
NOV. 96 1
LOBDELL
LEE
PORTACIO
WILLIAMS/JD

ABOVE:
Title panel from *Daredevil Vol. 2, #1* (November 1998). Script by Kevin Smith. Art by Joe Quesada (pencils), Jimmy Palmiotti (inks), Dan Kemp (colors), Liz Agraphiotis (letters).

classic styles. They included Busiek and Perez, who did extensive work on *The Avengers*, acclaimed by critics and readers alike, while *Captain America* featured stories written by Mark Waid and illustrated by Ron Garney that reached new qualitative heights. But some of the supporting characters still had a hard time catching the attention of the critics and fans. Frank Miller's legacy still weighed on *Daredevil*.

Other characters, like the Inhumans, had potential that for years went untapped. Taking its cue somewhat from the approach used for *Heroes Reborn*, Marvel brought in "outsiders" to develop those characters—in this case, Joe Quesada and Jimmy Palmiotti from Event Comics, both of whom had worked for Marvel in the past, as penciler and inker respectively. This time, however, the stories would not be set in a bubble-like parallel universe, but integrated within the regular continuity. The imprint would be called Marvel Knights. Fans and specialized periodicals mainly focused their attention on *Daredevil*. The imprint made its debut with the release of *Daredevil #1,* cover-dated November 1998, featuring artwork by Quesada, and written by Kevin Smith, a successful independent film director and comics fan.

Smith and Quesada's eight-part "Guardian Devil" story, which relied on updated versions of Miller-type atmospheres, was the first Marvel Knights hit, followed by the political fantasy series *The Inhumans*, written by Paul Jenkins, with artwork by Jae Lee; the brilliant ongoing series *Black Panther*; and new limited series for characters such as Black Widow and the Punisher. *The Punisher* series was designed to last only four issues, and featured the involvement of famed horror penciler Bernie Wrightson. A few years later, Frank Castle would return as the protagonist in a new Marvel Knights series, that shifted over to the new MAX imprint. It wasn't long before the imprint became synonymous with high-quality "adult" themes.

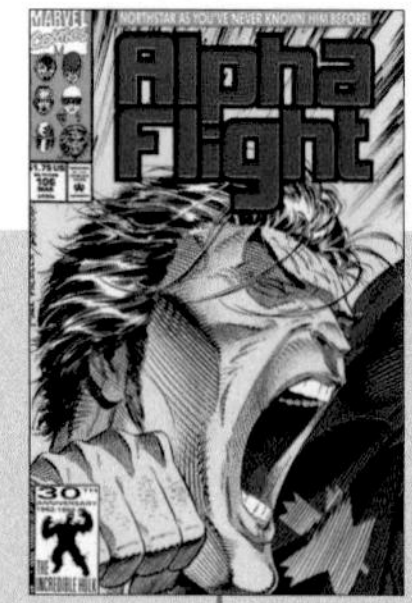
Alpha Flight

MARCH 1992

In *Alpha Flight #106* Northstar comes out soon after adopting a baby with AIDS. He is a Canadian Super Hero and Marvel's first openly gay character.

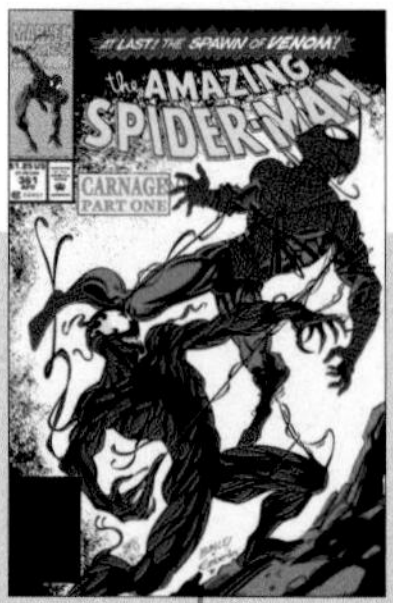
AT LAST! THE SPAWN OF VENOM!
The Amazing Spider-Man
CARNAGE PART ONE

APRIL 1992

The Amazing Spider-Man #361 marks the first appearance of one of Spidey's deadliest enemies (and a favorite of fans): Carnage!

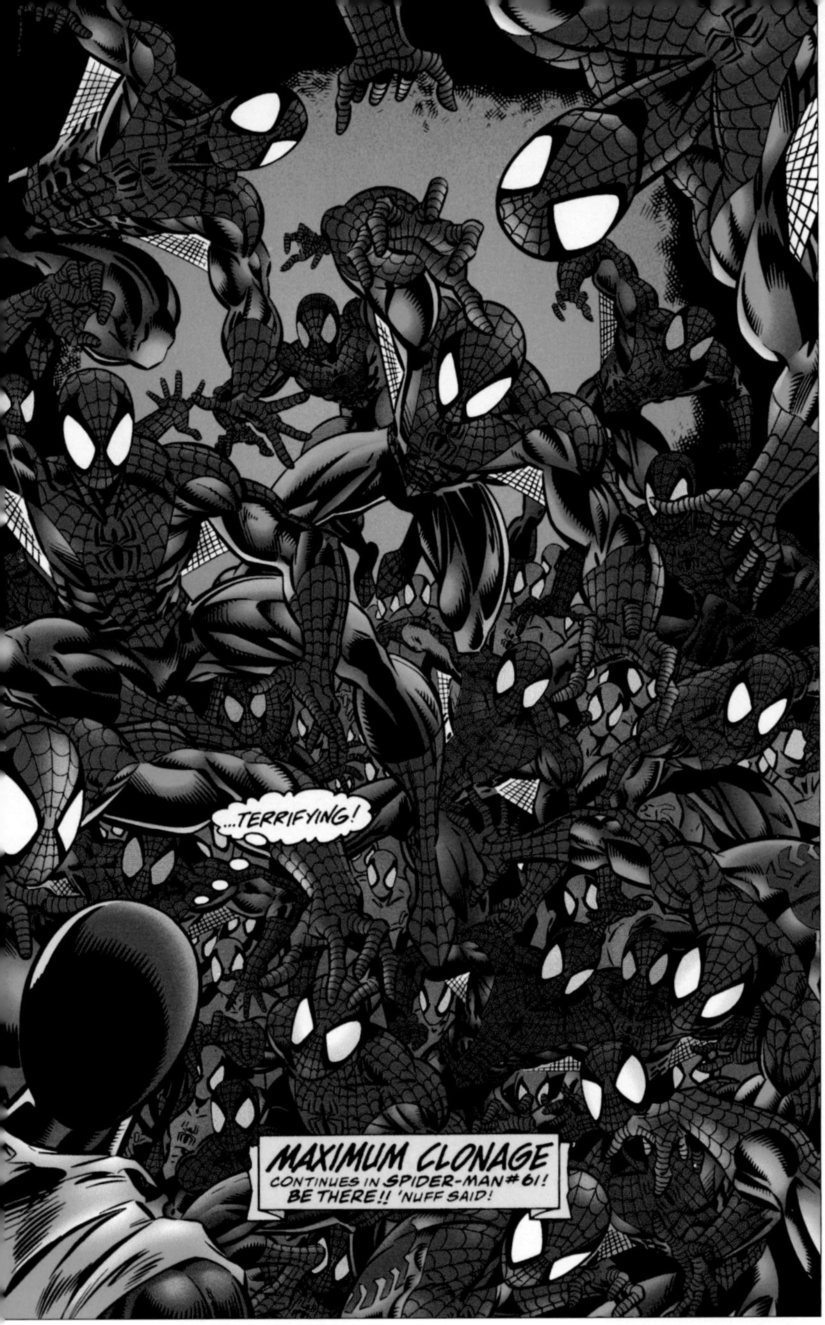
...TERRIFYING!
MAXIMUM CLONAGE
CONTINUES IN SPIDER-MAN #61!
BE THERE!! 'NUFF SAID!

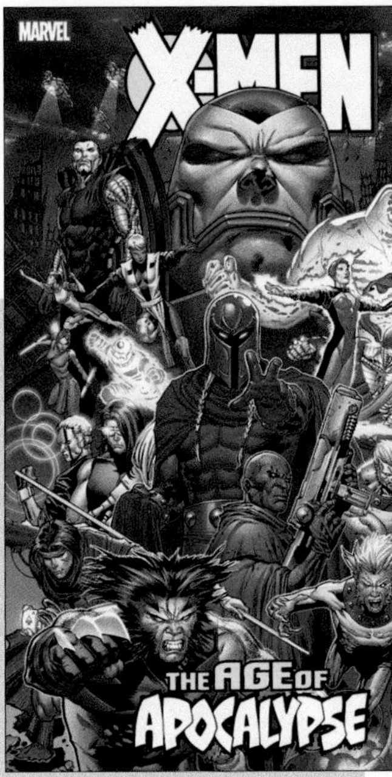
MARVEL
X-MEN
THE AGE OF APOCALYPSE

THE AGE OF APOCALYPSE

In 1995–96, the entire X-Men cast starred in one of the most ambitious comic book crossover events ever. Xavier's son Legion traveled back in time, seeking to murder a young Magneto so that his father's dream might prosper. But instead he mistakenly wound up killing Xavier himself, thereby altering the timeline. Thus Magneto brought together the X-Men, although they were not able to keep the immortal mutant Apocalypse from conquering half the world. It was risky business—the many series connected to the X-Men were shut down and replaced for four months by limited series with similar titles. The saga, which concluded with an inevitable return to normalcy, was a commercial success.

OPPOSITE PAGE: *Iron Man Vol. 2, #1* (dated November 1996, released September 18, 1996). Art by Whilce Portacio and Scott Williams.

LEFT: The "Clone Saga" from *The Amazing Spider-Man #404* (August 1995). Script by J. M. DeMatteis and Todd DeZago. Art by Mark Bagley (pencils), Larry Mahlstedt, Randy Emberlin, Josef Rubinstein (inks), Bob Sharen (colors), Bill Oakley (letters).

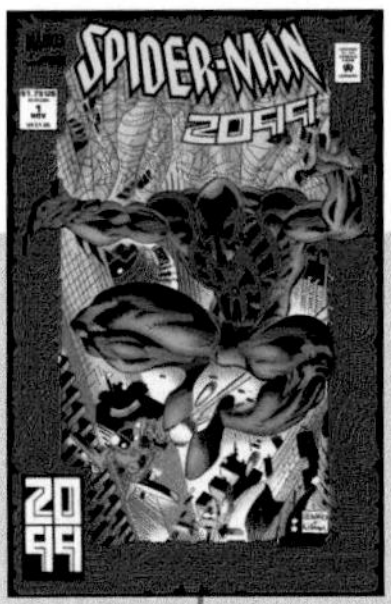
SPIDER-MAN 2099

NOVEMBER 1992

Marvel *2099*'s first release: *Spider-Man 2099*.

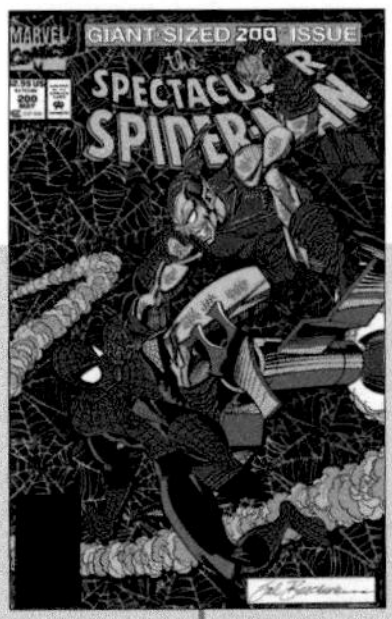
MARVEL
GIANT SIZED 200 ISSUE

MAY 1993

In *The Spectacular Spider-Man #200*, a touching story by J. M. DeMatteis and Sal Buscema, Harry Osborn dies.

THE OLD AND THE NEW

A wave of innovative concepts crests as Marvel reinvents classic characters and introduces new creations.

FIXER.
BEETLE.
SCREAMING MIMI.
GOLIATH.
AND MOONSTONE.
IN TIME, MY FRIENDS --

RIGHT: The team is gathered in *Thunderbolts #1*. Script by Kurt Busiek. Art by Mark Bagley (pencils), Vince Russell (inks), Joe Rosas (colors), Comicraft, Dave Lanphear, Oscar Gongorra (letters).

OPPOSITE PAGE: The cover to *Thunderbolts #1* (dated April 1997, released February 19, 1997). Art by Mark Bagley.

It must be said that the 1990s were steeped in a wealth of ideas. Besides giving fresh starts to characters from the past, the emergence of new writers and artists brought about the invention of all-new original concepts. Among them was Darkhawk, a violent, armor-clad crime-fighter who made his debut in March 1991, and the even more successful Deadpool, one of the many characters created by the explosive Rob Liefeld in stories that transitioned from the end of *The New Mutants* to the first issues of *X-Force*.

He was born a villain, and fans immediately picked up on him. In 1993 Deadpool went from supporting to main character in his first limited series, written by Fabian Nicieza, with illustrations by Joe Madureira, whose style came to symbolize 1990s comic book art, with influences from Japanese comics and video games.

AVENGERS WEST COAST
Soul Gauntlet

NOVEMBER 1993

Mockingbird dies in *The West Coast Avengers #100*. Two issues later, the series shuts down. The team returned with a new name and a new attitude in *Force Works*.

MARVELS

JANUARY 1994

Marvels #1 is released. The series depicts the Marvel Universe as seen through the eyes of everyday people, notably *Daily Bugle* photographer Phil Sheldon.

MARVEL COMICS
JUSTICE, LIKE LIGHTNING...
THUNDERBOLTS
DOUBLE-SIZED DEBUT EXCITEMENT!
APR '97 1
DISCOVER THE SHOCKING SECRET BEHIND MARVEL'S NEWEST CHAMPIONS!

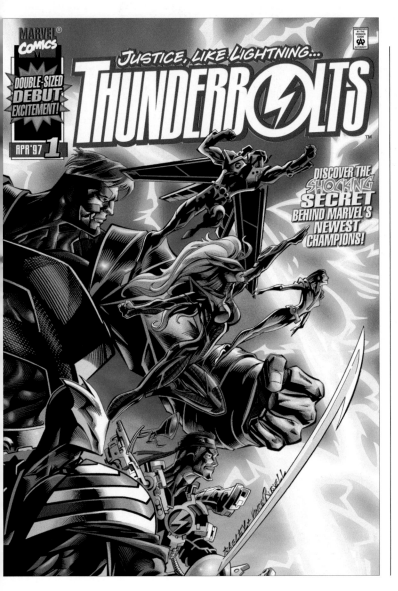

Other limited series followed for Deadpool, as did special appearances, until the launch of his first of many on-going series in 1997.

The 1990s also saw the consolidation of Wolverine's fame, and at one time his presence on a comic book cover guaranteed commercial success. In addition to his own ongoing series, the mutant called Logan guest-starred in countless annuals and one-shots. His attitude symbolized the Super Hero of the 1990s. The success of *X-Men: The Animated Series* also contributed to Wolverine's visibility and stature among the general public, on a par with iconic characters from the past like Spider-Man and Captain America.

Among the new series with links to the past, one of the biggest surprises proved to be the *Thunderbolts*. Kurt Busiek and Mark Bagley created the series that was launched to coincide with *Heroes Reborn*, so that while the most famous Super Heroes were busy in another universe, a new crew of crime-fighters would be protecting the Earth! But beneath the Thunderbolts' masks lurked the Masters of Evil, part of a complex plan orchestrated by Baron Zemo, Captain America's old foe. The series ran until 2003, and along the way many Thunderbolts actually did decide to become Super Heroes. Then there was Spider-Girl, introduced in one of the last issues of *What If?*, the series dedicated to Marvel Super Heroes involved in purely hypothetical situations.

WEB OF SPIDER-MAN

THE AMAZING SPIDER-MAN 400
"A DEATH IN THE FAMILY"

FEBRUARY 1994

On February 6, 1994, Jack Kirby, one of the founding fathers of the Marvel Universe, dies at his home in California.

NOVEMBER 1994

Peter Parker's clone, Ben Reilly, becomes Scarlet Spider in *Web of Spider-Man #118*.

APRIL 1995

The death of Aunt May was the focal point of *The Amazing Spider-Man #400*. Years later, readers learned this "Aunt May" was a fake, and that the real May was still alive.

YOU WANT A SPIDER-PERSON, NORMIE?
FACE IT, TIGER...YOU JUST HIT THE JACKPOT!

MARVEL COMICS
THE NEW MUTANTS
$1.00 US $1.25 CAN 98 FEB
APPROVED BY THE COMICS CODE AUTHORITY
02207
INTRODUCING THE LETHAL DEADPOOL
THE MYSTERIOUS GIDEON
AND THE DYNAMIC DOMINO!

ABOVE: The sensational Spider-Girl as she appeared in *What If? #105* (February 1998). Script by Tom Defalco. Art by Ron Frenz (pencils), Matt Webb (colors), Chris Eliopoulos (letters).

RIGHT: Deadpool makes his first appearance on the cover of *The New Mutants #98* (February 1991). Art by Rob Liefeld.

A few years earlier, Peter Parker and Mary Jane had had a daughter, who was kidnapped shortly after she was born and was never heard from again. But what would have happened had she grown up with her parents and discovered that she too possessed spider-powers? Dated February 1998, issue #105 of *What If?* answered that question and spawned the Spider-Girl series, featuring young May Parker donning "uncle" Ben Reilly's costume. Other new series would also be set in an alternative future known as MC2, which was decidedly less gloomy than life in 2099, although none achieved the success of Spider-Girl.

HEROES REBORN

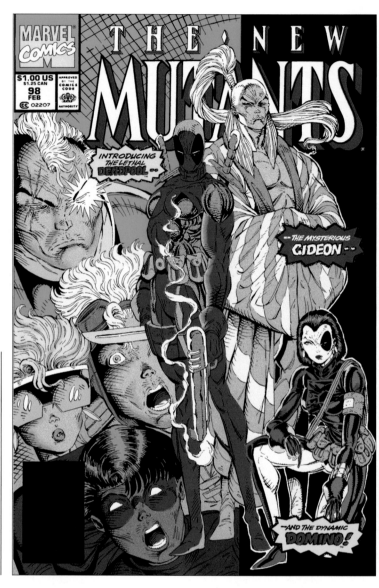

OCTOBER 1996

The Onslaught saga comes to an end. It opened the doors to *Heroes Reborn*.

ELEKTRA
FANTASTIC 1ST ISSUE
FOR THE FIRST TIME IN HER OWN MONTHLY SERIES

NOVEMBER 1996

Elektra is back, starring in her own series.

HEROES REBORN THE RETURN
THE COUNTDOWN BEGINS... AS WORLDS COLLIDE!

DECEMBER 1996

The Fantastic Four, the Avengers, and the Hulk all make a comeback in *Heroes Reborn: The Return*—in their original settings.

YOUNG MASTERS

A new wave of artists and writers from all areas of creative endeavor teams with Marvel to guide the Super Heroes into a new century.

As we mentioned, by the time the 1980s were drawing to a close, some comic book creators were already working their way into fans' hearts. They were mostly artists associated with Marvel's most celebrated Super Heroes, and this contributed to their commercial success. For example, after gaining notoriety for his grotesque, innovative style in *The Incredible Hulk*, Todd McFarlane made his way to *The Amazing Spider-Man*, where he redefined the main character's look. Now Spider-Man was capable of incredible moves, pushing the limits of physics and anatomy in spectacular, never-before-attempted shots. The eyes of his mask were larger and more expressive. Even his webbing had changed—it was no longer a set of straight lines, but spaghetti-like as it flowed from his web-shooters.

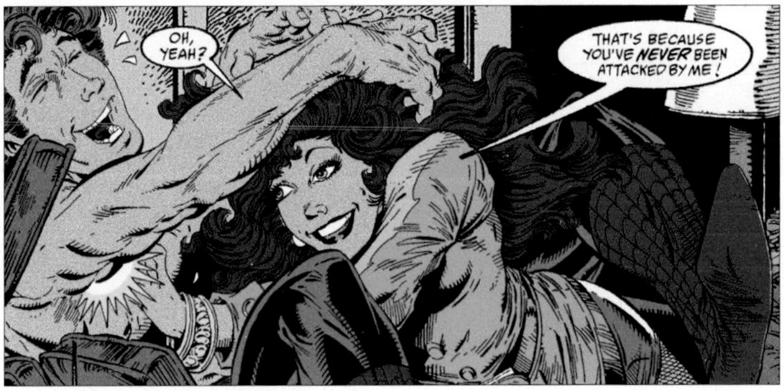
OH, YEAH?
THAT'S BECAUSE YOU'VE NEVER BEEN ATTACKED BY ME!

LEFT: A panel from *Spider-Man #1* (August 1990). Script and art by Todd McFarlane.

The revamped version was so successful that McFarlane was put to work on the series entitled simply *Spider-Man*, where he would also be involved in scripting stories. Something similar happened with the main artists working on the mutants at that time, Rob Liefeld and Jim Lee.

Liefeld transformed *New Mutants* into *X-Force*, introducing violent, musclebound and sexy characters into the cast. Among them were the highly successful mercenary Domino, and Cable, cyborg warrior of the future, who made an even bigger splash.

Jim Lee's *X-Men* was a staggering

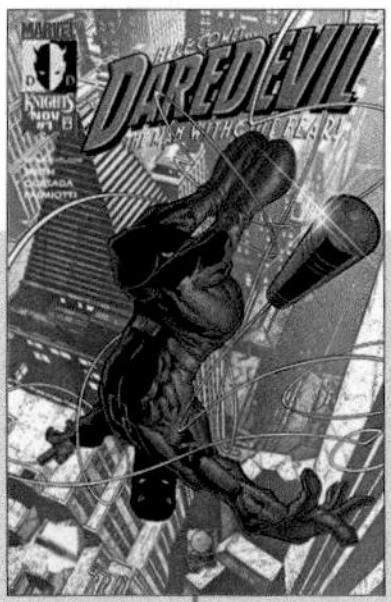
DAREDEVIL

NOVEMBER 1997

The Marvel Knights imprint debuts with *Daredevil #1*, by Kevin Smith and Joe Quesada.

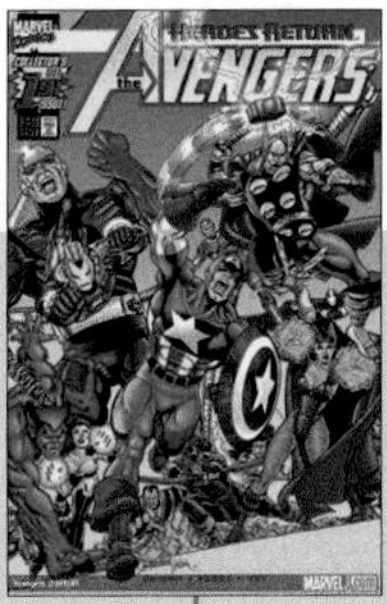
AVENGERS

JANUARY 1998

The Avengers and the Fantastic Four return from the pocket dimension of *Heroes Reborn*. Four new series are launched, such as *Avengers* by Kurt Busiek and George Pérez.

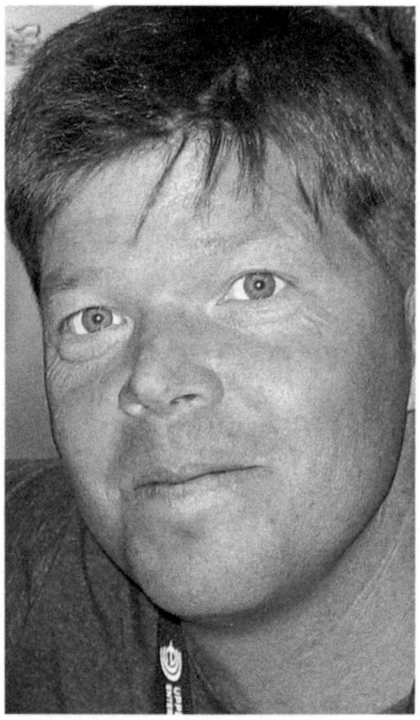

commercial hit. At first stories and dialogue were by Chris Claremont, but following his departure, Lee began cranking out subjects, and John Byrne, an old acquaintance of X-fans, was brought in to help with the dialogue. Other creators that were hailed by critics and fans in the early 1990s included Erik Larsen, who took over for McFarlane on *The Amazing Spider-Man*, and Marc Silvestri (cofounder of Image Comics, no coincidence there), who started out on *X-Men* and moved on to *Wolverine*.

Other artists received as much attention during the '90s, and those who did were almost all involved with best-sellers tied into the X-Men, like the Kubert brothers, Adam and Andy, sons of the legendary Joe Kubert, and Joe Madureira, as we have already seen. Others, like John Romita, Jr., and Mark Bagley, were able to combine quality and quantity, and were among the most reliable comic book artists in the business. By the late 1990s, when artist adulation had tapered off, it was Joe Quesada who won his way into fans' hearts. Marvel readers remembered his short but powerful *X-Factor* cycle, which was written by Peter David.

In *Daredevil*, which was part of the Marvel Knights imprint overseen by Quesada himself, he proved to be a versatile and mature illustrator, filling panels with details without compromising when it came to characters' spectacular feats and

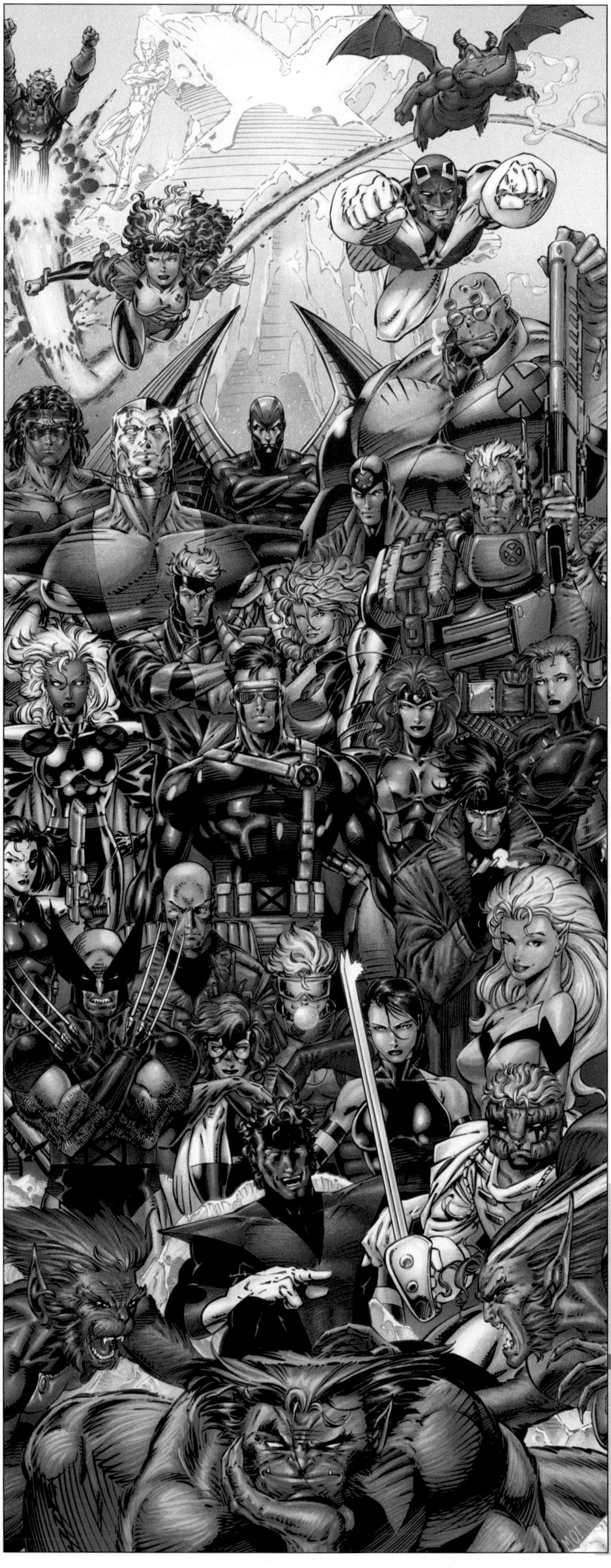

ABOVE: Artist Rob Liefeld.

RIGHT: Remastered X-Men *Forever Door Poster* by Jim Lee (June 2009).

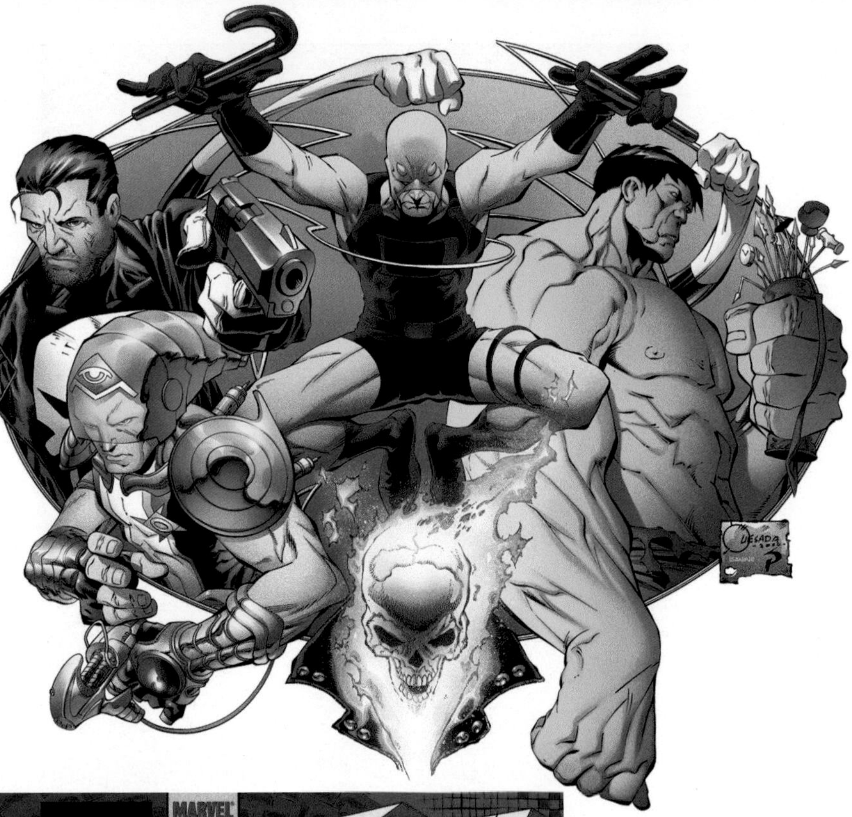

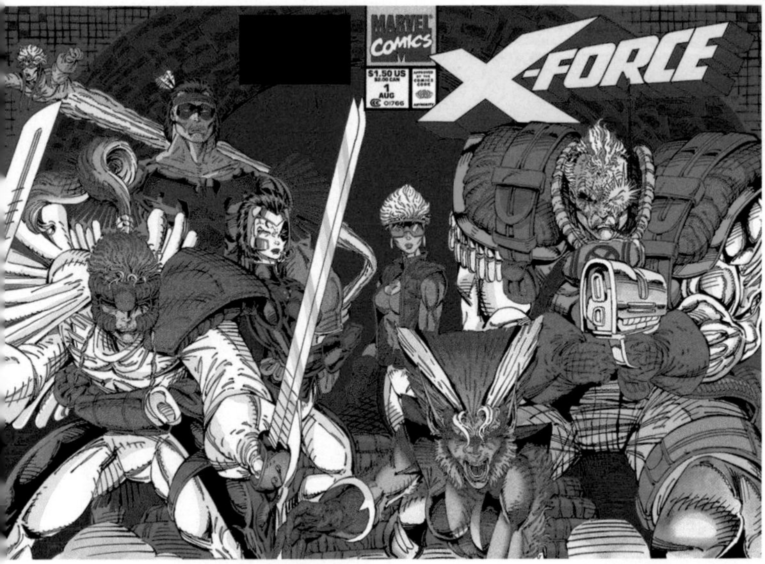
MARVEL COMICS
X-FORCE

acting. Such success was also thanks to Kevin Smith, who wrote one of the best-loved and best-told stories featuring Matt Murdock, "Guardian Devil." As Joe Quesada wrote years later, "While there have been some guys from Hollywood who came in and did good work, nobody came in with the cachet and cred a guy like Kevin had. Kevin's jumping into the pool resonated throughtout the Hollywood community and made a lot of Hollywood creators and writers who had thought about comics realize, 'You know, I could do that, too.'" In recognition of the huge success of the Marvel Knights imprint, Quesada would soon be handsomely rewarded by Marvel…

ABOVE: Promotional piece for the 20th anniversary of *Marvel Knights* (2018) by Joe Quesada.

LEFT: *X-Force #1* (August 1991). Cover and art by Rob Liefeld.

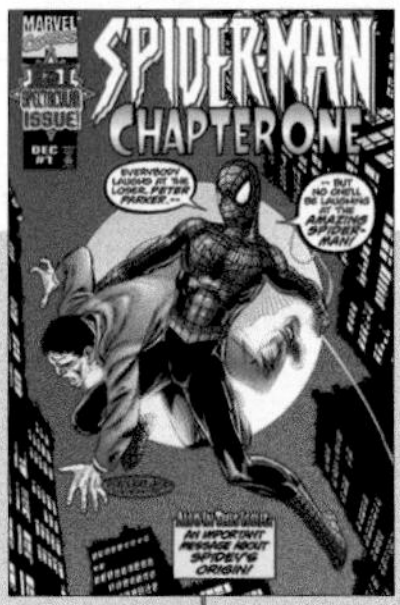
SPIDER-MAN
CHAPTER ONE

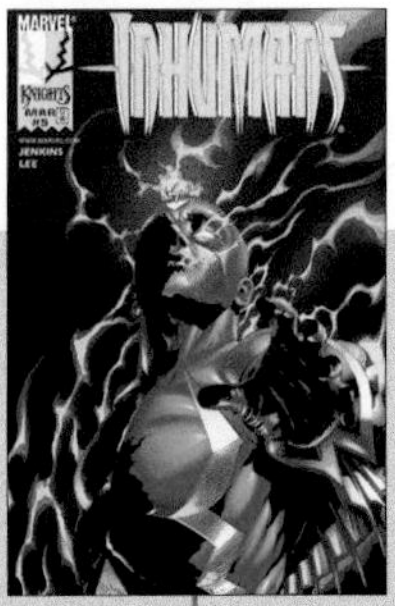
INHUMANS

2000

DECEMBER 1998

John Byrne is back at Marvel to write and draw *Spider-Man: Chapter One*, a limited series that retells Spidey's beginnings.

JUNE 1999

Seen for the first time in *Inhumans #5*, a new Black Widow, Yelena Belova, fights with Natasha Romanov in the mini-series *Black Widow*.

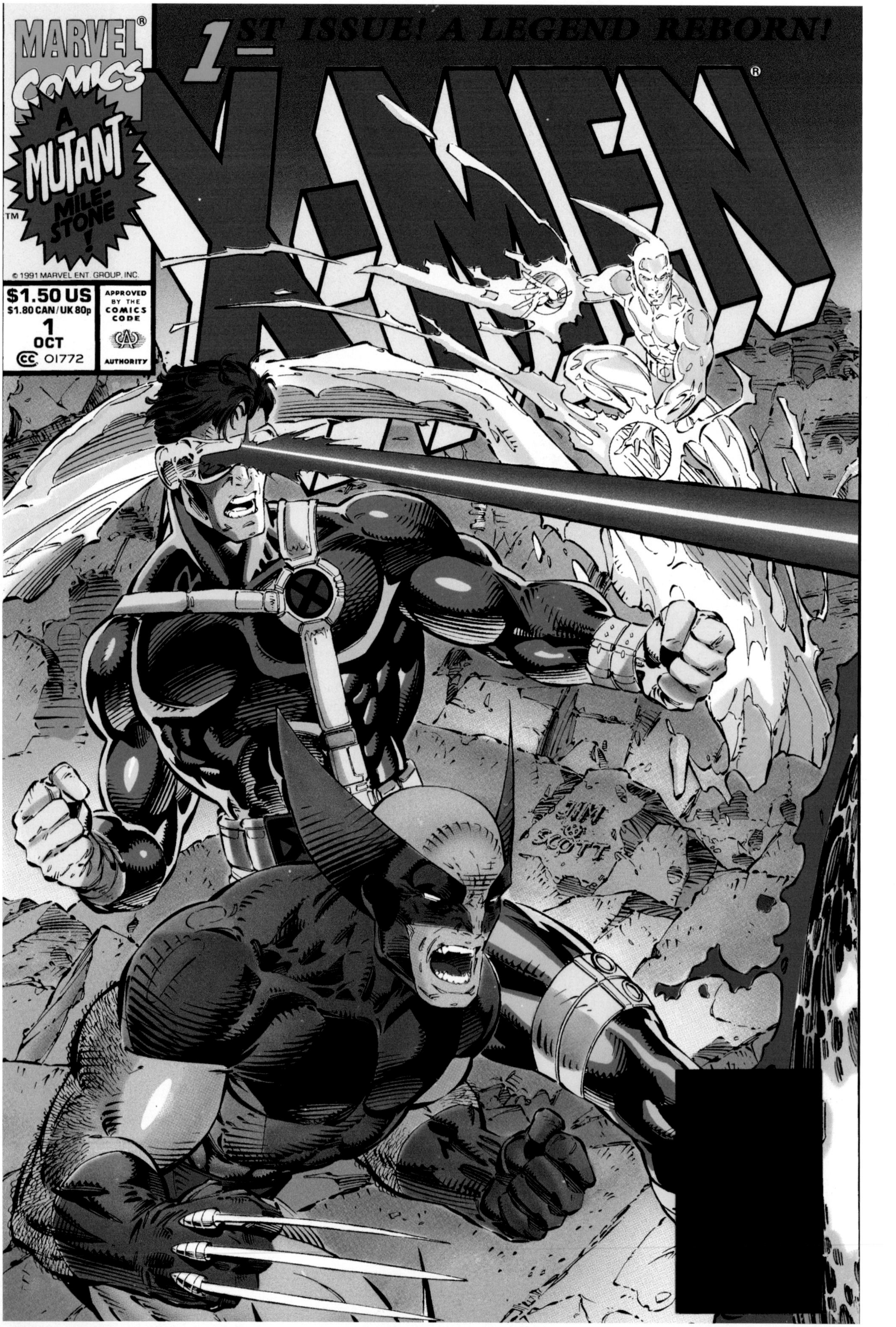
MARVEL®
COMICS
1ST ISSUE! A LEGEND REBORN!
X-MEN®
A MUTANT MILE-STONE!
TM
© 1991 MARVEL ENT. GROUP, INC.
$1.50 US
$1.80 CAN/UK 80p
1
OCT
01772
APPROVED BY THE COMICS CODE AUTHORITY
JIM & SCOTT

A NEW MILLENNIUM AWAITS

As the dawn of a new century looms, Marvel experiments and tackles the issues of the day in a way that only Marvel could.

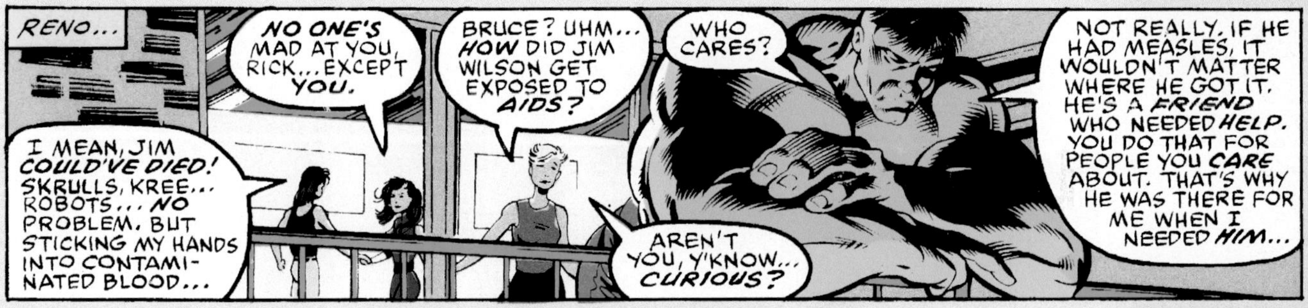
RENO...
I MEAN, JIM COULD'VE DIED! SKRULLS, KREE... ROBOTS... NO PROBLEM. BUT STICKING MY HANDS INTO CONTAMI- NATED BLOOD...
NO ONE'S MAD AT YOU, RICK... EXCEPT YOU.
BRUCE? UHM... HOW DID JIM WILSON GET EXPOSED TO AIDS?
WHO CARES?
AREN'T YOU, Y'KNOW... CURIOUS?
NOT REALLY. IF HE HAD MEASLES, IT WOULDN'T MATTER WHERE HE GOT IT. HE'S A FRIEND WHO NEEDED HELP. YOU DO THAT FOR PEOPLE YOU CARE ABOUT. THAT'S WHY HE WAS THERE FOR ME WHEN I NEEDED HIM...

The Cold War was over. The Berlin Wall had fallen. The threat of a nuclear war seemed to have subsided. Yet fear remained...fear sparked and stoked by invisible, microscopic threats, like viruses. Peter David and Gary Frank brought AIDS, a hot topic throughout the '90s, to the pages of comic books. Jim Wilson, nephew of the Falcon and sidekick to the Hulk in the 1970s, contracted the HIV virus and died in *The Incredible Hulk #420* (cover-dated August 1994) with the Jade Giant at his bedside. Even if at that time the Hulk possessed Bruce Banner's intelligence, he was helpless before his terminally ill friend.

The era of the speculators, who would buy up copies of comic books in bulk and sell them to collectors for a profit, was coming to an end. This was the start of a new and different chapter, which would be more focused on TV and the movies, and characters that loomed ever larger in the collective consciousness, in part due to the impact of cartoons and merchandising. In particular, trading cards became so popular that Marvel acquired one of the leading card manufacturers, the Fleer Corporation, to produce custom-designed collections, often

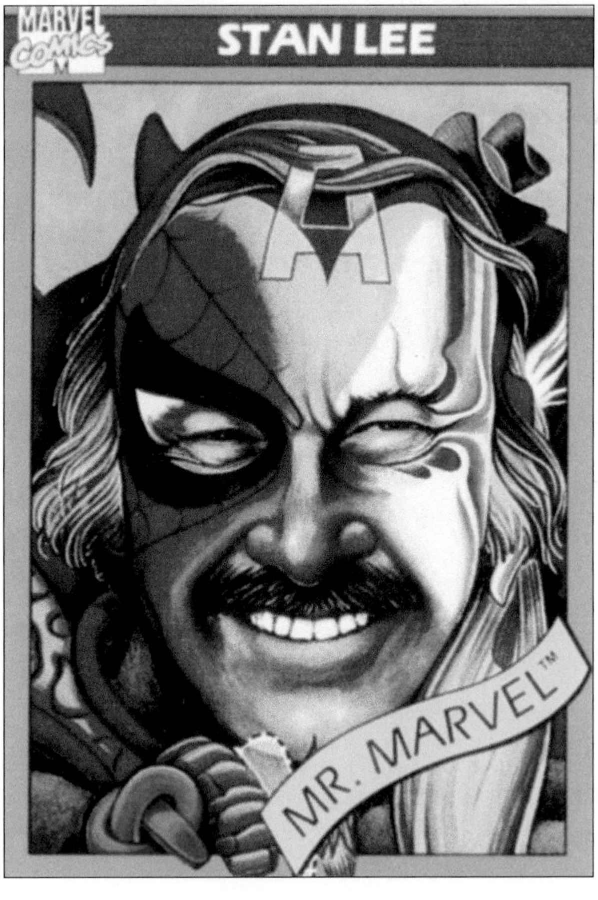
MARVEL COMICS
STAN LEE
MR. MARVEL™

OPPOSITE PAGE: *X-Men* #1 (October 1991). Art by Jim Lee.

LEFT: Stan Lee's Skybox trading card by John Romita, Sr.

ABOVE: Bruce Banner learns his friend Jim Wilson has HIV in *The Incredible Hulk #388* (December 1991). Script by Peter David. Art by Dale Keown (pencils), Mark Farmer (inks), Glynis Oliver (colors), Joe Rosen (letters).

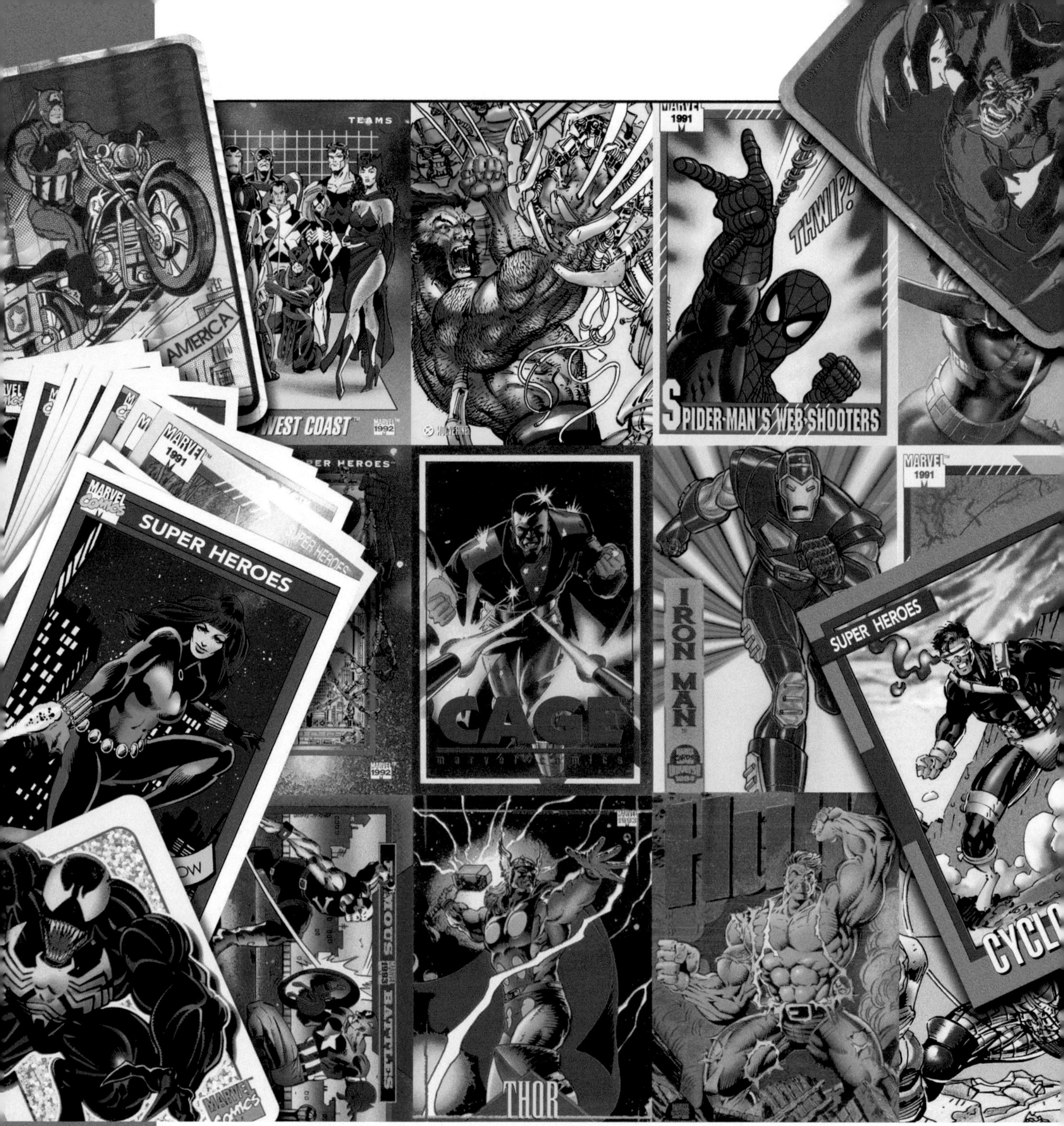
AMERICA
TEAMS
WEST COAST
THWIP!
SPIDER-MAN'S WEB-SHOOTERS
SUPER HEROES
CAGE
IRON MAN
SUPER HEROES
THOR

ABOVE
An assortment of Marvel trading cards from the early 1990s.

based on current comic book events. Cards contained replicas of special effects used on covers at that time—metallic, relief, holographic, and 3D effects were used. Collectors gobbled them up, and artists were glad to have further opportunities to illustrate the characters that had made them famous.

As for cartoons, after the incredible success of *X-Men: The Animated Series* (the longest Marvel cartoon series on record, with 80 episodes), the 1990s saw the return of Spider-Man. The 65 episodes of the *Spider-Man* cartoon series (1994–1998) weighed in on stories old and new, including the arrival of Venom. Each episode was introduced by the blistering guitar of Aerosmith's Joe Perry, who wrote an all-new theme for the web-slinger.

As arcade video games evolved, and later with the advent of the first consoles, games featuring Marvel Super Heroes became more complex too. They appeared on all the big platforms, from Sega to Nintendo, and took inspiration from comic book events like *Maximum Carnage*. The eponymous side-scrolling beat 'em up video game by Capcom gave players the chance to play in the roles of Spider-Man, the X-Men, and even the Punisher. Besides playing with action figures, kids could now maneuver their favorite Super Heroes with joysticks—first in arcades, later at home. Not all Marvel video games would be hits, although some did achieve cult status. Like *Marvel Super Heroes vs. Street Fighter*, a crossover fighting game with graphics that recalled the modern design seen in comic books at that time. It was followed by more games in which Marvel Super Heroes took on various Capcom characters. ■

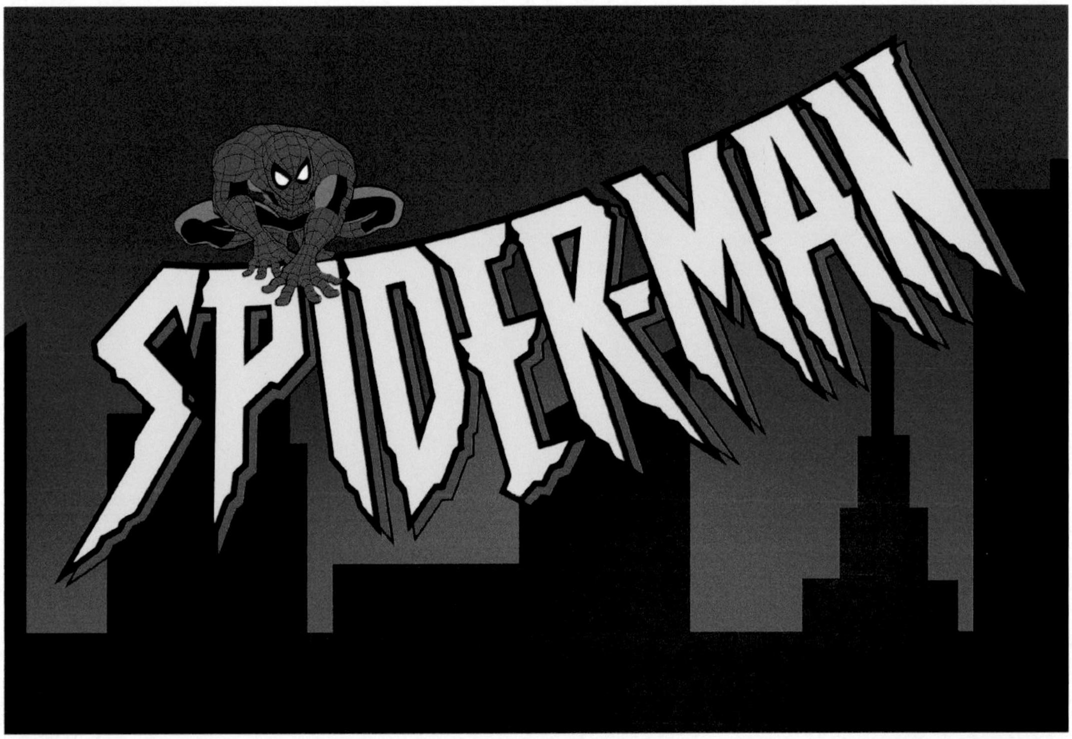
SPIDER-MAN

LEFT: The logo from the 1990s *Spider-Man* animated series.

BELOW: Marvel proved a popular video-game brand throughout the 1990s.

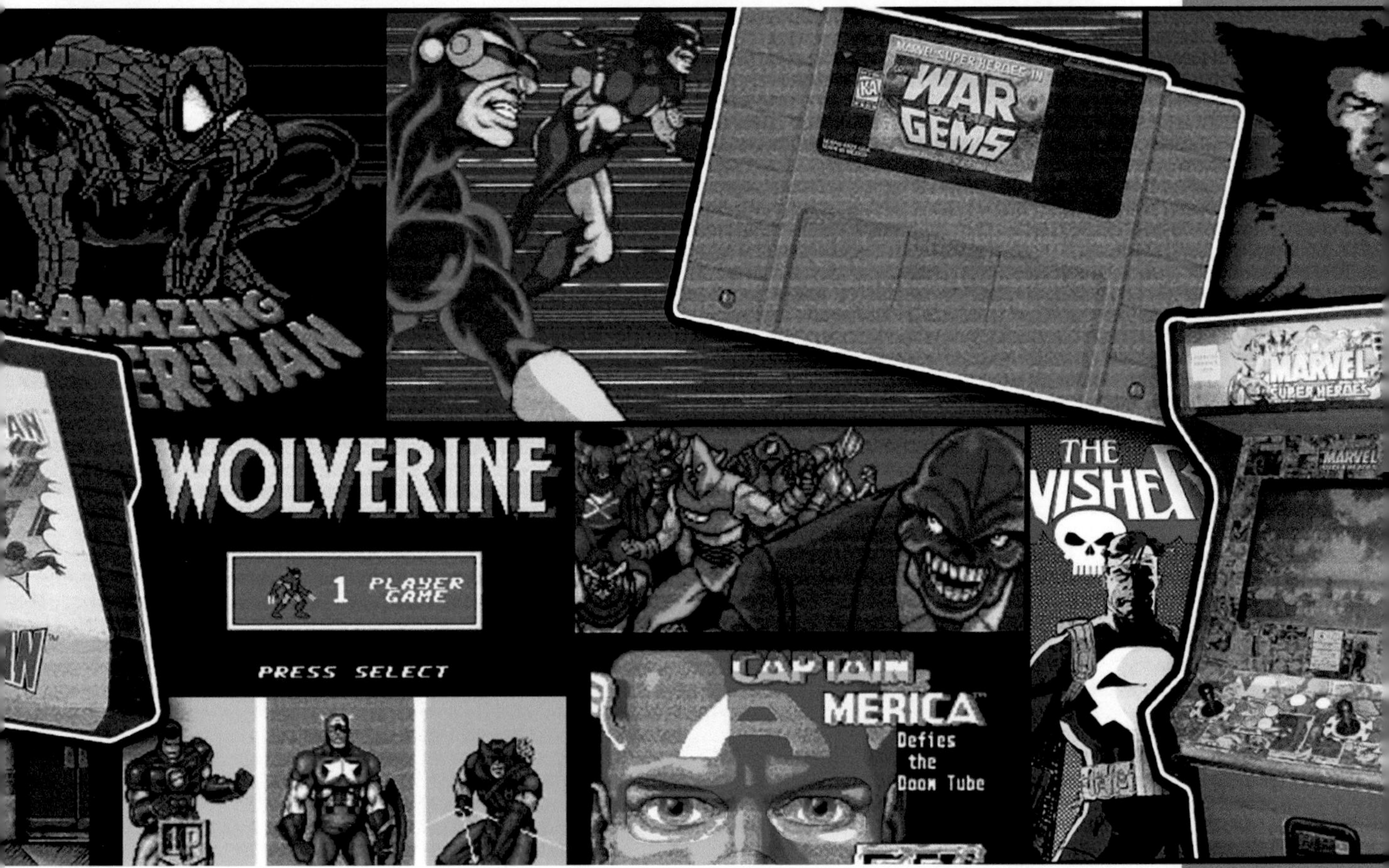
AMAZING
ER-MAN
MARVEL SUPER HEROES IN
WAR GEMS
MARVEL SUPER HEROES
WOLVERINE
1 PLAYER GAME
PRESS SELECT
THE
CAPTAIN
MERICA
Defies
the
Doom Tube

THE 2000s

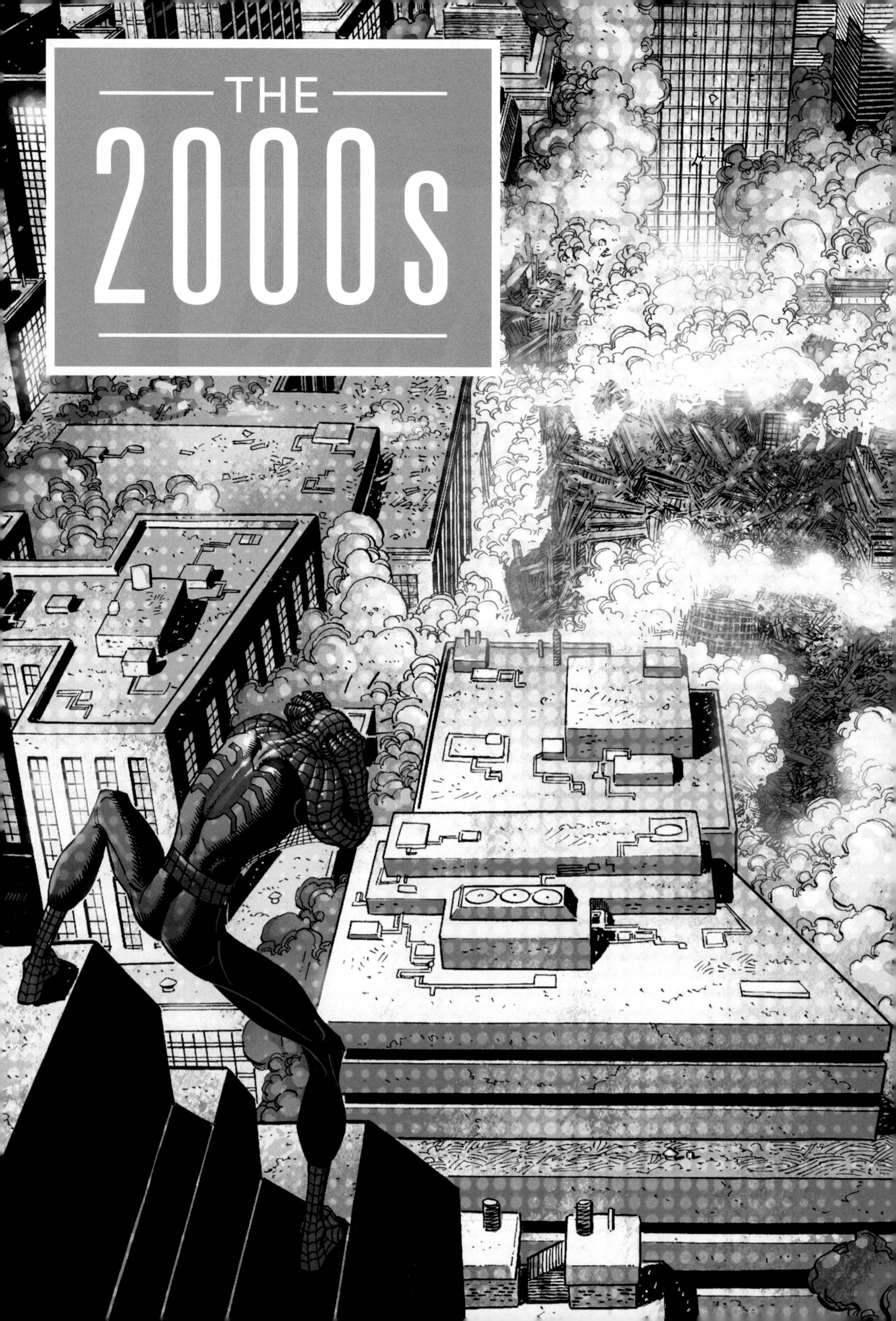

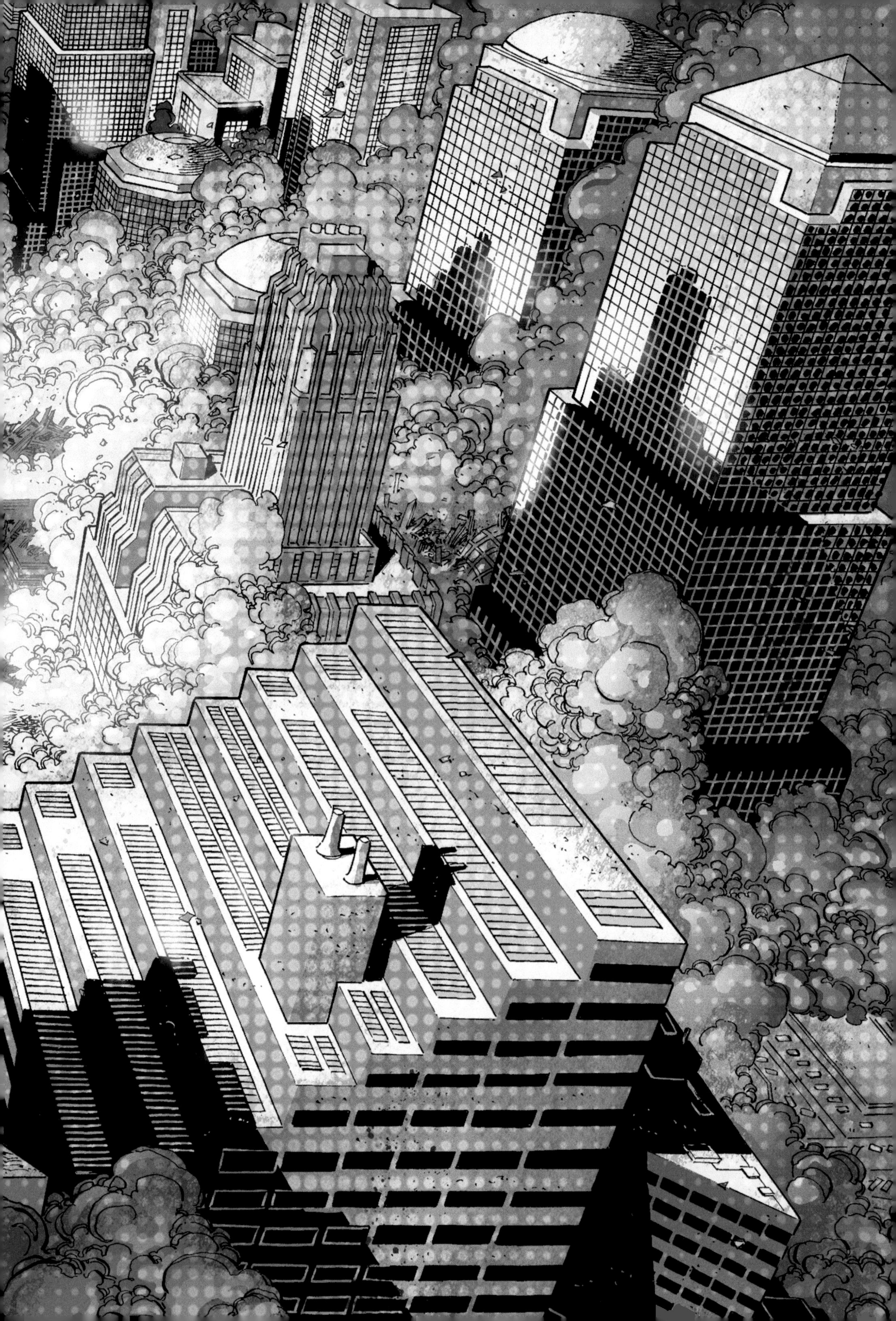

INTRODUCTION

OUT OF THE DARKNESS

As Marvel entered a new millennium, there would be new challenges and obstacles to overcome—and new success as well.

Who knows, once fear of the Millennium Bug had abated, whether anyone at the dawning of 2000s would have expected this to be a crucial decade for Marvel? Hot off his success with *Marvel Knights*, the imprint he headed, in August 2000 Joe Quesada was appointed Editor in Chief. "Joe Q" definitely played a part in making those stories among the most ground-breaking, revolutionary and adult-oriented in Marvel history. Readers had their first taste in April 2000, with the arrival of one of the biggest names in the business, Garth Ennis, who wrote *The Punisher*. The new Marvel Knights series dedicated to the vigilante turned out to be one of Marvel's most innovative and provocative productions of all time, also thanks to the artwork of Steve Dillon, one of Ennis's long-time partners.

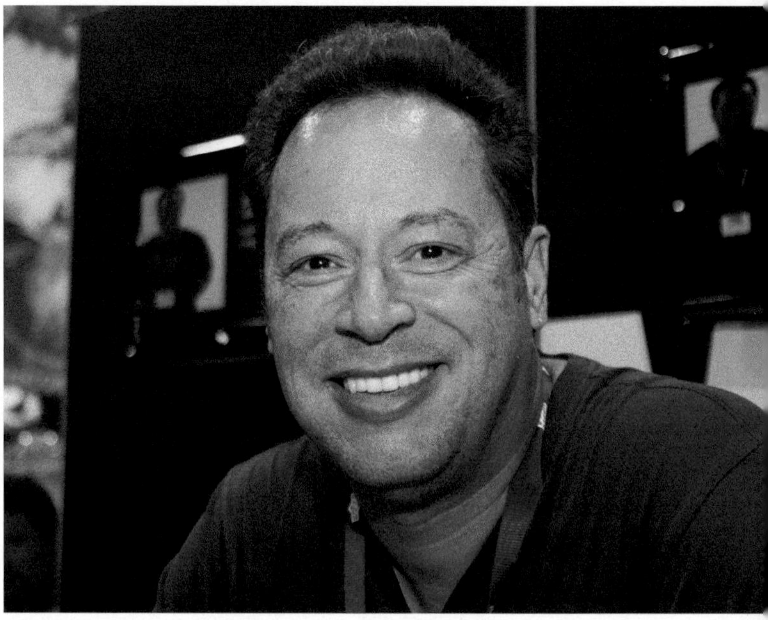

RIGHT: Joe Quesada, Marvel's Editor in Chief from 2000 to 2011.

2000

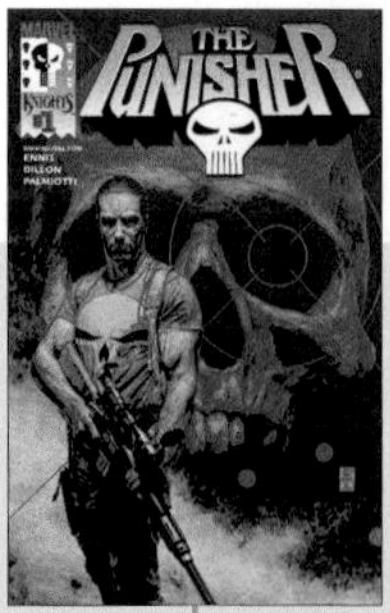
THE PUNISHER

APRIL 2000

The Marvel Knights imprint begins its longtime series *The Punisher*, written by iconoclast Garth Ennis.

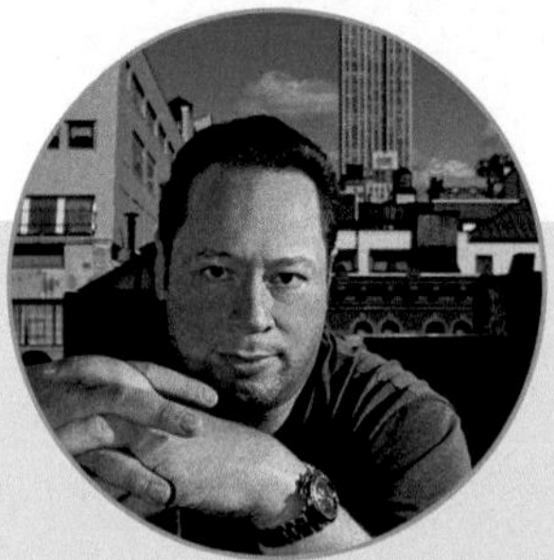

AUGUST 2000

Joe Quesada replaces Bob Harras as Editor in Chief. Bill Jemas is named president.

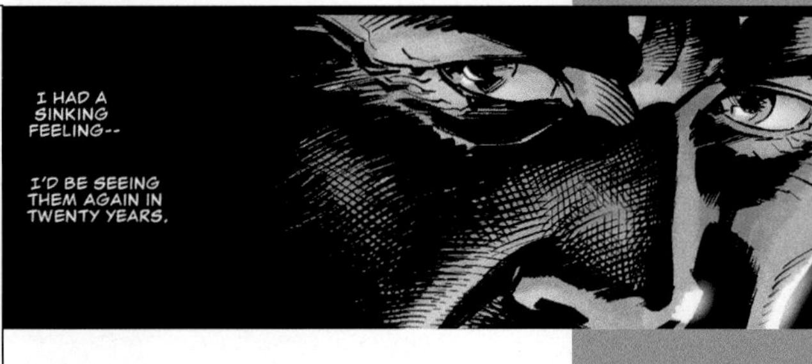
I HAD A SINKING FEELING--
I'D BE SEEING THEM AGAIN IN TWENTY YEARS.

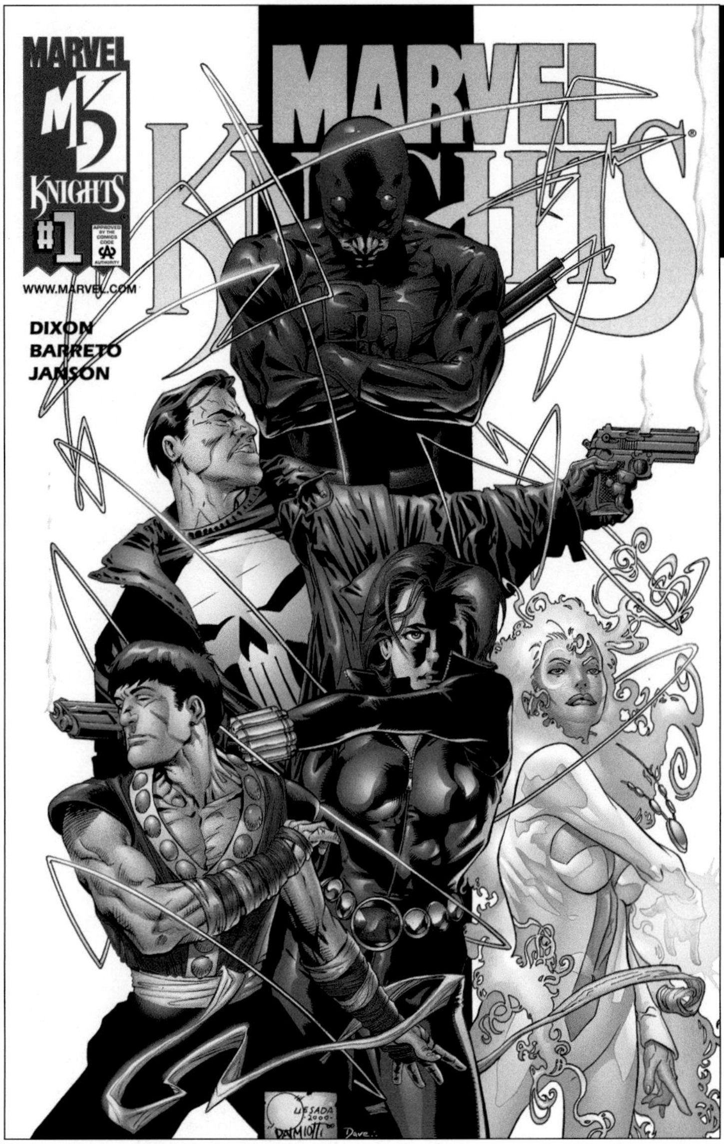
MARVEL
KNIGHTS
#1
MARVEL KNIGHTS
WWW.MARVEL.COM
DIXON
BARRETO
JANSON

With the promotion of Quesada and the arrival of a new president, Bill Jemas, who was very much involved in editorial decision-making, the recipe that had worked for *Marvel Knights* would be applied to the entire series. Writers from indie comics were called in, like Brian Michael Bendis, or from the competition, like Mark Millar and Grant Morrison, who's been active since the 1980s. Following the example of Kevin Smith, the 2000s saw more writers from Hollywood as well, such as Bob Gale (who wrote *Back to the Future*), Joss Whedon, idolized by fans for his *Buffy the Vampire Slayer*, and—most notably—J. Michael Straczynski, who at that time was riding high thanks to his sci-fi TV series *Babylon 5*. Throughout the 2000s these and other writers would relaunch history-making series featuring characters like the Avengers and Thor, consolidating sales, and winning back readers.

To reach out to new fans, however, it would be necessary to leave behind decades of continuity, just as Jim Shooter had done with the New Universe twenty years earlier. At the same time, characters that had long since made their way into the collective

ABOVE: Panel from *The Punisher #44* (March 2007). Script by Garth Ennis. Art by Lan Medina (pencils), Bill Reinhold (inks), Raul Trevino (colors), Randy Gentile (letters).

LEFT: *Marvel Knights #1* (dated July 2000, released May 31, 2000). Art by Joe Quesada, Danny Miki, and Dave Kemp.

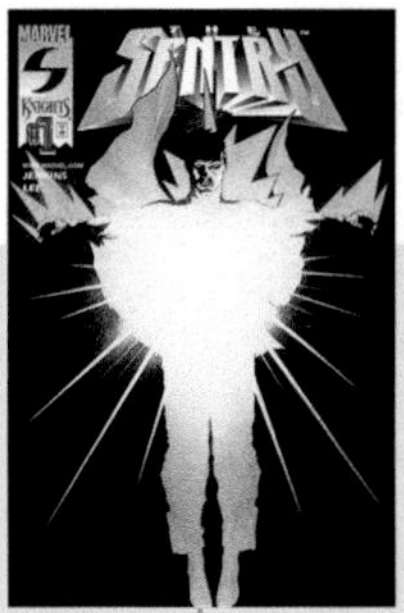

SEPTEMBER 2000

The debut of a new "old" Super Hero, Sentry: Created by Paul Jenkins and Jae Lee, the comic was released as if it was a lost work from the 1960s.

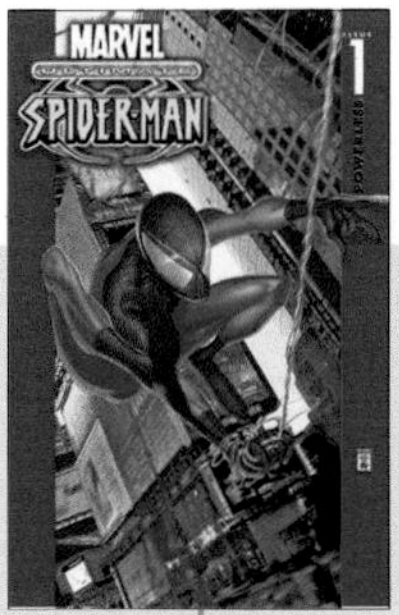
MARVEL
SPIDER-MAN
1

OCTOBER 2000

The Ultimate imprint is born with *Ultimate Spider-Man #1*, by Brian Bendis and Mark Bagley.

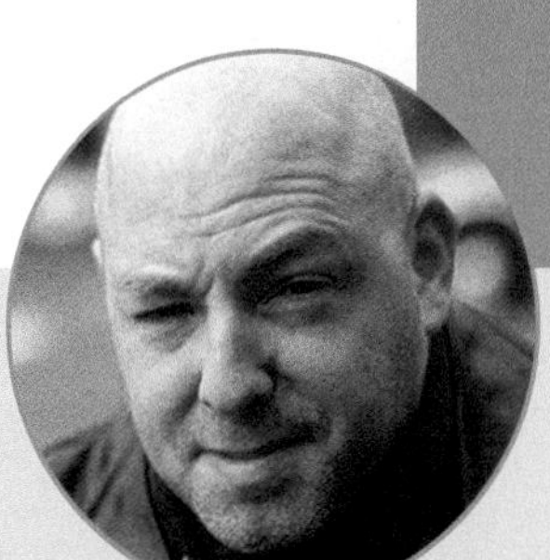

MAY 2001

Brian Bendis begins writing for *Daredevil*. His stint runs four years and is much acclaimed.

NEW X-MEN

The X-Men made their comeback in the 2000s thanks to Grant Morrison and Frank Quitely, who reinvented the characters in a lengthy run which, on the one hand paid tribute to classics by Claremont in terms of themes (space travel, a dystopic future, romantic intrigue), and on the other was brimming with modern solutions. They began with the look—spandex costumes were replaced by biker wear, like the gear seen in Bryan Singer's films. In 2004 Joss Whedon would take over as writer for *The Astonishing X-Men*. He brought back classic costumes, while maintaining an up-to-date spectacular style —and we have John Cassaday to thank for the artwork.

RIGHT: Variant cover for *House of M #1* (June 2005). Art by Joe Quesada.

NEW X MEN

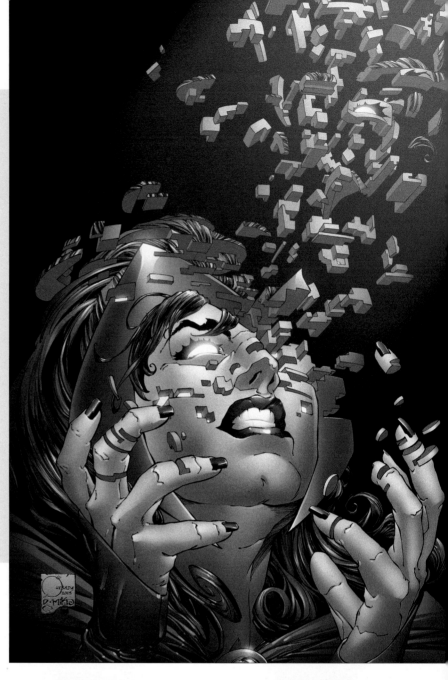

JULY 2001

Grant Morrison and Frank Quitely reinvent the mutants for the new millennium in *New X-Men #114* (following the old X-Men chronology).

MAX
ALI S
PARENTAL ADVISORY EXPLICIT CONTENT

NOVEMBER 2001

The MAX imprint is born with the release of *Alias*, the new hit written by Bendis.

MARVEL COMICS
the AMAZING SPIDER-MAN
36

DECEMBER 2001

J. Michael Straczynski and John Romita, Jr., dedicate *The Amazing Spider-Man #36* to the 9/11 attacks.

consciousness would have to remain recognizable, true to the classic series of the past. The Ultimate imprint was born. It wouldn't be long before even old fans were won over too. It was a parallel world where Spider-Man, the X-Men, the Fantastic Four and the Avengers (here called the Ultimates) took their first steps. They were written by the latest arrivals, and illustrated by Marvel superstars like Mark Bagley, Bryan Hitch, and Andy and Adam Kubert.

But no one had foreseen an event that would send comics creators for a loop, upend all certainty, and set the stage for story themes for the next ten years and beyond. The attack that destroyed the Twin Towers on September 11, 2001 sent shockwaves around the world. The sound of the crashes and explosions echoed through the offices at Marvel, at that time on 40th Street in Manhattan, not far from Ground Zero.

Marvel people lost friends and relatives. But there was no time to despair. It was time to rise again. Just like Marvel Super Heroes, who had won so many battles in New York. Marvel went immediately to work on tributes to victims and heroes like firemen, police officers, doctors, and rescue workers. Just five weeks after the attacks the 64-page *Heroes* was released, featuring artwork by a host of world-famous artists. The first print run of 100,000 sold out in two days, hundreds of thousands of more copies came rolling off the presses, all the proceeds going to the Twin Towers Fund.

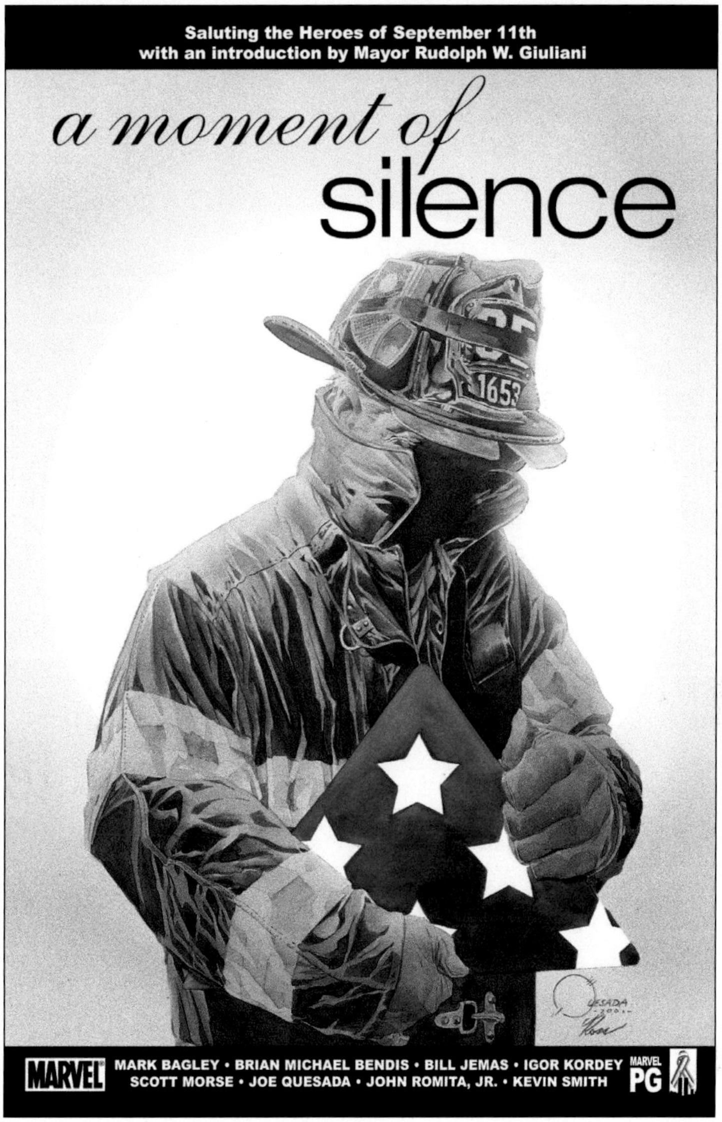
Saluting the Heroes of September 11th
with an introduction by Mayor Rudolph W. Giuliani
a moment of silence
1653
MARVEL
MARK BAGLEY • BRIAN MICHAEL BENDIS • BILL JEMAS • IGOR KORDEY
SCOTT MORSE • JOE QUESADA • JOHN ROMITA, JR. • KEVIN SMITH
MARVEL PG

LEFT: Saluting the heroes of September 11. *A Moment of Silence #1* (February 2002). Art by Joe Quesada, Alex Ross, Gene Ha, Shad Petoski.

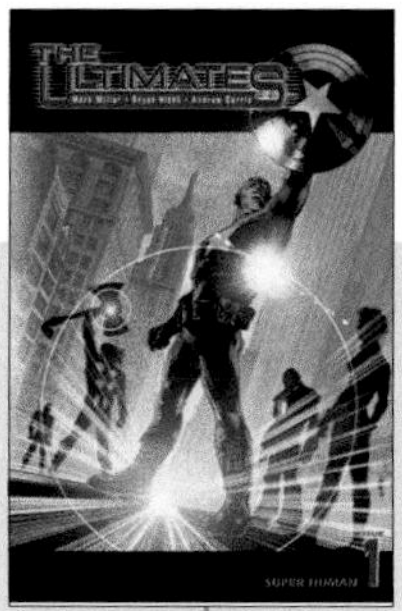
THE ULTIMATES

MARCH 2002

Following *The Ultimate Spider-Man* and *The Ultimate X-Men*, *Ultimates* is released.

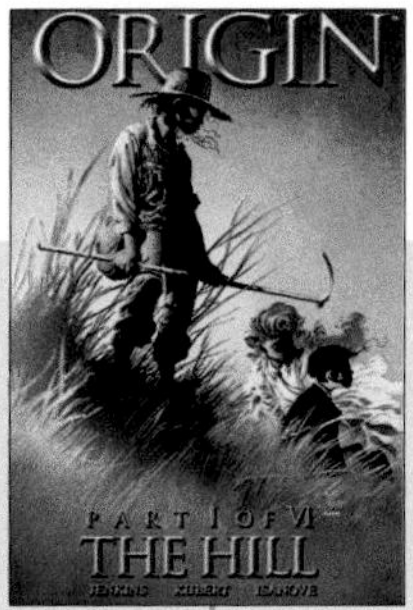
ORIGIN
PART I OF VI
THE HILL

APRIL 2002

With the conclusion of the limited series *Origin*, Wolverine's early years are revealed, along with other incredible details.

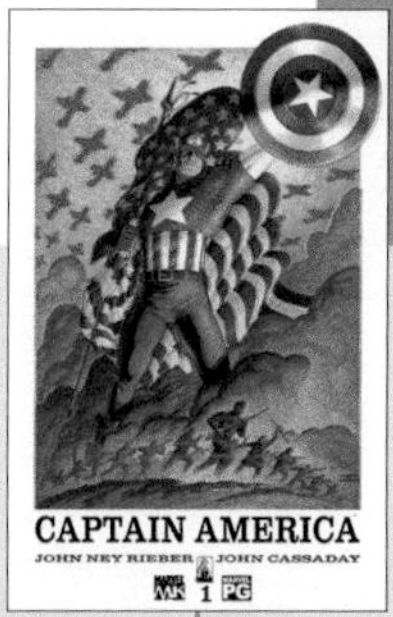
CAPTAIN AMERICA
JOHN NEY RIEBER JOHN CASSADAY
PG

JUNE 2002

Captain America deals with the consequences of 9/11 in a new series by John Ney Rieber and John Cassaday, battling it out with Islamic terrorists.

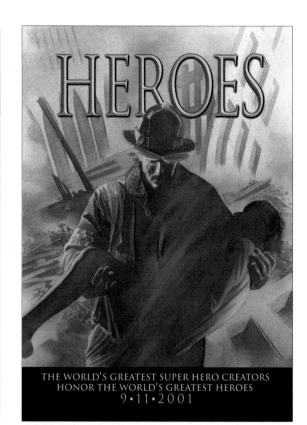

THE WORLD'S GREATEST SUPER HERO CREATORS
HONOR THE WORLD'S GREATEST HEROES
9•11•2001

RIGHT:
Mike Deodato, Jr.'s illustration of Captain America in the aftermath of the 9/11 attacks from *Heroes* (2001).

FAR RIGHT:
Marvel's *Heroes* (2001). Art by Alex Ross.

OPPOSITE PAGE
Spider-Man surveys the aftermath of 9/11, *The Amazing Spider-Man #36* (December 2001).Script by J. Michael Straczynski. Art by John Romita, Jr. (pencils), Scott Hanna (inks), Avalon Studios/Dan Kemp (colors), Richard Starkings, Wes Abbott (letters).

Another charitable initiative, the anthology *A Moment of Silence*, released the following February, was a collection of stories featuring fire fighters, cops, and everyday people. Apart from these two special editions, there was also a truly special issue of *The Amazing Spider-Man*, beginning with its all-black cover. Issue #36 of the new series was written by Straczynski and illustrated by Romita, Jr., and showed New York's own Spidey at Ground Zero aiding in the rescue effort just after the attacks.

His desperation is evident, even Dr. Doom and Magneto are aghast at the tragedy. Just as in real life, Super Heroes couldn't keep disaster from occurring, but as Spider-Man himself said in that story, "We could not see it coming. We could not be here before it happened. We could not stop it. But we are here now. You cannot see us for the dust, but we are here. You cannot hear us for the cries, but we are here."

The echo of 9/11 would continue to resonate in Marvel stories for years to come, recalling the creation of Marvel's New Universe—that imaginary world, even if inhabited by Super Heroes wearing costumes and by frightful villains, "is the world outside your window."

JULY 2003

The arrival of a group of new young Super Heroes, the *Runaways*.The series went on to achieve cult status.

NOVEMBER 2003

Laura Kinney (A.K.A. X-23) appears in *NYX #1*. She is a Wolverine clone who made her debut in the cartoon *X-Men: Evolution*, aired from 2000 to 2003.

NOVEMBER 2003

Also in November, Neil Gaiman's monumental *1602* is released—a reworking of the Marvel Universe set in the past.

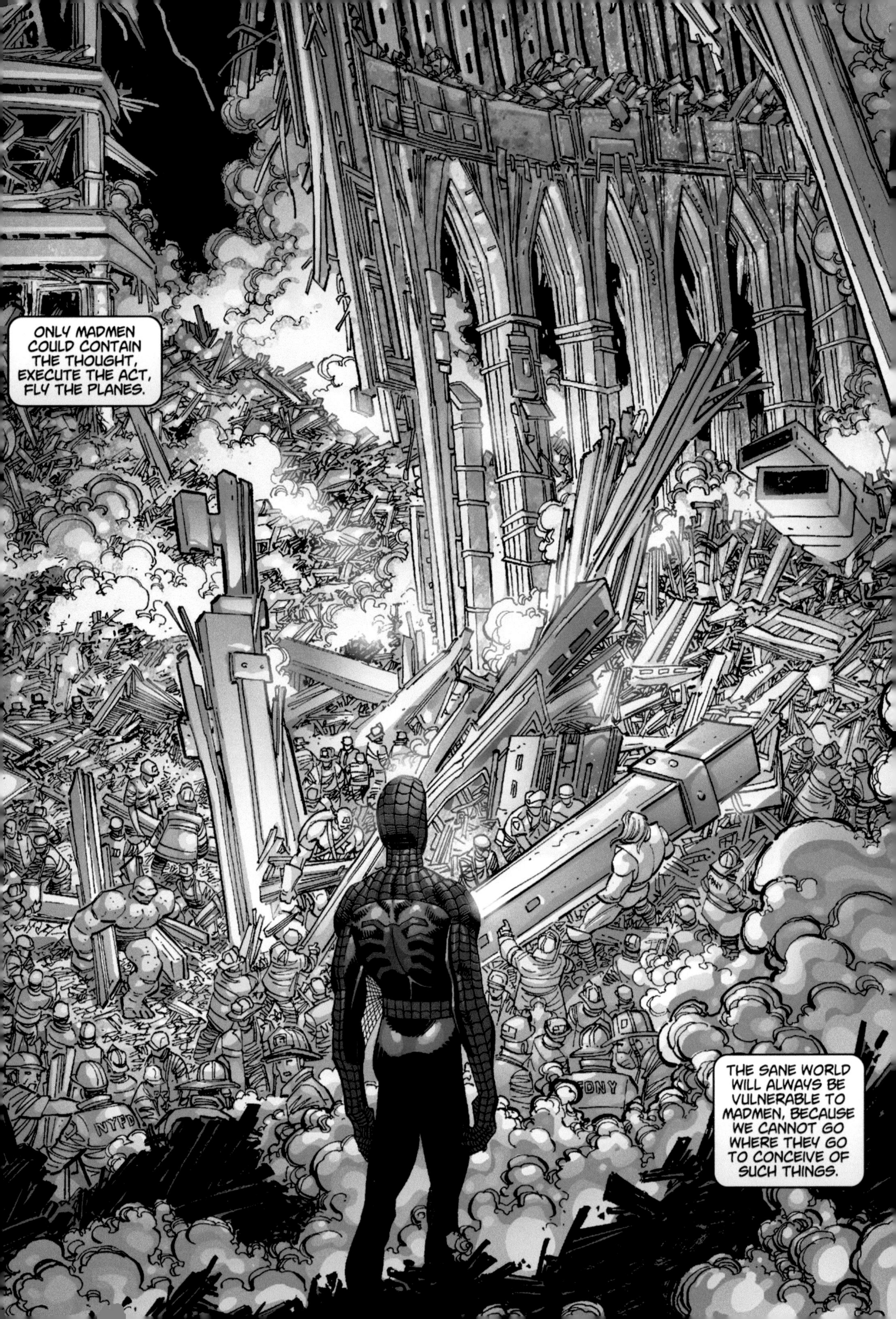
ONLY MADMEN COULD CONTAIN THE THOUGHT, EXECUTE THE ACT, FLY THE PLANES.
FDNY
NYFD
FDNY
THE SANE WORLD WILL ALWAYS BE VULNERABLE TO MADMEN, BECAUSE WE CANNOT GO WHERE THEY GO TO CONCEIVE OF SUCH THINGS.

NOIR AND FOUR-COLOR PRINT

Marvel experiments with new genres, and reinvents the Super Hero with its outstanding *Ultimates*.

When Brian Michael Bendis offered his services to Marvel, Quesada and Jemas knew that he was an excellent writer. He had already done great Hollywoodesque noir and combined hard-boiled fiction with fantasy in a series for Image Comics, *Sam and Twitch*. Taking him on as a writer was a natural choice. If anything was out of the ordinary, it was the series that started off his tenure at Marvel, *Ultimate Spider-Man*.

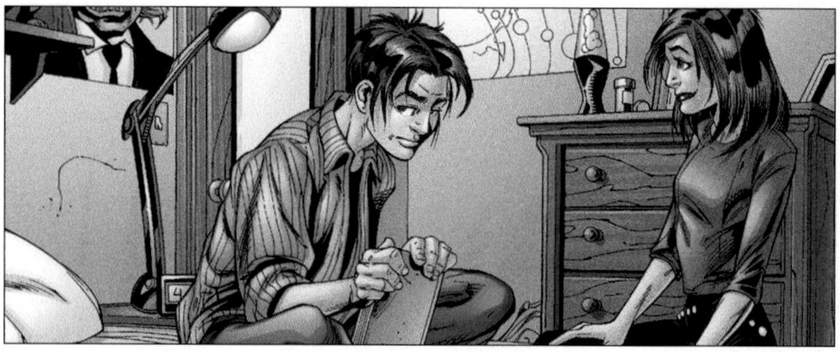

RIGHT: Panel from *Ultimate Spider-Man #13* (November 2001). Art by Mark Bagley (pencils), Art Thibert (inks), JC (colors), Albert Deschesne (letters).

OPPOSITE PAGE: Cover detail from *Fantastic Five #1* (September 2007). Art by Clayton Henry.

It reinvented Peter Parker for the new millennium, providing a contemporary take on his roots. We are treated to high schooler Peter's antics as he meets Mary Jane Watson and becomes a Super Hero fighting off villains the likes of Dr. Octopus and the Green Goblin. These stories, however, had a fresh, modern taste and rhythm, and at the same time were connected to the past thanks to illustrations by Mark Bagley, the benchmark artist who had drawn Spidey in the 1990s. Bendis and Bagley helmed the series for 111 issues, surpassing Lee and Kirby's record with *The Fantastic Four* for consecutive issues by the same pair of creators. Stuart Immonen would replace Bagley, and it wasn't long before he became one of Marvel's top artists, while Bendis worked on the Ultimate imprint until it was shut down in 2016. A few months after the *Ultimate Spider-Man* came the debut of *Ultimate X-Men*, written by Mark Millar, from Scotland, illustrated by brothers Andy and Adam Kubert, who were already favorites of X-fans everywhere. Their younger and morally ambiguous counterparts were a hit too.

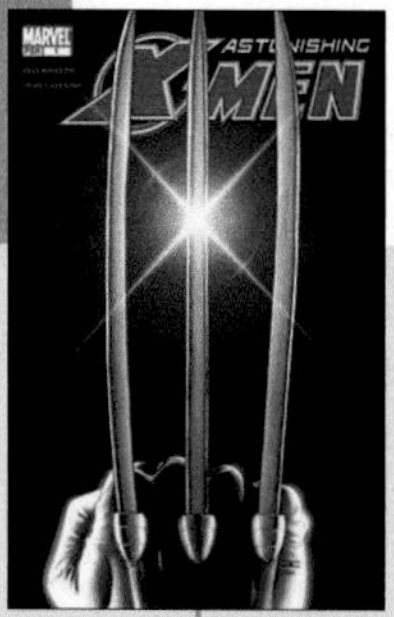

JULY 2004

Ever-popular Joss Whedon takes the reins of *Astonishing X-Men*, illustrated by John Cassaday.

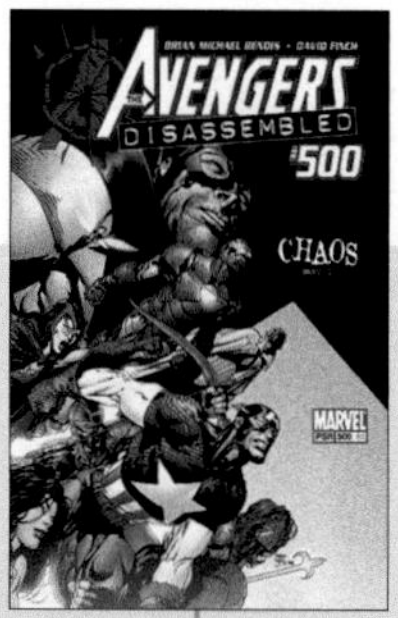
AVENGERS
DISASSEMBLED
#500
CHAOS

SEPTEMBER 2004

Brian Michael Bendis writes the Avengers' most devastating saga, "Avengers Disassembled." It would pave the way for the January 2005 release of *New Avengers*.

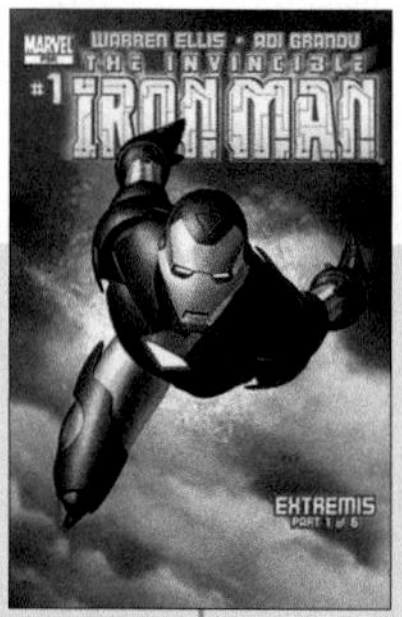
WARREN ELLIS • ADI GRANOV
THE INVINCIBLE
#1
IRON MAN
EXTREMIS

JANUARY 2005

In the saga "Extremis," writer Warren Ellis and artist Adi Granov redefine Iron Man's look for the 21st century.

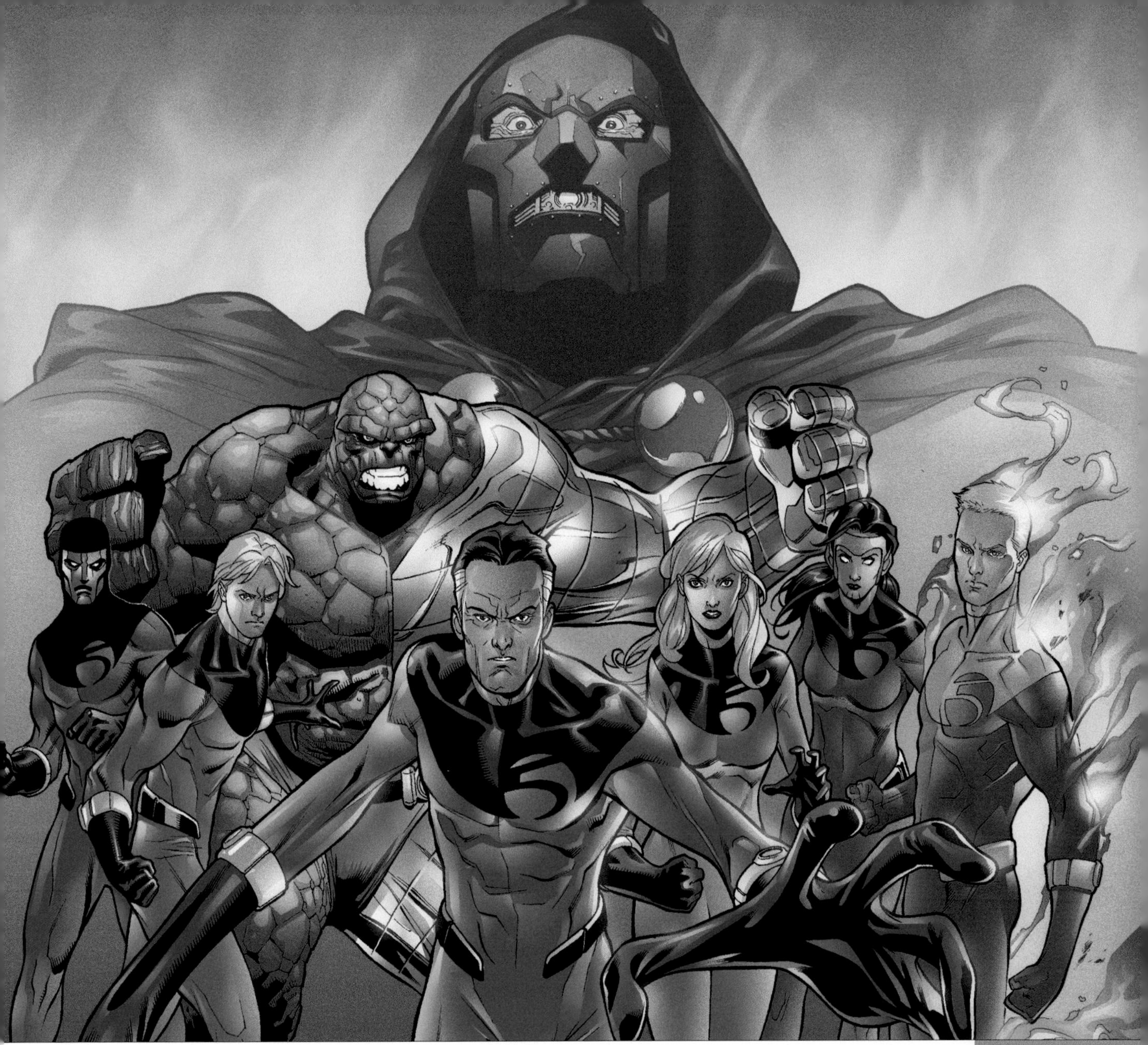

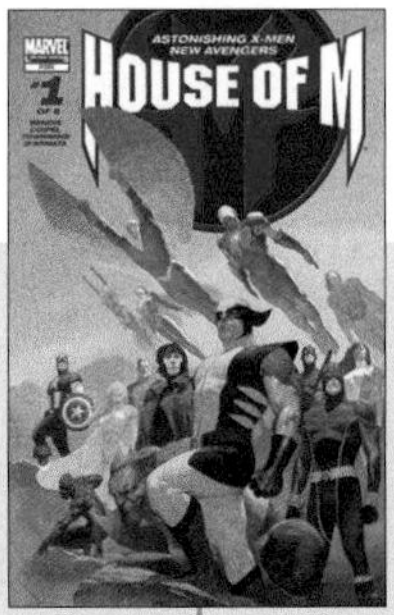
ASTONISHING X-MEN
NEW AVENGERS
HOUSE OF M

AUGUST 2005

The crossover *House of M* reunites the X-Men and the Avengers. It would relaunch the career of Carol Danvers, who would go on to become Captain Marvel.

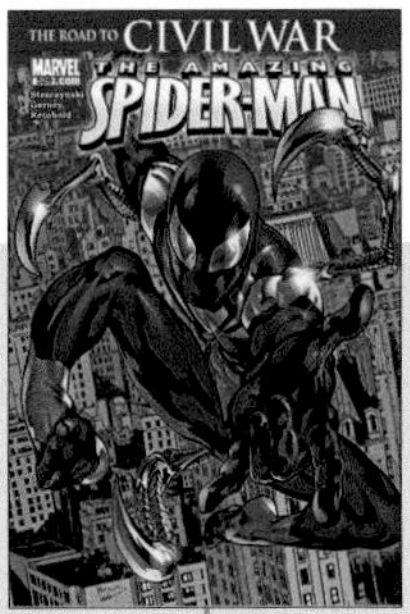
THE ROAD TO CIVIL WAR
THE AMAZING
SPIDER-MAN

APRIL 2006

Tony Stark gives Peter Parker custom-made armor with the arrival of the Iron Spider. The costume is similar to the one seen in *Avengers: Infinity War*.

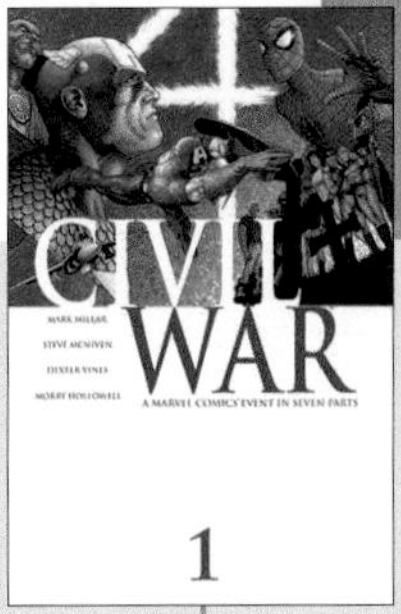
CIVIL
WAR
1

JULY 2006

The beginning of the greatest modern crossover: *Civil War*.

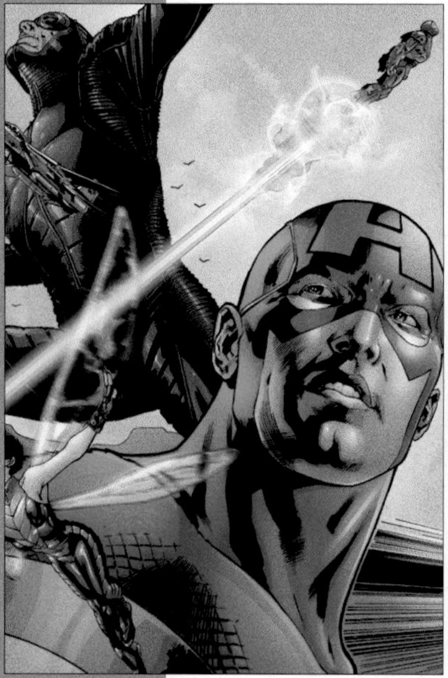

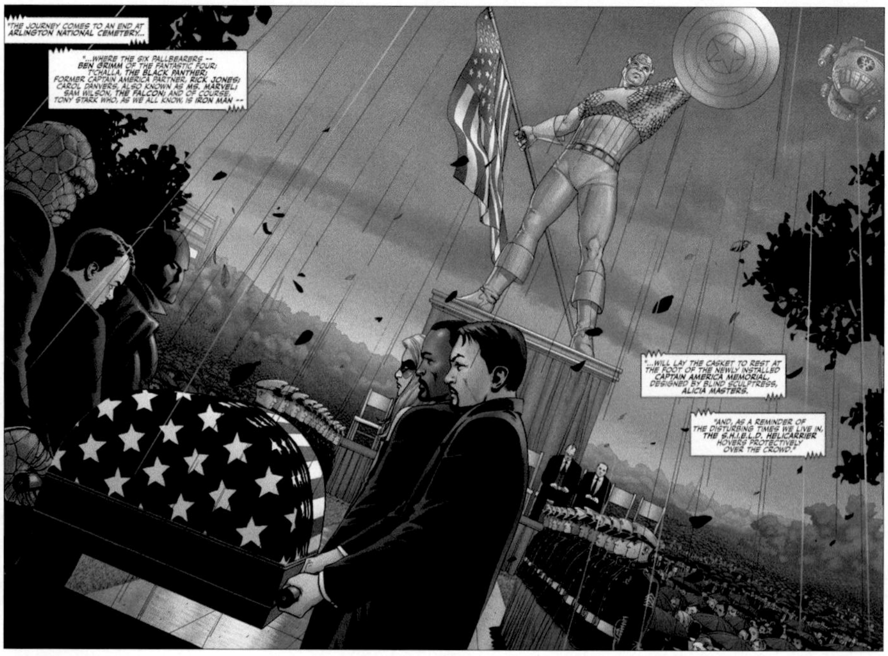

"THE JOURNEY COMES TO AN END AT ARLINGTON NATIONAL CEMETERY...
"...WHERE THE SIX PALLBEARERS -- BEN GRIMM OF THE FANTASTIC FOUR; T'CHALLA, THE BLACK PANTHER; FORMER CAPTAIN AMERICA PARTNER, RICK JONES; CAROL DANVERS, ALSO KNOWN AS MS. MARVEL; SAM WILSON, THE FALCON; AND OF COURSE, TONY STARK WHO, AS WE ALL KNOW, IS IRON MAN --
"...WILL LAY THE CASKET TO REST AT THE FOOT OF THE NEWLY INSTALLED CAPTAIN AMERICA MEMORIAL, DESIGNED BY BLIND SCULPTRESS, ALICIA MASTERS.
"AND, AS A REMINDER OF THE DISTURBING TIMES WE LIVE IN, THE S.H.I.E.L.D. HELICARRIER HOVERS PROTECTIVELY OVER THE CROWD."

ABOVE: Back cover detail from *The Ultimates #1* (March 2002). Art by Bryan Hitch and Paul Mounts.

ABOVE: Panel from *Fallen Son: The Death of Captain America #1* (dated June 2007, released April 4, 2007). Script by Jeph Loeb. Art by Leinil Yu (pencils, inks), Dave McCaig (colors), Richard Starkings and Comicraft (letters).

In 2002 Millar came out with *Ultimates*, this universe's counterpart to the Avengers. Illustrator Bryan Hitch was known for his spectacular and highly detailed panels that smacked of scenes out of a Hollywood blockbuster. *Ultimates* offered an almost realistic approach to Super Heroes, with its sanctimonious Captain America, a cannibal Hulk, and a Thor who was not believed when he claimed to be a god. Standout enemies included Chitauri aliens. More Ultimate series followed, including *Ultimate Fantastic Four*. Ultimate was a survivor alongside the "regular" Marvel Universe, and had a decisive impact on future styles and themes.

The *Civil War* event (see sidebar, page 141) that would soon follow would change the status quo of the Super Heroes for years, especially the fates of Captain America and Iron Man. The series became the standard bearer for trenchant Super Hero action. Shortly after the end of the *Civil War*, Steve Rogers was assassinated. Handcuffed, he was hit by a shooter as he walked down the steps of the Capitol. His death would spark repercussions throughout the Marvel Universe! In the months immediately prior, writer Ed Brubaker and artist Steve Epting brought back Cap's old sidekick Bucky Barnes in *Captain America*.

He didn't die on his last mission, but had been captured by the Soviets, who brainwashed him and transformed him into the killer Winter Soldier. Once back with the good guys, Bucky took Steve's place after his death. A few years later Steve came back. He brought his shield with him.

Another character that went through some major issues was Spider-Man. Initially, Peter sided with Iron Man in the *Civil War* and had publicly revealed his secret identity, before regretting it. In a 2008 story co-written by Straczynski and Quesada and illustrated by Quesada, "One More Day," Peter makes a deal with the demon Mephisto to save the life of Aunt May... in exchange for which, his marriage to Mary Jane would never have happened. At the end of the saga, Peter Parker is once again single. The bond with Mary Jane was still a lifeline for Spider-Man, who experienced new adventures in "Brand New Day." As for Hulk, he gained new popularity in the 2000s thanks to two long sagas—*Planet Hulk* and *World War Hulk*.

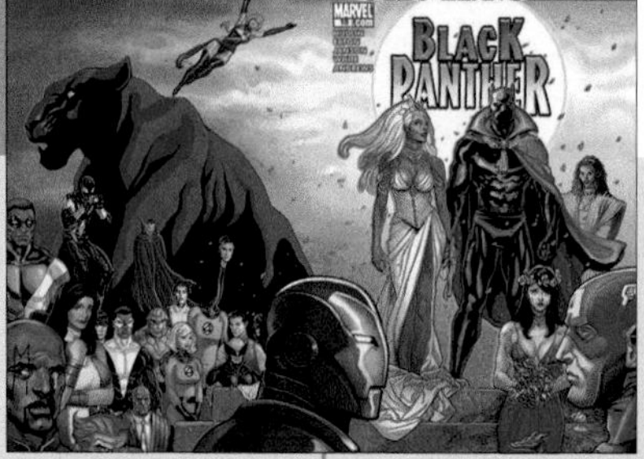

CIVIL WAR CEASE-FIRE
BLACK PANTHER

SEPTEMBER 2006

Super Heroes reunite during a truce in their *Civil War*: Black Panther and Storm, of X-Men fame, are married!

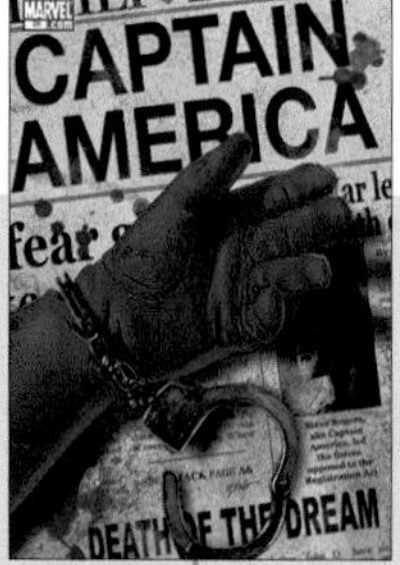

CIVIL WAR EPILOGUE
CAPTAIN AMERICA
DEATH OF THE DREAM

APRIL 2007

At the end of the *Civil War*, Captain America is killed by a mysterious sniper. All part of Red Skull's complex plan.

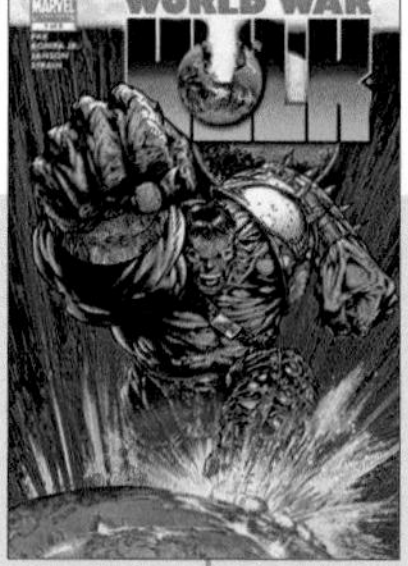

WORLD WAR HULK

AUGUST 2007

After a year of exile in slavery, as a gladiator and a commander of troops on another planet, Hulk is back on Earth declaring war on the Super Heroes in *World War Hulk*.

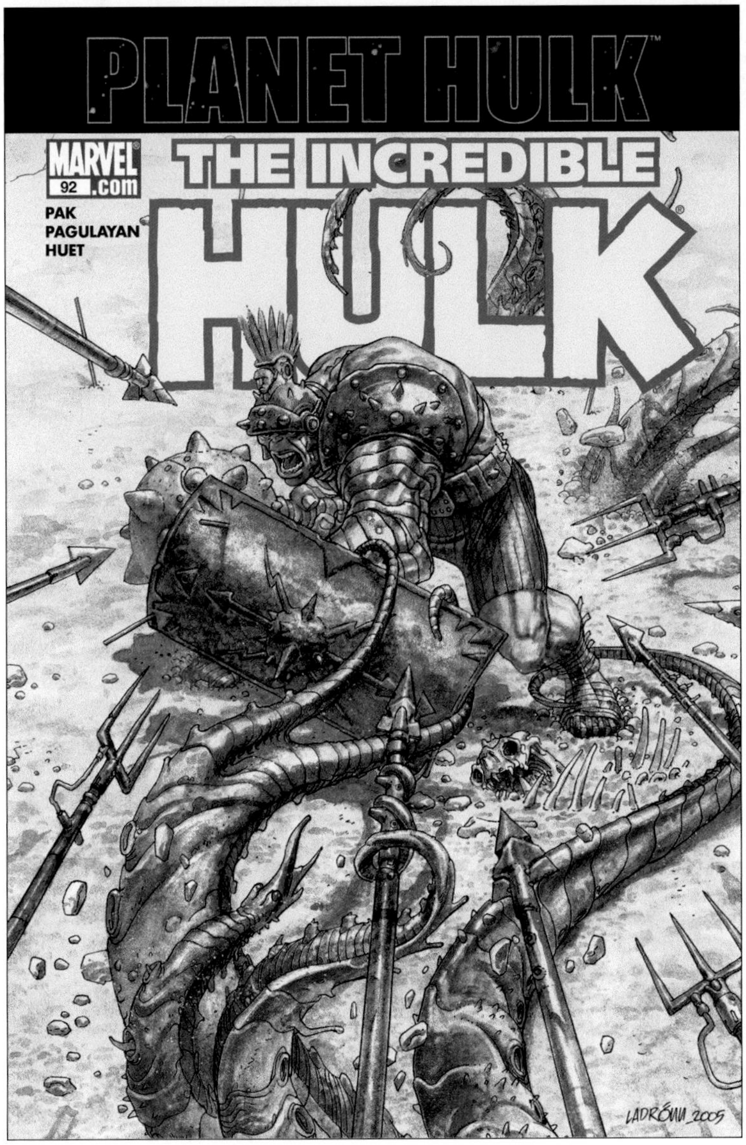
PLANET HULK
MARVEL
92 .com
THE INCREDIBLE
HULK
PAK
PAGULAYAN
HUET
LADRÖNN 2005

CIVIL WAR

Following the success of Ultimate Comics, Mark Millar went to work on the Super Heroes of the Marvel classic *Earth-616*. It was an event that influenced all the plots and the many characters to come. In the 2006 *Civil War* limited series, illustrated by Steve McNiven, Captain America and Iron Man went their separate ways over the issue of the government's new law that Super Heroes had to be officially registered. Under the law, Super Heroes had to reveal their secret identities to the government. The question readers and characters alike were asked: Whose Side Are You On? Captain America's and the freedom of choice, or Iron Man's and the security option? Heroes split into two factions. Stories focused on characters' choices and the consequences. The Avengers would never be the same...for a few years, at least.

LEFT: Part one of the "Planet Hulk" storyline from *The Incredible Hulk #92* (April 2006). Art by José Ladrönn.

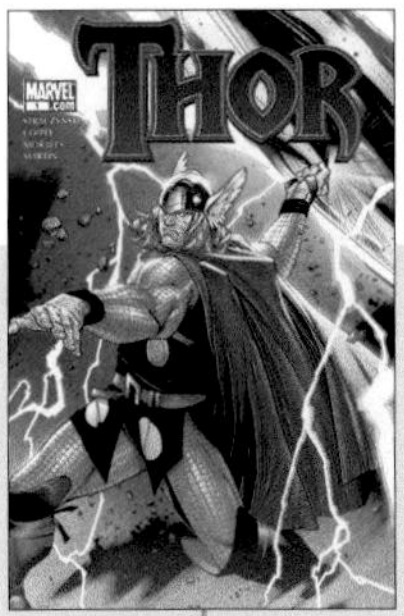
THOR
MARVEL

SEPTEMBER 2007

Absent since "Avengers Disassembled," following the cyclical Asgard apocalypse, Ragnarok, Thor returns in a new series by J. M. Straczynski and Olivier Coipel.

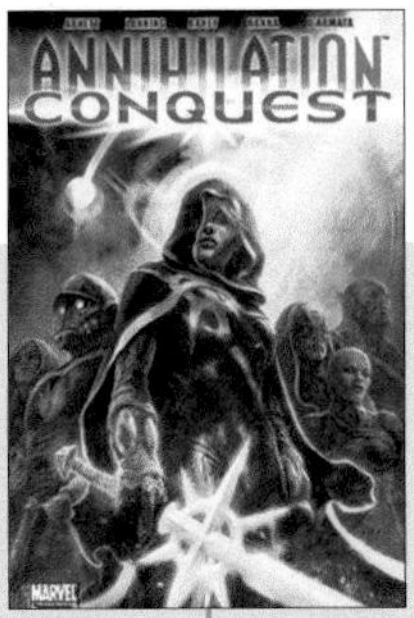
ANNIHILATION
CONQUEST

JANUARY 2008

The crossover storyline *Annihilation: Conquest* is the sequel to the big hit Annihilation, upending Marvel's "cosmic" universe and spelling trouble for the Guardians of the Galaxy.

NEW AVENGERS, NEW HEROES

A team of incredible creators comes together to introduce a new take on a classic team as new heroes come into the fold.

After the success of *Ultimate Spider-Man*, Bendis was put to work on one of Marvel's flagship series, *The Avengers*. The question was, if Spider-Man and Wolverine were the most popular characters, why not put them on the team? Bendis's first approach with Earth's Mightiest Heroes saw the destruction of the classic formation in the saga "Avengers: Disassembled." Some characters died; others, like Scarlet Witch and She-Hulk, went crazy. Their headquarters was destroyed.

A few months later, in *The New Avengers*, a new team was born, featuring old members like Cap and Iron Man, as well as Spidey, Logan, Luke Cage, and Spider-Woman. The 2000s also saw the emergence of two new groups of young heroes. In *Runaways*, Brian K. Vaughan and Adrian Alphona presented a team of teenagers who rebelled against their parents, who turned out to be Super Villains and mob leaders in

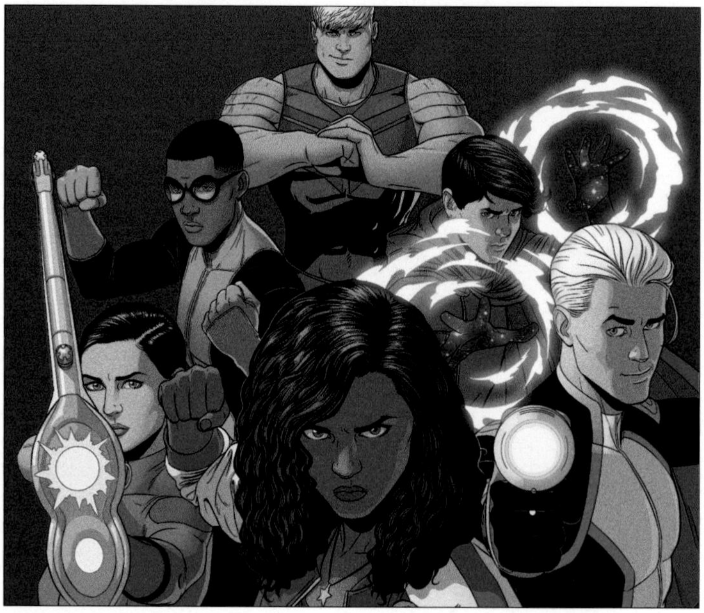

RIGHT: Detail from the cover to *Young Avengers #13* (dated February 2014, released December 4, 2013). Art by Jamie McKelvie.

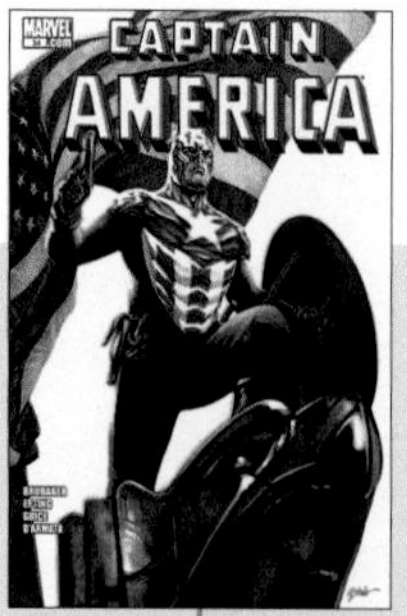
CAPTAIN
AMERICA

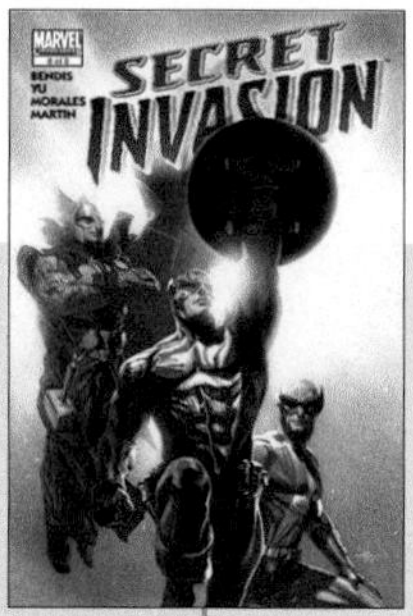
SECRET
INVASION

MARCH 2008

Bucky Barnes inherits Captain America's shield in *Captain America #34*, by Ed Brubaker and Steve Epting.

JANUARY 2009

The crossover *Secret Invasion* comes to an end with the discovery that shape-shifting Skrull aliens have infiltrated the Super Hero community.

Los Angeles. Taking advantage of money from merchandising and their inherited powers, they became true runaways and Super Heroes. Allan Heinberg, who scripted the TV series *The O.C.*, wrote *Young Avengers*, a spin-off dedicated to the young "heirs" of Iron Man and company. Both soon became cult hits. Remarkably innovative was the project behind Sentry: Marvel Knights hyped him as a character Stan Lee had created in the 1960s who had at last seen the light of day. As for continuity, he was considered outside the realm of collective memory in order to protect his dual nature—heroic Sentry and evil Void.

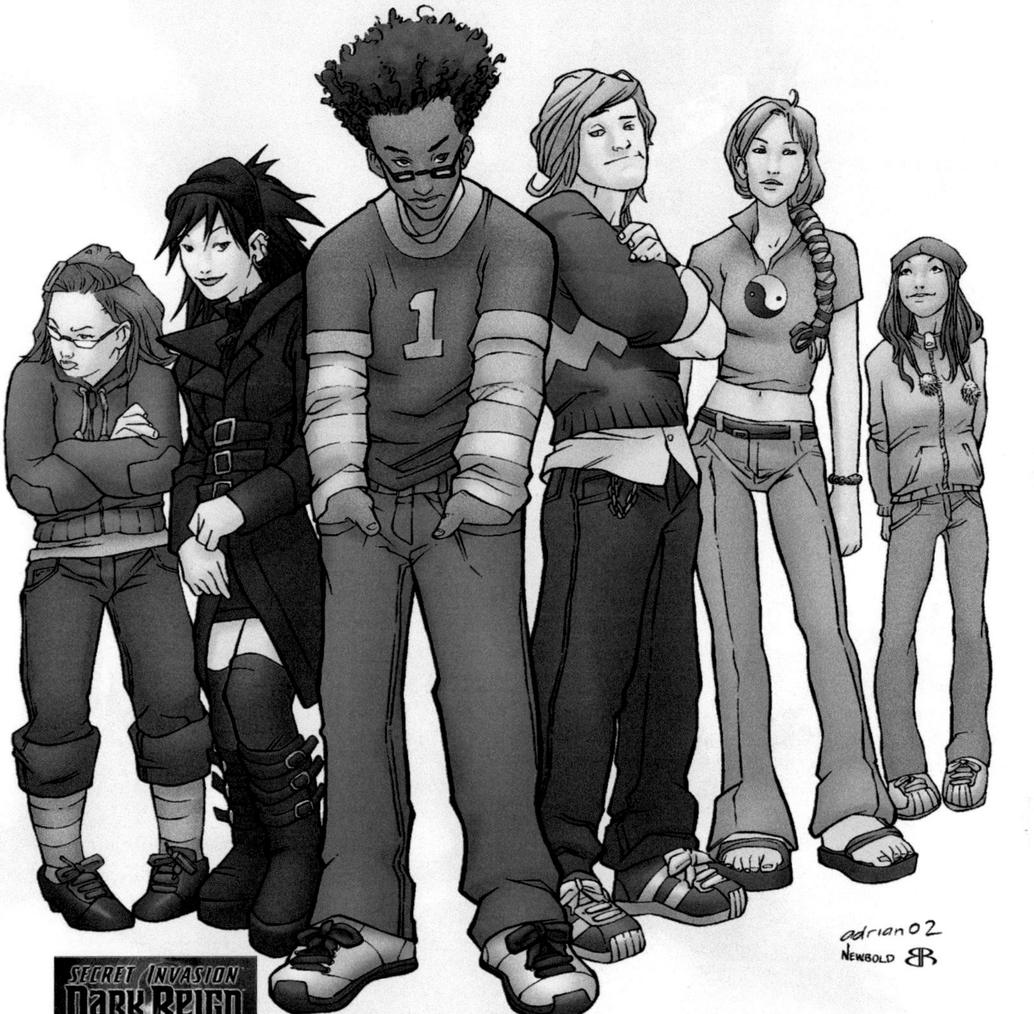

LEFT: Cover detail for the *Runaways Volume 1* hardcover edition (August 2005). Art by Adrian Alphona.

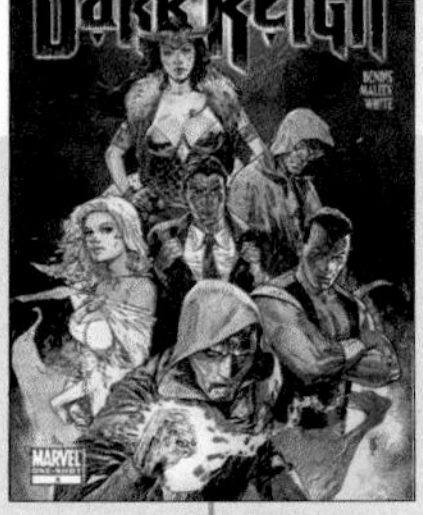
SECRET INVASION
DARK REIGN

The Walt Disney Company

2010

FEBRUARY 2009

Dark Reign is released. As a result of what happened in *Secret Invasion*, Norman Osborn is charged by the U.S. government to lead the Super Heroes.

AUGUST 2009

The Walt Disney Company acquires Marvel. It's the start of a new era.

THE AGE OF THE WRITERS

An amazingly talented team of writers assembles, making their mark on the mighty heroes and villains of Marvel.

T he 2000s ushered in an era that saw a focus on writers, which was curious at a time when the Editor in Chief was Quesada, an illustrator. This was thanks to the success of Brian Michael Bendis and Mark Millar.

Ultimate Spider-Man and *The New Avengers* had made Bendis a star. He came back with a long *Daredevil* run, adding new heights in quality, also thanks to illustrations by Alex Maleev, and *Alias*, which opened the R-rated MAX imprint, which also published the new *Punisher* series. *Alias* narrated the adventures of Jessica Jones, a former Super Hero turned alcoholic private investigator.

Mark Millar went on to limited series that Marvel fans couldn't get enough of. Besides *Civil War*, he also wrote the storyline "Old Man Logan," which featured an elderly Wolverine in a dystopia where villains had beaten almost all the Super Heroes, and *1985*, set in "our" world, starring a young comic book reader who meets up with his favorite characters. His contributions to historical series include an unforgettable *Fantastic Four* cycle illustrated by Bryan Hitch. Less prolific, but fundamental, was the award-winning Neil Gaiman, who wrote two high-quality limited series, *1602* and *Eternals*.

ABOVE:
Comics writer
Mark Millar.

RIGHT:
Writer Brian
Michael Bendis.

**OPPOSITE
PAGE:**
Cover from
*Fantastic Four
#560* (November
2008).Art by
Bryan Hitch.

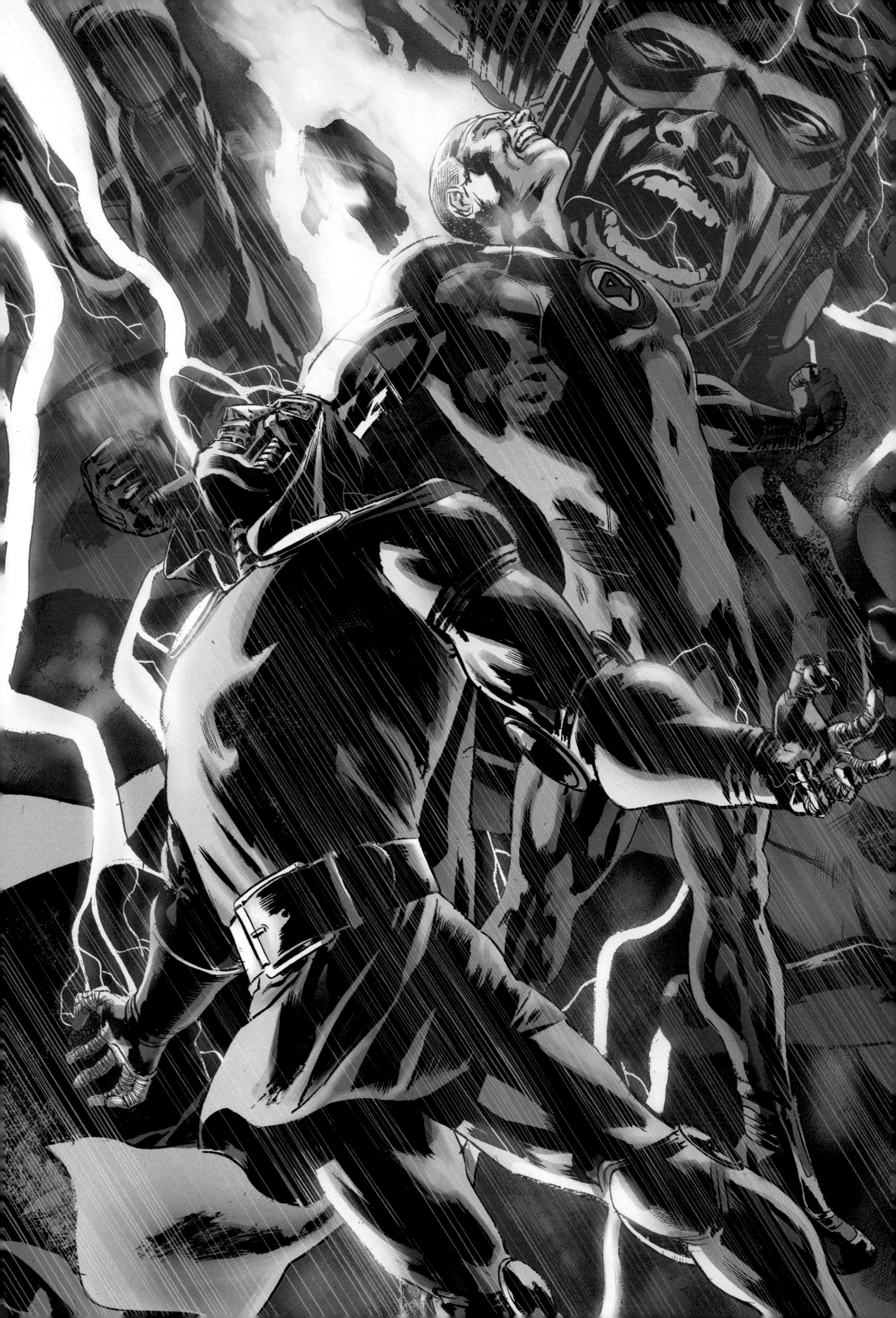

INTO THE FUTURE

Marvel's influence extends beyond comics and into the world of popular culture, growing its audience.

Marvel readers had grown up. People who read comics in the 1970s and '80s were now adults hankering for more mature stories. Readers young and old found what they were looking for in *Alias*, *Daredevil*, and *X-Statix* by Peter Milligan and Mike Allred (featuring Super Heroes that were depraved, unscrupulous celebrities), and in Garth Ennis's *The Punisher*.

It was time for Marvel to leave the Comics Code Authority behind. Self-censorship hampered creators while hardly affecting sales. Marvel adopted its own rating system. By the end of the 2000s Marvel had legions of new readers and garnered media attention thanks to the Super Heroes' success at the movies. Marvel had become a force to be reckoned with in pop culture.

Characters were quoted and T-shirts sold, as new attention, even by the mainstream media, was lavished on the world of comics like never before. The seeds Stan Lee had planted in the 1960s have sprouted, and Marvel's cross-cultural influence continued to grow. ■

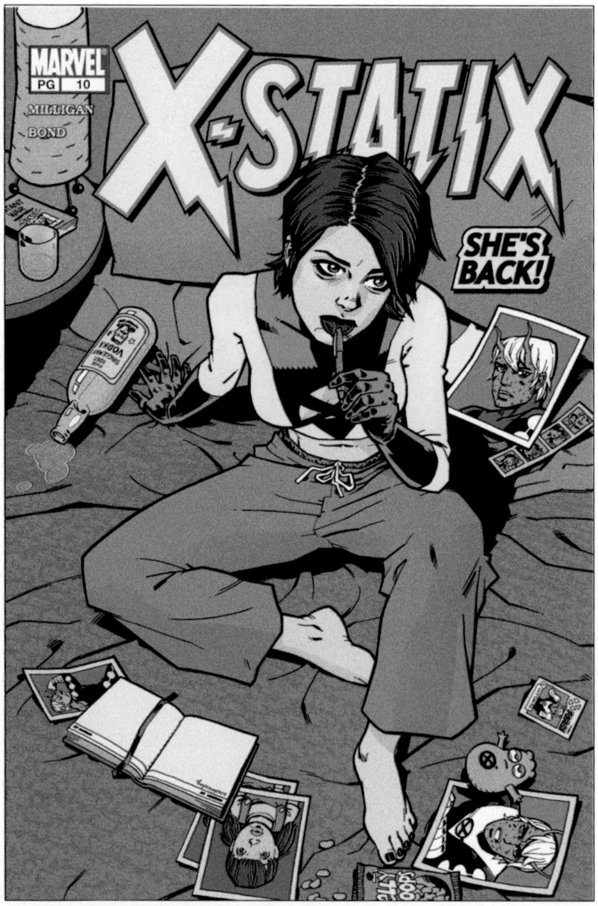
MARVEL
PG 10
MILLIGAN
BOND
X-STATIX
SHE'S BACK!
VODKA

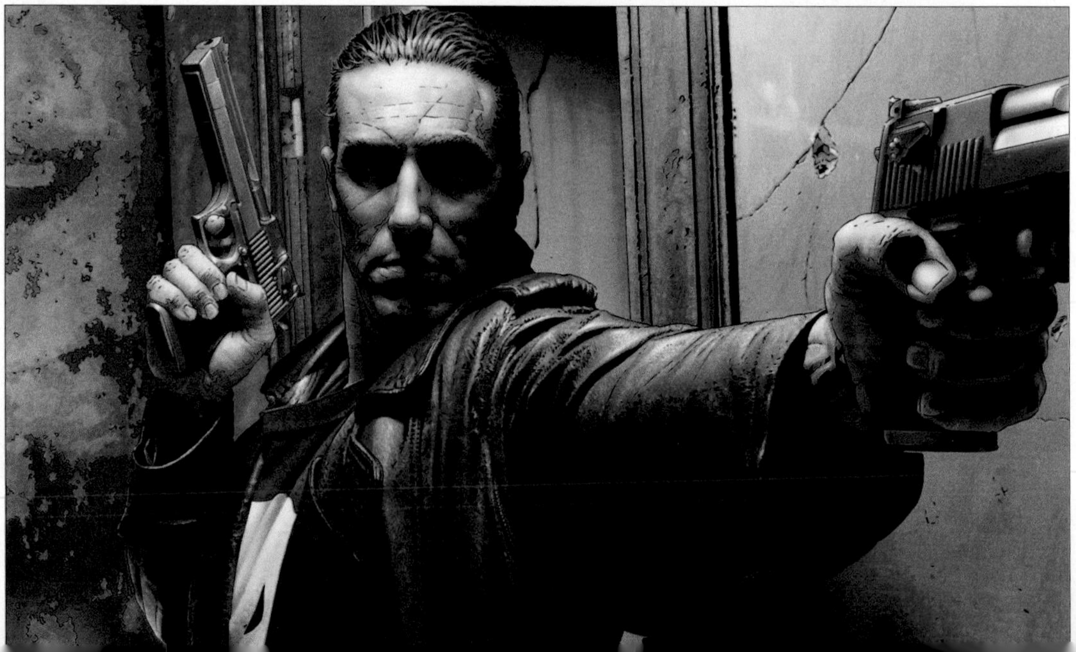

ABOVE: *X-Statix #10* (June 2003). Art by Philip Bond

RIGHT: Cover detail from *The Punisher MAX Volume 2: Kitchen Irish* (December 2005). Art by Tim Bradstreet (pencils).

OPPOSITE PAGE: *Stan Lee Meets the Amazing Spider-Man #1* (November 2006). Art by Olivier Coipel.

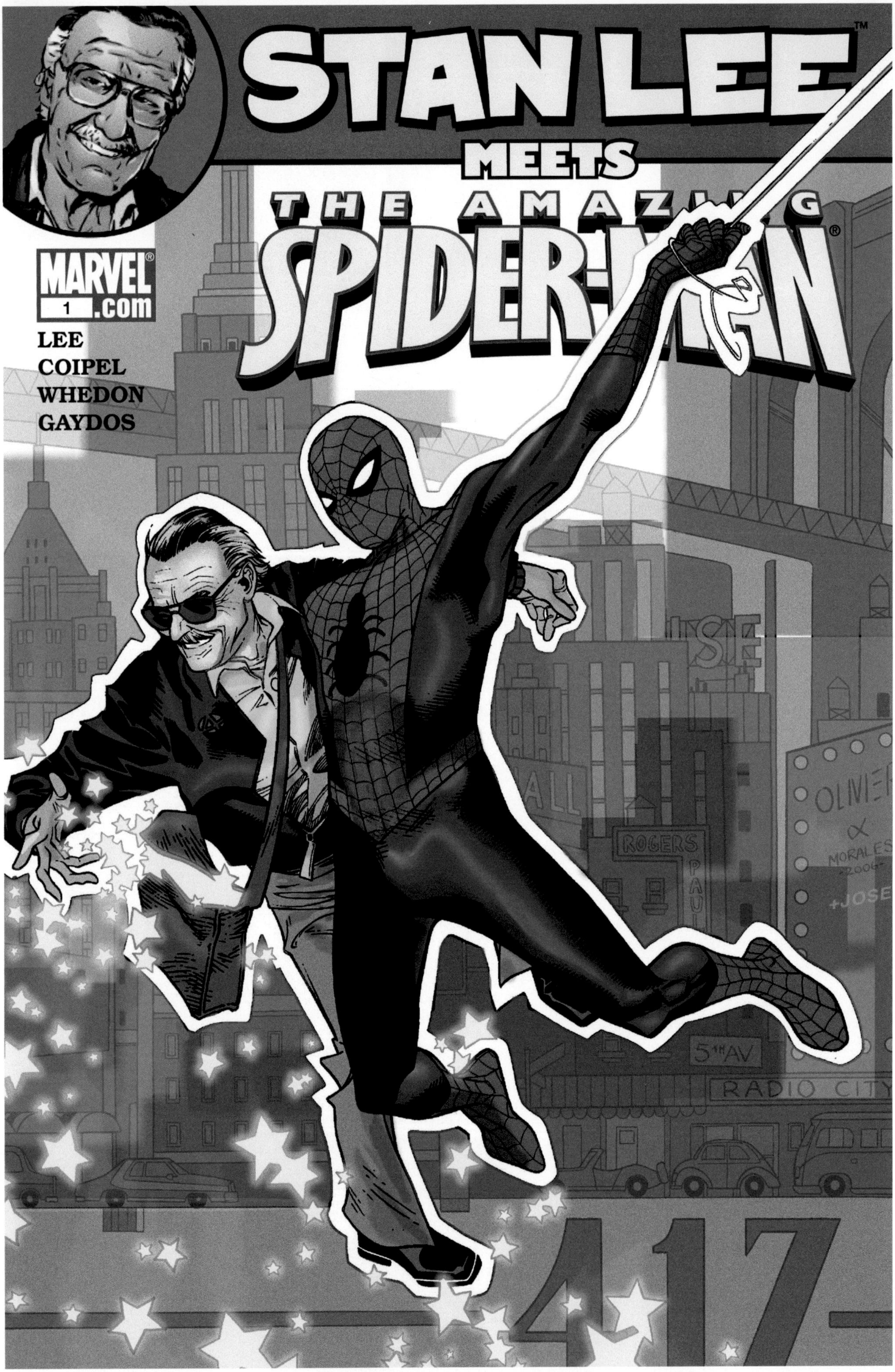
STAN LEE™
MEETS
THE AMAZING
SPIDER-MAN®
MARVEL®
1 .com
LEE
COIPEL
WHEDON
GAYDOS
ROGERS
5TH AV
RADIO CITY
417

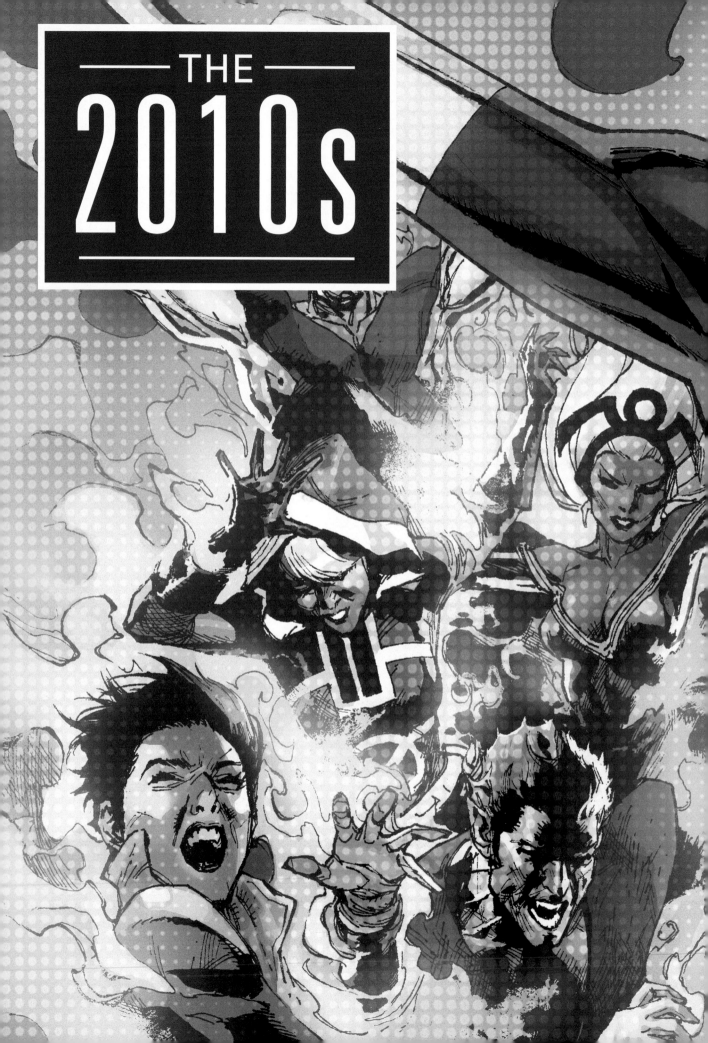

THE
2010s

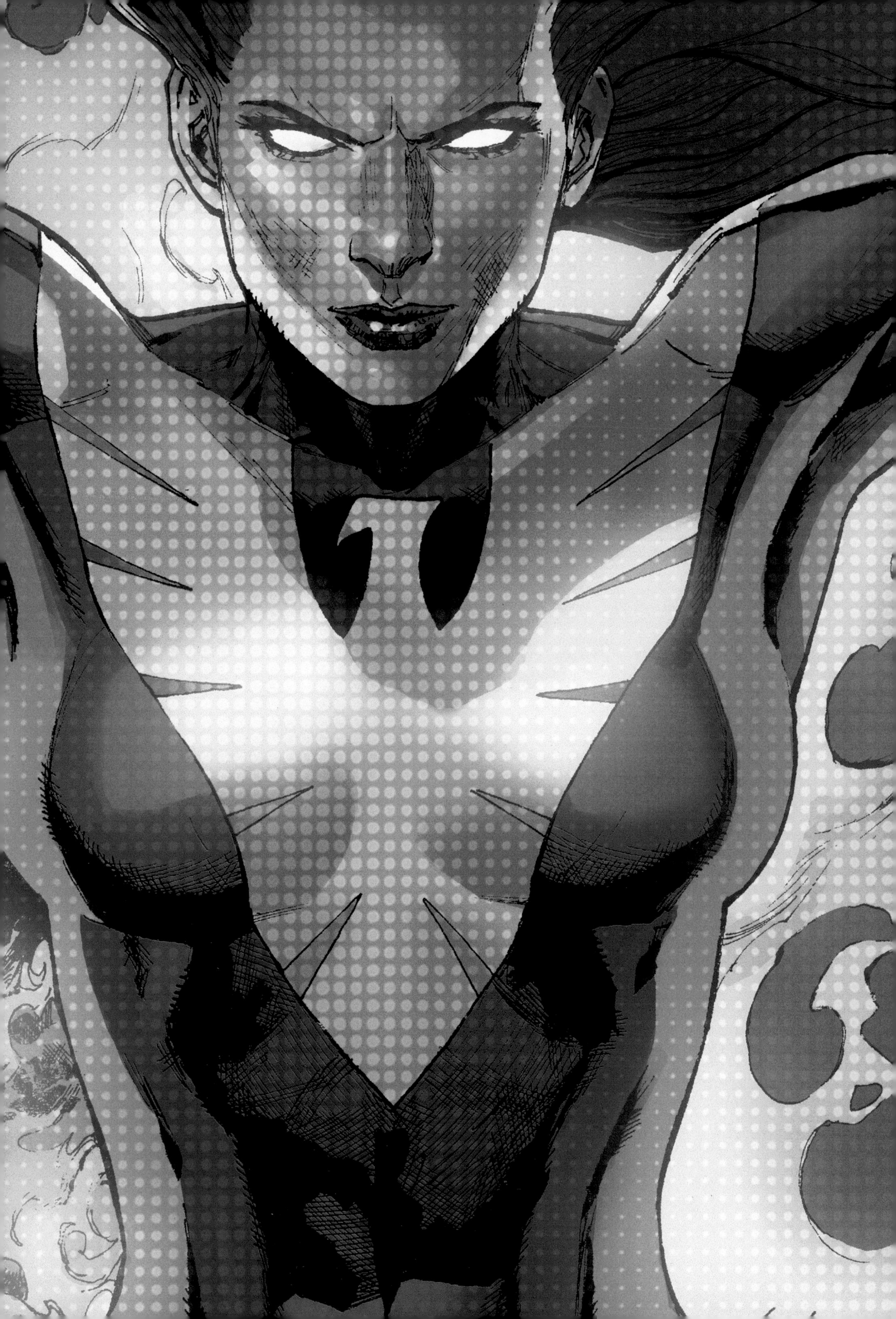

NEW HORIZONS

As the 21st century continued, Marvel adapted even more to the changing demands of the audience and the culture.

It was finally happening—what for decades so many artists and writers had worked so hard for. Marvel characters had become part of the world's common heritage, household names, icons of the collective consciousness.

Meanwhile, Marvel wasn't resting on its laurels. Readership was growing, but they were constantly enticing new readers to the fold. The Ultimate line was by now ten years old and had its own baggage of continuity, while the Super Heroes from *Earth-616*, the ones from the classic Marvel Universe, maintained a strong following. The 2010s thus saw a number of relaunches, with series starting from issue #1, that provided new beginnings as writers crafted their stories so that they would also be accessible to new readers.

These relaunches were usually limited to individual series or to "families," but in 2012 Marvel took a chance on something much bigger with the *Marvel NOW!* initiative: a new starting point for all the series. It was not a reboot, since continuity would not be altered or disavowed. Simply put, all the series would start fresh from issue 1, with creative teams shifting from book to book. For instance, Brian Michael Bendis, who for years had worked on the *Avengers*, became the new creator behind the *X-Men*, while Jason Aaron, the versatile and highly talented writer from Alabama, moved from *Wolverine* to *Thor*. And if this were not enough, new characters would appear as protagonists in the Marvel Universe: a new Ms. Marvel, the young Kamala Khan, a Pakistani-American; a new formation for Guardians of the Galaxy; the Korean-American Cindy Moon as Silk, who teamed up with Spider-Man; and others. The audience had grown more diverse, and Marvel along with it.

The world was changing; readers' ethnicity and the places they called home became increasingly diversified. What's more, women were beginning to take a more active interest in comic books, and comic book creators could

2.47PM
X-MOBILE
PHOTO
VIDEO

RIGHT: Ms. Marvel and Wolverine pose for a selfie on the cover of *Ms. Marvel #7* (October 2014). Art by Jamie McKelvie and Matt Wilson.

OPPOSITE PAGE: The wedding of Northstar and Kyle Jinadu—the first gay wedding seen in Marvel comics. *Astonishing X-Men #51* (dated August 2012, released June 20, 2012). Art by Mike Perkins (pencils, inks), Andrew Hennessy (inks), Andy Troy, Jim Charalampidis, Rachelle Rosenberg (colors), Joe Caramagna, Cory Petit, Clayton Cowles (letters).

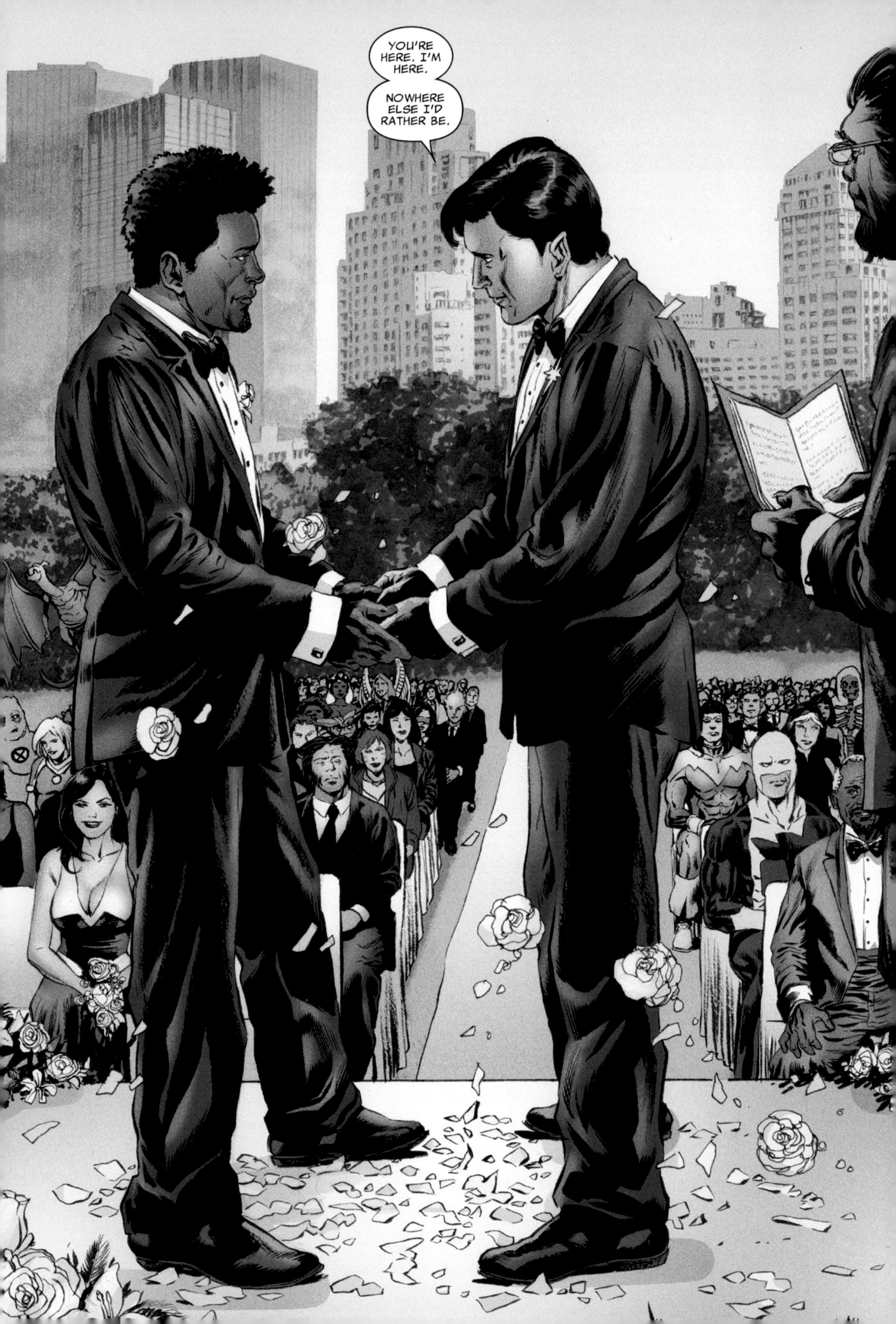
YOU'RE HERE. I'M HERE.
NOWHERE ELSE I'D RATHER BE.

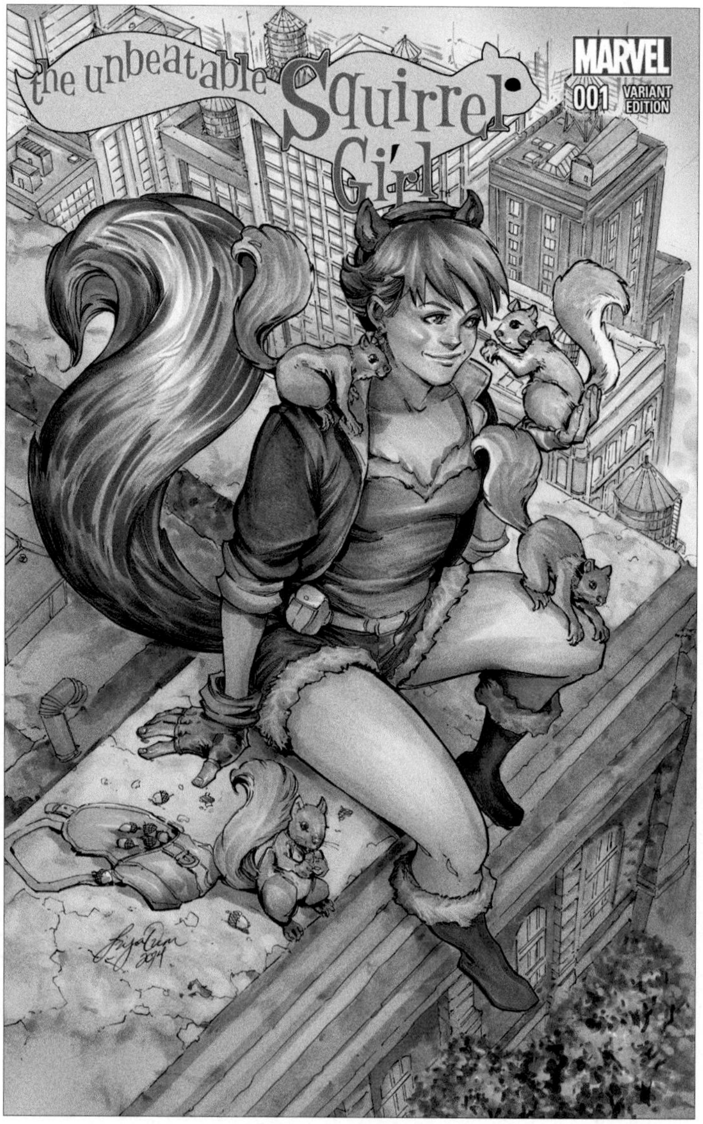
the unbeatable Squirrel Girl
MARVEL
001 VARIANT EDITION

RIGHT: *The Unbeatable Squirrel Girl #1* variant cover (March 2015). Art by Siya Oum.

not ignore all the progress made in expanding the legal rights and visibility of the LGBTQ community. More and more, Marvel Super Heroes and Heroines would reflect readers' backgrounds and lifestyles, and the world they lived in.

Formats were also changing. Over the years, new distribution channels came to the fore, and increasingly readers waited for the conclusion of a story arc to read it in its entirety. Like other publishers, Marvel responded with an increasing number of collections in digital, trade paperback, or hardcover form, which met the needs of both occasional readers and collectors interested in volumes that contained complete story arcs.

As a result, writers often sought out complete cycles within any given series which might easily appear in a single volume. This gave rise to an approach that eventually spelled success for characters that otherwise would have been considered minor. Instead of being relegated to supporting roles in comic books alone, they became stars in their own right, and included characters like Moon Girl and Devil Dinosaur, Squirrel Girl, and, of course, Ms. Marvel.

Toward the end of the decade, new readers and new writers would join in the celebration of Marvel's 80th anniversary.

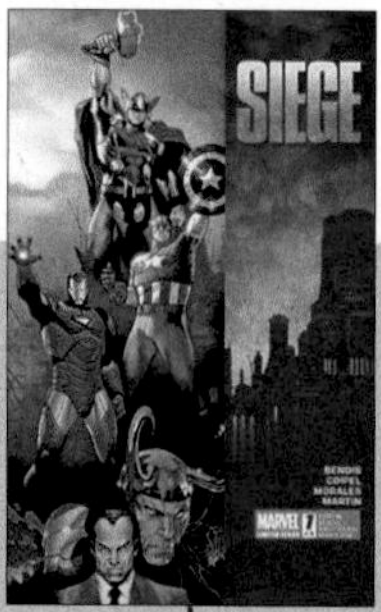
SIEGE

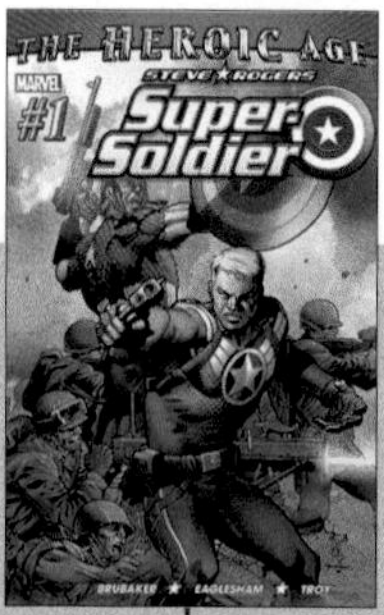
THE HEROIC AGE
STEVE ROGERS
#1
Super Soldier

2010

JANUARY 2010

With the event series *Siege*, Norman Osborn attempts to conquer Asgard, and the end to the Dark Reign era is nearly in sight.

JULY 2010

Steve Rogers becomes the new head of SHIELD and assumes the identity of Super Soldier.

MOON GIRL
AND
DEVIL DINOSAUR
#1
REEDER
MONTCLARE
BUSTOS
BONVILLAIN
MARVEL
BONUS
DIGITAL
EDITION

MARVEL NOW! POINT ONE
001
VARIANT EDITION

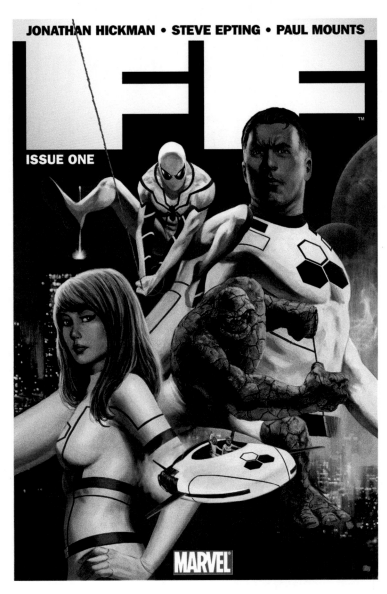

JONATHAN HICKMAN • STEVE EPTING • PAUL MOUNTS
FF
ISSUE ONE
MARVEL

TOP LEFT: *Moon Girl and Devil Dinosaur #1* (dated January 2016, released November 25, 2015). Art by Amy Reeder.

BELOW LEFT: Promotional image for *Marvel NOW!* by Joe Quesada, 2012.

LEFT: *FF #1* (dated May 2011, released March 23, 2011). Art by Steve Epting.

FEAR
ITSELF
BOOK ONE

APRIL 2011

The *Fear Itself* crossover recounts the end of the Dark Reign and the return of Iron Man, Thor, and Captain America, leading the way for the Avengers.

THE MIGHTY
THOR

JUNE 2011

Matt Fraction and Olivier Coipel relaunch the new *Mighty Thor* series with issue #1. His first adversary is Galactus!

JUNE 2011

In Jonathan Hickman and Steve Epting's *FF #1*, with the Human Torch gone, Spider-Man joins the team. The Future Foundation is born.

A NEW AGE FOR NEW READERS

2010 began with a bang, as Marvel reunited the trinity of Super Heroes—Captain America, Iron Man, and Thor—and blazed new trails.

Following the gloom of *Secret Invasion* and *Dark Reign*, crossover events that had an impact on all the series put out at the end of the 2000s, the times were once again ripe for Super Heroes to be portrayed as positive examples of law and order. Marvel kicked off the 2010s with the limited series *Siege*, which laid the foundations for the relaunch of the Avengers family and marked the end of the bleak scenarios commandeered by Norman Osborn.

The so-called trinity made its return, now cast in roles that hadn't been seen since the pre–Civil War days: Thor, Captain America, and Iron Man would once again be fighting side by side. Tensions in the Super Hero community did not abate altogether, however, and exploded in a new maxi-crossover, *Avengers vs. X-Men*. The two factions

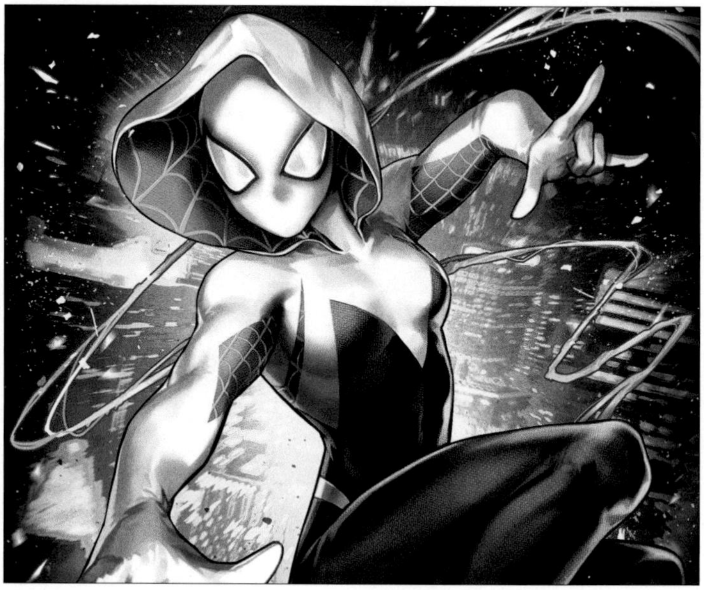

RIGHT: Cover detail from *Spider-Gwen: Ghost Spider #1* variant (December 2018). Art by Sujin Jo.

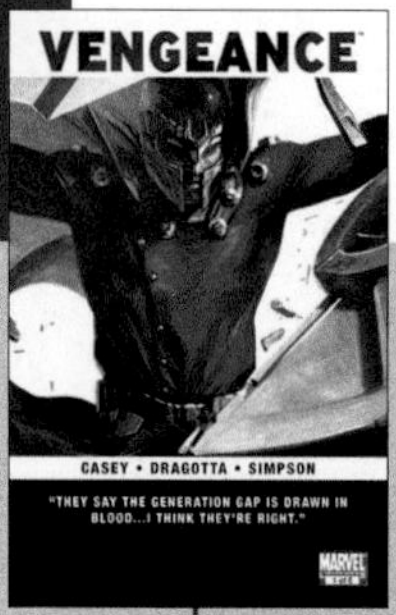
VENGEANCE
CASEY • DRAGOTTA • SIMPSON

SEPTEMBER 2011

America Chavez, from another dimension, makes her debut in *Vengeance #1*. Soon she would become one of Marvel's top LGBT icons.

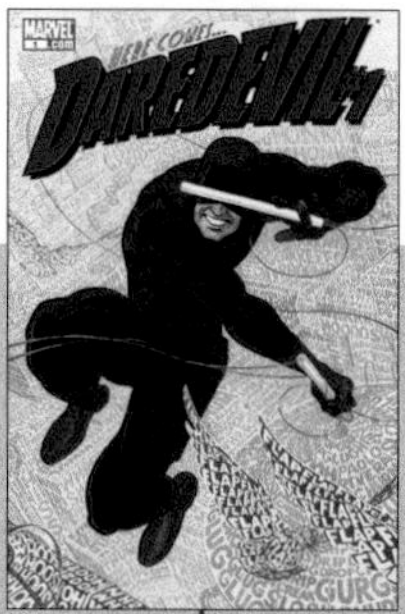
DAREDEVIL

SEPTEMBER 2011

Writer Mark Waid begins his long award-winning run on *Daredevil*, which concludes in 2015. Illustrators: Paolo Rivera, Marcos Martin, and the big gun Chris Samnee.

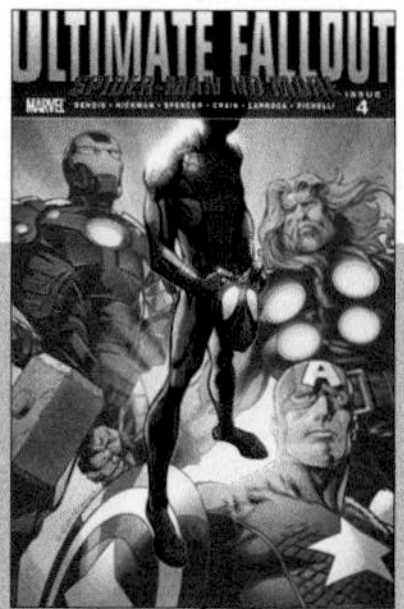
ULTIMATE FALLOUT

OCTOBER 2011

Miles Morales debuts as the new Spider-Man in *Ultimate Fallout #4*.

ABOVE: Cyclops stands over the body of the slain Professor X. *Avengers vs. X-Men* #11 (dated November 2012, released September 12, 2012). Art by Olivier Coipel (pencils), Mark Morales (inks), Laura Martin (colors).

clashed over control of the Phoenix Force, heading straight for Earth in the form of a flaming bird.

The war that broke out between the two sides was recounted in a 12-issue series written and illustrated by the hottest names at that time. At the end of the saga, the longtime leader of the X-Men, Cyclops, was corrupted by the power of Dark Phoenix, as had happened many years earlier in the case of Jean Grey.

The mutant family was subject to various acts of vengeance at the hands of this evil Cyclops (he even murdered his mentor, Charles Xavier), although the Avengers wound up with an apparent victory. This event marked the end of a long run of stories that had begun with *Civil War* and proved to be the perfect opportunity for a relaunch, known as Marvel NOW! Banners like All-New Marvel NOW!, Ultimate Marvel NOW! and Marvel NOW! 2.0 heralded the relaunch of the entire Marvel line and paved the way for all-new series. They included *Guardians of the Galaxy*, which gave readers a taste of what was to come in the 2014 film, featuring characters like Star-Lord, Drax the Destroyer, Rocket Raccoon, and Gamora, in a series written by Bendis and illustrated by Steve McNiven, who had provided the artwork for *Civil War*.

Each year of the 2010s would see the release of a new crossover event, based on the model of *Secret Wars* from the 1980s. Each event was a

ULTIMATE COMICS
SPIDER-MAN
BENDIS PICHELLI PONSOR
ISSUE 01

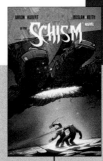

AUGUST 2011

Peter Parker meets up with Miles Morales for the first time in *Ultimate Comics Spider-Man*, by Brian Michael Bendis and Sara Pichelli.

AVENGING
SPIDER-MAN
FREE

NOVEMBER 2011

The *Avenging Spider-Man* series marks the return of artist Joe Madureira, whose work in the 1990s became legendary.

SCHISM

DECEMBER 2011

In the finale of the limited series *X-Men: Schism*, written by Jason Aaron and illustrated by an all-star list of artists, the mutants split into two factions led by Wolverine and Cyclops.

chance to reshuffle the cards and serve up starting points for readers new to the comic book experience, or who enjoyed maneuvering the characters on PlayStation, Xbox, or their mobile devices. The most important of all these events, beating out even *Avengers vs. X-Men*, was entitled *Secret Wars*, a tribute to the old saga by Jim Shooter and Mike Zeck.

2016 saw the shutdown of all the ongoing series, symbolizing the end of the Multiverse, under attack by powerful aliens. They were replaced by various limited series, whose titles echoed the great sagas of the past, such as *Inferno*, *Civil War*, *Planet Hulk,* and so on. The stories gave readers glimpses of alternative worlds, and ran parallel to the main limited series, *Secret Wars*, written by Jonathan Hickman and illustrated by Esad Ribic. There, Doctor Doom assumes divine powers and re-creates the world in his image after the destruction of the Multiverse.

Once again, an alliance among Super Heroes was necessary in order to bring about his defeat and return the world to normalcy...or nearly so. After 15 years of honorable service, the Ultimate Universe was destroyed, although there were some survivors. Like Miles Morales, who had been the Ultimate Spider-Man in that universe. *Secret Wars* was perhaps the most important of Marvel's new starting points, especially considering the massive amounts of planning that went into the series. The Fantastic Four were left to recreate the Multiverse, keeping them out of action in the main Marvel Universe until 2018.

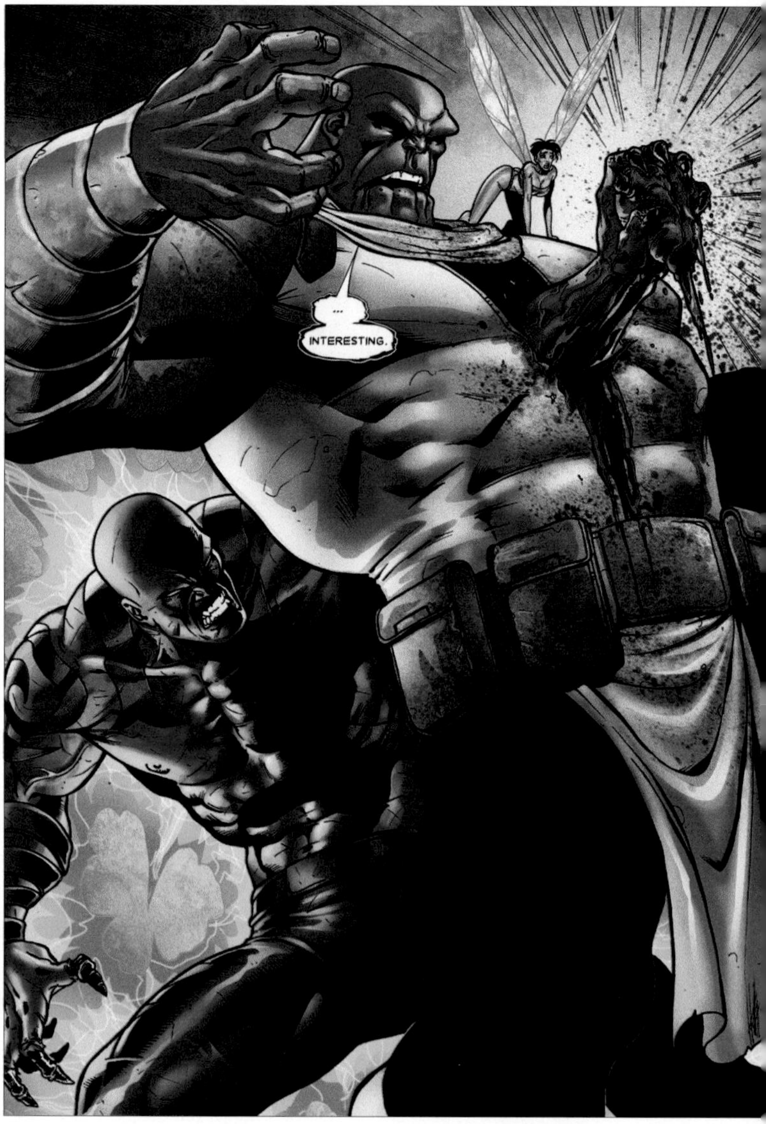
...
INTERESTING.

RIGHT: Drax destroys Thanos in *Annihilation #4* (January 2007). Script by Keith Giffen. Art by Andrea Di Vito (pencils and inks), Laura Villari (colors), Cory Petit (letters).

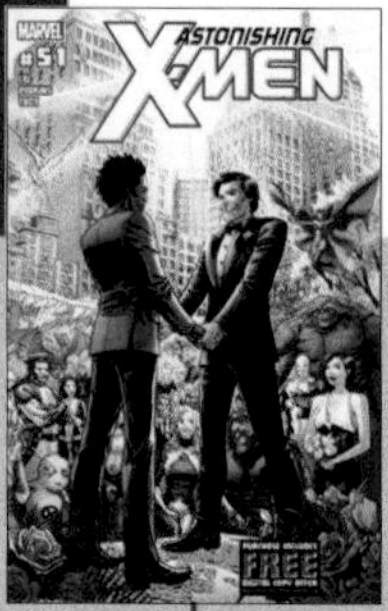
ASTONISHING X-MEN
51
FREE

AUGUST 2012

The mutant Northstar marries partner Kyle in *Astonishing X-Men #51*, written by Marjoire Liu and illustrated by Mike Perkins. It is the first gay marriage in a mainstream comics.

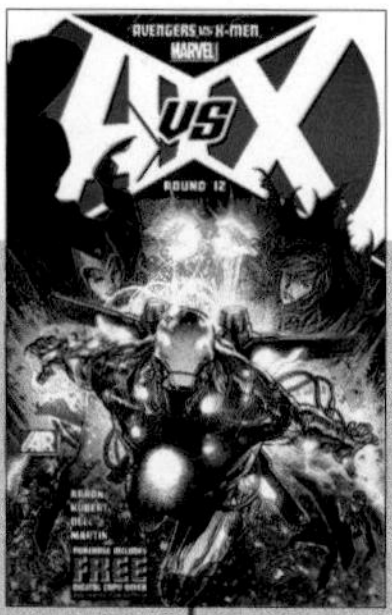
AVENGERS vs X-MEN
VS
ROUND 12
FREE

DECEMBER 2012

The crossover event *Avengers vs. X-Men* comes to an end, paving the way for the Marvel NOW! initiative.

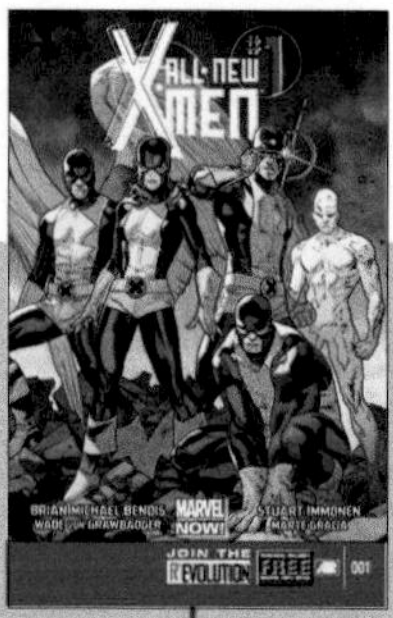
ALL-NEW X-MEN
MARVEL NOW!
JOIN THE EVOLUTION
FREE

JANUARY 2013

In *All-New X-Men 2*, by Brian M. Bendis and Stuart Immonen, the five original X-Men travel into the future—the present-day Marvel Universe!

SPIDER-MAN
#1
"SITTING IN A TREE!" STARTS
NOW!
MARVEL
#12
BENDIS
PICHELLI
PONSOR
BONUS
DIGITAL EDITION

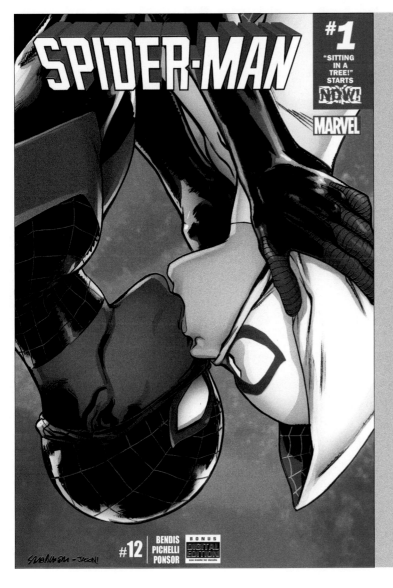

MILES & GWEN

As the *Ultimate* Universe grew, writers and illustrators realized that they could take things well beyond what went on in the classic Marvel Universe. Shocking turns of events soon took place, like the killing of Peter Parker. Taking his place in the role of Spider-Man would be young Miles Morales, the son of an African-American father and a Puerto Rican mother. He got his spider powers much the same way that Peter had gotten them. Conceived by Bendis and illustrator Sara Pichelli in 2011, Miles soon showed himself to be a valid replacement. Following the second incarnation of *Secret Wars* and the destruction of the Ultimate Universe, he turned up alongside the adult Spider-Man in *Earth-616*. Today Miles is one of the world's best-loved Super Heroes. As is Spider-Woman from *Earth- 65*, better known as Spider-Gwen. In that world it was Gwen Stacy, who received the bite of a radioactive spider. She became a Super Heroine who made contact with the Spider-Men of the Multiverse in the 2014 saga *Spider-Verse*.

LEFT: *Spider-Man Volume 2 #12* (January 2017). Art by Sara Pichelli and Jason Keith.

JUNE 2013

The last issue of the *Age of Ultron* event, over the course of which, the evil robot Ultron uses a time travel paradox to take over the world.

GHOST RIDER
#1

MAY 2014

Robbie Reyes becomes the new Ghost Rider. He drives a flaming car instead of a motorcycle.

SPIDER-MAN 2099
#1

SEPTEMBER 2014

Peter David returns to write *Spider-Man 2099*, featuring the wall-crawler in all-new adventures set in the present.

ALL-NEW, ALL-DIFFERENT

The classic Marvel heroes were reborn in the 2010s, taking on new forms that spoke to new audiences.

Under the leadership of Editor in Chief Axel Alonso, who followed Joe Quesada after years as a go-to editor, Marvel approached the 2010s hailing diversity. At the same time, Marvel succeeded in consolidating the popularity of its most iconic Super Heroes by making choices that proved to be of watershed magnitude. At a certain point, it almost seemed like the 1980s all over again.

By the mid-2010s, some of the greatest Marvel Super Heroes had once again been replaced. The Hulk was zapped of his strength and apparently dead, until young genius Amadeus Cho assumed his identity, taking the place of Bruce Banner. In a brilliant move by writer Jason Aaron, Jane Foster, Thor's old love interest, took possession of Mjolnir and transformed into Thor after he lost his ability to

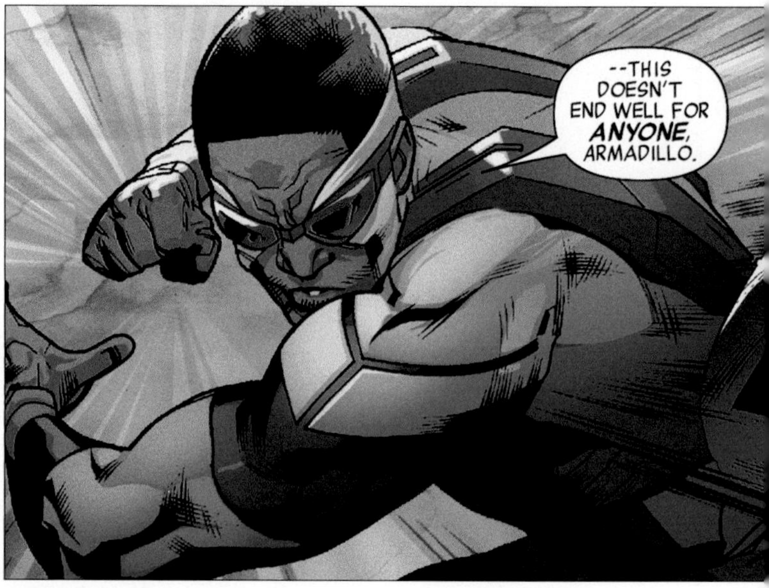
--THIS DOESN'T END WELL FOR *ANYONE*, ARMADILLO.

RIGHT: Panel from *All-New Captain America #4* (dated April 2015, released February 18, 2015). Art byStuart Immonen, Wade Von Grawbadger, Marte Gracia.

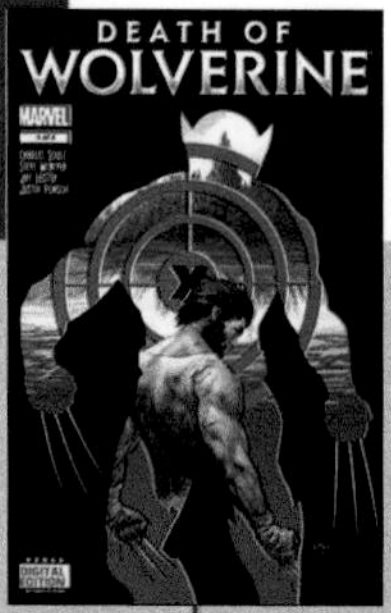
DEATH OF WOLVERINE
MARVEL

NOVEMBER 2014

Logan loses his final battle in the limited series *Death of Wolverine*. A few months later, X-23 takes his place in *All-New Wolverine*.

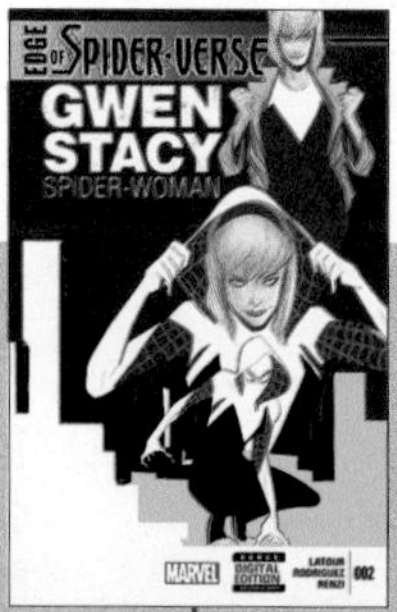
EDGE OF SPIDER-VERSE
GWEN STACY
SPIDER-WOMAN
MARVEL

NOVEMBER 2014

Spider-Gwen makes her debut in *Edge of Spider-Verse #2*, the prequel to the Spider-Verse crossover event.

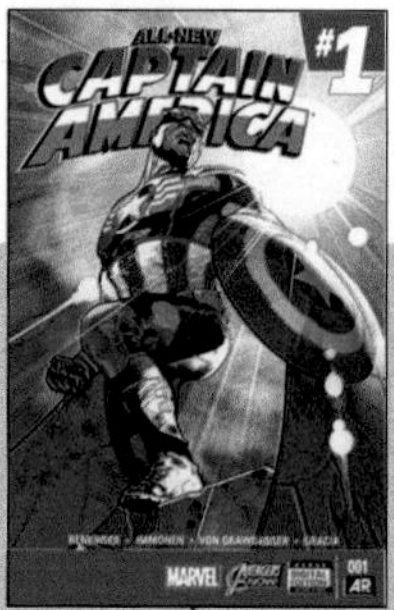
ALL-NEW
CAPTAIN AMERICA
#1
MARVEL

DECEMBER 2014

Steve Rogers, suddenly grown old, taps Sam Wilson, A.K.A. Falcon, as the new Captain America.

use his hammer—a transformation that eased the side effects of Jane's cancer treatment. Steve Rogers lost the benefits of the Super Soldier Serum and aged suddenly. His place was taken by Sam Wilson, Cap's former sidekick as Falcon, who became a Captain America fighting for civil rights and against racism, putting him on a collision course with the U.S. government.

Steve returned two years later in the *Secret Empire* saga, where we learn that Rogers' evil doppelganger, teamed up with Hydra, had taken his place. As for Iron Man, in a cycle written by Bendis, he was replaced by Ironheart, A.K.A. the brilliant young inventor Riri Williams; later, a Doctor Doom in search

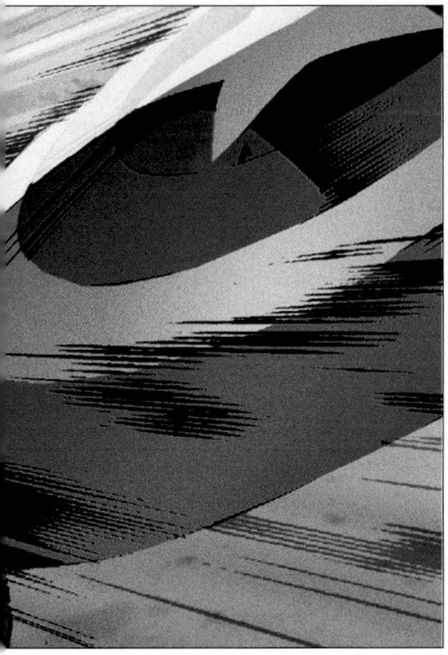

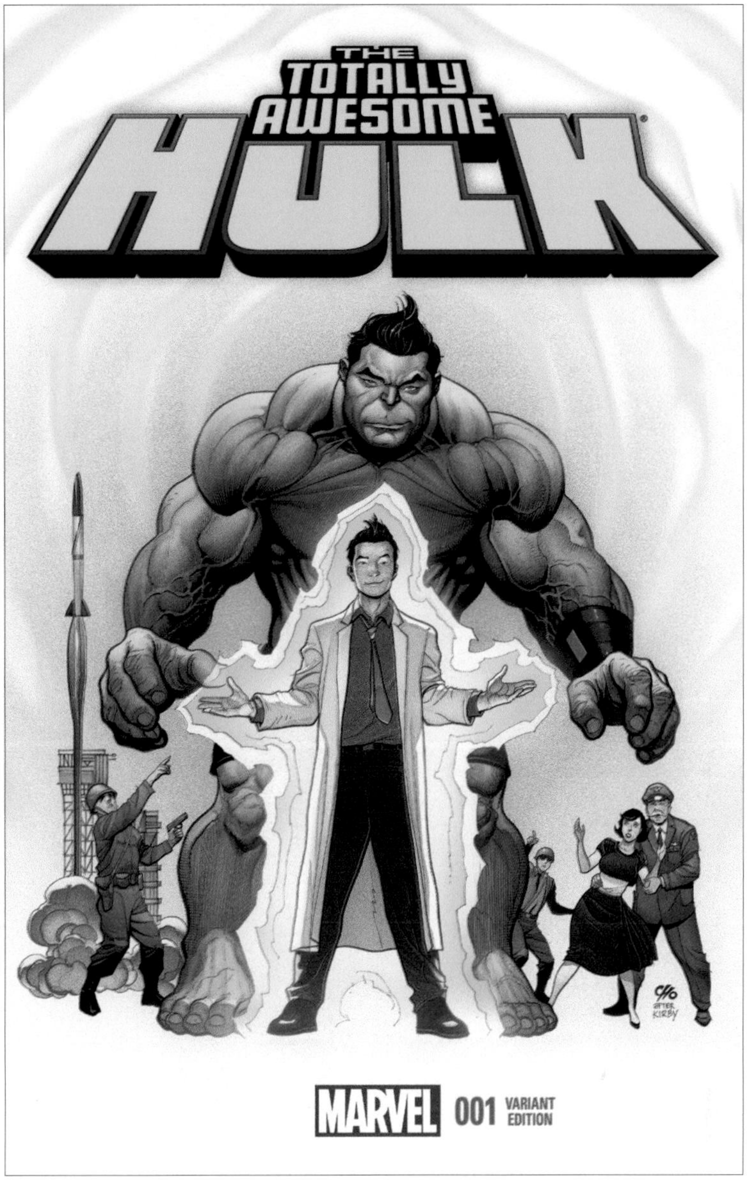
THE TOTALLY AWESOME HULK
MARVEL 001 VARIANT EDITION

LEFT: Cover to *The Totally Awesome Hulk #1* variant cover. Art by Frank Cho; Colors by David Curiel.

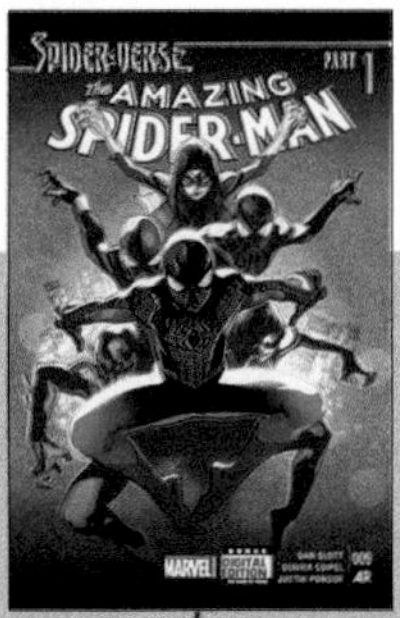
SPIDER-VERSE PART 1
THE AMAZING SPIDER-MAN

JANUARY 2015

In the *Spider-Verse* event, Peter Parker meets up with Spidey's alter egos from other dimensions.

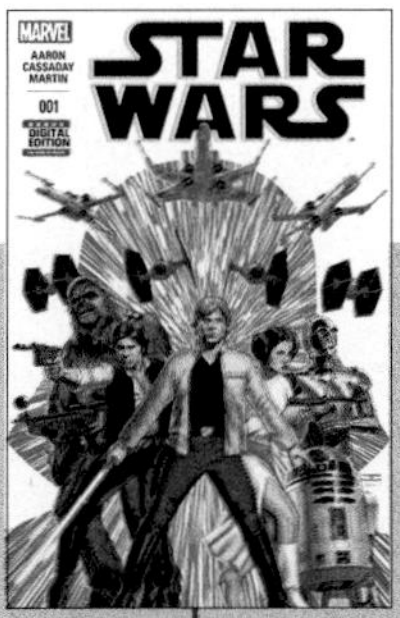
STAR WARS

MARCH 2015

The new *Star Wars* series returns to Marvel Comics, and issue #1 sells more than one million copies.

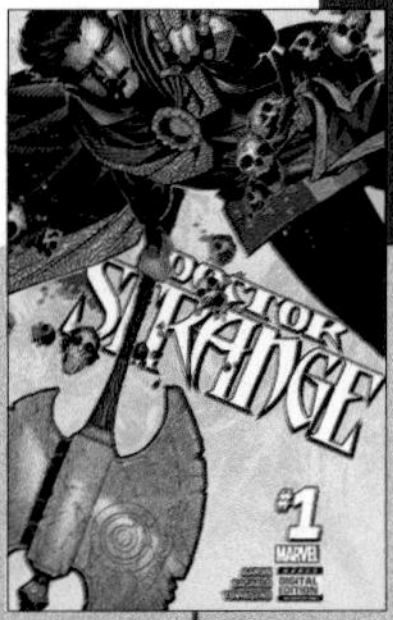
DOCTOR STRANGE
#1

DECEMBER 2015

Jason Aaron and Chris Bachalo create the new *Doctor Strange* series.

of redemption would become the third incarnation of Iron Man. Tony Stark, as it turns out, had wound up in a coma after *Civil War II*, the latest clash among Super Heroes, which pitted him against Carol "Captain Marvel" Danvers. Carol was still in circulation and had earned the right to call herself Captain Marvel, while young Kamala Khan became Ms. Marvel. Kamala had received her powers through terrigenesis, after being caught up in the Terrigen Mists, a mutation causing vapor unleashed by Black Bolt, able to bestow incredible powers on humans who possess traces of Inhuman DNA.

Even if things had pretty much gone back to the old status quo by the end of the decade, the new Super Heroes were here to stay. Many of the younger characters joined the team known as the Champions, adding a new twist to the old League of Champions from the 1980s.

The spirit of renewal continued with the installment of a new Editor in Chief, C. B. Cebulski, in November 2017. Among other credits, Cebulski had had lengthy experience as a talent scout, and recruited top young writers and authors from around the world for Marvel. Within a year of signing on as Editor in Chief, he had relaunched numerous series whose starting points coincided with the arrival of new creative personnel.

Relaunches garnered both commercial and critical success, and included *The Immortal Hulk*, a horror-tinged version of the big guy written by Al Ewing and illustrated by Joe Bennett; the return of *Fantastic Four*, written by Dan Slott and illustrated by Sara Pichelli; and the new *Daredevil* series, written by Chip Zdarsky and illustrated by Marco Checchetto.

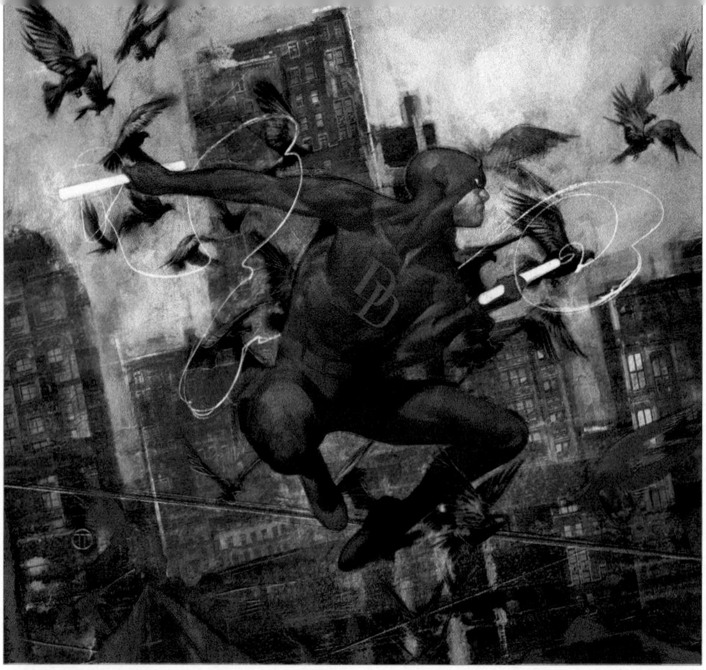

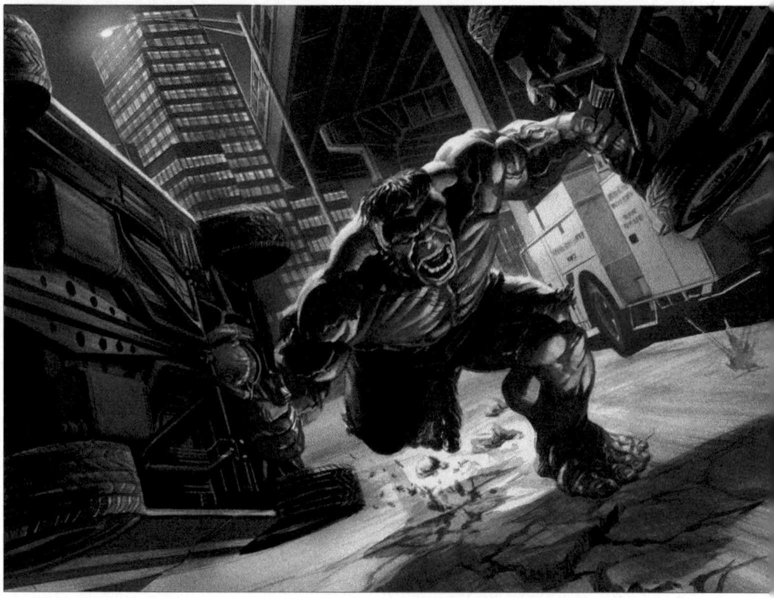

ABOVE: Cover detail from *Daredevil Vol. 6, #2* (dated April 2019, released February 27, 2019). Art by Julian Tedesco.

RIGHT: Cover detail from *The Immortal Hulk #4* (dated October 2018, released August 1, 2018). Art by Alex Ross.

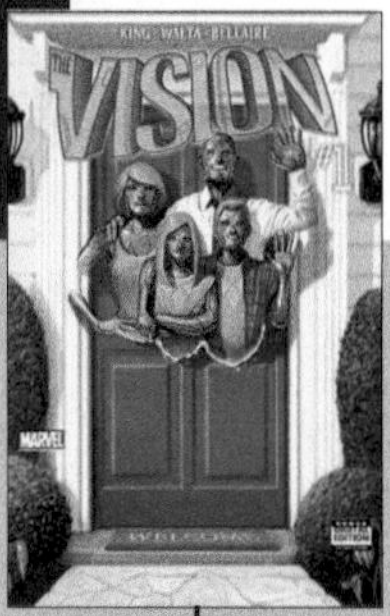
VISION

JANUARY 2016

Debut of the maxi-series *Vision*, written by Tom King and illustrated by Gabriel H. Walta. The android Avenger starts a family in a story line that ends in tragedy.

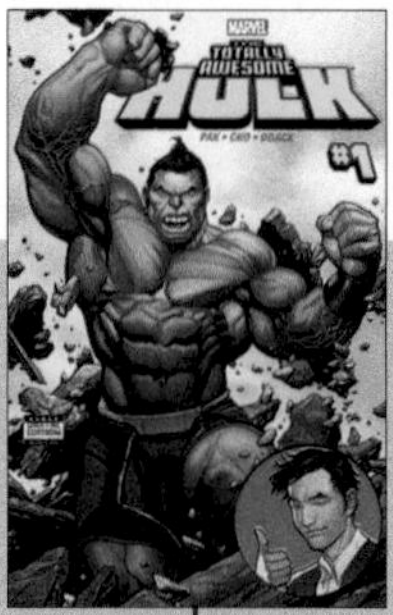
TOTALLY AWESOME
HULK
#1

FEBRUARY 2016

In *The Totally Awesome Hulk* #1, written by Greg Pak and illustrated by Frank Cho, Amadeus Cho becomes the new Hulk.

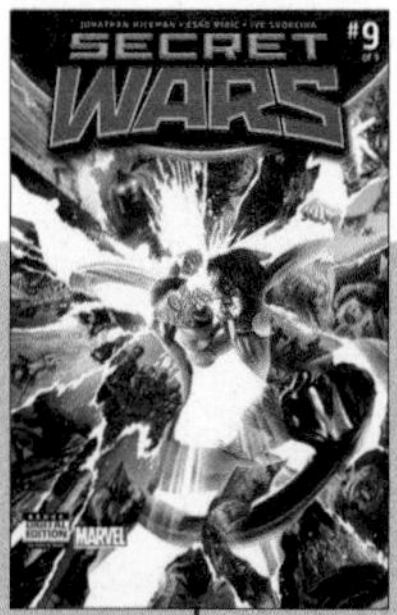
SECRET
WARS
#9

MARCH 2016

The monumental limited series *Secret Wars* brought on the destruction of the Multiverse, including the Marvel and Ultimate universes.

RISE OF THE PANTHER

The 2000s had seen the arrival of writers from outside the world of comic books. Following guest appearances by directors and screenwriters for television, in 2016 Marvel opened its doors to author, journalist, and opinion leader Ta-Nehisi Coates. His impressive list of credits includes the memoirs *The Beautiful Struggle: A Father, Two Sons, and An Unlikely Road to Man-hood*, and the nonfiction bestseller *Between the World and Me*. Coates was hired by Marvel to relaunch the new *Black Panther* series, illustrated by Brian Stelfreeze. The series' esthetics had a major impact on the film dedicated to the King of Wakanda. The first issue of the new *Black Panther* sold over 300,000 copies, and the series was a hit with readers and critics alike. Coates' name on the cover catalyzed media attention, with reviews and interviews in magazines and on TV. In 2018 he was also tapped to write *Captain America*, and true to his creed, it put the spotlight on some of the day's most important issues.

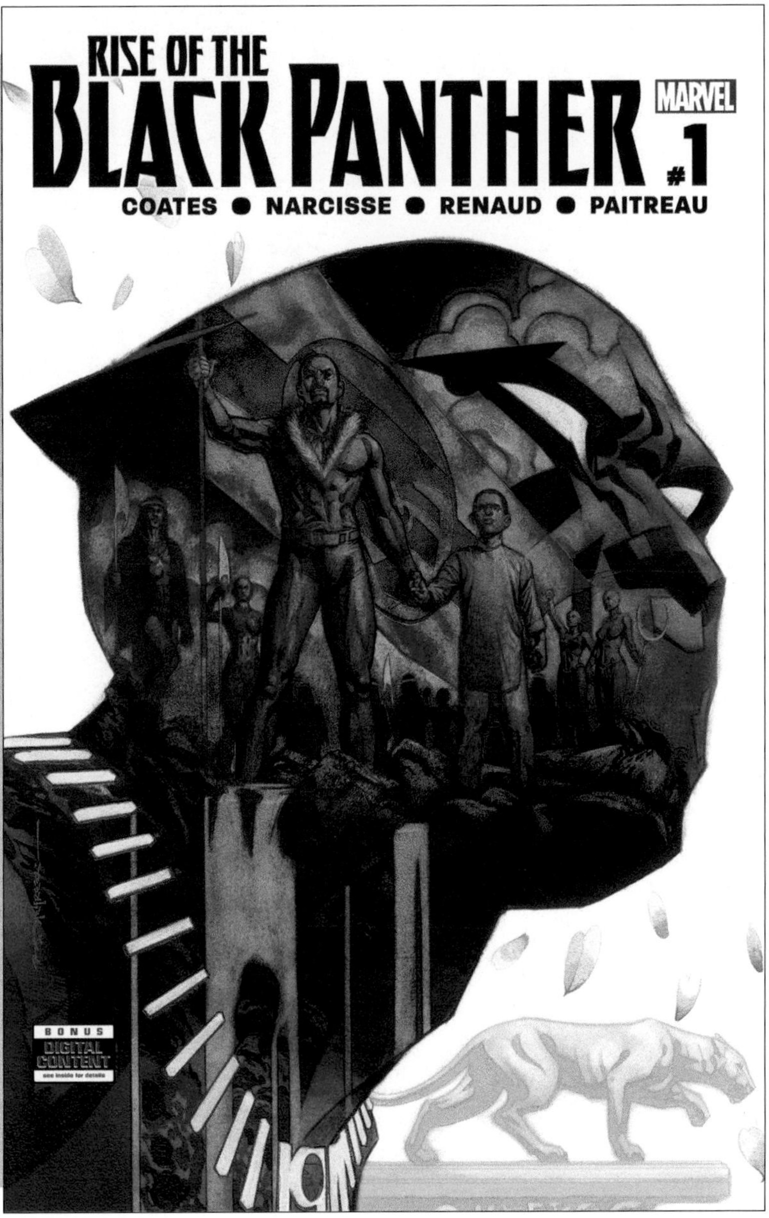
RISE OF THE
BLACK PANTHER
MARVEL
#1
COATES ● NARCISSE ● RENAUD ● PAITREAU
BONUS
DIGITAL CONTENT

LEFT
Rise of the Black Panther #1 (dated March 2018, released January 3, 2018). Art by Brian Stelfreeze.

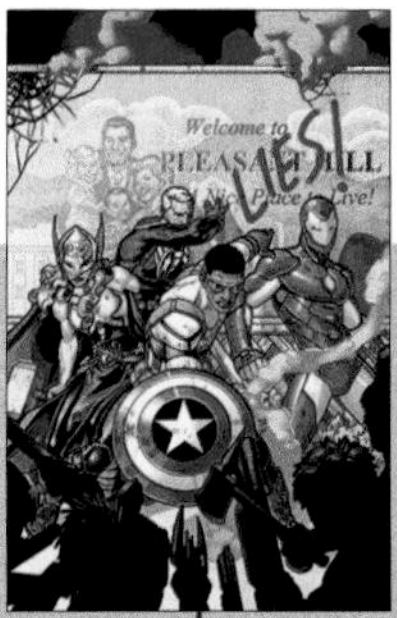

MAY 2016

The *Avengers: Standoff* event gets underway, with unexpected consequences for Steve Rogers and Sam Wilson, who at that time wore the Captain America uniform.

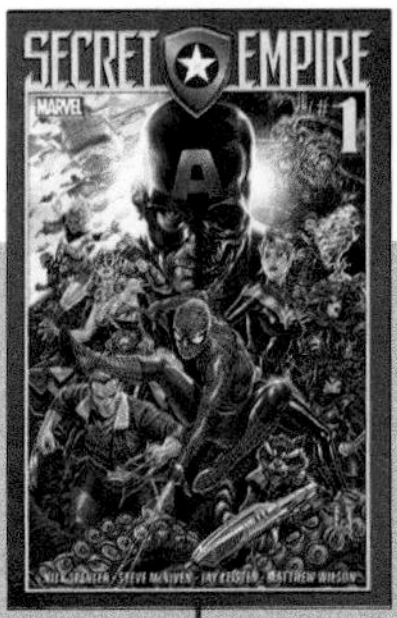
SECRET EMPIRE
MARVEL
#1

JULY 2017

The beginning of the limited series *Secret Empire*, which sees a villainous Captain America conquer the U.S. thanks to the backing of Hydra.

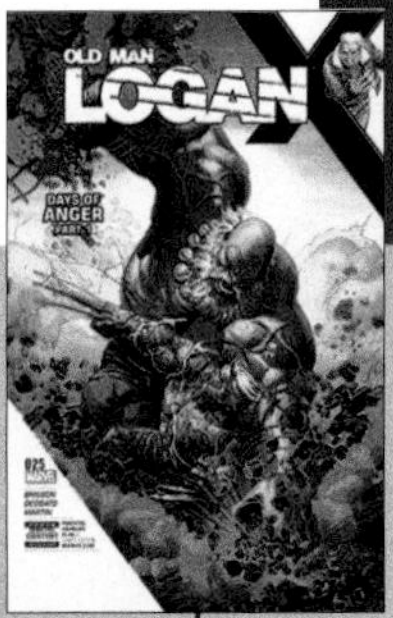
OLD MAN
LOGAN
DAYS OF ANGER

AUGUST 2017

Old Man Logan, the aging Wolverine from a parallel future who took the place of Wolvie, faces off against the Maestro, a mean old future version of Hulk, in *Old Man Logan #25*.

ARCHITECTS OF THE FUTURE

A new wave of comics creators would rise to prominence in the 2010s, reflecting the diverse audience of Marvel fans.

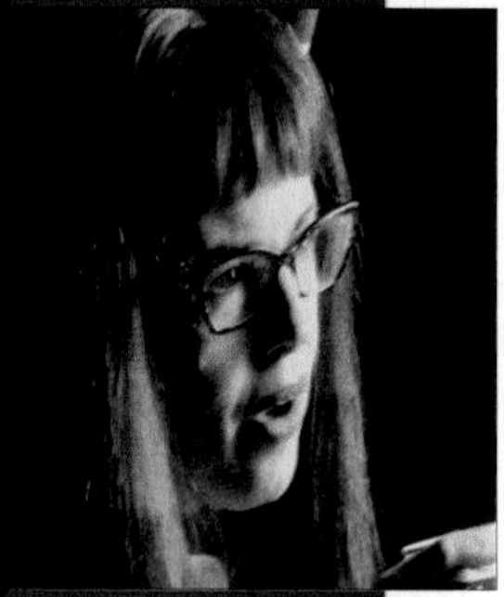

Since the early 2000s, much of readers' attention had been focused on writers. Of course, they were also interested in the artists, but the advent of more complex and detailed artwork meant that any given run might include the work of a team of artists. Writers, on the other hand, tended to stay on for the duration of long story arcs, and thus became stars in their own right, much the way that artists had been idolized by readers in the 1990s.

As far as writers go, Dan Slott is a record holder. From 2010 to 2018, Slott was pretty much the sole writer behind Spidey's adventures, which were studded with electrifying story arcs that kept readers throughout the world on the edges of their seats with nonstop plot twists and cliffhangers—from *Spider-Verse*, featuring alliances among various Spider-Man incarnations in the

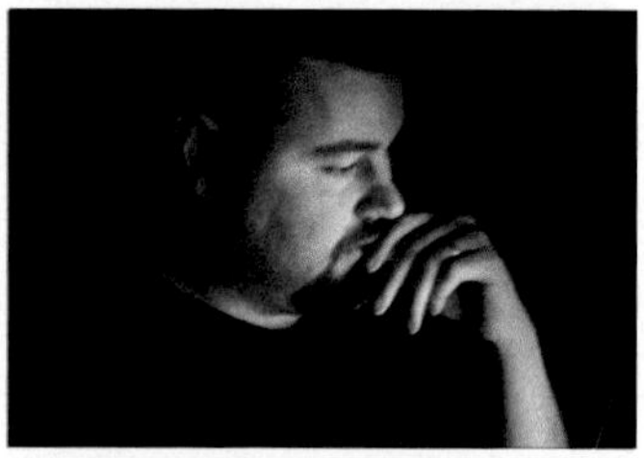

Multiverse against common enemies, to the *Superior Spider-Man* series, which sees Doctor Octopus taking possession of Spidey's mind and identity. During his long run he also transformed Peter Parker into a rich industrialist who eventually slipped into rack and ruin, had Aunt May marry J. Jonah Jameson's father, and created Cindy Moon, A.K.A. Silk, a new Super Heroine with spider-powers.

After *Spider-Man* and an award-winning *Silver Surfer* series illustrated by Mike Allred, Slott went on to write for *Iron Man* and the *Fantastic Four*. Other big-name writers included Matt Fraction and his wife Kelly Sue DeConnick. In the late 2000s and early 2010s he revitalized *Iron Man*, while she breathed new life into *Captain Marvel*. Fraction's version of Tony Stark was very similar to the one created by Robert Downey, Jr., which was a huge hit with fans, for the series *The Invincible Iron Man*, with all artwork by Salvador Larroca. DeConnick transformed Carol Danvers from a minor Super Heroine into one of the main characters in several recent Marvel sagas and a leader of the Avengers.

G. Willow Wilson was another writer who left her mark. A novelist besides her work in comics, Wilson teamed with editor Sana Amanat to come up with the Kamala Khan character, creating a Super Heroine that many would call the Peter Parker of the 21st century, in terms of the way she reflected aspects of

ABOVE: Writer Kelly Sue DeConnick.

RIGHT: Writer Jonathan Hickman.

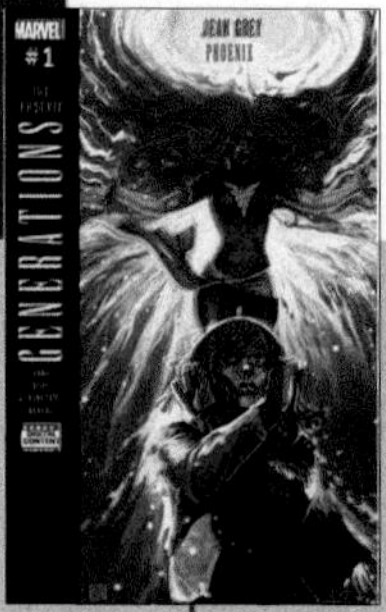
MARVEL #1
GENERATIONS
JEAN GREY PHOENIX

SEPTEMBER 2017

In the anthology *Generations*, Marvel Super Heroes meet their younger counterparts: Wolverine faces his clone Laura Kinney, Kamala Khan deals with Carol Danvers in the past...

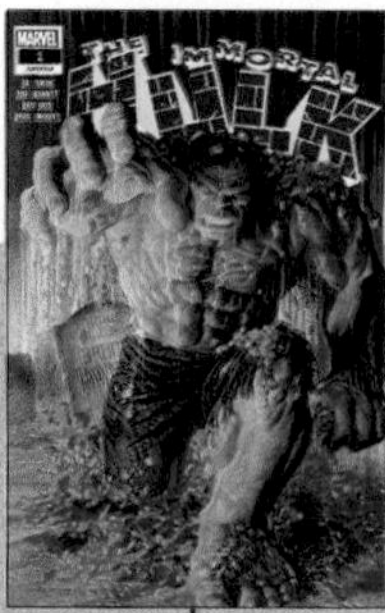
MARVEL
THE IMMORTAL HULK

AUGUST 2018

Al Ewing and Joe Bennett come up with an all-new horror version of Hulk in the acclaimed series *The Immortal Hulk*.

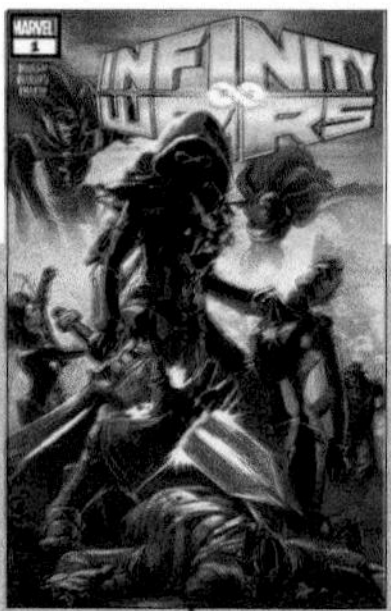
MARVEL
INFINITY WARS

OCTOBER 2018

The Infinity Gems return to the center of the Marvel universe in the saga *Infinity Wars*. The first victim of this quest: Thanos!

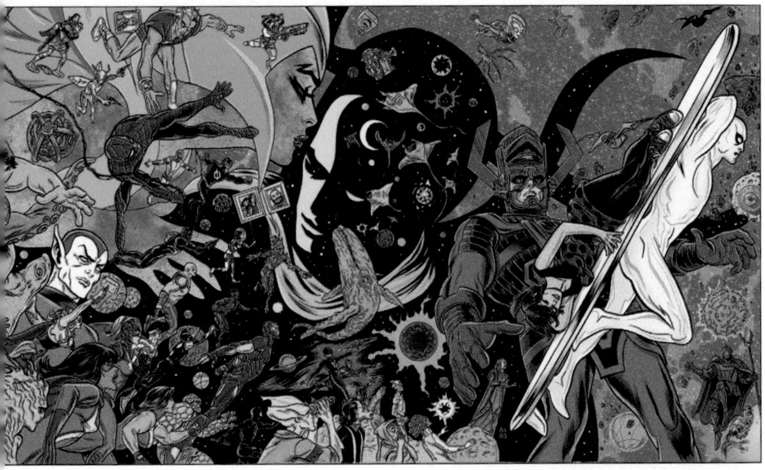

audience. Lastly, among the great writers in recent years, we can't leave out Jonathan Hickman, who gained fame thanks to several series he created for Image Comics. He is known for his long, complex story lines that crisscross and intertwine before reaching perfect solutions.

Besides masterminding the recent *Secret Wars* series and the spy saga *Secret Warriors*, featuring a team led by Nick Fury, Hickman also wrote a long run for *Fantastic Four*. From 2009 to 2012, on the pages of that old-time favorite, he "killed" the Human Torch and brought him back to life, transformed the Fantastic Four into the Future Foundation, and made Doctor Doom a reluctant ally. In 2012 Hickman began work on *The Avengers* and *The New Avengers*, leading the teams to a monumental clash with Thanos in the Infinity saga. In 2019 he made his debut in *X-Men*.

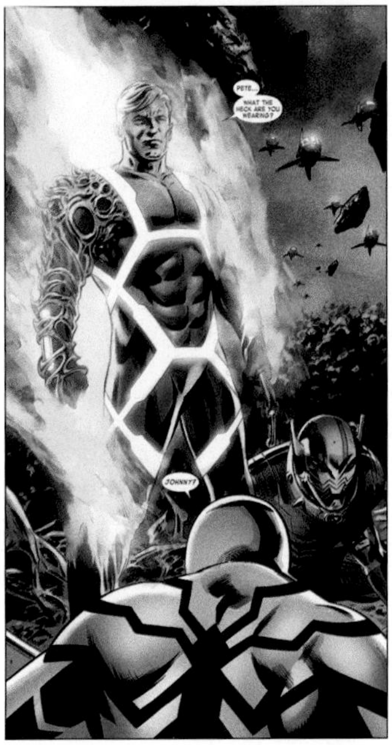
PETE...
WHAT THE HECK ARE YOU WEARING?
JOHNNY?

STAR WARS STRIKES BACK!

The Walt Disney Company acquired Lucasfilm in October 2012, just three years after picking up Marvel Entertainment. Fans worldwide hankered for the return of *Star Wars* to the world of comic books, and Marvel did not disappoint them. The initial *Star Wars* series made its debut in January 2015, written by Jason Aaron and illustrated by John Cassaday. The first issue sold over one million copies, making it the biggest-selling comic of the past two decades. More series followed, featuring the work of artists like Simone Bianchi, Stuart Immonen, and others. The limited series *Star Wars: Princess Leia*, written by Mark Waid and illustrated by Terry Dodson, was the first of several series dedicated to characters from the saga; *Star Wars: Darth Vader*, written by Kieron Gillen and illustrated by Salvador Larroca, ran from 2015 to 2016. To this day, *Star Wars* comics rank among Marvel best-sellers and feature some of the leading writers and artists in the business, with all-new stories that have become part of the franchise's canon.

ABOVE: Cover detail from *Silver Surfer Omnibus* (November 2018). Art by Mike Allred (pencils).

LEFT: Johnny Storm returns in *Fantastic Four #600* (dated January 2012, released November 23, 2011). Script by Jonathan Hickman. Art by Steve Epting (pencils and inks), Rick Magyar (inks), Paul Mounts (colors), Clayton Cowles (letters).

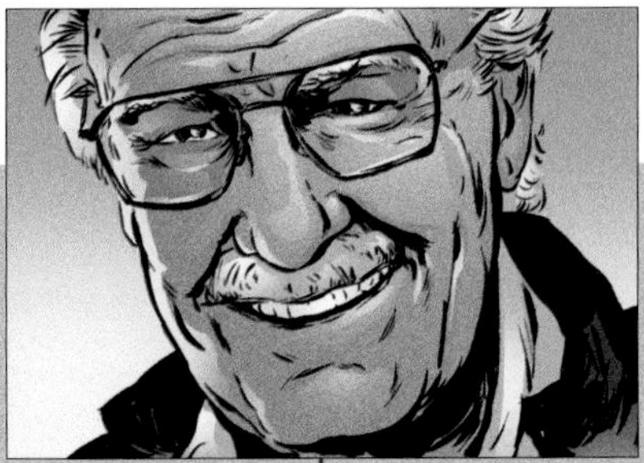

NOVEMBER 2018

On November 12, fans all over the world mourn the death of Stan Lee.

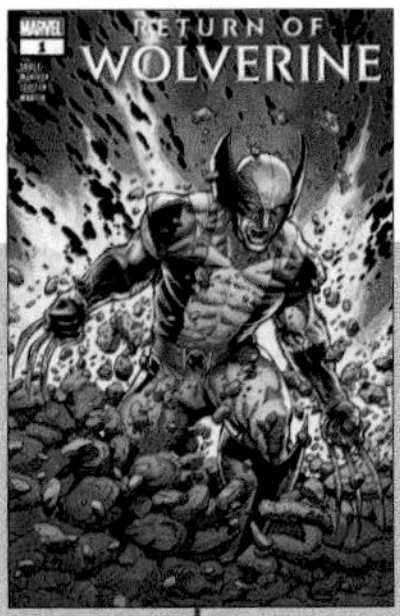
RETURN OF WOLVERINE

NOVEMBER 2018

After an absence of two years, Logan returns among the living in the limited series *Return of Wolverine*.

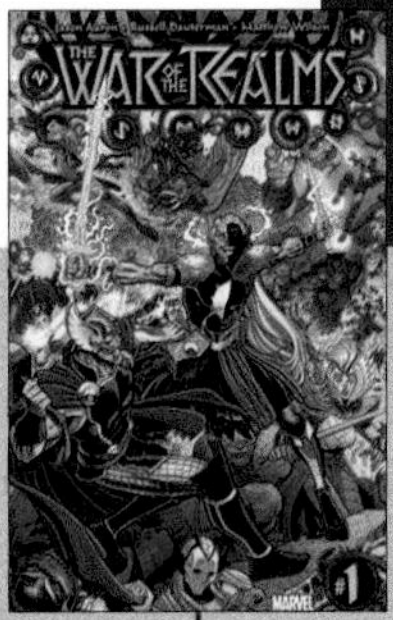
THE WAR OF THE REALMS
#1

JUNE 2019

Jason Aaron caps his Thor run with the storyline *War of the Realms*, which sees the participation of the greatest Super Heroes from the Marvel Universe.

A NEW GOLDEN AGE

RIGHT: Detail from *Captain Marvel #2* (dated June 2014, released April 9, 2014). Art by David Lopez.

OPPOSITE PAGE: TOP LEFT: America Chavez gets her own series with *America #1* (dated May 2017, released March 1, 2017). Art by Joe Quinones.

OPPOSITE PAGE: TOP MIDDLE: *Miles Morales: Spider-Man* (Marvel YA Novel; August 2017). By Jason Reynolds (author), Kadir Nelson (illustrator).

The reach of Marvel extends far beyond the comic-book world, taking global audiences by storm.

After years of television popularity, Marvel Super Heroes had at long last become hits at the movies as well. In just a few years, characters created by Stan Lee, Jack Kirby, Steve Ditko, and others were no longer legends whose fame was limited to a privileged group of aficionados, but had cemented their status as icons of pop culture, recognizable the world over. Today, it's not rare to overhear people not necessarily attuned to comic book culture discussing the powers of Thor or the dilemmas of Peter Parker.

Today, even the world's most celebrated newspapers indulge in breaking news about the latest developments and disclosures from the world of comics, like *Entertainment Weekly*'s announcement in 2014 that Sam Wilson would take over as Captain

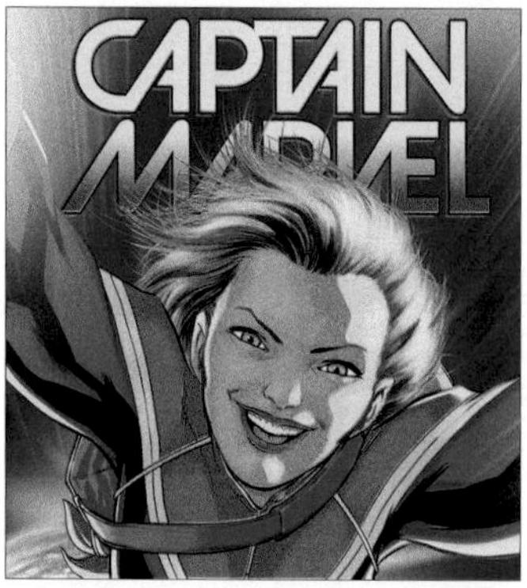
CAPTAIN MARVEL

America, or recent reporting in the *New York Times* that a new *Captain Marvel* series was on the way. What's more, today tons of merchandising products, which may have been impossible to fathom back in Marvel's early days, invade the homes of not just collectors, but of children and adults that have come to know and love Marvel characters through films, cartoons, and the ever-expanding world of video and mobile games. The young—and the young at heart—often see Marvel Super Heroes as role models that drive their ambitions and fire their dreams. Today, characters like Kamala Khan, Miles Morales, and America Chavez are idolized by new legions of fans because they reflect their cultural heritage or sexual orientation, the same way nerdy kids in the 1960s could relate to a shy guy by the name of Peter Parker.

Reveling in a glorious past and enjoying the extraordinary present, the future looks bright for Marvel's star-studded cast of Super Heroes. The sad news is that Stan Lee, one of the fathers of so many illustrious characters that populate the Marvel Universe, won't be around to see it. Just as his own popularity and that of his creations reached stunning new heights, Lee left us on November 12, 2018, at the Cedars-Sinai Medical Center in Los Angeles, at the age of 95. Lifelong readers, brand-

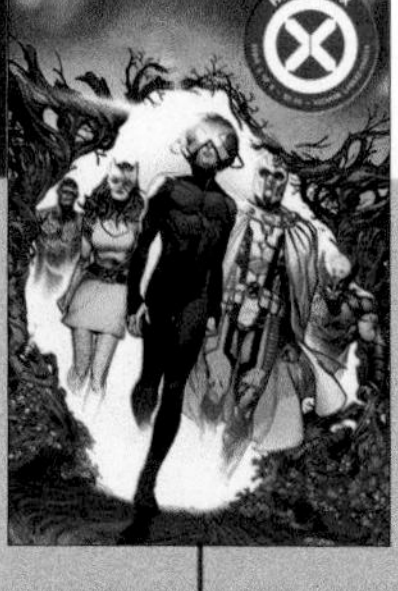
MARVEL
HOUSE OF X

SEPTEMBER 2019

Writer Jonathan Hickman begins work on the X-Men, shaking up the status quo with two limited series, *House of X* and *Powers of X*.

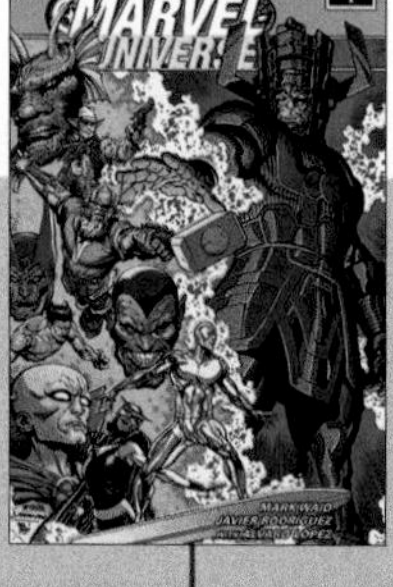
HISTORY OF THE MARVEL UNIVERSE
MARVEL
1

SEPTEMBER 2019

Mark Waid and Javier Rodriguez collect years of story lines to create the ultimate *History of the Marvel Universe*, a new and ambitious limited series.

2020

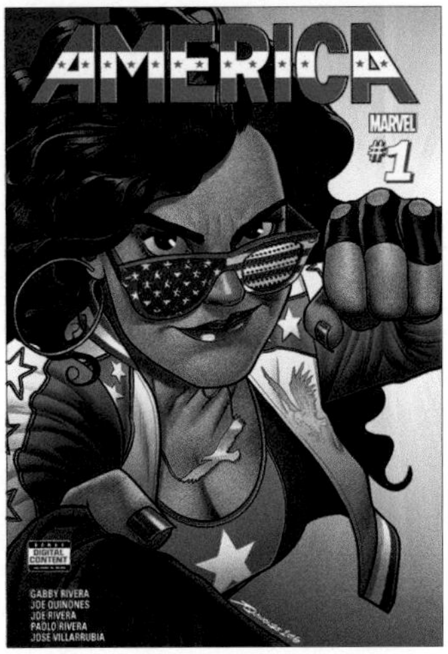
AMERICA
MARVEL
#1
GABBY RIVERA
JOE QUINONES
JOE RIVERA
PAOLO RIVERA
JOSE VILLARRUBIA

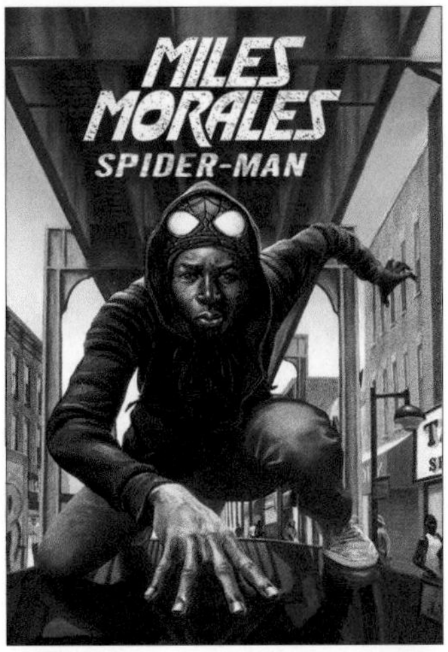
MILES MORALES
SPIDER-MAN

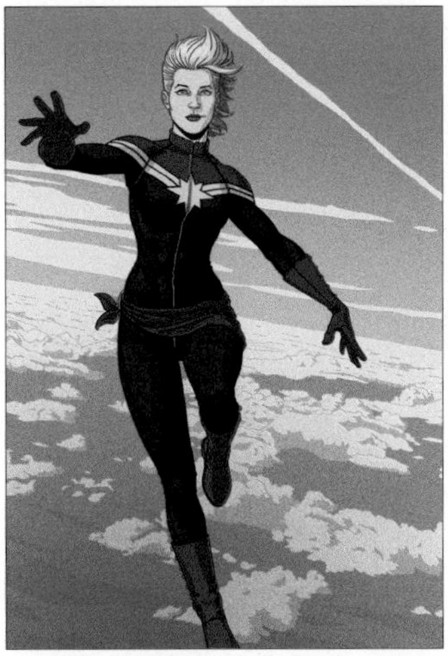

new fans, and moviegoers who thrilled to his many delightful cameo appearances, all shared in mourning the loss as they relived with one another the slew of memories he left behind.

His death made the front pages of newspapers across the globe; news shows and TV specials paid tribute to him. Although he won't be with us to celebrate Marvel's 80th anniversary, Lee was able to pull of the dream he'd carried with him since his youth—penning the Great American Novel…in his own way, of course. He created a saga that spanned so many of his characters' lifetimes, one destined to last through the ages, and considered by many experts and sociologists to be the annals of modern-day mythology. Few people would ever remember him by the name he was born with, which he was holding in reserve for that novel of his—Stanley Lieber. But many people instinctively link his pen name, Stan Lee, to the flood of quintessential characters seen in today's movie theaters, streamed over the

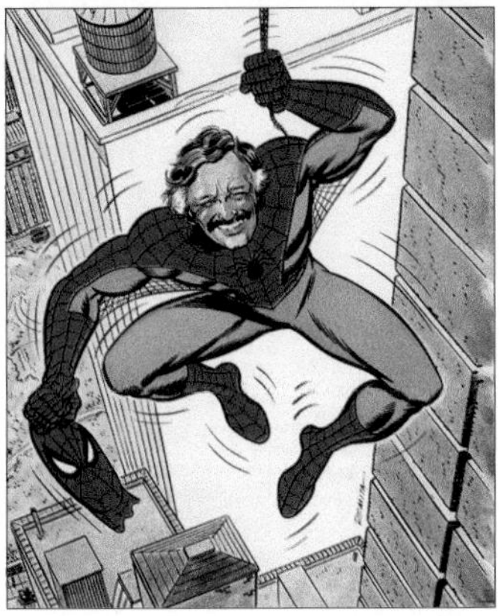

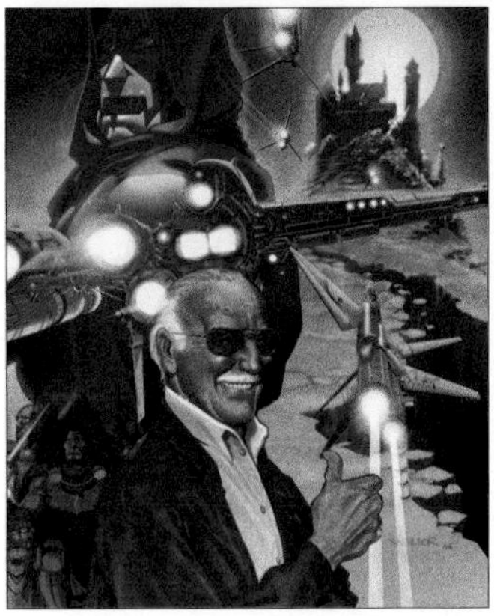

Internet, maneuvered in video and mobile games, immortalized in statues, their likenesses in action figures, on T-shirts, bags and cereal boxes, and shaped into snack foods, not to mention their appearance on the thousands of pages of comics produced every year by Marvel and its writers and artists.

To this day, the idea of Super Heroes with super problems, living in a world very similar to our own, remains the ingenious driving force behind the latest incredible creations that readers have already come to love. New writers and artists will come, as will new Super Heroes and new readers. And all of them will be grateful to Stan Lee for his masterful insight. ■

BULLPEN BULLETINS

STAN'S SOAPBOX

Hey, gang, I think I'm in big trouble, and since misery loves company, I might as well let you worry along with me! Y'see, I've got this Soapbox column to write and it's due at the printer tomorrow morning! So, I've gotta wrap it up in the next hour, or else! But, for the first time in about twenty years, I can't think of anything to write about! Oh sure, I could tell you to latch on to the second great issue of EPIC, or one of our many new regular comicbook titles, but I've been trying to avoid the big sell here in the Soapbox. Or, I could give you some gossip about what's happening amongst our batty bullpen bigwigs, but Jolly Jim Shooter and his capricious cohorts usually like to feed you those illuminating items themselves. So here I sit, staring at an emotionless typewriter with fear and panic welling up within my noble breast, while the clock keeps — HEY! Hold it! I thought of something! Wow — saved by the bell! And, best of all, it's something you can help me with!

Ever since I've been out here in Los Angeles, working on Marvel's many magnificent tv and film projects, one thought's been bugging me. I have a feeling that I don't really understand what makes the Saturday morning animated cartoon shows tick on tv! They're so different from the mighty masterworks you find in our mags that they might have originated on another planet. Okay, then, here's what you can do to help me — and perhaps to help the entire world of tv cartoons...

Just send me a short note, no more than 100 words, saying "Here's what I like about tv cartoons: ————", "Here's what I hate about tv cartoons: ————", and "Here's how to make them better: ————". I'll have our staff of thousands (Irving Thousands, the boss's uncle!) read 'em, and tabulate your opinions. Then, we'll print a summary of your suggestions in a future Soapbox (thereby guaranteeing that I'll have another topic for at least one more column)! Remember, what you write may change the entire tv industry — or, at the very least, give us a case of eyestrain! Just address your oh-so-meaningful missives to STAN LEE'S TV SURVEY, 575 Madison Ave., NYC, NY 10022. Culture lovers everywhere will be eternally in your debt!

Till we meet again, stay cool, stay happy, and stay in touch with the EPIC Epidemic! (Might as well get a plug in somewhere)!

Excelsior!

Stan

TOP RIGHT: As Marvel looks to the future, its commitment to diversity and strong female characters like Captain Marvel will guide the House of Ideas to even greater heights. Captain Marvel illustration by Jamie McKelvie.

MIDDLE: Spider-Man reveals his "true" secret identity. Art by John Romita, Sr.

ABOVE: Cover art to Stan Lee *Meets Doctor Doom* (December 2006). Art by Salvador Larroca.

LEFT: Stan Lee's last Stan's Soapbox column from the original run, August 1980.

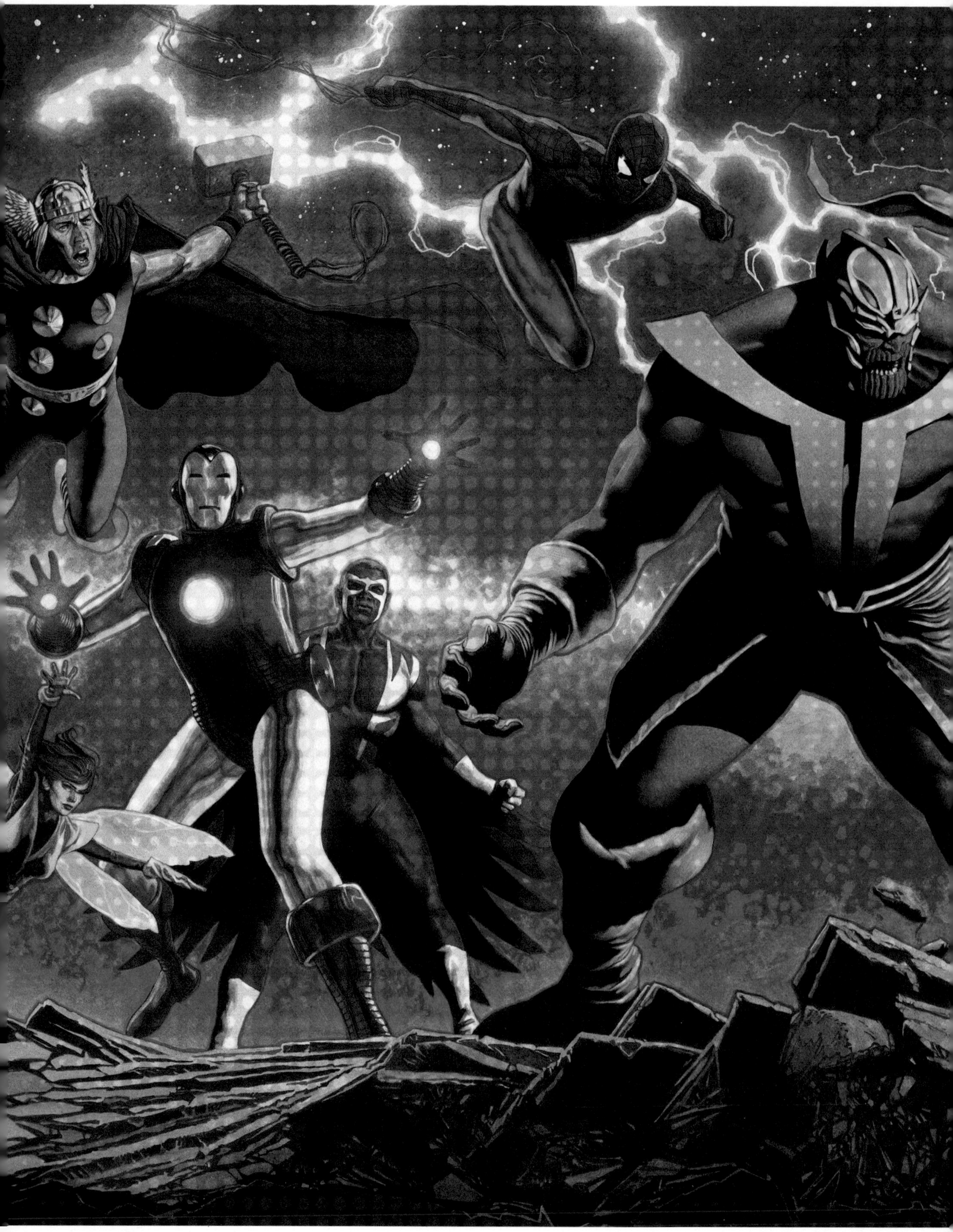

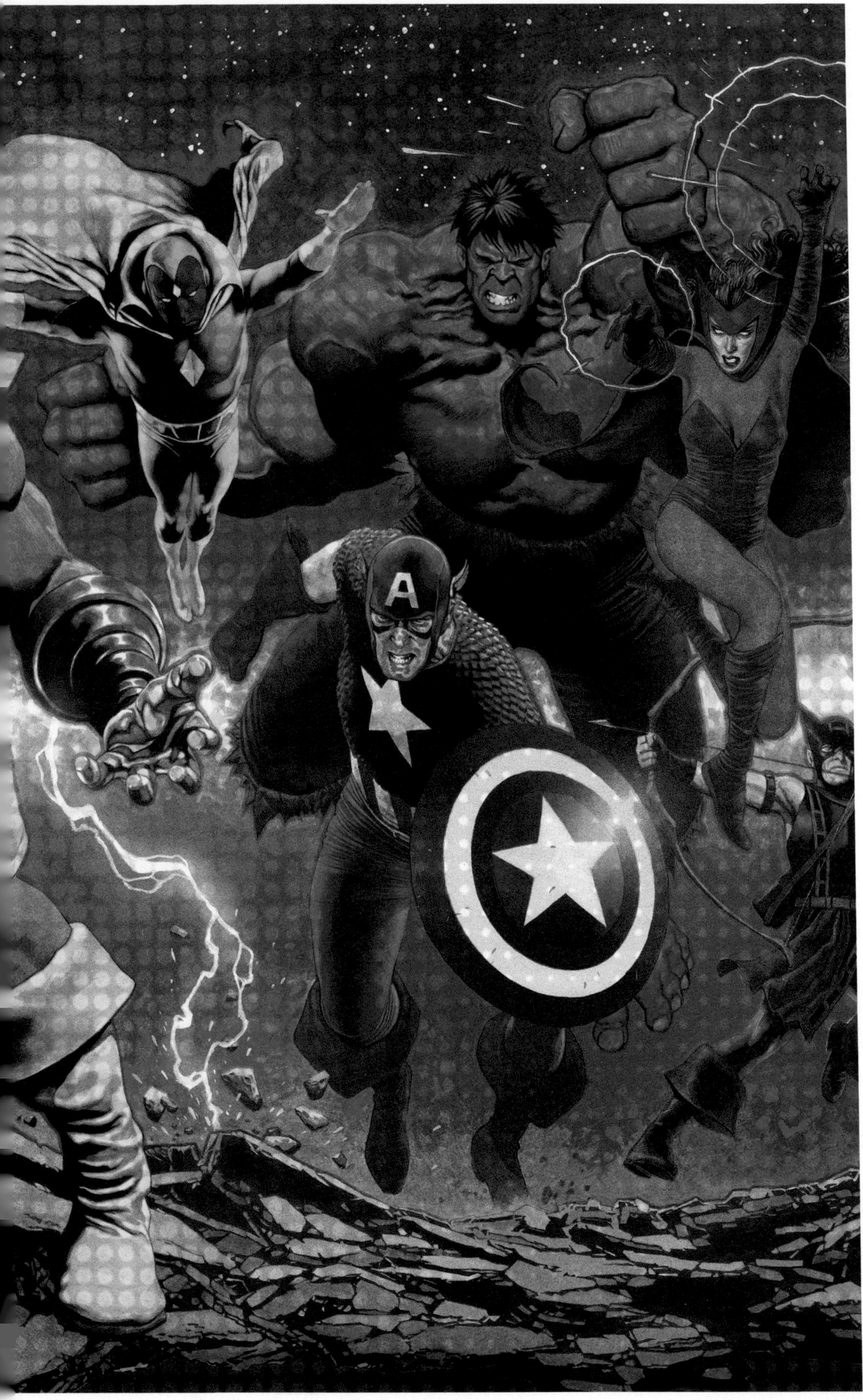

IMAGE CREDITS

All photos and artwork from Marvel archives

pp. 2-3 *Spider-Man vs. the Sinister Six: Alex Ross (painting).*

pp. 4-5 *Marvel Mystery Comics #13 (November 1940): Jack Kirby (pencils).*

pp. 20-21 *Journey Into Mystery #1 (June 1952): Russ Heath, Stan Goldberg.*

pp. 32-33 *The Incredible Hulk King-Size Special #1 (October 1968): Jim Steranko, Marie Severin.*

pp. 60-61 *The Amazing Spider-Man #80 (January 1970): John Romita, Sr.*

pp. 82-83 *Wolverine #1 (September 1982): Frank Miller (pencils), Joe Rubenstein (inks).*

pp. 100-101 *Marvels (trade paperback): Alex Ross (painting).*

pp. 122-123 *The Amazing Spider-Man #36 (December 2001): John Romita, Jr. (pencils), Scott Hanna (inks), Avalon Studios/Dan Kemp (colors).*

pp. 140-141 *Phoenix Resurrection: The Return of Jean Grey #1 (February 2018): Leneil Francis Yu, Sunny Gho.*

pp. 158-159 *The Avengers vs. Thanos: Travis Charest (painting).*

MARVEL LIBRARY

MARVEL CLASSIC NOVELS
- **SPIDER-MAN** THE VENOM FACTOR OMNIBUS
- **X-MEN AND THE AVENGERS** GAMMA QUEST OMNIBUS
- **X-MEN** MUTANT FACTOR OMNIBUS

NOVELS
- **ANT-MAN** NATURAL ENEMY
- **AVENGERS** EVERYBODY WANTS TO RULE THE WORLD
- **AVENGERS** INFINITY
- **BLACK PANTHER** WHO IS THE BLACK PANTHER?
- **CAPTAIN AMERICA** DARK DESIGNS
- **CAPTAIN MARVEL** LIBERATION RUN
- **CIVIL WAR**
- **DEADPOOL** PAWS

THE X-MEN AND THE AVENGERS
GAMMA QUEST
A MARVEL OMNIBUS BY GREG COX

THE X-MEN AND THE AVENGERS
GAMMA QUEST OMNIBUS

- **SPIDER-MAN** FOREVER YOUNG
- **SPIDER-MAN** KRAVEN'S LAST HUNT
- **THANOS** DEATH SENTENCE
- **VENOM** LETHAL PROTECTOR
- **X-MEN** DAYS OF FUTURE PAST
- **X-MEN** THE DARK PHOENIX SAGA
- **SPIDER-MAN** HOSTILE TAKEOVER

ART BOOKS
- **MARVEL'S *SPIDER-MAN*** THE ART OF THE GAME
- **MARVEL *CONTEST OF CHAMPIONS*** THE ART OF THE BATTLEREALM
- ***SPIDER-MAN: INTO THE SPIDERVERSE***
- ***THE ART OF IRON MAN*** 10TH ANNIVERSARY EDITION

THE OFFICIAL MOVIE SPECIAL
MARVEL
BLACK WIDOW

MARVEL STUDIOS' BLACK WIDOW:
THE OFFICIAL MOVIE SPECIAL

SPECIALS
- **MARVEL STUDIOS' *ANT-MAN AND THE WASP***
- **MARVEL STUDIOS' *AVENGERS: ENDGAME***
- **MARVEL STUDIOS' *AVENGERS: INFINITY WAR***
- **MARVEL STUDIOS' *BLACK PANTHER* (COMPANION)**
- **MARVEL STUDIOS' *CAPTAIN MARVEL***
- **MARVEL STUDIOS' *SPIDER-MAN: FAR FROM HOME***
- ***MARVEL STUDIOS'* THE *AVENGERS: A COMPLETE GUIDE TO THE AVENGERS FILMS***
- **MARVEL STUDIOS: THE FIRST TEN YEARS**
- **MARVEL STUDIOS' *THOR: RAGNAROK***
- ***MARVEL: THE FIRST 80 YEARS***

- ***SPIDER-MAN: INTO THE SPIDERVERSE***

STAR WARS LIBRARY

- ***ROGUE ONE: A STAR WARS STORY*** THE OFFICIAL COLLECTOR'S EDITION
- ***ROGUE ONE: A STAR WARS STORY*** THE OFFICIAL MISSION DEBRIEF
- ***STAR WARS: THE LAST JEDI*** THE OFFICIAL COLLECTOR'S EDITION
- ***STAR WARS: THE LAST JEDI*** THE OFFICIAL MOVIE COMPANION
- ***STAR WARS: THE LAST JEDI*** THE ULTIMATE GUIDE
- ***SOLO: A STAR WARS STORY*** THE OFFICIAL COLLECTOR'S EDITION
- ***SOLO: A STAR WARS STORY*** THE ULTIMATE GUIDE
- **THE BEST OF *STAR WARS INSIDER*** VOLUME 1
- **THE BEST OF *STAR WARS INSIDER*** VOLUME 2
- **THE BEST OF *STAR WARS INSIDER*** VOLUME 3
- **THE BEST OF *STAR WARS INSIDER*** VOLUME 4
- ***STAR WARS:*** LORDS OF THE SITH
- ***STAR WARS:*** HEROES OF THE FORCE
- ***STAR WARS:*** ICONS OF THE GALAXY
- ***STAR WARS:*** THE SAGA BEGINS
- ***STAR WARS*** THE ORIGINAL TRILOGY
- ***STAR WARS:*** ROGUES, SCOUNDRELS AND BOUNTY HUNTERS
- ***STAR WARS*** CREATURES, ALIENS, AND DROIDS
- ***STAR WARS: THE RISE OF SKYWALKER*** THE OFFICIAL COLLECTOR'S EDITION
- ***STAR WARS: THE EMPIRE STRIKES BACK*** THE OFFICIAL COLLECTOR'S EDITION
- ***STAR WARS: THE RISE OF SKYWALKER:*** THE OFFICIAL COLLECTOR'S EDITION
- ***STAR WARS: THE SKYWALKER SAGA*** THE OFFICIAL MOVIE COMPANION
- ***THE MANDALORIAN*** THE ART AND IMAGERY VOLUME 2

THE 40TH ANNIVERSARY SPECIAL EDITION
STAR WARS
EPISODE V: THE EMPIRE STRIKES BACK

STAR WARS: THE EMPIRE STRIKES BACK: THE OFFICIAL COLLECTOR'S EDITION

STAR WARS
THE MANDALORIAN
THE ART & IMAGERY
COLLECTOR'S EDITION
VOLUME ONE

THE MANDALORIAN
THE ART AND IMAGERY VOLUME 1

DISNEY LIBRARY

THE OFFICIAL MOVIE SPECIAL
DISNEY
DUMBO

DISNEY DUMBO
THE OFFICIAL MOVIE SPECIAL

DISNEY PIXAR
TOY STORY 4
THE OFFICIAL MOVIE SPECIAL

DISNEY•PIXAR TOY STORY 4
THE OFFICIAL MOVIE SPECIAL

DISNEY
THE LION KING
THE OFFICIAL MOVIE SPECIAL

DISNEY THE LION KING
THE OFFICIAL MOVIE SPECIAL

THE OFFICIAL MOVIE SPECIAL
DISNEY
FROZEN II

DISNEY *FROZEN 2*
THE OFFICIAL MOVIE SPECIAL

AVAILABLE AT ALL GOOD BOOKSTORES AND ONLINE

TITAN-COMICS.COM | **TITAN**BOOKS.COM